Underwriting Commercial Property

Underwriting Commercial Property

Joseph F. Mangan, CPCU
Insurance Consultant

Connor M. Harrison, CPCU, AU
Director of Underwriting Education
American Institute for CPCU/Insurance Institute of America

Second Edition • Thirteenth Printing

American Institute for Chartered Property Casualty
Underwriters/Insurance Institute of America
720 Providence Road, Suite 100
Malvern, Pennsylvania 19355-3433

Second Edition • Thirteenth Printing • November 2009
Library of Congress Catalog Number: 97-77729
ISBN 978-0-89462-120-8

Foreword

The American Institute for Chartered Property Casualty Underwriters and the Insurance Institute of America (the Institutes) are not-for-profit organizations committed to meeting the evolving educational needs of the risk management and insurance community. The Institutes strive to provide current, relevant educational programs in formats that meet the needs of risk management and insurance professionals and the organizations that employ them.

The American Institute for CPCU (AICPCU) was founded in 1942 through a collaborative effort between industry professionals and academics, led by faculty members at The Wharton School of the University of Pennsylvania. In 1953, AICPCU coordinated operations with the Insurance Institute of America (IIA), which was founded in 1909 and remains the oldest continuously functioning national organization offering educational programs for the property-casualty insurance sector.

The Insurance Research Council (IRC), founded in 1977, is a division of AICPCU supported by industry members. This not-for-profit research organization examines public policy issues of interest to property-casualty insurers, insurance customers, and the general public. IRC research reports are distributed widely to insurance-related organizations, public policy authorities, and the media.

The Institutes' customer- and solution-focused business model allows us to better serve the risk management and insurance communities. Customer-centricity defines our business philosophy and shapes our priorities. The Institutes' innovation arises from our commitment to finding solutions that meet customer needs and deliver results. Our business process is shaped by our commitment to efficiency, strategy, and responsible asset management.

The Institutes believe that professionalism is grounded in education, experience, and ethical behavior. The Chartered Property Casualty Underwriter (CPCU) professional designation offered by the Institutes is designed to provide a broad understanding of the property-casualty insurance industry. Depending on professional needs, CPCU students may select either a commercial or a personal risk management and insurance focus. The CPCU designation is conferred annually by the AICPCU Board of Trustees.

In addition, the Institutes offer designations and certificate programs in a variety of disciplines, including the following:

- Claims
- Commercial underwriting
- Fidelity and surety bonding
- General insurance
- Insurance accounting and finance
- Insurance information technology
- Insurance production and agency management
- Insurance regulation and compliance
- Management
- Marine insurance
- Personal insurance
- Premium auditing
- Quality insurance services
- Reinsurance
- Risk management
- Surplus lines

You can complete a program leading to a designation, take a single course to fill a knowledge gap, or take multiple courses and programs throughout your career. The practical and technical knowledge gained from Institute courses enhances your qualifications and contributes to your professional growth. Most Institute courses carry college credit recommendations from the American Council on Education. A variety of courses qualify for credits toward certain associate, bachelor's, and master's degrees at several prestigious colleges and universities.

Our Knowledge Resources Department, in conjunction with industry experts and members of the academic community, develops our trusted course and program content, including Institute study materials. These materials provide practical career and performance-enhancing knowledge and skills.

We welcome comments from our students and course leaders. Your feedback helps us continue to improve the quality of our study materials.

Peter L. Miller, CPCU
President and CEO
American Institute for CPCU
Insurance Institute of America

Preface

The profitable selection of applicants for commercial property insurance coverages is the focus of *Underwriting Commercial Property*. Because of the variety of coverages included in this subject area, the text covers a number of property topics. Understanding the COPE (construction, occupancy, protection, and external exposure) framework for analyzing exposure to fire is basic to underwriting the fire cause of loss. Since fire remains the key cause of loss for most property accounts, COPE remains an essential approach even for accounts that request more comprehensive coverage.

Underwriters cannot evaluate every cause of loss included in insurance coverage forms. In some instances, the occurrence of a cause of loss is extremely rare, and for other causes of loss, the total amount of loss is insignificant. For these reasons, this text does not discuss every cause of loss, though it does discuss most. A fuller understanding of the causes of loss that represent the majority of claims in frequency and severity enables underwriters to better assess the potential exposures facing an account. With this knowledge, the underwriter can then evaluate the profit potential from an account and determine whether modifications in the account, its pricing, or the coverages requested will mutually satisfy the majority of the applicant's insurance needs and the insurer's objectives.

Underwriting Commercial Property is one of a series of four textbooks, all of which were written for students working toward the Insurance Institute of America's Associate in Underwriting (AU) designation. This course of study assumes that students already have a mastery of commercial property insurance coverages. Such an understanding can be obtained by studying and preparing for CPCU 551—*Commercial Property Risk Management and Insurance*. Likewise, this text is the second of two textbooks used for AU 65—*Commercial Underwriting: Principles and Property*. Students should thoroughly understand underwriting principles before reading this text. The course guide exercises and the national examination for AU 65 will assume an understanding of all these topics.

Underwriting Commercial Property and the other textbooks in the Associate in Underwriting program are successors of four very fine textbooks that were used to prepare the more than 5,000 students who have already earned the AU designation. This text and the others used in the AU program were made possible because of the insights of members of three specific groups. These groups are the AU advisory committee, the AU grading panels, and the Underwriting Interest Section of the CPCU Society. Additionally, many AU graduates took an active role in reviewing manuscripts. We are deeply indebted to their continued commitment to the Institutes and the insurance underwriting profession. These people are:

Julie S. Angstadt, CPCU, AU

Diane L. Blake, CIC, AU, AAI

Sheila Enger Coleman, CPCU, AAI, AU

Joseph R. Dodd, CPCU, AU, AFSB

Philip W. Dumont, CPCU, AU

Martin J. Ermanis, AU

Steve Farnsworth, CPCU, AU, ALCM

John Ferry, CPCU, CLU, AU

Dick Fox, CPCU, ARM, ALCM

Lorie Graham, CPCU, AU, ALCM

Joseph L. Grauwiler, CPCU

Ferdinand Innes, AU

Lois Jacobs, CPCU, AU

Richard Kline, CPCU, AIM, AU

Norman E. Lucas, AU

Scott A. MacAdam, AU

W. Paul Mandt, CPCU, CIC, AU

Eugene M. Maresca, CPCU, AU, CIC

David Rispoli, CPCU, AU

Marian Rucks, AU

Brian Salz, CPCU, AU, AIM

James "Skip" Spencer, AIAF

Carol Sukchai, AU, ARM

Johnn E. Trotter, CIC, AU

Pete Tyler, CPCU, AU, ARM

Joseph W. Warren, Jr., CPCU, AU, AIAF

Thomas Weiant, CPCU, AU

Gwendolyn K. Young, AU

Mark L. Young, AU

Three outside reviewers were asked to review all of the manuscripts. Their help has been invaluable not only because they found inconsistencies but also because they made significant last-minute contributions to ensure the manuscript's accuracy and completeness. We wish to thank Shelly Arnold, CPCU, AU, ARM, Roger P. Carlson, CPCU, ARM, AU, and Richard E. Hess, AU, for their contributions.

For more information about the Institutes' programs, please call our Customer Service Department at (800) 644-2101, e-mail us at customerservice@cpcuiia.org, or visit our Web site at www.aicpcu.org.

Joseph F. Mangan
Connor M. Harrison

Contributing Authors

Extensive selections from the IIA texts *Principles of Property and Liability Underwriting*, *Personal Lines Underwriting*, *Commercial Property and Multiple-Lines Underwriting*, and *Commercial Liability Underwriting* were incorporated into this text and the others used in the Associate in Underwriting program. We are indebted to the authors listed below for these materials. Even more so, we are indebted to them because their ideas and contribution to the AU program have influenced how we think about underwriting.

Principles of Property and Liability Underwriting

J. J. Launie, PhD, CPCU
Professor of Finance and Insurance
California State University

J. Finley Lee, PhD, CLU
Julian Price Professor of Business Administration
University of North Carolina

Norman A. Baglini, PhD, CPCU, AU
American Institute for CPCU/Insurance Institute of America

Personal Lines Underwriting

G. William Glendenning, PhD, CPCU
Chairperson and Professor
Department of Insurance and Risk
Temple University

Robert B. Holtom, LL.B., CPCU, AU
Assistant Vice President
Farmers Insurance Group

Commercial Liability Underwriting

Larry D. Gaunt, PhD, CPCU
Professor of Risk Management and Insurance
Georgia State University

Numan A. Williams, PhD, CPCU, AU
Professor of Insurance
Ball State University

Everett D. Randall, CPCU, CLU, AU
American Institute for CPCU/Insurance Institute of America

Commercial Property and Multiple-Lines Underwriting

E. P. Hollingsworth, CPCU, ARM
Vice President
Frank B. Hall & Co., Inc.

J. J. Launie, PhD, CPCU
Professor of Finance and Insurance
California State University

Contents

Chapter 1

Construction

Construction is one of four interdependent elements that commercial property underwriters analyze when evaluating submissions for property insurance. The other three elements are *occupancy*, *protection*, and *external exposures*. These four elements are collectively referred to by the acronym **COPE** and are discussed in this and the two following chapters.

Of the four COPE elements commonly used by property underwriters, construction stands out as a key factor in underwriting property insurance. Construction is a tangible property characteristic that underwriters can evaluate. A property's construction is less likely to change than are the nature and quality of occupancy, protection, and external exposures.

Fire is usually considered the most likely cause of loss to occur, and underwriters commonly evaluate first the desirability of an insured based on its susceptibility to this cause of loss. Other causes of loss such as windstorm and earthquake could have a significant effect on the underwriting decision in some parts of the country. If, however, a risk is not acceptable because of the possibility of a loss caused by fire, it will not be acceptable for the less likely causes of loss included in commercial property policies.

The construction of a building has a direct bearing on the extent of damage a fire can cause as well as the building's ability to resist damage from other perils. When considering construction, underwriters are concerned with far more than the basic construction classification used in pricing property insurance.

(The building construction classification system used by Insurance Services Office is described in depth later in this chapter.) Underwriters should be concerned with how various structural features will resist the effects of a fire and how the structural features contribute to the spread or containment of fire. Additionally, structural features are important in analyzing the effects of other perils on the structure.

Underwriters often treat construction incidentally because applications normally provide information about construction. Underwriters should not, however, treat construction superficially. Construction features are not standard, and additional investigation by the underwriter will usually reveal information that will make a risk either more or less desirable.

Fire Resistance and Flame Spread

In determining the appropriate classification for a particular structure, underwriters often analyze the fire resistance of materials used in construction. In the interior of buildings, the flame spread of the interior construction materials or finish is important. **Interior finish** consists of materials used to form the exposed interior surfaces of walls and ceilings in a building. Interior finish includes such items as carpets, ceiling tiles, wallboard, insulating materials, and decorative materials.

Fire Resistance

Fire resistance refers to the ability of a structure or material to withstand the effects of a large-scale, severe fire. Fire resistance is evaluated by exposing structural elements to fire in a controlled setting. Materials are classified by their fire-resistance capabilities, according to the Standard Methods of Tests of Fire Endurance of Building Construction and Materials, NFPA Standard Number 251. Such an evaluation is conducted by using a test tunnel developed by Underwriters Laboratories, Inc. (UL). NFPA standards are established by the National Fire Protection Association, which is an organization dedicated to safeguarding people and property from destruction by fire. In this test tunnel, materials are exposed to a standard fire so that their performance can be measured and classified relative to other materials.

Those specimens are exposed to a reproducible standard fire following a time-temperature curve, as shown in Exhibit 1-1. The structural elements being evaluated are loaded with the weight that they are supposed to hold when put into actual use. The unit passes the test if it resists its prescribed superimposed

Exhibit 1-1
Time-Temperature Curve—Standard Fire

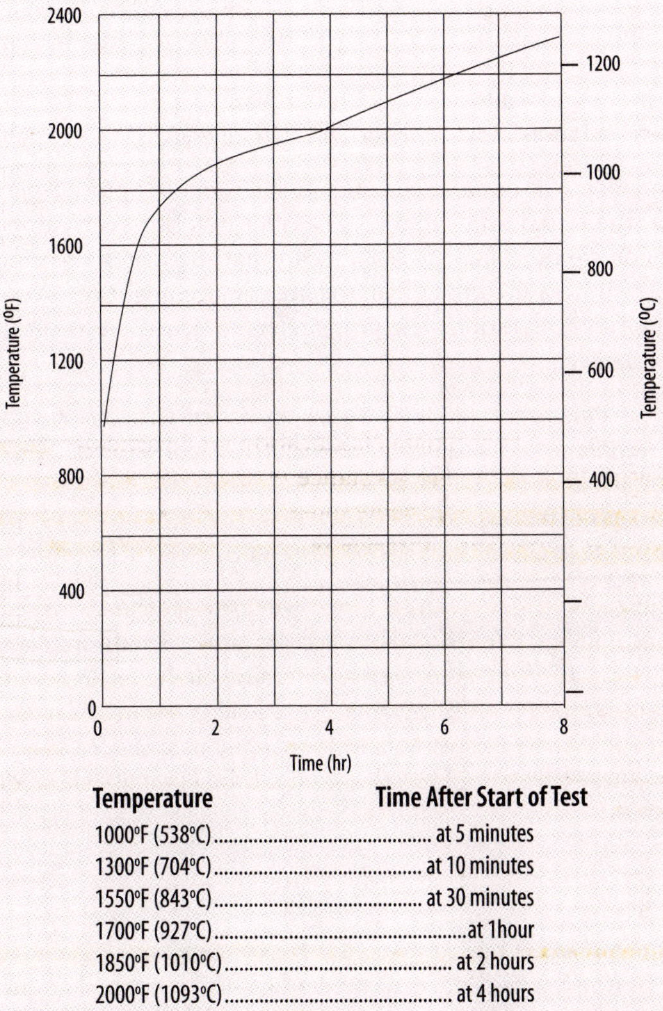

Temperature	Time After Start of Test
1000°F (538°C)	at 5 minutes
1300°F (704°C)	at 10 minutes
1550°F (843°C)	at 30 minutes
1700°F (927°C)	at 1hour
1850°F (1010°C)	at 2 hours
2000°F (1093°C)	at 4 hours
2300°F (1260°C)	at 8 hours or over

The concept of a **standard test fire** to evaluate building materials was developed by the American Society for Testing Materials (ASTM) in 1918. It is the benchmark for evaluating the fire-resistive characteristics of building components.

The temperatures listed above are temperatures of the exposing fire and represent increments of increase over the ambient temperature in the furnace at the start of the test.

load. Partitions, walls, floors, and roofs pass the test if they resist the spread of fire for a specified period of time. Underwriters Laboratories conducts most of the tests. The minimum sizes for test specimens are the following:[1]

- Columns 9 feet
- Beams and girders 12 feet
- Partitions and walls 100 square feet
- Floors and roofs 180 square feet

Structural elements or materials are rated in terms of hours, depending on the time that the tested unit survives. These ratings, however, can be confusing. A two-hour fire resistance does *not* mean that the materials being tested can survive a two-hour fire unscathed; the fire damage might be severe, even with exposure of short duration. The rating refers to structural integrity, not to the degree of damage.

The test evaluates the likelihood that an actual structure composed of the same materials would survive a fire under like conditions. The underlying assumptions are that the specimens tested are the same type as those used in a structure, that the actual fuel load does not exceed the fuel load tested, and that the duration of the fire does not exceed the time tested.

Fuel load (sometimes referred to as **fire load**) is the expected maximum amount of combustible material in a given area. In a normal building the fuel load consists of the combustible structural elements and the combustible contents contained within the area. Fuel load is usually expressed as weight of combustible material per square foot. It is, in essence, a measure of the maximum heat that would be released if all the combustibles in a given area were to burn.

Flame Spread

The **flame spread** of materials is also determined by using a test tunnel. As with measuring fire resistance, a standard gas fire is applied at one end of the tunnel, and the rate of flame spread is measured. Exhibit 1-2 illustrates a test tunnel used for measuring flame spread.

As a baseline of the evaluation of materials and to determine whether the test tunnel is set to the uniform conditions, a relative scale has been created using a piece of red oak and a piece of asbestos cement board. The results obtained from testing those materials are classified as 0 (asbestos cement board) and 100 (red oak flooring). The volume of smoke that the fire generates and the amount of fuel that the fire consumes are also measured.[2]

Exhibit 1-2
Test Tunnel for Measuring Flame Spread

The test tunnel, often referred to as a Steiner Test Tunnel, is a chamber of uniform size. A gas-fueled fire is applied to material at one end of the chamber. Viewing ports allow observers to watch the spread of the fire, and this observation serves as the basis for the flame spread rating. Temperature and smoke density are also measured.

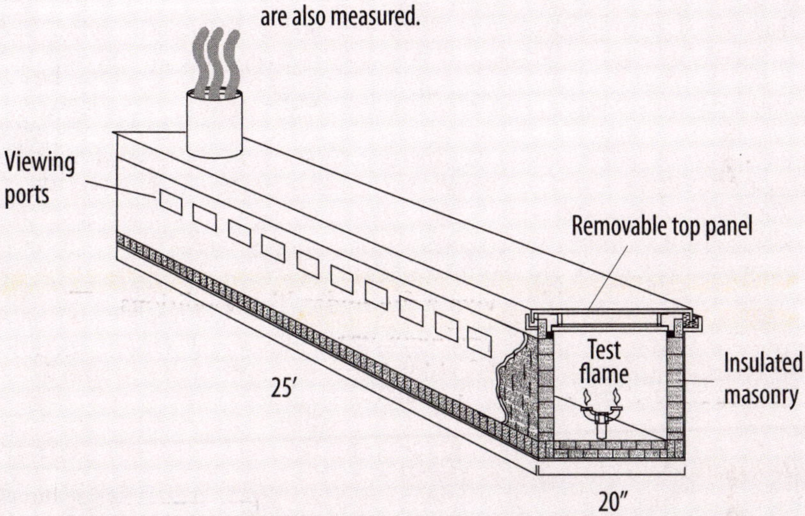

Test tunnels (at least fifteen of which are operating in the United States and Canada) were developed by A. J. Steiner at Underwriters Laboratories, Inc. UL proposed procedures for testing building materials in the early 1940s, but not until the occurrence of three disastrous hotel fires in 1946 were testing procedures adopted.

A set of gradings (A through C) and a numerical rating are also used. The letter grade is often used for interior finish classifications. A tested material with a rating of 100 would exhibit the same flame spread and combustion byproducts as the red oak. Flame-spread classifications provide references that building planners can use for different finishes. Builders should use Class A materials in exit areas and Class B or C materials in other areas of the building. Exhibit 1-3 shows flame-spread ratings.

Components of Structural Strength

The materials used for load-bearing components have the greatest effect on how different types of construction are classified. **Load-bearing components** carry the weight of the structure and its contents. Walls and columns bear the

Exhibit 1-3
Flame-Spread Ratings

Classification	Flame Spread Range
A	0 to 25
B	26 to 75
C	76 to 200

Flame-spread ratings are integrated into NFPA's Life Safety Code for Interior Finish. Class A is more fire-resistive than Classes B or C. The Life Safety Code provides that exits, access to exits, and other spaces for different occupancy classes be one of those classes.

Adapted with permission from *Fire Protection Handbook*, 17th edition, Copyright © 1991, National Fire Protection Association, Quincy, MA 02269.

vertical load, and other structural components spread the load horizontally. Builders attach columns to beams that provide horizontal support, and this combination is called the "structural frame." The materials used for load-bearing components and the arrangement of those components determine the building's ability to withstand damage.

Components That Carry the Vertical Load

Some types of construction have load-bearing *exterior* walls that serve a dual purpose. They enclose the building and support its weight and that of its contents. In a small structure, those walls might carry the full weight of the building and all that it contains, but larger structures require additional vertical support in the form of load-bearing *interior* walls and columns. The load-bearing components of noncombustible and fire-resistive structures are usually columns, but walls made of concrete are sometimes load bearing.

The design and planned use of the building dictate the choice between walls and columns for interior load-bearing components. Columns create the large open spaces that many occupancies require but demand massive materials that are not easy to conceal. Load-bearing partition walls divide the inside space into compartments or rooms and spread the load over a large quantity of light materials that the walls can conceal within themselves.

Components That Spread the Load Horizontally

A structure would be useless if the entire weight of the building and its contents had to rest directly on a load-bearing wall or column. Something is needed to spread the load horizontally to vertical load-bearing components.

Floors, beams, and joists perform this task. In addition to spreading the weight of the structure and its contents, floors, beams, and joists tie the vertical load-bearing components together and stabilize them.

Generally, in concrete construction only floors made of pre-stressed and poured-in-place reinforced concrete are strong enough to support their load and their own weight. Floors made of virtually any other material require beams for horizontal support. Beams are substantial components made of wood, steel, or concrete that are laid horizontally and fastened securely (or "tied") to vertical load-bearing components. Beams spread the weight of the floor and the load it carries to load-bearing columns and walls. Beams also provide all the support required by floors made of heavy timber, metal, or poured concrete over steel decking. The light floors typical of masonry and wood frame constructions need additional support from joists, which are light wood components generally laid across the beams at right angles.

Structural Components That Do Not Carry the Load

Certain structural components are not strong enough to carry any weight other than their own, so they are called **non-load-bearing components**. Non-load-bearing components include exterior walls that only enclose the building, including masonry walls in masonry noncombustible and fire-resistive structures. Those walls are sometimes referred to as curtain walls. Interior partition walls do not always bear part of the load, and columns are sometimes decorative rather than load bearing.

Building Construction Classifications

For the fire cause of loss, Insurance Services Office (ISO) divides building construction into six classifications:[3]

- Class 1—frame
- Class 2—joisted masonry
- Class 3—noncombustible
- Class 4—masonry noncombustible
- Class 5—modified fire-resistive
- Class 6—fire-resistive

The classes are often referred to simply by the class numbers. Those classifications are based on three essential factors:

1. The materials used for the load-bearing portions of exterior walls
2. The materials used in the roof and floors of the building, especially the supports of the roof and floor
3. The fire-resistance rating of materials used in the building construction

Frame

In **frame construction**, the load-bearing components of the building are wood or other combustible materials. Although most building codes differentiate between protected and unprotected frame buildings, a frame building might require certain firestop devices. A **firestop** is an element of construction inserted in a concealed space, either a wall or roof area, that prevents the passage of flame from one point to another. Firestops may contain a fire for a time, thereby increasing the chance that the fire can be extinguished before it spreads further. Exhibit 1-4 illustrates the use of firestops in frame construction.

Exhibit 1-4
Examples of Firestopping

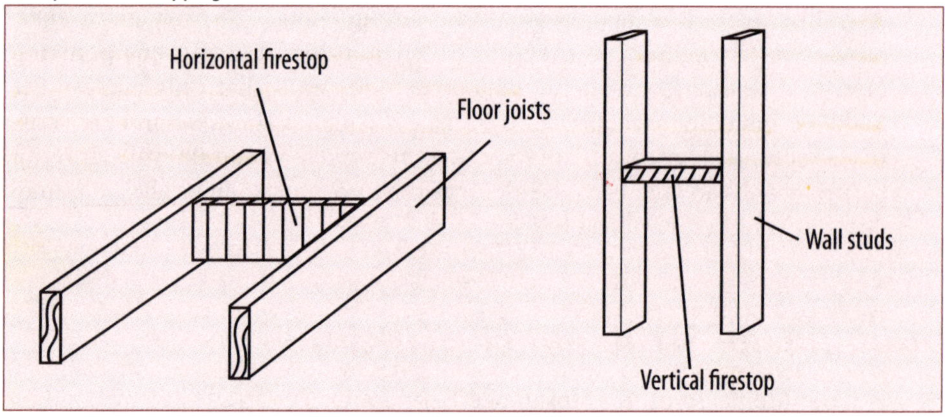

In frame construction, materials other than wood can be used without changing the construction classification. Various composition boards and many other exterior wall-covering materials can be used in place of wood, including the following:

- Brick or stone veneer, consisting of a single thickness of brick or stone (two to six inches thick) over a wood-framed structure, and depending on bonding to the wood structure for stability. Veneer gives a building the appearance of standard brick or stone construction but is not equivalent to brick or stone construction. However, veneer provides some protection against external exposures such as grass or brush fires.

- Metal-clad or asbestos-clad construction, consisting of a sheet metal (steel or aluminum) covering fastened to the wooden structure, or cement asbestos shingles or corrugated cement asbestos sheets over wood siding. Although the covering can prevent ignition of the wood by minor fires, little protection is provided against external exposure fires of any magnitude, such as when a neighboring building is on fire.
- Stucco, consisting of cement plaster on lath over wood-frame construction, which adds a slight degree of resistance to fire, depending on the type of lath used and the thickness of the plaster.
- Concrete block walls of unknown fire resistance, which are also classified as frame buildings for insurance rating purposes. In fact, any building that cannot be properly classified because of lack of information is tentatively classed and rated as a frame building.

Exhibit 1-5 shows a skeletal view of frame construction. As illustrated, wood studs provide structural support to the building components, even if stone masonry facades are used.

Although frame construction is less desirable than other, more fire-resistive construction classifications, some occupancies are acceptable in the frame construction classification. Offices and other occupancies that present few hazards and a high level of protection are suitable for frame buildings. The weight-bearing frame structural components can be protected against both the vertical and horizontal spread of fire. The inherent problem of combustible external surfaces remains. In extreme cases, exposure fires can be reduced by an external sprinkler system. Such systems are not common, however, and are rarely found in colder climates.

Frame construction is common throughout the United States, particularly where other building materials, such as clay bricks, are unavailable or expensive. The northwest and south-central areas of the country contain many large frame buildings. Because of the earthquake hazard, many small frame structures are found throughout California. A frame structure's ability to bend with earthquake tremors makes it a more desirable risk for that peril than is a masonry structure. However, masonry structures are prevalent in the Southeast, where hurricanes are a great concern.

Joisted Masonry

Joisted masonry construction has load-bearing exterior walls of brick, adobe, concrete, gypsum block, stone, tile, or similar materials with combustible floors and roofs. Most discussions of joisted masonry construction refer to its two subclassifications, ordinary construction and mill construction.

Exhibit 1-5
Examples of Wood Frame Platform and Balloon Construction

Wood frame platform construction (also called western construction) is the most common method used in residential construction. The "platform" is the foundation and floor structure. Walls are built on this base. If there is a second story, another platform is built on top of the first. Wood frame platform construction has replaced balloon framing, which was the standard building practice until about 1930. With **balloon frame construction**, the bearing wall studs rest on the foundation. The second-floor joists rest on a ledger strip notched into the studs.

Wood Frame Platform Construction

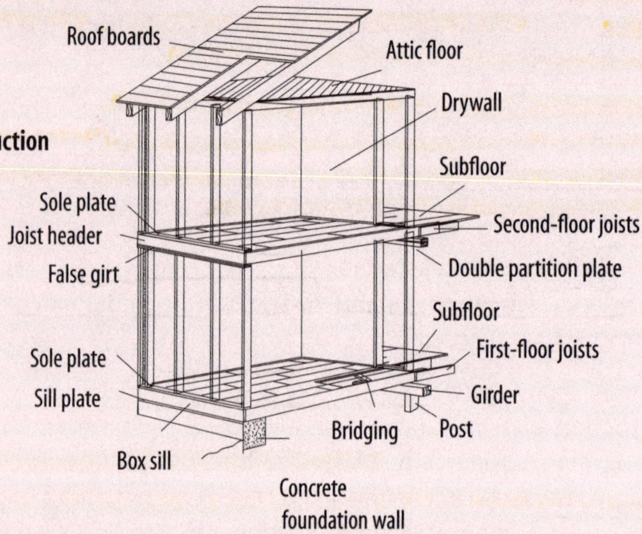

Balloon Frame Construction

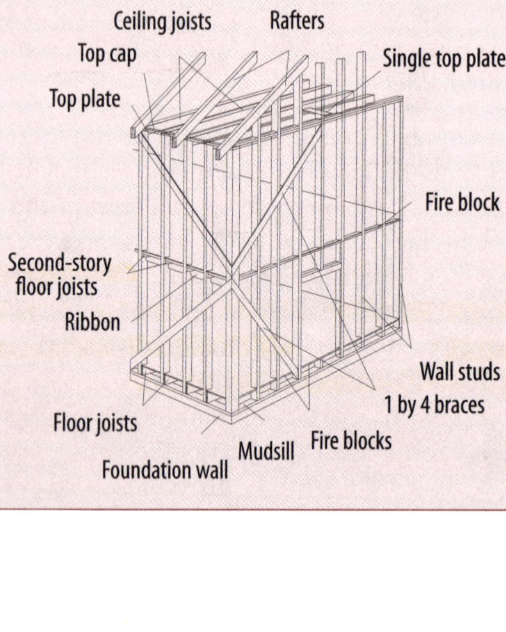

Exhibit 1-6
Example of Ordinary Construction

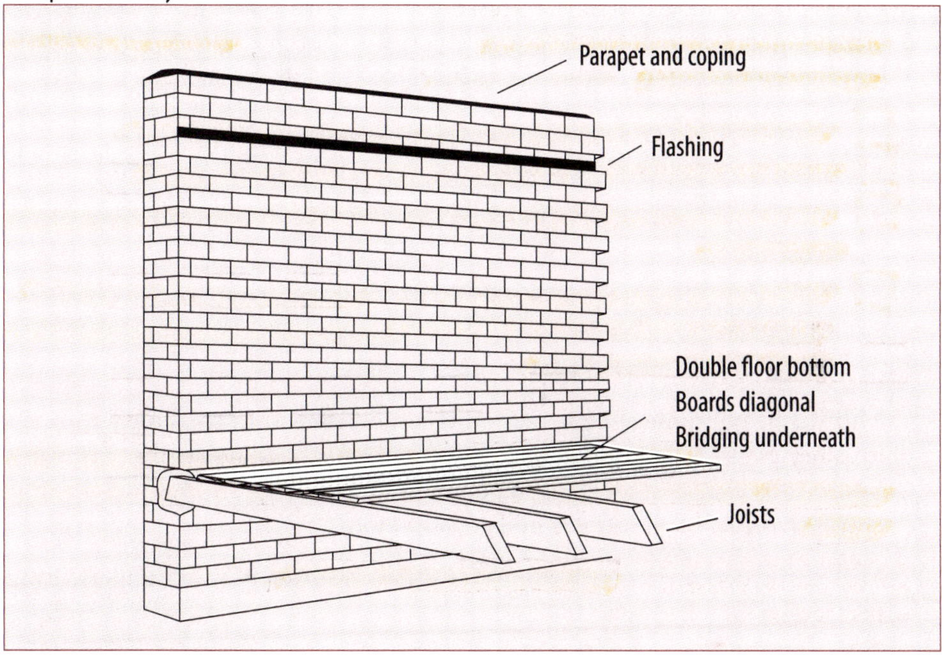

Ordinary Construction

Ordinary construction has exterior load-bearing walls of noncombustible materials with at least a one-hour fire-resistance rating. The materials used for floors, roofs, and interior surfaces are usually combustible. Ordinary construction is referred to as brick, wood joisted, or brick joisted. Exhibit 1-6 is an illustration of ordinary construction.

Ordinary construction has many of the inherent hazards of frame construction because of the possibility of horizontal and vertical fire spread. Therefore, firestops are just as important in the horizontal and vertical areas in ordinary construction as in frame construction.

Buildings of ordinary construction are usually found in major metropolitan areas in the northern states. The buildings are usually no more than six stories high because the exterior walls, which are the bearing walls, cannot support a taller structure. Many of those buildings were constructed before World War II. Consequently, age and deterioration are potential problems. Achieving proper amounts of insurance to value is often a problem. Although a building of ordinary construction is less desirable in an area subject to earthquakes, ordinary construction has proven to be adequate in areas subject to hurricane-force winds.

Mill Construction

Occasionally, underwriters are presented with risks that can be classified as heavy timber or mill construction, which is sometimes referred to as "slow-burning construction." **Mill construction** has the following characteristics:

- A minimum two-hour fire-resistance rating on the bearing walls
- Wood columns that are at least eight inches thick on every side
- Wood beams, supports, and ties that are at least six inches wide or ten inches deep
- Floors that are tongue and groove planks and at least three inches thick with a one-inch overlay and roof decks that are on heavy timbers with at least a two-inch thickness

Mill (or heavy timber) construction is a subclass within the broader joisted masonry class. A major characteristic of mill construction is the *absence* of floor joists, which means the absence of hidden spaces through which fire can spread. Exhibit 1-7 illustrates mill construction.

Mill construction has two important characteristics from an underwriting perspective:

- The heavy floors, built without concealed spaces, constitute a firestop, retarding the spread of flames.
- The heavy timbers of the beams and columns give the building great structural strength, reducing the possibility of collapse.

Mill construction is very expensive, but it nonetheless would survive a severe fire. Buildings of mill construction are primarily found in the Northeast.

Occasionally, a mill construction building with laminated beams is found in a western state. A risk of that type is usually a relatively new building, and, if of true mill construction, the risk is highly acceptable for most occupancies, such as shopping centers, churches, or wineries. Those buildings often have unique architectural designs and configurations, making proper valuation difficult.

Noncombustible

The **noncombustible construction** classification includes buildings with exterior walls, floors, and roofs of noncombustible materials supported by noncombustible supports such as metal, asbestos, and gypsum. Buildings are usually made of metal, but the metal is unprotected and hence not fire resistive.

Underwriters should be knowledgeable enough of noncombustible construction to address a common misconcception that noncombustible construction

Exhibit 1-7
An Example of Mill Construction

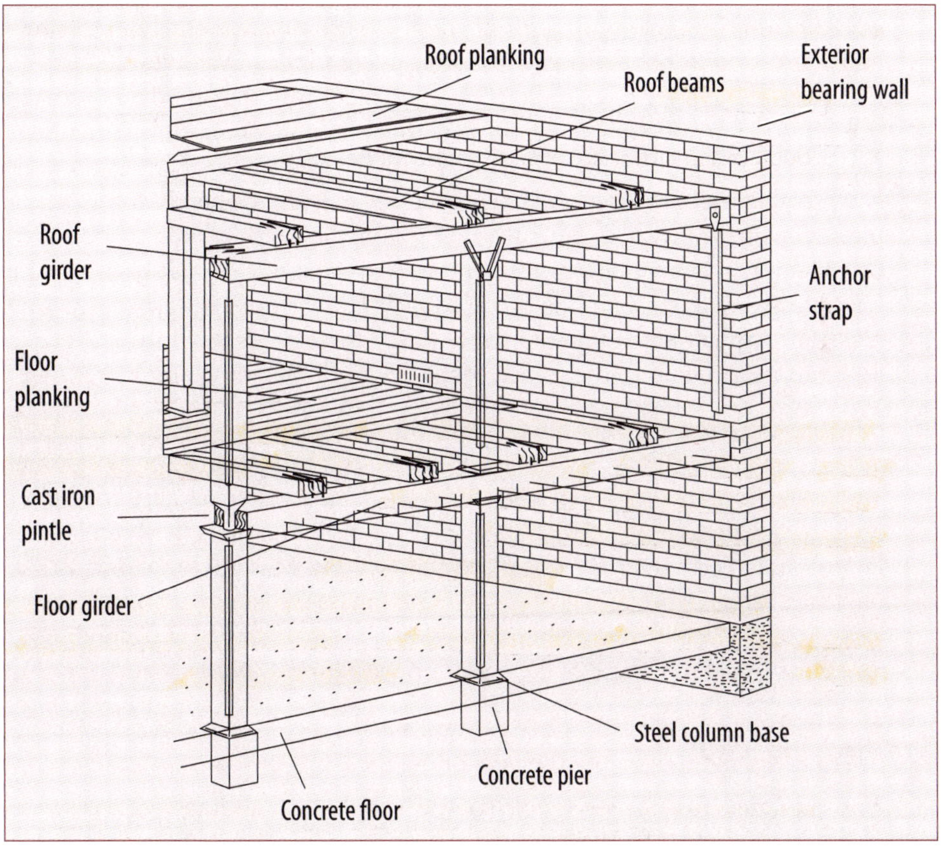

is a close equivalent to fire-resistive construction. Risk managers, agents, and brokers sometimes overestimate the capacity of noncombustible buildings to withstand damage by fire. They assume that because load-bearing components of the structure will not burn, they will stand up to fire without significant damage. This is not true.

When exposed to the heat a fire generates, unprotected metal columns, beams, and joists rapidly lose tensile strength. They buckle and warp, raising the prospect that the entire structure will collapse and become a total loss. This is especially true of the light-metal construction that has become popular for many commercial structures. As discussed later in this section, the structural members of a fire-resistive structure are insulated against the destructive effects of heat.

Masonry Noncombustible

The **masonry noncombustible** classification includes buildings with exterior walls of masonry and noncombustible or slow-burning floors and roofs. A slow-burning floor or roof has a flame spread rating of twenty-five or less (Class A). The main benefit of noncombustible construction is that it will not aid in the spread of fire. Occasionally, the integrity of a noncombustible structure is violated by the use of materials such as asphalt or felt vapor barriers on noncombustible roof deckings. A large loss in 1953 at the General Motors transmission plant in Livonia, Michigan, of a noncombustible building occupied by a metalworking operation was attributed to the use of asphalt barriers. The heat of the fire in the building began to melt and vaporize the asphalt roofing material. Asphalt vapor entered the building through joints in the steel deck roof and contributed to the spread of the fire in the building's interior.[4]

The typical masonry noncombustible building has a masonry nonbearing wall surface, a concrete floor, some type of metal deck roof, and unprotected steel webbing supported by unprotected columns. Underwriters usually encounter light to moderately severe fuel loads in those risks and must be careful in selecting risks because of the potential for collapse. Masonry noncombustible buildings have withstood major windstorms and earthquakes with little or no damage. Low initial cost, low maintenance, and the ability to withstand those perils have made this type of construction extremely popular.

Modified Fire-Resistive

The **modified fire-resistive** classification includes buildings with exterior walls, floors, and roof constructed of masonry or fire-resistive materials with a fire-resistance rating of between one and two hours.

Fire-Resistive

The **fire-resistive** classification includes buildings constructed of any combination of the following materials:[5]

- Exterior walls or exterior structural components made of the following:
    - Solid masonry, including reinforced concrete
    - Hollow masonry block at least twelve inches thick
    - Hollow masonry block less than twelve inches thick, but at least eight inches thick, with a listed fire-resistance rating of at least two hours
    - Materials used have a fire-resistance rating of at least two hours

- Floors and roofs made of the following:
  - Floors and roof of reinforced concrete with slabs at least four inches thick
  - Construction known as "joist systems" with slabs supported by concrete joists spaced not more than thirty-six inches apart with a slab thickness of at least two and three-quarters inches
  - Floor and roof assemblies with a fire-resistance rating of not less than two hours
- Structural metal supports:
  - Horizontal and vertical load-bearing protected metal supports (including horizontal pre-stressed or post-tensioned concrete units) with a fire-resistance rating of at least two hours

From a fire underwriting standpoint, fire-resistive is the best construction. Buildings have walls, floors, columns, and roofs constructed of a noncombustible material. The materials either have a fire-resistance rating in excess of two hours or are protected by a noncombustible covering, such as plaster or gypsum, to achieve a two-hour rating. "Fire-resistive construction" is a general term that encompasses buildings with ratings between two and four hours. In terms of structural integrity, this is a wide range. Exhibit 1-8 illustrates fire-resistive construction.

Virtually all types of occupancy classes can be found in fire-resistive buildings. Most high-rise office and apartment buildings are in that classification. Other fire-resistive occupancies include heavy manufacturing plants in which large structural supports for machinery are required and warehouses with heavy fuel loads.

Mixed Construction

Underwriters often encounter buildings that do not fit into any single construction classification. These types of construction are known as **mixed construction**. The architectural design might mix building types, or owners might have made additions and changes over the years.

Construction Design

The construction design characteristics of a building affect its underwriting desirability. A structure's size (height and shape), number of fire divisions, and building openings (windows and doors) influence the ease with which fires can be controlled and extinguished.

Exhibit 1-8
Fire-Resistive Construction

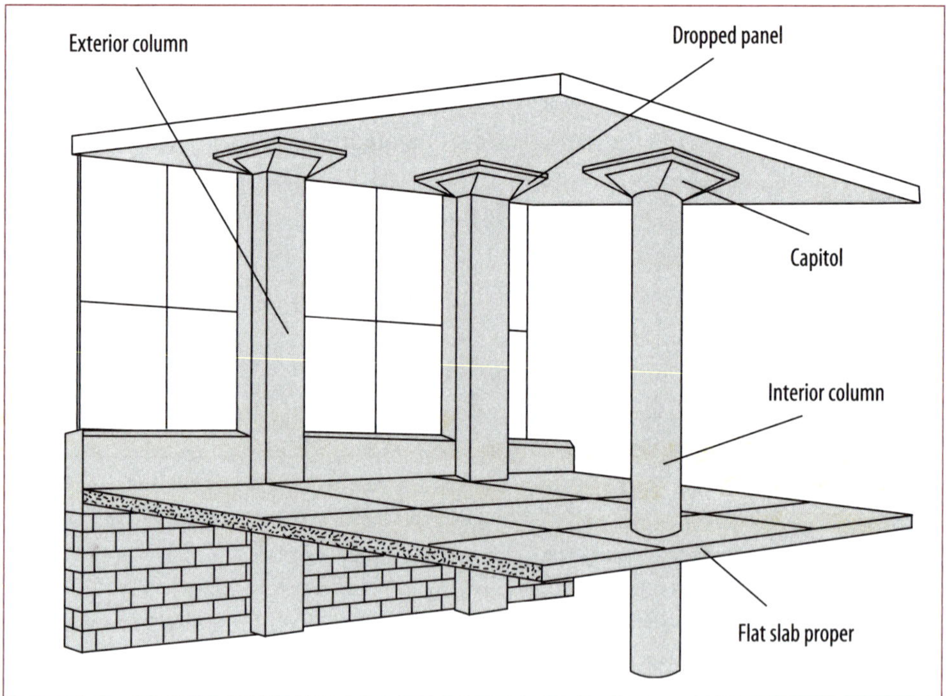

High-Rise Buildings

The height of a structure also influences the risk's general desirability. A 50,000-square-foot building could be one, two, three, or more stories high. A thorough description of the structure's design or a diagram is helpful in evaluating how the square footage is used. Underwriters must try to evaluate the design of the structure according to the following criteria:

- Its ability to confine fire
- Its ability to resist fire
- The capabilities of the exterior firefighting force, especially in view of the structure's design (for example, low, windowless buildings)
- The nature of the occupancy

In recent years, structures that rise beyond the reach of municipal fire service ladders have become more common. Buildings such as the Sears Tower and the Canadian National Tower in Toronto rise more than 1,000 feet above street level and present unique problems. Most municipal fire departments cannot handle a fire from the exterior of a building taller than 120 feet. A building 120 feet tall would have ten to twelve stories. The underwriter must accept that the fire department cannot be of much assistance from the exterior of the premises in a modern high-rise.

Buildings that are taller than the tallest ladder available to the fire service are commonly referred to as "high-rises," but not everyone agrees on exactly what constitutes a **high-rise building**. NFPA defines any structure taller than seventy-five feet as a high-rise, but some underwriters prefer a more flexible definition. They consider buildings up to six stories high (approximately the seventy-five feet that the NFPA uses) as low-rise.

Taller structures are divided into two classes that depend on the equipment available for fighting fires. High-rise buildings are those that rise above the reach of the tallest aerial ladder available to the local fire service, and anything in between is medium-rise. For many years, no aerial ladder reached beyond 100 feet, so 100 feet defined where high-rise construction began. Some fire services now have aerial ladders that rise to 120 feet and that change the definitions of high-rise and medium-rise in the communities they protect. If the fire service has no aerial ladders, any structure above six stories (or 75 feet) is a high-rise. In the future, improved technology could extend the reach of aerial ladders and alter those definitions.

If a fire started in a high-rise, the fire department would have to attack the fire from inside, which could delay the firefighting response. When fire struck a midtown Manhattan high-rise office building several years ago, the second fire company to arrive did nothing more than rescue the first fire company on the scene. Units that arrived later had to fight their way through the rescue efforts and devote their initial attention to saving the building's occupants. As a result, fire service units were on the scene for several critical minutes before they could start to attack the blaze. Damage to property was much more severe than it might otherwise have been. The fire also posed a serious threat to both firefighters and the occupants of the building. That incident was one of several that prompted the city council to revise New York City building codes in order to require the retrofitting of buildings with sprinklers.

Underwriters should pay particular attention to the structure's fire-resistive characteristics and to the presence or absence of approved horizontal and vertical barriers that confine the fire to its area of origin. Underwriters should also evaluate the internal protection, such as sprinklers, standpipes, and hoses. For example, in a high-rise, heating and air-conditioning ducts often penetrate vertical and horizontal barriers. This can contribute to the spread of fire unless the ducts are equipped with automatic shutoffs and dampers.

Elevator shafts and stairwells, unless properly constructed, can also spread fire and smoke.

High-rise structures require control of heavy fuel loads. Occupancies should not contain high fire hazards as a result of the tenants' operations or heavy fuel loads caused by storage. High-rise structures are often office and residential occupancies with relatively fewer combustibles than other types of occupancies and few ignition sources. Most offices have storage areas, duplicating areas, small kitchen areas, and areas containing data processing equipment, and such areas usually have a large amount of paper. The potential for a severe fire might exist in what are normally considered light hazard areas.

High-rise buildings sometimes have restaurants or bars located on the upper floors to take advantage of attractive views, and those businesses are high-hazard occupancies. Without adequate loss control measures or private protection with control monitored by a central station, they constitute a significant concern to the underwriter.

In fighting a high-rise fire, the fire department breaks out windows for ventilation. If high wind conditions are present, the high winds can increase the spread of the fire.

In addition, underwriters should be concerned with life safety. A 100-story structure might have as many as 25,000 occupants. If a severe fire occurs on the fiftieth floor, over 12,000 people (on the average) would be located above the fire and subjected to potential injury from flame, smoke, and gas. The occupants of fire-resistive buildings are often instructed to go to a certain area and wait for further instructions. Again, evaluating the integrity of the structure is important because occupants might not be able to pass through the fire area unless the structure is equipped with specialized evacuation facilities. Life safety is important to fire underwriters not only out of concern for the occupants, but also because firefighters arriving at the scene of the fire will concentrate on rescuing the occupants before attacking the fire.

Fire Divisions

Large horizontal structures present a different type of problem than that present in a high-rise building. Structures with a total horizontal area approaching 1 million square feet are more common than they once were. The solution to many high-rise structure fire problems is vertical integrity, and a corresponding solution for large horizontal areas is the use of fire divisions.

A **fire division** restricts the spread of fire. For insurance rating, a fire division must meet specific requirements. The buildings must be separated by two independent walls or one continuous, common masonry wall that divides two adjoining properties. Exhibit 1-9 illustrates two approaches that qualify as fire divisions.

Exhibit 1-9
Fire Divisions

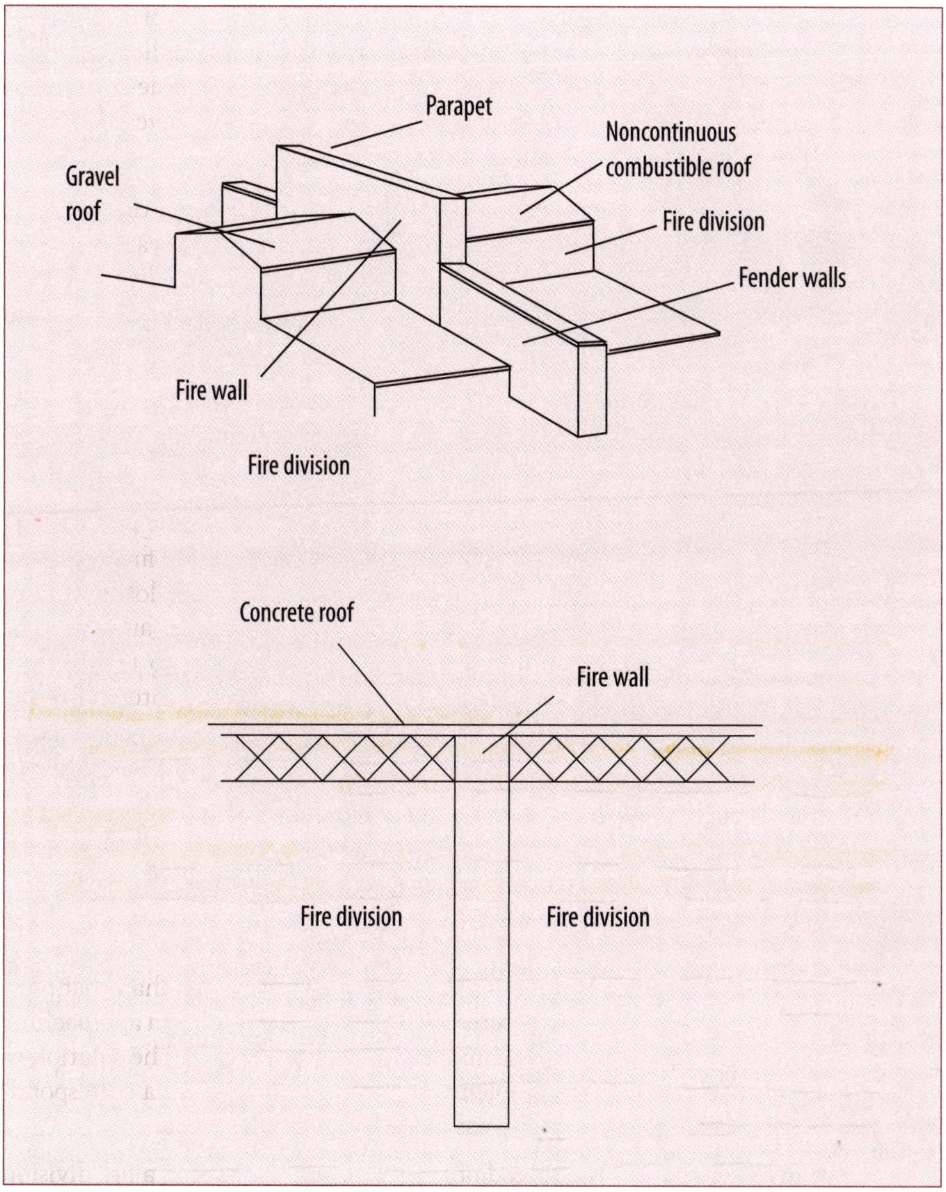

Exhibit 1-10
Typical Freestanding Fire Wall

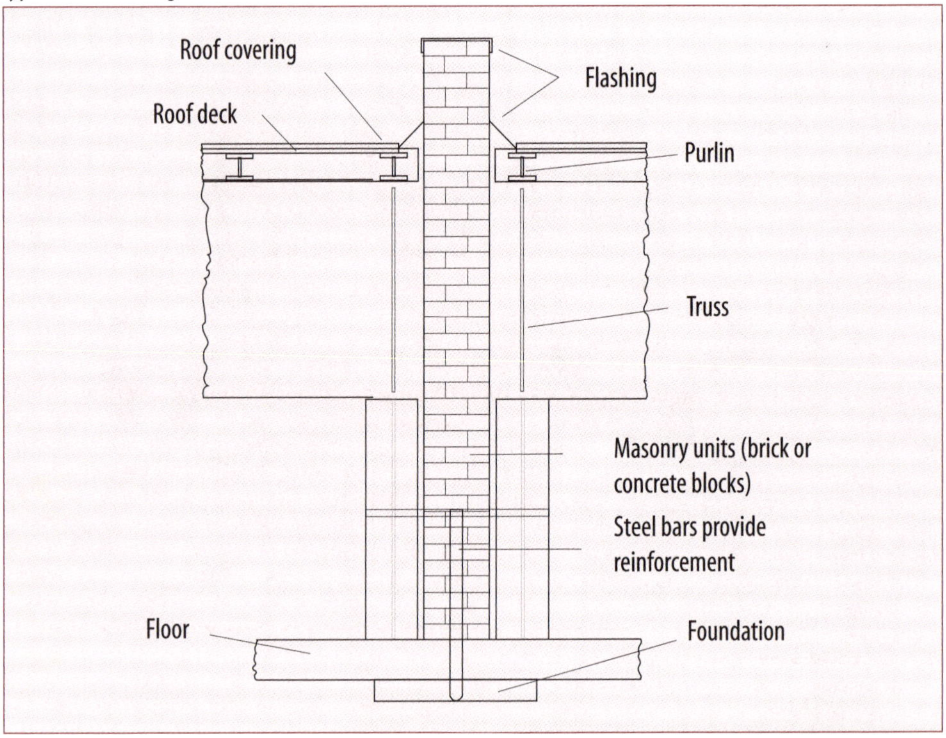

Fire walls are essential to fire divisions. A fire wall is an interior wall erected to prevent the spread of fire and to "withstand the effects of the severest fire expected to occur in the building. Fire walls must provide a complete barrier to the spread of fire."[6] They must be fire-resistive or very slow burning. Also, they must not stop short of the ceiling or floor (a stream of superheated gas can pour through a one-inch opening like a blow torch), and they must not interfere with the safe exit of the building occupants. A wall must be at least eight inches thick and of masonry material to be classified as a fire wall. Exhibit 1-10 depicts a typical fire wall.

The combustibility of the contents of the building determine the adequacy of fire walls. What is adequate for a school building might be inadequate to prevent fire spread in a paper mill. In fire-resistive buildings, interior walls that extend from floor to ceiling might be of sufficient fire-resistive quality to be called fire walls.

In a masonry or frame building, a fire wall must extend beyond the roof line to be effective. Since fire can spread via the roof in such buildings, those fire wall extensions, or **parapets**, extend above the normal roof line. Parapets should be eighteen to forty-eight inches high, depending on the occupancy of the building. In buildings of frame construction, fire walls must also extend through combustible exterior walls to have full effect. Those extensions, called fender walls, act as a horizontal parapet that would prevent the spread of fire through the outside wall and around the fire wall. Builders of apartment houses and hotels use them to provide balconies and enhance privacy.

Frequently, industrial firms adopt automated processes to increase production and decrease unit cost. Automation is best adapted to processes with uninterrupted horizontal production lines. In these instances, fire loss control can often conflict with economies of scale. Although loss control considerations may suggest the introduction of a fire wall or other protection device for a building opening, those fire barriers could interfere with efficient production.

The underwriter must consider the building occupancy and its fuel load when determining acceptable fire divisions. A 100,000-square-foot warehouse used to store steel presents few problems. However, a flammable-liquid storage area in excess of 5,000 square feet is a severe problem.

Underwriters should suggest the physical separation of occupancies to prevent losses. The segregation of the finished-goods warehouse from the production facilities and the raw-material warehouse could prevent a major business income loss and possibly reduce the size of the direct loss. The risk manager or plant owner, however, might be faced with a conflict between production efficiency and exposure reduction.

Underwriters can also rely on **curtain boards**, which are illustrated in Exhibit 1-11. Those partial fire walls, when installed in conjunction with roof vents, help contain the hot smoke and gases in the area of origin, aiding the exterior venting of the property and simplifying the task of fire suppression.

Building Openings

An underwriter might decide that a certain construction type appears to be appropriate for the intended occupancy. However, during the construction process, subcontractors, such as electricians and heating and air conditioning technicians, have installed electrical conduit and ductwork throughout the structure to distribute electricity, heat, or air conditioning. Those subcontractors might have violated vertical and horizontal firestops or fire walls.

A loss involving a high-rise structure near completion that occurred in New York City illustrates the consequences of unplanned building openings. The structural components of that building were noncombustible and had originally been adequately protected to provide a minimum of a two-hour

Exhibit 1-11
Curtain Boards and Roof Vents

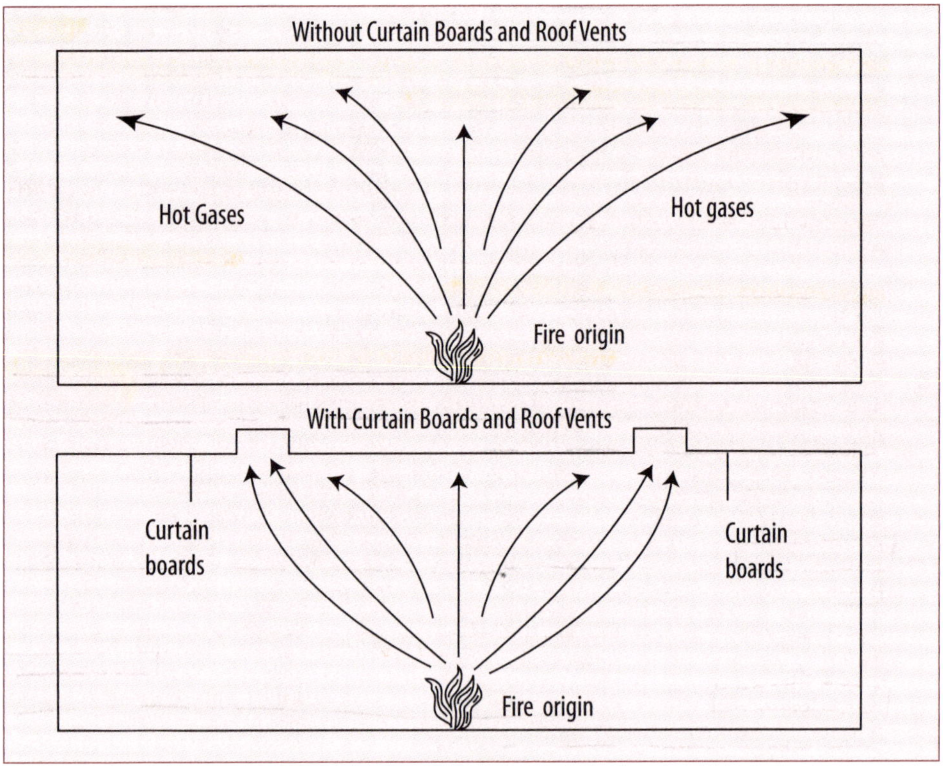

fire rating. Installation work by subcontractors, however, diminished that protection. The effect was to lay bare the structural steel components. The structure's completion did not include resurfacing those structural components with a protective coating. A subsequent fire weakened the steel enough that the steel had to be replaced before the structure was occupied. Although the damage to those components was minimal and their original cost was not high, the cost of replacing major building supports within a structure nearing completion resulted in a multimillion dollar loss.

In addition to the other ducts and passageways present within a structure, buildings are often equipped with door openings between fire divisions and with floor openings for stairs between floors. Elevators, dumbwaiters, conveyor belts, and air and light shafts are also often present. All of those openings violate the basic integrity of a fire division. In rare instances, some of those openings cannot be protected, although most can be corrected with approved fire doors. Fire doors are usually rated according to their fire-resistive hourly rating, such as a three-hour fire door. To be most effective, a fire door in a fire wall should be capable of withstanding the same intensity of fire as the wall itself. Even with a fire door and other fire protection devices in operation, an opening will likely have less resistance to fire than a fire wall that has not been compromised by an opening.

A vertical opening is protected only when it is wholly segregated into a separate fire division. Elevators and stairwells, when properly constructed, constitute a building within a building. If this design is achieved, a fire cannot spread from one floor to another unless it moves horizontally through one floor, through a barrier door, into the stairwell, up the stairwell, and through a second barrier door.

Fire doors are approved when they meet design specifications of NFPA. Manufacturers of fire doors have their products tested by Underwriters Laboratories or the Factory Mutual Engineering and Research Corporation. An approved door is granted a seal, which is usually placed on its edge, indicating its rating.

Fire doors are rated according to hourly ratings, but an alphabetic designation (or a combination of a specific time rating and a letter classification) is also used. For example, fire doors can be rated in descending order of fire resistance, A through E. (Class A fire doors have a three-hour rating; Class E doors have a forty-five-minute rating.) Those ratings measure the door's ability to prevent the passage of heat, smoke, and other products of combustion. The rating might vary, depending on the occupancy and the location of the door within the building.

An approved fire door is obviously useless if propped or blocked open. Therefore, each door must be automatically self-closing and unobstructed. Doors that must be left open to permit efficient industrial operations are fitted with fusible links that permit automatic self-closing when heat activated.

Construction Materials

The interior finish of a structure affects the desirability of a risk. For example, assume that a structure is of superior fire-resistive construction, with all building components rated at four hours' fire resistance. The structure has a light-hazard occupancy such as an apartment or an office. However, the interior finish is highly combustible. The characteristics of interior finishes that are most relevant to fire problems include their ability to do the following:

- Spread fire
- Contribute fuel to the fire
- Emit smoke and noxious gases when burning

Those three characteristics affect the overall property loss potential and the safety of the occupants. Several disastrous fires have occurred in Korea and in South America in which little structural physical damage was done but during which severe loss of life occurred as the result of highly combustible interior finishes. The MGM Grand Hotel fire in Las Vegas involved highly combustible decor that contributed to loss of life as well as physical damage to the structure.

Noncombustible interior finishes that are relatively less combustible include plaster, gypsum, and wall board coverings. Combustible interior finishes include wood or plywood, fiber ceiling tiles, and plastic wall coverings. Surface coatings such as paints, varnishes, plastic ornamentation, and wallpapers, when added to other combustible finishes, could significantly contribute to the fuel load. Even adhesives used in floor or ceiling tile can add substantially to a building's capacity to sustain or fuel a fire.

The hazard created by an interior finish arises when the finish is installed. During construction, interior finishes can serve as additional fuel. Once the finish is installed, a small fire can ignite the interior finish to quickly engulf the entire room, a process referred to as a flashover. (Flashover is caused by heat radiating off ceilings and upper walls that gradually heats the combustibles in the room. When the combustibles are heated to ignition temperatures, all the combustibles burst into flame simultaneously.) Even a small fire involving a highly combustible interior finish can generate toxic gases that can be distributed quickly throughout the building. The toxic fumes and smoke from the MGM Grand fire killed many people.[7]

A high degree of interior combustibility can generate a fire that will climb the outside of a building, moving from one floor to the next, even when the vertical openings within the interior of the structure are well protected. Fire can climb the outside of a noncombustible or fire-resistive structure by escaping through windows. Hot gases rising along the outside wall can radiate enough heat through the windows of floors above the fire to ignite nearby combustibles. Although the structure itself is of fire-resistive construction and the occupancy is of low combustibility, the interior finish must also be examined to determine the building's actual combustibility. The combustibility of interior finishes can be measured analytically, using flame-spread tests.

On February 18, 1981, a fire started in the eighth floor lobby of the Las Vegas Hilton Hotel, next door to Clark County Fire Department Station 18. To enhance the atmosphere of luxury, the hotel had covered the walls of the lobby with plush carpet. The fire blew out the lobby window and spread to the floor above by radiating intense heat through the windows. Drapes in guest rooms and carpet covering hallway walls ignited quickly. The poured-in-place reinforced concrete floors could not inhibit the vertical spread of the fire by this route. Firefighters found a fire that had already involved two floors and watched it spread to a third before they could reach the hotel. They were ready to call for the help of additional units before they could get all their apparatus out the firehouse door. Of the hotel's thirty floors, twenty-two sustained damage; 200 guests suffered injuries, and 8 died.[8]

Three factors enabled the Las Vegas Hilton fire to spread so quickly and do so much damage, despite early detection. First, the exterior walls contained vast expanses of glass, a material that does not create a barrier to radiated heat. Second, the highly combustible drapes and wall coverings that were at or very close to windows allowed the fire to break through the building's exterior and move up the outside of the building. Third, emergency procedures contributed to the fire's severity. Hotel security staff decided to investigate the alarm before calling the fire service. Station 18 received the alarm a full seven minutes after hotel security did. By then, the fire was spreading so rapidly that the fire service had no chance to keep up with it.

Factory Mutual Engineering and Research Corporation has developed standards for safely sizing and spacing windows to prevent the spread of fire up the outside of a building. Increased vertical spacing and reduced window size can limit both the escape of heat from the fire scene and the amount of heat radiated back through the windows of floors above the fire. Architects, owners, and tenants, however, find larger windows more pleasing.

Insulation

Just as the interior finish of a structure has a great effect on the structure's combustibility, insulation can also add to combustibility. A common form of insulation is fiberglass that usually has a combustible paper backing. Insulation material includes combustible substances such as recycled paper and wood chips formed into fiberboard. Insulation is used not only for heat conservation, but also as a sound barrier. Combustible insulation can be found in the interior walls of highly fire-resistive buildings.

Whether the insulation is installed to conserve heat or to suppress sound, underwriters should try to determine the insulation's flame spread, as well as its fuel- and smoke-contribution characteristics. Both rigid foam board and sprayed- on cellular plastic foam insulation produce high volumes of toxic smoke when burned. Building codes typically require foam insulation to be protected with fire-resistive barriers.

Environmental awareness has led to renewed interest in energy conservation, so underwriters should direct loss control personnel to determine whether additional insulation has been added to a structure. For example, if a roof and wall structure were designed and originally constructed in accordance with a standard fire rating, a problem would occur if additional combustible insulation were added. That insulation, if improperly installed, could have the adverse effect of holding the heat being generated by the fire within the structure, concentrating it on other building components without insulation and possibly weakening them to the point of early collapse.

Roofing

The exterior surface of a roof is used for two basic purposes. The first is as a weather seal. The quality of this weather seal can be important to an underwriter who writes commercial property policies that normally include weather-related causes of loss. Second, the surface of a roof is a barrier against fires outside the building to which the building is exposed. In its role as a fire protection barrier, the roof should be as noncombustible as possible.

Roofs are subject to fire from two sides: heat, sparks, and falling embers from outside fires and heat from inside fires. The combustibility of both the exterior and interior surfaces of a roof is therefore important. Untreated wooden shingles invite spread of fires to other structures. Resistive coverings are classified as A (safest), B, and C (some fire resistance). Treated cedar shingles and zinc sheets over asphalt-saturated organic felt are C. Other metal roofs and various combinations of asphalt, felt, and gravel in layers range from A to C. Concrete, tile, and slate are A. Tile and slate, however, are subject to other damage, such as wind damage.

Asphalt shingles are probably the most common roof covering. When properly constructed and installed, asphalt shingles act as an excellent barrier against even severe fire exposures. Combustible materials such as wood shakes or shingles and tar paper afford almost no protection from fire. In recent California brush fires, high winds caused wood shake roofs to send sparks and embers great distances downwind.

Other Building Construction Materials

Two other aspects of building construction materials that underwriters must consider are the materials used for interior and exterior decoration.

Interior Decoration

Underwriters must be aware of features such as pictures, drapes, and wall hangings in a building. Such items add not only significant value but also potential hazards. In occupancies such as restaurants, bowling centers, bars, theaters, clubs, and funeral parlors, the interior decor should be scrutinized. Otherwise, the underwriter might inadvertently judge that a risk is of low combustibility when, in fact, it is not. For example, unless made of flame-retardant fabric, upholstered furniture in offices can be highly combustible. Unless care is taken, an underwriter might easily underestimate the fuel load of an office building. In restaurants, open flames from candles used for their atmospheric effect can create additional sources of ignition.

Foyers of some high-rise office buildings have murals, fountains, pools, sculptures, and friezes. Those decorations might obscure architectural faults or engineering features such as ductwork, and they could constitute collapse or breakage hazards as well as attract vandals.

Exterior Decoration

Vermiculite and marble veneer panels are often present on the exterior of the lower floors of office buildings. Those veneers cover protected steel components or hide the residual form markings in poured concrete structures. They are subject to breakage and cracking from the effects of ice in loose joints. Older buildings could have glazed tiles capping parapets that can fall or be blown off in windstorms.

Age

A key factor affecting the underwriting desirability of a building is its age. Following are underwriting considerations regarding older buildings (although they are not all specifically construction-related):

- A different building code in force at the time of construction
- Possible deterioration of heating and electrical systems
- Possible changes in occupancy relative to the use originally intended for the building
- Potential increases in losses imposed by current building codes
- Possible deterioration or erosion by dry rot, rust, termites, settling, or excessive wear

Although proper maintenance will mitigate the effects of age and deterioration, all buildings eventually wear out. The degree of deterioration is directly related to the basic type of construction, the occupancy, the use of the building, and the quality of the owner's maintenance.

A frame structure will normally show its age faster than a joisted masonry structure; a joisted masonry structure will show its age faster than a fire-resistive structure. However, an office occupancy in a frame structure with good maintenance can outlive a fire-resistive building occupied by a drop-forge operation with minimal maintenance.

The method of constructing buildings and their style change significantly with time. Building materials that were used in the 1920s or 1930s are obsolete today. Today's plumbing systems seldom use cast iron, galvanized iron, or brass piping. Iron is susceptible to corrosion and rusting. Brass pipes are susceptible to vibration and subsequently loose fittings. Electrical systems of forty, fifty, and sixty years ago were designed primarily for lighting, but modern wiring systems are designed to accommodate space heating, computer systems, and heavy appliances.

A building that was designed for a dry-goods retailing occupancy fifty years ago might be inadequate for a laundry, a printer, or a beverage distributor today. Weight loadings for machines and bottled goods might exceed the original specifications. Equipment demands for electricity have increased greatly. The structural integrity of buildings also deteriorates over time. Underwriters should determine whether the plumbing and electrical systems have been brought up to the current codes.

Fire

From the perspective of fire underwriting, newer structures are more desirable risks than older structures. As the construction industry has advanced technologically, structures more appropriate for their occupancies have been built. Those structures can be easily replaced or repaired.

Modern technology has increased the use of noncombustible materials, introduced high-capacity electrical systems, improved space heating and cooling systems, and changed the predominant fuels used on premises.

When examining a submission on a building more than twenty years old, some underwriters request loss control inspections to verify the condition of key elements of the structure such as the electrical, heating, air conditioning, and plumbing systems. Loss control reports provide valuable information regarding the desirability of the risk.

Windstorm and Hail

The elemental forces of wind, rain, and hail all take their toll on the exterior of a building. Even a structure that is adequately maintained will show its age in its exterior surfaces, particularly the roof. If the shingles or the roof surfaces are not replaced on a twenty- or thirty-year cycle, losses can be expected from hail or wind. The design of roof surfaces in the past did not include such features as self-sealing shingle tabs, which are commonplace today. Without such features, shingles can easily be torn off by gales or hurricanes.

Collapse

Most policies that cover broad named perils or risks of direct loss provide protection against collapse. Collapse has probably produced more extensive damage to structures, including total losses, than any other peril except fire and wind. Collapse is often not underwritten because many underwriters consider it to be inconsequential. Age influences the desirability of a risk being insured for collapse because structures weaken through fatigue, misuse, or exposure to weather, such as the weight of ice, sleet, and snow.

Several factors, many related to age, can cause an apparently sound building to collapse suddenly and without warning. A once exclusive hotel in New York City collapsed even though prior inspections had revealed no hint of danger. A later investigation revealed structural fatigue as the cause of the failure. The design of the nineteenth-century structure did not contemplate the vibrations generated by passing traffic and a subway line later built under the street in front of the building. Trains and heavy trucks contributed to the fatigue, but poor maintenance was probably a factor.

Hard Use

A structure that is heavily loaded with contents will begin to show its age or wear through such symptoms as depressed wooden floors or spalling (scaling) concrete surfaces. Just as a metal spring will begin to lose its strength after it has been compressed numerous times, a building will begin to lose the ability to support its design load after continued excessive use. Hard use can greatly affect potential losses. A risk that is well constructed but lightly occupied, such as an office or a condominium, will have a useful life of many years. A structure designed and used for heavy manufacturing will have a shorter useful life. The occupancy can wear out the building, creating a potentially catastrophic collapse exposure.

Weather

The effects of wind, rain, hail, and heat and cold also affect a structure's useful life and potential desirability. Wooden surfaces that are not adequately maintained rot and lose their strength. Concrete or brick surfaces also need protection against the effects of weather, although to a lesser degree than wood. As those surfaces and structural supports begin to weaken, they will no longer support the structure's design load. Symptoms such as hairline cracks in columns or bearing walls must be recognized as potential loss causes. Water markings from floods or leaks can also be vital signals of potential loss causes.

Underwriters should remember that weather can also cause new structures to collapse. The collapse of the new Hartford (Connecticut) Civic Auditorium in the winter of 1977-78 from heavy, wet snow was precipitated by faulty design.

Sources of Construction Information

Underwriters should understand the types of basic construction that are within their territory, and they should know what construction types predominate as well as the current construction trends. General knowledge, however, is only a basis on which inferences can be drawn in the absence of more specific data. Specific data are available from the following sources:

- Applications
- Specifically published rates and class rating manuals
- Bureau reports
- Inspection reports and diagrams (usually accompanying the inspection report)
- Local building codes

Applications

Applications for insurance provide the name of the insured, which often includes some generic phrase indicating the occupancy of that structure; for example, David Schneider dba Schneider's Philadelphia Cheesesteaks. The application generally provides the address of the building, its age, and possibly additional data regarding construction type, types and age of plumbing and heating systems, and the presence or absence of special protective devices such as automatic sprinkler systems. The application only provides sufficient data for an underwriting decision on smaller and less sophisticated property accounts.

Specifically Published Rates and Class Rating Manuals

Property insurance risks are either class rated or specifically (schedule) rated. A **class rate** applies to an entire category of similar risks and does not vary based on the specialized features of any particular risk within the class. Each class is categorized based on general construction type and occupancy. Class rates are found in the insurer's manuals. Those rates are usually developed from loss costs published by insurance advisory organizations. Insurance Services Office (ISO) is the largest of those organizations.

A **specific rate,** on the other hand, is developed for each structure, based on a fire rate inspection during which the structural features are identified and graded according to published standards.

Specific rates were previously published on individually printed rate cards and microfiche. However, Commercial Risk Services (CRS), an ISO subsidiary, now stores the information electronically. Companies can access information in many ways, including on-line communication through ISOTEL, ISO's computer-based system for published rates. For each address, an underwriter can obtain a number of pieces of objective information regarding the building at that location. CRS has two numbers associated with each address—the distribution area number (DA) and risk number—that can be used to access a specific risk more quickly than looking up the town or township, the street, and the address.

In addition to the DA and risk numbers, the information contained for each location includes the following:

- Address
- Name of the occupancy or occupancies
- Building and contents loss costs
- SCOH (Standard Classification of Occupancy Hazards) code (almost obsolete)
- Class code (a four-digit numerical description of the occupancy)
- RCP code (a four-digit number denoting whether the building is sprinklered or nonsprinklered, the building's construction classification, and its protection classification)
- An effective date of the information

By reviewing both the application and the CRS data, underwriters can obtain useful information about construction, occupancy, protection, and external exposure, the COPE factors. Exhibit 1-12 shows a sample specific rate card.

The producer can provide additional information. An inspection can also reveal specific information on internal operations, private protection, housekeeping, and exposures.

Advisory Organization Reports

On some risks, highly detailed reports, promulgated by the engineering department of CRS or an advisory organization similar to ISO, are available. Those

Exhibit 1-12
Specific Rate Card

WARREN 1402 W PENNSYLVANIA AVE				PAGE 11964.00					37 PENNSYLVANIA WARREN			
Risk No	Line No	Risk Identification: Location	Risk Identification: Description	Dist Area	Adj Eff Date 07 17 91	Group I	Group II	Comm Stat Plan: CLS.	Comm Stat Plan: RCP	Prot Safe Gard	Terr Code	Schedule Applied Date MM-DD-YY
011680		1402 W Pennsylvania Ave		2010							620	08-16-85
	010	(File PA06867)	Pizza & Sub shop			.496	.119	0542	1204			
	015		Pizza shop			.557	.119	0542				
011690		2R 1408 W Pennsylvania Ave		2010							620	04-25-89
	010	(File PA34079)	Keystone Stamping Mtle 83 (1)			.578	.119	6810	1204			
	015		Maintenance Shop			.643	.119	6810				
011681		1413 W Pennsylvania Ave		2010							620	07-06-88
	010	(File PA29466)	Gilbert's Restaurant			.640	.119	0434	1104			
	015		Restaurant			.824	.119	0542				
	020		Apts (Landlord's Furnishings)			2.641	.119	0321				
011682		1501-1503 W Pennsylvania Ave		2010							620	01-18-91
	010	(File PA33324)	G & R Machine Co Bldg 1 (1S)			.915	.119	6850	1204			
	015		General Metal Working			.933	.119	6850				
011683		1R 1501-1503 W Pennsylvania Ave		2010							620	01-18-91
	010	(File PA33324)	G & R Machine Co Bldg 2 (1S)			1.148	.119	6850	1104			
	015		Mixed Stg of Equipment			1.328	.119	6850				
011684		2R 1501-1503 W Pennsylvania Ave		2010							620	01-18-91
	010	(File PA33324)	G & R Machine Co Bldg 3 (13)			.387	.119	6850	1104			
	015		Metal Scraps			.387	.119	6850				
011685		1517 W Pennsylvania Ave		2010							620	05-05-86
	010	(File PA14125)	Plastic Tent Pegs & Rec Station			.317	.041	0567	1404			
	015		Plastic Products			.505	.041	0567				
011760		1600-1800 W Pennsylvania Ave		2010							620	09-22-85
	010	(File PA05593)	Betts Industries IAC Bldg 1			.128	.119	6850	1404			
	015		Metal Manhole Truck Covers			.170	.119	6850				
011762		1601 W Pennsylvania Ave		2010							620	08-04-82
	010	(File E 8713)	Tres Pros Inc T/A Twin Kiss West			.463	.041	0542	1404			
	015		Restaurant			.545	.041	0542				
010680		1701 W Pennsylvania Ave		2010							620	05-15-80
	010	(File E-1240)	Bldg (13)			.373	.119	0933	1204			
	015		Auto Body Paint Shop & Serv Sta			.381	.119	0933				

reports normally describe risks with sprinkler protection or risks larger than 15,000 square feet that are not eligible for class rating.

The report includes the class of the risk, the owner and occupant, construction, fire divisions, observed hazards, external exposures, private protection systems, the history of the risk, and often a diagram of the building. The report also points out major problem areas and contains recommendations for necessary improvements.

Other types of advisory organization reports are also developed in geographic areas of special concern. For example, reports are available from CRS's San Francisco office concerning special earthquake situations.

Inspection Reports and Diagrams

Diagrams are included with many bureau reports and company inspection reports. A well-drawn diagram is almost as valuable as an on-site inspection by the underwriter. The ability to interpret a diagram properly is an essential property underwriting skill.

Exhibit 1-13 shows a complete building sketch. That sketch includes not only information about the structure of the building, but also information about the fire protection and internal processes of the plant. A sketch of this type includes a great deal of valuable underwriting information.

The question of when an underwriter should order an inspection can be perplexing. For example, assume that a submission of a light-hazard occupancy with high values comes in from a producer with whom the underwriter is unfamiliar. If the application does not provide complete information, the underwriter should have the risk inspected. Although inspections cost money, poor risks, over the long run, cost even more money. In any event, the request for an inspection should clearly state the information required.

Low-value submissions present a major problem because the average cost of a company loss control representative is at least $100 per hour. Therefore, a risk that might produce a minimum premium of $250 cannot support the cost of an inspection. In such cases, the underwriter might rely on personal knowledge of the risk and its locale. Reviewing the CRS report might be sufficient. The underwriter might request that the producer provide a photograph to supplement the application on low-value submissions.

To develop a successful book of business, underwriters must make decisions based on information and knowledge. Since underwriters cannot visit all premises, they must rely on others to furnish adequate information. The cost of information is an important consideration. Underwriting management should

Exhibit 1-13
Building Sketch

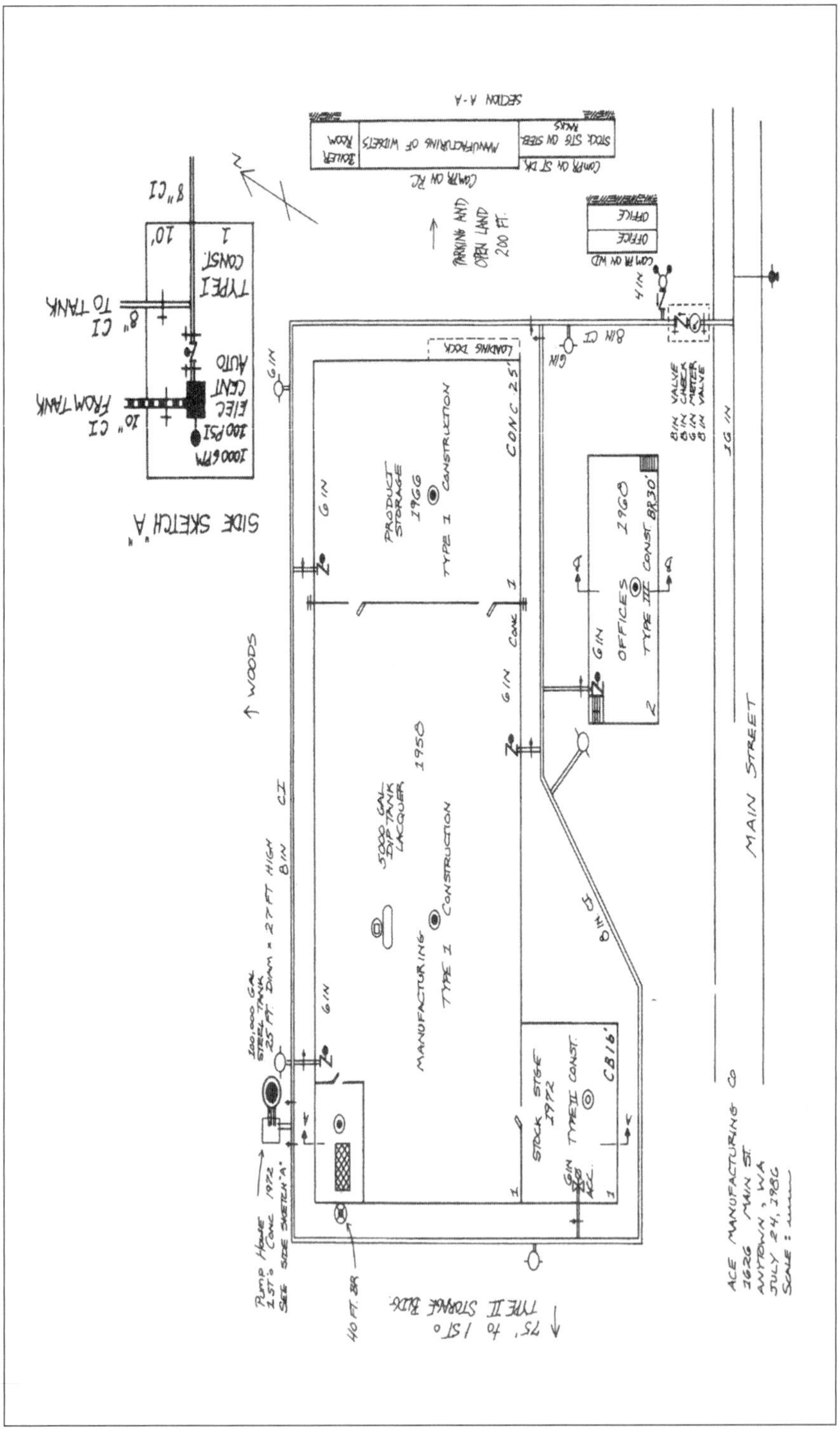

Reprinted with permission from *The Fire Protection Handbook*, 17th ed., Quincy MA: National Fire Protection Association, p. 10-135.

provide written guidelines for ordering inspections either by company personnel or by outside firms.

Local Building Codes

Local building codes can provide the underwriter with information regarding the construction of buildings erected under the provisions of those codes. Older buildings might have been constructed according to the provisions of a code different from that which is in effect. Building codes are of two types:

- **Specification codes** state in detail the size, type, and installation techniques for all structural and other building components.
- **Performance codes** establish criteria that structural and other building components must meet.

Building codes are an important tool used by communities to ensure that contractors build to specific standards. Because there are several building code systems in use in the United States and multiple editions of each of these building codes that local communities must adopt, underwriters are unlikely to know what building code standards are actually in place. Compounding this problem is the varied enforcement of building codes. In some communities, building code enforcement is given a high priority and provision is made to fund the cost of inspections. In other communities, contractors are expected to be self-policing because there are not enough inspectors to enforce the code.

In 1995, ISO and the Insurance Institute for Property Loss Reduction began grading communities based on their building codes in an approach similar to the grading system used for grading municipal fire protection. This new grading system is called the Building Code Effectiveness Grading Schedule (BCEGS) and will be implemented over a period of years. The first areas in which this system will be used are the states of Florida, North Carolina, and South Carolina, where communities are most likely to be adversely affected by peril of windstorm.

Summary

Commercial property underwriting begins with an analysis of the physical hazards. The acronym COPE, which stands for construction, occupancy, protection, and external exposures, describes the major categories of physical hazards.

Building construction is divided into six classes:

- Frame
- Joisted masonry
- Noncombustible
- Masonry noncombustible
- Modified fire-resistive
- Fire-resistive

The design of the structure is very important. High-rise buildings and buildings with large horizontal spaces present unique underwriting problems. The combustibility of interior finishes and interior decorations must also be determined. The age of a building can affect its acceptability; older buildings are often constructed on the basis of outmoded building codes.

Information concerning a particular building can be obtained from the application, rating data (whether it is specific or class rated), bureau reports, inspection reports, diagrams drawn by inspectors, and local building codes.

Chapter Notes

1. NFPA 251—Standard Methods of Tests of Fire Endurance of Building Construction and Materials (Quincy, MA: National Fire Protection Association, 1995), p. 251.
2. *Fire Protection Handbook*, 17th ed. (Quincy, MA: National Fire Protection Association, 1981), pp. 6-39
3. Insurance Services Office, *Commercial Fire Rating Schedule* (New York, NY: Insurance Services Office, 1977), pp. 3-4. Also in the ISO *Commercial Lines Manual*.
4. *Fire Protection Handbook*, p. 6-32.
5. Insurance Services Office, *Commercial Fire Rating Schedule*, Revision No. 4, p. 4, 4-78.
6. *Fire Protection Handbook*, p. 5-33.
7. Rhonda L. Rundle, "Liability Limits May Not Cover MGM Fire Claims," *Business Insurance*, December 1, 1984, p. 1.
8. Steve Taranella, "NESCO to Pay Most of Hilton Settlement," *Business Insurance*, October 21, 1985, p. 1.

Chapter 2

Occupancy

Occupancy—how a structure is used—is a prime consideration in commercial property underwriting. Occupancy is also a valuable source of information to the underwriter. Just as construction, protection, and external exposures affect loss potential, the operations and processes conducted within a structure introduce hazards that influence loss frequency and severity. The occupancy for which the builder designed the structure affects the characteristics of the building itself in most cases. In addition, the compatibility of the actual use of the structure with its design occupancy affects the characteristics of the building from an underwriting standpoint. For example, the structures in a chemical refinery differ markedly from those in a steel mill.

The evaluation of occupancy requires concrete details; occupancy cannot be considered in abstract terms. This chapter begins with a discussion of how occupancy classification affects pricing. Next, the chapter considers how to classify occupancy hazards. Finally, it examines occupancy hazards related to specific kinds of applicants for commercial property insurance.

Occupancy Hazards Rating

Commercial fire rating systems, such as the method used by ISO, indicate the degree of hazard that an occupancy presents in a particular classification. In the ISO system, each occupancy is assigned a **Commercial Statistical Plan (CSP)** code. For specifically rated risks, the CSP code is part of the rating information that ISO supplies.

The CSP codes evolved from an earlier classification system, the Standard Classification of Occupancy Hazards (SCOH). Because one set of codes replaced the other and the two systems are similar, some experienced underwriters continue to refer to the CSP codes as "SCOH codes." Both the old and new classification systems provide a classification of occupancy hazards that is highly relevant to the exposure to loss by fire, but they often ignore the propensity for loss from other causes. Underwriters have to be aware of the limitations inherent in this system. The same CSP code, for example, is assigned to both airport control towers and airport office buildings. If an underwriter considers only the potential for loss by fire, grouping these exposures is appropriate. Airport control towers, on the other hand, have a significant exposure to windstorm and aircraft as causes of loss. The underwriter's analysis should take these differences concerning occupancies within a single CSP classification into consideration.

The ISO occupancy rating system includes the following four factors:

- Basic occupancy charge
- Combustibility
- Susceptibility
- Additional occupancy hazards

Basic Occupancy Charge

The **basic occupancy charge** reflects the relative hazard of an occupancy for pricing purposes. It is expressed as a percentage of the base rate, and it ranges from 10 percent to 1,000 percent. A great difference in the occupancy hazards clearly exists between a parking garage with a charge of 10 percent and a dry log sawmill sawing unbarked logs with a charge of 800 percent.[1]

The purpose of every rating system is to produce a premium that is commensurate with the hazard, and the degree of hazard presented by a particular occupancy is still a major underwriting consideration for three reasons. First, the degree of hazard affects the amount of fire insurance that an underwriter is willing to accept. Second, occupancy is an important characteristic that must be evaluated in the analysis of the composition of all the policies written or an insurer's book of business. A book of fire business made up entirely of sawmills would produce an attractive premium per unit. It would also represent a high level of exposure to loss that is not likely to be acceptable to reinsurers. Third, the hazards reflected in the basic occupancy charge provide an insight into the importance of additional hazards that might be present in a particular risk. Poor housekeeping, for example, is never desirable. That hazard has much less effect, however, in an office building than in a sawmill. A high basic occupancy charge magnifies the effect of any additional hazards.

Combustibility

Combustibility refers to the ability of something to ignite and burn. The combustibility of the contents usually found in a particular occupancy is a major determinant of the overall fire hazard. The ISO Specific Commercial Property Evaluation Schedule ranks the combustibility of contents according to five classes, from noncombustible to rapid or flash burning, as described below.[2] Each class considers the merchandise or materials, including the furniture, stock, or equipment typical of the occupancy. The ISO classification system is shown in Exhibit 2-1.

Exhibit 2-1
Combustibility Classifications

Class	Description
C-1	Noncombustible
C-2	Limited combustibility
C-3	Combustible
C-4	Free burning
C-5	Rapid burning or flash burning

Used with permission from Insurance Services Office, *Specific Commercial Property Evaluation Schedule* (New York, NY: ISO, July 1990), p. 4-4.

Noncombustible

The **noncombustible** class (C-1) includes occupancies with "merchandise or materials, including furniture, stock or equipment which in permissible quantities do not in themselves constitute an active fuel for the spread of fire." An example of such an occupancy would be a building containing clay or glass products or metalworking (manufacturing) operations. Since the basis of the combustibility grading system is the effect of the contents on the structure, the noncombustible classification cannot be used if the occupancy contains sufficient combustible material to cause structural damage.

Limited Combustibility

The limited combustibility class (C-2) includes occupancies that contain (1) merchandise or materials of low combustibility and (2) limited concentrations of combustible materials. Occupancies in this classification might include offices, banks, barber and beauty shops, habitational occupancies, and hospitals.

Combustible

The **combustible** class (C-3) includes occupancies with merchandise or materials of moderate combustibility. This classification includes mercantile occupancies such as food markets and most wholesale and retail occupancies.

Free Burning

The merchandise or materials usually found in the **free burning** class (C-4) burn freely and constitute an active fuel. These materials include baled cotton, furniture stock, and wood products.

Rapid Burning or Flash Burning

The **rapid** or **flash burning** class (C-5) includes occupancies that contain merchandise or materials representing an extreme fire hazard to the structure. The contents in these occupancies include materials that can do the following:[3]

- Burn with a great intensity
- Ignite spontaneously and are difficult to extinguish
- Give off flammable or explosive vapors at ordinary temperatures
- Produce large quantities of dust or other finely divided debris subject to flash fire or explosion as a result of an industrial process

Examples of occupancies in this class include the manufacturing of ammunition, explosives, mattresses, and upholstery.

Susceptibility

In addition to combustibility, another factor that determines how severely a fire will damage personal property is susceptibility. Contents that do not burn can also sustain damage from fire, smoke, and water. **Susceptibility** measures the extent to which fire and its effects will cause damage to materials typical of the occupancy. A relatively small fire can produce a large financial loss if the contents of the building lose their value when contaminated by smoke. Federal law, for instance, regulates the manufacture and sale of furniture and certain household furnishings. If materials intended for use in those products sustain smoke or water damage, the insured will not be able to use them for their intended purposes. The materials can be sold only as scrap, so even a very small loss can easily destroy most of their value. ISO classifies the contents, furniture, and fixtures of occupancies, ranging from occupancies that would likely suffer minimal damage to those that would suffer extreme loss. Those classifications are shown in Exhibit 2-2.

Exhibit 2-2
Susceptibility Classifications

Class	Description	Examples
S-1	Minimal damage	Pig iron, marble, heavy metals
S-2	Slight damage	Sheet metal, green hides or skins
S-3	Moderate damage	Boots, shoes, household appliances
S-4	Heavy damage	Books, clothing, furniture
S-5	Extreme loss (total loss possible)	Animals, birds, explosives, flowers, furs

Used with permission from Insurance Services Office, *Specific Commercial Property Evaluation Schedule* (New York, NY: ISO, July 1990), p. 4-5.

Additional Occupancy Hazards

In addition to the basic occupancy charge and the determination of the combustibility and susceptibility of the materials found in the occupancy, surcharges can be made for extra hazards found in a risk. An example is the surcharge for cooking. Since cooking is included in the basic occupancy charge of restaurants, that hazard is usual for that occupancy. A small industrial plant, however, could have a complete employee cafeteria with a full commercial kitchen. A cooking hazard charge would be added to the basic occupancy charge of the manufacturing classification. The underwriter should keep those hazards in mind since their presence can make a risk less desirable. Additional occupancy hazards are shown in Exhibit 2-3.

ISO also classifies occupancies for rating purposes with regard to exposure to sprinkler leakage (slight, moderate, or high); vandalism or malicious mischief (a rating of one to four); earthquake (a rating of one to four); and the sprinkler protection occupancy class, or SPOC (a rating of one to six to determine the sprinkler system water supply requirements). The susceptibility to sprinkler leakage can also provide valuable information if the insured requests "all-risks" coverage or specified causes of loss that include coverage for water damage.

Exhibit 2-3
Additional Occupancy Hazards

Chemicals, acids, or gases—storage and handling
Combustible or flammable liquids—storage and handling
Combustible or flammable liquids—painting or coating
Highly combustible materials
Cooking and cooking equipment
Dust collection and refuse removal systems
Heat producing or utilizing devices
High piled stocks
Smoking control (control of smoking in hazardous areas)
Miscellaneous hazardous conditions:
a. Electrical equipment defects
b. Housekeeping
Auxiliary or incidental operations or processes

Used with permission from Insurance Services Office, *Specific Commercial Property Evaluation Schedule* (New York, NY: ISO, July 1990), pp. 7-5 to 7-21.

Common and Special Hazards

Physical hazards can be most thoroughly analyzed if they are divided into the following three groups:

- Common hazards
- Special hazards of the class
- Special hazards of the risk

Common hazards are those conditions or features that are typical of any structure regardless of its use and that can cause or aggravate a loss. Common hazards include housekeeping, electricity, heating, ventilating, and cooling equipment.

Special hazards of the class are characteristics typical of all occupancies in a given class that can cause or aggravate a loss. Cooking is a special hazard of the restaurant class. It is common to restaurants, but not to other occupancies, such as clothing stores. Some underwriters prefer to use the term "common hazards of the class," but the difference is purely semantic.

Special hazards of the risk are conditions that can cause a loss but that are not typical of the occupancy. The use of welding torches in an auto repair shop and a janitorial service that uses toluene for wax removal are examples.

Those three hazard groups are not mutually exclusive. The circumstance in which a hazard occurs in a particular occupancy can change a common hazard. The housekeeping hazard, for instance, is a concern for all occupancy classifications, but it can range from a minor concern in an office occupancy to a major consideration for sawdust and wood chips in a furniture manufacturing occupancy. Chapter 4 will describe common hazards in detail. Chapter 4 does not use the term "common hazard," however, because it is primarily used in discussing occupancy.

Examples of special hazards include welding and the use of volatile chemicals in an industrial process. The list of possible occupancies is considerable, as evidenced by the number of classifications in the ISO manual. The number of special hazards that might exist is even larger. The analysis of occupancy hazards is a full-time task for commercial property underwriters because building materials and industrial processes do not remain static. The remainder of this chapter discusses broad industry classes and some of their major characteristics. It also examines a small number of occupancy classes and indicates the types of hazards that are present.

Occupancy Hazards Grouped by Major Categories

Occupancy hazards fall into the following six broad categories:

- Habitational
- Office
- Institutional
- Mercantile
- Service industry
- Manufacturing

When analyzing occupancy hazards, underwriters should consider each of the following factors:

- Ignition sources
- Fuel (fire) load
- Combustibility and susceptibility of contents, furniture, and fixtures

- Interior finish of the structure
- Efficiency of management, encompassing:
    - Control over housekeeping
    - Employee training and skills
    - Loss control programs

This and the next section will address several of those factors. The last factor, however, is usually specific to an individual risk and can be addressed only when underwriting the risk. This section does not address each of the factors separately, since some are not of major concern for some occupancies. Rather, this section tries to highlight the hazards of major concern, both common hazards and special hazards.

Habitational Occupancies

Habitational occupancies include apartments, hotels, motels, and nursing homes. Habitational occupancies have a wide variety of common hazards and additional special hazards that arise from the occupancy. Engineering an account to reduce the loss potential from special hazards is difficult for these occupancies.

The maintenance of the location itself by its owners might be the most desirable situation, but the activities of tenants are difficult if not impossible to supervise. The carelessness of one tenant is a source of potential loss and can undo the loss control efforts of both the owner and the other tenants.

Habitational occupancies range from modern high-rise structures to old, converted buildings. New construction usually conforms to current building codes, but converted buildings might include renovations that never met building codes or that met building codes proven to be inadequate and since revised. Therefore, older buildings require closer analysis of wiring, heating, and trash disposal systems than do newer structures.

The financial stability of the owner is an important underwriting consideration for the habitational class. In addition to the usual financial ratios, the vacancy rate is an important indicator of business success. Seasonal factors influence hotel and motel vacancy rates, but the vacancy rate of the particular risk under consideration can always be compared with that of successful operations of the same size and type within the same geographic area.

Ignition Sources

For most habitational occupancies, smoking and incendiary or suspicious causes are the primary **ignition sources**. For example, smoking accounted for

30 percent of all fires in health-care facilities. Fires that were, or were suspected to have been, set intentionally represented another 13 percent of those fires.[4] Given the nature of those occupancies, management can never sufficiently control the incidence of smoking. Loss control efforts in habitational occupancies must focus on structural characteristics that limit damage from covered causes of loss. Fire doors and smoke curtains help contain the damage that fire causes. Private detection and suppression systems promote early response to fire, which can help reduce losses significantly. Fire and smoke alarm systems alert the occupants of a structure and often the local fire service as well. Automatic fire sprinklers attack a fire at its source and in its formative stages, when less water is required to suppress the blaze.

Combustibility and Susceptibility of Contents

The presence of combustible contents in habitational occupancies contributes to fire severity. Mattress fires caused by careless smoking in bed have resulted in extremely serious apartment, hotel, and nursing home fires. Contents typical of habitational occupancies are not only subject to serious fire loss; they are also susceptible to loss from smoke contamination and water damage, breakage, and other consequences of fighting the fire.

The arrangement of the fuel load in habitational properties is unique and presents some problems in fighting fires. Mercantile and industrial occupancies tend to distribute the fuel load horizontally, which helps to retard the spread of fire. Heated gases tend to move away from the fuel load as they rise. In spaces designed as dwellings, however, large open areas are important. As a result, major portions of the fuel load are typically arranged vertically along the walls. Tall furniture, window curtains, and drapes all contribute to the vertical fuel load. This normal arrangement of furniture and furnishings allows fire to travel upward more rapidly, distributing the fire horizontally. Because hot gases concentrate just below the ceiling, losses develop more quickly than in many other occupancies, and flashover becomes a more serious consideration. Fire service response time and automatic systems to suppress fire might be more important in habitational occupancies than in other types of occupancies.

Many hotels and motels have carpentry workshops in which furniture is repaired, refinished, or reupholstered. Those operations present many of the hazards of a furniture factory or upholstering shop, such as the storage of paint and volatile solvents and the use of combustible stuffing materials and fabrics. In addition, many hotels and motels have storage areas for surplus furniture, mattresses, and other items. To reduce the possibility of loss, those rooms should be sprinklered and separated from the rest of the building by fire walls in properly enclosed noncombustible rooms. Enclosed metal storage closets should be used for storing paints and solvents, and the room should be ventilated to carry off fumes. Upholstering supplies should also be stored in metal storage bins.

Storage areas available to tenants of an apartment house present several hazards. Many types of personal property, flammable and often highly damageable, are found in those areas with often questionable housekeeping. Controlling those hazards is difficult because storage areas are often accessible to both tenants and others. Children often use them as play areas. The hazards of smoking and children playing with matches might exist. Preventing fires in storage areas requires exceptional enforcement of security measures.

Cooking

The cooking hazard exists in the majority of habitational occupancies and essentially becomes a special hazard of the class. Every apartment dwelling has a kitchen or kitchenette with a domestic type of gas or electric stove. Hotel or motel eating facilities range from kitchenettes to coffee shops to full restaurant facilities. Nursing homes have fully equipped commercial kitchens. Regardless of the type of cooking involved in these occupancies, the hazard exists, and loss control measures must be taken.

Heating and Air Conditioning

Heating systems vary from complex plants installed in large metropolitan hotels to wall heaters in seasonal hotels. The systems may provide heat by way of a hot-air duct system, steam radiators, hot-water pipes, or electrical or gas space heaters. Regardless of the type, heating systems should be properly installed and maintained. Space heaters operated by tenants should be installed so that combustibles are unlikely to be stored near them. Because space heaters are dangerous, some cities do not permit them.

Most hotels, motels, apartments, and other habitational units are built with air conditioning. This often means that ducts run throughout the building. Unless properly protected, they will transmit flames and smoke. Automatic dampers, which act as fire doors within the duct system to prevent the spread of smoke or fire, effectively control this hazard. The dampers serve as cutoffs, particularly where a duct pierces a wall or goes through a floor. With the air being pushed through the ductwork by a motorized fan, automatic controls (or firestats) sometimes stop the fan if a fire breaks out within the equipment or in the structure.

In the event of fire, state-of-the-art ventilating systems will evacuate smoke-laden air from the building and replace it with fresh air from outside. Those systems assist firefighting in several ways. They enhance human life safety because residents will not become disoriented or overcome by fumes and can therefore evacuate the premises in a swift and orderly fashion. That evacuation relieves fire service personnel of the need to mount a massive rescue effort and allows them to attack the blaze as soon as they arrive. Along with smoke, ventilating systems also vent heat and products of combustion, helping to reduce the intensity of the fire. This venting more than offsets the effects of the fresh supply of oxygen that it introduces to the fire. Lower temperatures and clearer air aid the efforts of firefighters, as they reduce the need to rely on protective gear and self-contained breathing apparatus.

Plumbing

The amount of plumbing in habitational occupancies is extensive. The kitchens and bathrooms of nursing homes are sizable. Apartments, hotel rooms, and motel rooms require a network of cold- and hot-water pipes and sanitation pipes running throughout the building to service bathrooms and kitchens. Tenants who permit water to overflow from sinks and toilets can cause severe damage to their contents, warp wooden floors, and damage contents and building property on lower floors of the building.

In addition to the plumbing installed for sanitation and drinking purposes, a building heated by steam or hot-water systems also requires a network of pipes. If the building is sprinklered or has standpipes, the leakage hazard is increased. To avoid freezing during cold spells, property owners should insulate those systems.

Panel heating or radiant heating systems with hot-water pipes embedded in the walls, ceilings, or floors are subject to several hazards. Unless those systems are properly insulated, the pipes can freeze and break. If there is building subsidence, the piping is also subject to breakage. The pipes can be affected by wind damage to the walls in which the pipes run. Whatever the cause of the damage, repairs are costly.

Because plumbing must go through walls and floors, all openings should be refitted so that fire will not easily spread through gaps between the wall and piping (firestopped). In one recent fire, a fire-resistive apartment house sustained serious damage to several floors because of the lack of firestopping around plumbing between floors. The fire spread through two floors and was so intense that the steel in the flooring buckled.

Office Occupancies

The office occupancy is a relatively low hazard classification. Materials found in offices are usually of limited combustibility and relatively less susceptible to damage than those found in other occupancies. Certain office buildings might include features such as restaurants or heliports that represent special hazards. Office occupancies range from fire-resistive high-rises to suites of offices located over a mercantile occupancy in a two-story frame building.

Ignition Sources

The primary ignition source affecting office occupancies is incendiary acts. Other sources of ignition are heating and electrical distribution systems, portable heating equipment, other appliances, torch and other maintenance operations, matches and lighters, and smoking.[5] The emergence of personal computers has contributed to a rapid growth in the demand for electric service in office buildings. Wiring systems are clearly a cause for concern in office occupancies. This is particularly true of older buildings built to now-outdated codes. Buildings in which substantial remodeling has occurred are a concern because of the increased electrical loads placed on old wiring and because modifications are often given little attention by building officials.

Fuel Loads

Fuel loads vary considerably among office occupancies. Materials used in office furnishings and decorations have changed over the years. Older wooden desks and filing cabinets have given way to steel equipment. This development measurably reduces the fuel load, because metal furniture does not contribute to the fuel load and the steel cabinets can protect contents from fire.

Recent trends in modern offices tend to increase the fire hazard. One is the increased use of plastics in office machines, decor, and interior finish. Plastics are found in many of the synthetic fabrics used as both batting and covers for upholstered furniture. Computer media, particularly diskettes and tapes, are frequently made of combustible plastics. Plastics burn easily and emit noxious gases and thick smoke.

A second trend is the increased use of movable partitions and wall modules to provide more flexibility in the use of office space. Partitions are usually lower than ceiling height. As compared to small offices with traditional walls, dividers that do not meet the ceiling provide a feeling of spaciousness, particularly when dividing a large room into a number of small offices and reception areas. Since partitions stop short of the ceiling, the result is an open area that is one fire division and a single draft area. That open area makes prevention of ignition of paramount importance, since fire can quickly involve the entire room if flashover occurs.

Hazards

Today, most office occupancies have eating facilities for employees. Those facilities range from a simple coffee urn to a lounge with domestic cooking appliances or a cafeteria that provides hot meals. A frayed electrical cord on the coffee urn is an obvious source of potential loss. Automatic flame failure relays should protect gas-fired domestic ranges. Those relays will prevent an explosion if an office employee carelessly permits the water to boil over, thereby extinguishing the flame in a gas burner. Employee cafeterias often have the characteristics of a full-scale restaurant, and the underwriter must evaluate them as such.

Solvents used for cleaning office machinery should be stored in secure containers in locked cabinets. Employees should keep only a one-day supply of combustible liquids in self-closing metal cans. Bulk supplies of flammable liquids in manufacturers' cans should be stored in accordance with NFPA standards. A separately vented fire-resistant cabinet is preferable.

Computer systems range from highly complex installations to desktop computers used for record keeping in offices of all sizes. A fire will result in a heavy loss, because the equipment is susceptible to damage from heat, fire, corrosive fumes, gases, and smoke. Water used to fight the fire might also damage equipment if the equipment is not dried out immediately. NFPA has established standards for computer installation and wiring.

Large computers are usually located in a separate room. This room should be kept clean, air conditioned, and under strict supervision. The furnishings should be noncombustible, and necessary supplies of combustible materials, such as paper and recording media, should be enclosed in metal file cases or cabinets. The quantities of combustible material in use at any one time should be kept to a minimum.

Institutional Occupancies

This category includes schools, churches, municipalities, and hospitals, as well as special-purpose facilities such as prisons and police and fire stations. Some experts place nursing homes in this category as well.

Many of these institutions present unique occupancy hazards as well as obstacles to controlling those losses that occur. For example, patients in a hospital are not particularly mobile, and surgical procedures cannot necessarily be suspended. Likewise, prisons are designed to contain prisoners, and such a design could impede prison personnel fighting a fire.

Old buildings are common among institutional occupancies. Schools in changing or deteriorating areas are often left unrepaired. Church congregations dwindle, and the remaining congregants find maintaining old church buildings financially impossible. Well-established hospitals in cities are often in old buildings; modernization and upkeep are very expensive. Also, older buildings often do not have necessary firewalls or ductwork cutoffs.

The problem of accumulating operating funds can produce excessive zeal to reduce expenses. Upkeep and maintenance of the premises might be neglected if cost-cutting programs are implemented. Everything else being equal, an insured strapped for operating funds is a poor underwriting risk.

Ignition Sources

Because of the wide variety of occupancies within this category, generalizing with respect to fire ignition sources and forms is difficult. Arson is clearly a major underwriting problem. In virtually all of those cases, the arson is against the insured, so moral hazard of the insured is not a major factor. Another factor is the trend to make churches, schools, and colleges the focal point for social movements and unrest. The social issues causing unrest have changed with the years, but the acts of arson persist. Many social issues arouse deep, emotional responses in the community, and those feelings can lead to violence, destruction of property, and arson. For example, hospitals and clinics have become targets in the debate over abortion.

Combustible, Explosive, or Susceptible Supplies

School, college, hospital, or municipal occupancies often contain hazardous supplies. Those supplies include chemicals used in science programs, cleaning solvents, and the contents of hospital laboratories and pharmacies. The most effective loss control measures call for storing supplies in metal-enclosed receptacles and dispensing only a limited amount for use at any one time. Only amounts being used should be outside the receptacles. Rooms in which flammables are used should have adequate ventilation to carry off fumes and gases that could explode. Bunsen burners should be set on a metal base and connected to the gas source with rubber tubing. The supervision of chemistry students and the security of laboratory supplies should raise concern at schools and colleges. Maintenance shops and storage rooms in schools, hospitals, and similar institutions can contain high-hazard wood- and metal-working operations and supplies of combustible materials. Craft shops in schools and hospitals can contain highly combustible supplies.

Some institutional contents are highly susceptible to damage. These include hospital technical equipment and church artifacts that not only are easily damaged by fire, smoke, and water but that also represent high values. Stained and leaded glass windows, vestments, and church fixtures are especially vulnerable and are also subject to vandalism or theft.

Cooking

The cooking hazard can be less severe in an institutional risk than in a restaurant. Food preparation is not continuous, being limited to the number of meals provided by the institution. Grade schools and high schools as a rule prepare only lunches, whereas hospitals prepare three meals each day. Dietary considerations in many institutions limit the amount of deep-fried foods served. Those cooking facilities nevertheless require proper maintenance with hoods and ducts being routinely cleaned. Institutions should also install automatic hood-and-dust extinguishing systems.

Cooking in a church is usually limited to "church suppers" and similar events. Appliances are often of the household variety. Since the cooking is done by the church group sponsoring the meal, many people are responsible for keeping the equipment clean. Housekeeping is not easily controlled, and carelessness can be a hazard. Ignorance of how to properly operate the equipment and inexperience are also concerns.

Municipalities, depending on the services provided, could have a wide range of cooking hazards, such as employee cafeterias and institutional cooking for prisons, youth homes, and nursing homes. A city commissary might exist for purchasing foodstuffs in quantity and bulk preparation of food. Fire prevention measures such as sprinkler systems, fire extinguishers, prompt removal of combustibles and trash, and careful housekeeping should be maintained.

Heating and Air Conditioning

The heating systems in institutional occupancies are usually substantial. Large boiler and furnace systems might require a full-time engineer. Many churches are not used continuously, and heat is often turned down or off between services. Often the thermostat is turned very high just before the church service. This forcing of an excessive amount of heat could result in a boiler explosion or a fire. Because of its infrequent use, the church heating system might not be properly maintained, and combustibles might be stored near the unit.

An institutional heating unit, because of its large size, should be in a separate, enclosed room isolated from the rest of the building by firewalls. The furnace room should never be used as a storage area.

Many institutions are housed in old buildings whose air conditioning systems were added during remodeling. Loss control personnel should evaluate the adequacy of wiring, the protection of vertical and horizontal wall and floor openings, and the location of fire dampers during a loss control survey.

Heat Treatment

Engineering and vocational schools are likely to contain hazards that are comparable to those found in industrial plants, such as the heat treating of metals. Those metals are heated in an oven or furnace and then bathed in a coolant that can be fish oil, salts, or chemicals. The temperature of the coolant must be carefully controlled to prevent fire or explosion. The immersion tank itself must be protected with a hood to prevent water from coming in contact with the contents and causing an explosion.

Oxygen and Gas Hazards

The use of oxygen and gases, as in a hospital, is a serious hazard. Gases used for anesthesia constitute an explosive mixture. The sealed atmosphere of a hospital operating room gives it all the characteristics of a bomb. Anesthetics are usually combustible, and open flames or electric sparks should be avoided where anesthetics are used and stored.

Welding in school craft shops or city garages involves acetylene gas. Welding produces sparks, which, unless shielded, can fly several feet from the work. Welding should be done in well-ventilated areas or separate rooms having a fire-resistant shield to contain flying sparks. No combustibles should be in the area. When welding is performed, an attendant should be on hand with a fire extinguisher and a bucket of sand, ready to extinguish a fire. If the welding takes place on a wooden floor, the floor should be wetted down or protected by a fire-resistant covering during the process.

Gases, anesthetics, oxygen, and acetylene must be properly stored in approved metal cylinders. Those cylinders should be stored in a fire division separate from the main building and chained upright to prevent accidental upset. The area should be well-ventilated. If electrical motors and fans are used in the storage area, they should be explosion-proof with blades and bearings made of nonsparking materials.

Plumbing Systems

Plumbing systems in institutions are extensive because of the requirements of sanitation, cooking, laboratory, and other needs. In addition, piping is frequently installed throughout the building to supply water for private fire protection consisting of sprinklers, standpipes, pumps, and gravity tanks. Property owners should secure a service that will ensure that private fire protection devices are properly maintained.

Trained personnel should make routine flow and pressure tests. The equipment should be protected from freezing in unheated areas such as in entryways and attics and beneath floors and platforms.

Institutional occupancies, like habitational and office occupancies, are subject to abuse by the public. Toilet and sink overflow and plugged drains often result in water damage. Preventing such situations is extremely difficult and requires constant monitoring and education of the institutional population. Plumbing systems in schools are especially susceptible to vandalism.

Mercantile Occupancies

This category includes wholesale and retail stores such as department stores, clothing stores, hardware stores, specialty shops, and grocery stores. Shopping centers, particularly those with enclosed malls, represent a rapidly growing segment of this group.

Ignition Sources

Incendiary fires and fires of suspicious origin are leading contributors to the frequency of fires in retail occupancies. Moral hazard is an important underwriting consideration. Analysis should include any past history of suspicious fire losses, the prosperity of the business, and the length of time the business has been in operation. Other factors include the credit standing of the owner, the existence of labor problems, and the possible effects of technological or market changes on the particular store.

Other sources of ignition that contribute significantly to mercantile occupancy fires include electrical arcing or overloading electrical circuits and the use of tobacco products.

Cooking in a supermarket or department store restaurant and cooking demonstrations (for example, warming samples of new foods) combine the hazards of a commercial restaurant and the hazards related to cooking in close proximity to merchandise highly susceptible to fire.

Combustible or Susceptible Contents

In mercantile occupancies, the combustibility of the contents varies, depending on the merchandise being sold. Usually an entire inventory is susceptible to fire, smoke, and water damage.

Many mercantile operations carry highly combustible items in inventory or as operating supplies. A sporting goods store usually stocks ammunition and fuel for camping stoves and portable lanterns. Hardware stores stock paints, varnishes, solvents, and other combustible liquids. A rapidly growing variation of the traditional hardware store is the home center, which, in addition to the items just listed, stocks lumber and building supplies. A furniture store might have refinishing chemicals and polishes as operating supplies. The store might also provide an upholstering service. Even appliance and television retailers might operate a repair service that requires the use of combustible liquids.

Retail operations should provide adequate space for shelving, showcases, displays on the selling floor, and storage facilities off the selling floor. Unless proper care is taken, the operation can become congested with accumulations of cartons, packing materials, and other debris. Housekeeping is important because the unpacking of merchandise can generate a high volume of combustible trash. This trash and other debris should be promptly removed from the premises. Proper containers and storage facilities should be provided for highly combustible items. The public should be prohibited from entering storage and service areas, and smoking should not be permitted in these areas.

Most stocks of merchandise are subject to water and smoke damage. Clothing is especially susceptible to severe loss from smoke and water damage. The stock of a hardware store can rust from the water used in fighting a fire. Residual damage such as smoke and water, therefore, can turn a small fire into a large loss.

Health authorities will usually destroy food in a neighborhood store, supermarket, or wholesale outlet that has been damaged by fire or smoke. A small fire in these types of businesses can produce a large loss.

Fuel Loads

Many mercantile risks maintain substantial space for storing their inventory. The back of a retail store might resemble a warehouse. A wholesale distributor might require extensive warehouse facilities. Large undivided areas and high ceilings characterize a warehouse. Warehouses can contain one product or a wide variety of products. High-rack storage can aid the spread of fire and hinder firefighting efforts. Underwriters must consider the wholesale occupancy in terms of the products involved and the nature of the operation. Some wholesalers do a great deal of packing and crating that entails the hazards of highly combustible packing materials, but other operations are limited to storage and shipping.

A new kind of retail store has many of the characteristics of a warehouse. Large home centers and wholesale clubs rely on high sales volume and low overhead to maintain their profit margins. Many of the stores began operations in unused warehouse space. Today, the more successful chains build to suit their needs, but even the new stores resemble warehouses. These retail stores essentially remain warehouses, but they are newer and are the right size and shape for the occupancy. The problem of high-rack storage, in particular, remains.

Service Industry Occupancies

The service sector of our economy is growing rapidly. The list of service businesses is long, and it includes businesses such as dry cleaners, laundries, automobile rental services, automobile service stations, barber shops, repair shops of various types, cable subscription companies, and car washes, just to name a few.

Ignition Sources

Because the service category includes such a diverse assortment of occupancies, generalizations regarding the fire ignition sequence are not helpful. This does not mean that underwriters should ignore fire ignition sources for these occupancies. Data regarding the usual fire causes for these classes, however, must be developed either from company files or from statistics gathered by industry associations. One ignition source that is common to many service industries is flammable liquids such as gasoline in service stations and solvents in dry cleaners.

Flammable or Combustible Liquids

Solvents, oils, paints, and grease are highly combustible. Because of the combustibility of solvents, dry cleaning operations should be done in a separate area. This area should be well-ventilated, all equipment should be grounded, and lighting and other switches should be explosion-proof. To reduce the possibility of fire or explosion, most cleaners use a standard solvent with a flash point comparable to that of kerosene. Repair shops use flammable paints, refinishing fluids, and cleaning solvents that should be used with care in a well-ventilated area.

Housekeeping

In both dry cleaners and laundries, lint escapes from drying units and might settle on machinery, motors, and equipment. Lint accumulation presents both fire and explosion hazards that are compounded in dry-cleaning operations by the accumulation of vapors from the solvents that permeate the premises. Therefore, housekeeping is of prime importance. Timely cleaning of the lint traps and regular removal of lint from machinery are essential. Proper ventilation to remove lint and accumulated vapors from the air is also necessary.

Often, the tidiness of a commercial occupancy's storage areas is a good indication of the overall quality of housekeeping. The inventory should be stored in a manner that is prescribed for the type of commodity. Flammable items such as solvents, fluids, and paints should be stored in metal, enclosed lockers. Metal containers with self-closing lids should be used for trash. Trash and rubbish should be routinely removed to an outside storage area away from the building.

Welding and Painting

Service stations and auto repair shops, in addition to gasoline, oil, and other flammable liquids, might have acetylene tanks to provide gas for welding and cutting. Welding and cutting in rooms in which vapor from flammable gases exists are extreme hazards. Spray painting is also hazardous unless the station area is kept clean and ventilated and unless the hazard is properly controlled. The best control is to limit welding and cutting to an area isolated from gasoline and vapors. Spray painting should be done only in an approved spray booth.

Heating Processes

Dry cleaners and laundries require a sizable boiler that should be in a separate room fully isolated from the rest of the premises by firewalls. In addition, hand irons, dryers, mangles, and presses all use heat-generating equipment. Electrical equipment should have "on-off" warning lights, be adequately grounded, and have master cutoff switches. Steam pipes from the boiler should be insulated, and combustibles should not be stored close to the pipes.

Soldering irons in television and appliance repair shops should have "on-off" lights and be used on a metal table with a metal resting stand.

Although the refrigeration unit might not be thought of as a heat-producing system, the motors do generate heat. Motor installations have a grill or screen permitting air circulation. Blockage of that ventilation will cause the motor to run hot, constituting an ignition source.

Other Hazards

Self-service operations represent a growing segment of this category. Self-service laundries and gas stations are common. Although self-service equipment is designed for easy operation, a trained attendant should be on hand. The attendant should be ready to react to an emergency if the equipment is misused or if a defect should develop. Self-service operations are subject to vandalism. Self-service laundries, which could operate on a twenty-four-hour basis, are especially susceptible to vandalism. If no attendant is present, the underwriter might find such a risk unacceptable for *any* property coverage.

Gas stations are also subject to vehicle damage to their gas pumps, spillage of gasoline from overfilling, and gasoline leakage from underground storage tanks.

Manufacturing Occupancies

The occupancies within the manufacturing category vary according to the nature of the product being manufactured. Each occupancy must be considered on its own merits, with the underwriter's evaluation based on the special hazards found in that occupancy.

For example, steel manufacturers have blast furnaces, rolling mills, and associated steel processing equipment. Pasta manufacturers use an extensive drying process that poses a severe dust hazard. The physical layout of the manufacturing plant could be extensive, with separate buildings for each phase of the manufacturing process, or it could be a small, one-product operation with a few employees concentrated in a small area of a multitenant building.

Ignition Sources

Generalizing with respect to the fire ignition sequence is difficult because of the diversity of the manufacturing category. However, within the industrial sector, underwriters should note certain characteristics of fire ignition.

Most fires in industrial occupancies are caused by the specialized equipment being used. According to NFPA statistics, such equipment caused 21 percent of those fires.[6] Given the vast array of machinery and equipment found in the industrial category, underwriters should stress the quality of maintenance as an underwriting variable. Desirable manufacturing risks have not only good housekeeping but also an ongoing program of equipment inspection and maintenance.

Inventory Combustibility and Susceptibility

The combustibility and susceptibility of inventory vary widely among manufacturers. Underwriters must consider the characteristics of not only the finished product or commodity but also the stocks of raw materials and semi-finished goods. In manufacturing, finished products of relatively low hazard can have highly combustible or susceptible components. A manufacturer of jewelry or precision instruments, for instance, will sustain a more serious loss than the manufacturer of a more durable type of stock, such as wood flooring or concrete paving stones, which can be readily refinished if damaged.

Paper products not only provide fuel for fires but are also highly susceptible to damage by fire and heat. Paper stocks are commonly damaged extensively by water even when the actual fire loss is minimal. Technological development has produced many plastic substitutes for metal as components of a variety of products. Most plastics are highly susceptible to fire and heat and emit noxious fumes and heavy smoke that hamper firefighting efforts.

Clothing and cloth products are susceptible to severe damage from fire, smoke, and water. Salvaging part of an inventory permeated by the odor of smoke or reprocessing water-soaked merchandise is an expensive process. Selling damaged clothing as new is not possible, which reduces the value of the salvage.

Wood product inventories are highly combustible and susceptible to damage from smoke and water. They are not limited to furniture, but also include musical instruments and toys and novelties. Recreational vehicles and mobile homes generally contain wood furniture designed for their living space. Manufacturers of these products typically have extensive inventories of these furniture components.

A metal fabricator working with magnesium, beryllium, and similar metals is subject to extreme fire and explosion hazards. The metal itself can be highly combustible. This hazard is increased by the manufacturing processes of grinding, burning, forging, and welding.

Regardless of the commodity, underwriters must evaluate the physical arrangement of the inventory and housekeeping. A congested layout contributes to loss severity. Aisle space should be adequate, with stocks stored on steel shelving or on pallets. High piling of stock should be avoided, particularly when the risk is sprinklered and high piling could block the sprinkler heads. Flammable commodities should be stored separately from nonflammable stock. The storage of flammable items should be in accordance with NFPA standards.

Combustibility of Materials and Supplies

The type of supplies necessary to an occupancy can introduce hazards that might not be as obvious to the underwriter as those presented by the inventory. Most occupancies include some form of packing and shipping materials, together with materials and supplies necessary for the production or warehousing of the inventory. Those supplies should be evaluated in terms of storage, combustibility, and handling.

Paper goods such as cardboard cartons are commonly used for packing and shipping finished products. Packing material such as shredded paper or excelsior is no longer common for protecting fragile items such as glassware; other combustibles have replaced them. Recent technology has resulted in increased use of plastic packing material that can be molded to fit the item being packed. When the commodity requires crating, such as for export, wooden crates provide the needed strength.

The type of packing material will dictate the necessary loss control techniques. The packing and shipping area should be isolated from the rest of the operation, preferably in a separate fire division with no accumulation of debris. All packing materials are combustible and should not be stored near boilers or any source of heat. Storage of supplies in stacks or piles can present the problem of excessive weight. This is particularly true with respect to cardboard, which is water-absorbent. If stacks of cardboard become wet during a fire, structural damage to the building could result if their weight exceeds the floor load capacity. To reduce the possibility of this occurrence, such stock should be stored on pallets.

Depending on their chemical content, plastics can burn or melt and should be stored in separate metal bins. Small pieces of styrofoam, called peanuts, will fill an irregular space and prevent the contents of a shipping package from moving. These properties and their low cost have made styrofoam peanuts a popular packing material. Like other forms of plastic packing, peanuts burn easily and emit noxious fumes that interfere with fire suppression efforts. Because they have a large surface in relation to their total mass, styrofoam peanuts are easier to ignite than other types of plastic packing materials.

Manufacturers usually maintain storage facilities for raw stock, materials and supplies, and finished goods. Because of the quantity of contents they have to store, manufacturers often use rack storage systems. Rack storage provides both a horizontal and a vertical flue in which a fire can spread. In addition, overloading the rack facility will cause it to collapse. The racks in a warehousing operation might be not only high but also long. Sometimes having sprinklers within the racks and not just at the ceiling is advisable. Early suppression fast response (ESFR) sprinklers afford the best available protection for high rack storage, but the technology is new and approved only for certain warehouse occupancies.

When an extensive amount of wood is used for crating, the operation has many of the elements of a woodworking or carpentry occupancy. Rough wood must be stored, cut to size, and trimmed. This results in dust and shavings and requires an exhaust system and careful housekeeping.

Janitorial supplies are common to every occupancy. As previously noted, cleaning solvents and polishes are usually flammable and should be stored on metal shelving or in metal lockers. Although good housekeeping might exist in the overall occupancy, it might not be as good as it must be to control the dangers presented by flammable solvents.

Heat Sources

Heat sources include special power sources such as steam pressure vessels and turbines. Those power sources can be direct-drive electric motors, steam-powered engines or turbines with belts and shafts, or internal combustion engines.

Electric motors should be of the proper size and type for their intended use. Constant operation of these motors can cause overheating to the point at which insulation can burn, and a short circuit could cause a fire. Equipment should be clean, well-lubricated, and routinely inspected, in order to prevent overheating. A simple test for overheating is to place the palm of the hand on the motor casing. If it is too hot for comfort, the motor is overheated.

With steam power, pressure is built up within the boiler. Unless the pressure is controlled, the boiler will explode. The safety pressure relief valve is an important component of any steam boiler. It relieves excessive pressure and should be inspected frequently. Steam pipes should be fully insulated to avoid heat loss and to reduce the hazard of heat transfer to combustibles. Bearings can become overheated unless kept clean and well-lubricated. Drive belts should be kept taut at the proper tension to prevent the possibility of slippage and friction.

Internal combustion engines present several fire hazards. The exhaust system should be arranged so that clearance between the exhaust stack and combustibles is adequate. Exhaust systems commonly run underground outside the building. In this case, the exhaust system should be kept free from weeds and trash that could ignite from the hot exhaust gases and possible backfires. If the fuel tank is fastened to the engine, it should be secure and not permitted to vibrate and loosen the fuel lines. The area in which the engine is located should be properly vented to carry off accumulations of fumes.

Heat Treatment Processes

Oil baths, annealing, hardening and tempering, high frequency induction heating, and molten salt baths are heat treatment processes that operate at extreme temperatures. The process area must be kept free of combustible materials. Hot sparks or slag could splash on combustibles, or hot metal objects could be placed on combustibles, if they are present. Tempering vats containing oil are usually used for quenching or rapid cooling of metal objects. Those vats should have temperature controls, self-closing covers, and overflow pits with drains. Hoods should cover the vats to prevent water from getting into the vats.

Welding and Cutting

In manufacturing occupancies, as in other occupancies, welding and cutting operations are a principal cause of fires primarily because of the sparks and hot slag deposited on combustibles. Hazardous welding and cutting operations are found in a variety of plants, and their presence is a problem.

Manufacturers ordinarily have a special advantage in controlling this ignition source. Welding and cutting are often part of the production process and performed at a fixed location. The manufacturer can design the area to accommodate the hazards. Usually, no one employee is responsible for controlling that hazard.

Finishing Processes

A finishing process will usually be hazardous because of either the flammability of the material used or the inherent nature of the process. Painting and finishing operations involve using oils and solvents that are subject to flash fires and explosion. Rags that become paint-soaked should be disposed of in self-closing metal containers with tightly fitting covers. The finishing method used can be by hand, spraying, or dipping. Spray painting is the most hazardous of these.

Spray painting should be done in a well-ventilated area cut off from the rest of the operation or at least in an approved booth that contains the paint spray. Electrical fixtures should be explosion-proof, and the booth should be kept clean. Dip tanks should be constructed of metal and secured to prevent overturning. Chemical extinguishers should be kept close to a dip tank or spray booth. All paints, oils, and solvents should be stored in metal lockers, and only the amount needed for the operation should be out in the open.

Sanding and buffing of wood products create wood dust that settles on all surfaces, including any exposed overhead components of structural members. Therefore, an explosion hazard exists, and flash fires can occur. Disposing of the dust and chips that accumulate necessitates not only routine cleaning but also an adequate exhaust system to remove the dust from the air.

Spontaneous Heating

Spontaneous heating is "the process of increasing the temperature of a material without drawing heat from its surroundings."[7] If the material is heated to ignition, it is called **spontaneous ignition** or **spontaneous combustion**. Spontaneous heating is actually an oxidation process, and the result of the process depends on the rate of heat generation or oxidation, air supply, and the insulation properties of the immediate surroundings.

Spontaneous combustion will result, for example, if oily mops are left in a poorly ventilated closet. Vegetable fibers that have been processed for their oil content, such as cottonseed and copra, and other fibers with a naturally high oil content, such as hemp and sisal, are extremely hazardous. Such material should be in low piles and moved frequently. High piles of coal, wet hay, and sawdust are subject to spontaneous heating and should be checked regularly with probes or should have thermocouples inserted to warn of heat buildup.

Spontaneous heating can also result from paint residue or oils that are not particularly dangerous at ordinary temperatures but that can be adversely affected by the heat of industrial drying ovens.

Friction and Static Electricity

Any manufacturing operation using machinery is subject to possible fire from friction as heat is built up between a pulley and sheave and a fast-moving, rubberized fabric belt. If the belt is ignited, flaming pieces will be thrown over a wide area. Occupancies that involve grinding, milling, or crushing of noncombustible materials are subject to possible buildup of friction that might ignite nearby combustible materials.

Friction also creates static electricity. Static electricity is dangerous in grinding, milling, or crushing operations in which dust is present or operations in which flammable vapors or gases are present, since it provides an ignition source for fire and explosion. Detection equipment indicating the presence of static electricity should be installed. A common device used for detection purposes is a neon tube tester, which glows when it comes in contact with an object charged with static electricity. Since **static electricity** occurs when the atmosphere is clear and dry and static charges are eliminated when the relative humidity is high, the relative humidity should be kept as high as possible around milling, grinding, and crushing operations. Electrical equipment should be well-grounded to prevent electrical charges from accumulating in the machinery. Grounding the equipment permits static electricity to discharge harmlessly into the ground, thus eliminating it as a potential ignition source.

Numerous industrial fires can be attributed to friction and static electricity as well as to mechanical breakdown, so machinery should be carefully inspected and maintained. Also, combustible material should not be placed close to equipment, and the ventilation system should be adequate to carry off any flammable vapors, gases, or dust.

Industrial Materials Handling Equipment

Most manufacturers' warehouses use industrial lift trucks for handling materials within the plant or warehouse or on the loading dock. Industrial lift trucks can be electrically operated using storage batteries as a power source or equipped with gasoline, diesel, or liquefied petroleum (LP) gas internal-combustion engines. Vehicles with internal-combustion engines create exhaust fumes and have the potential for leaking or spilling fuel. In addition, fuel must be stored for their operation. Careless operation of a lift truck can result in collision with the building structure or machinery and equipment. The vision of the operator can be hindered by the size of the load being carried, and sprinkler pipes, refrigerant pipes, or steam pipes can be damaged.

Areas in which such equipment is used should be well-ventilated to carry off the exhaust fumes. Operators should be trained and qualified to use the equipment. Aisle space should be adequate, and potential obstructions should be removed or protected to minimize damage from collision.

Fuel supplies for the equipment should be stored, and equipment should be refueled outdoors and away from the building. If gasoline is stored in underground tanks, the fittings should be tight to prevent leakage, and the tanks should have vents for discharging vapors during filling. Dispensing hoses and nozzles should have automatic shutoff valves to stop the flow of gasoline when the tank of the lift truck is filled.

LP gas can be stored under pressure in either bulk tanks or cylinders. In either situation, the storage location should be outdoors and away from the building, protected from possible damage from collision or vandalism. Battery-powered vehicles require frequent charging. If overcharged, the batteries emit hydrogen gas, which is flammable and odorless. The charging of the batteries should be confined to a well-ventilated, detached building and handled by properly trained individuals.

Flammable Liquids

Storing and using flammable liquids, solvents, and paints are hazards that exist in most manufacturing risks to some degree. The volatile material might be inherent to the operation, as in a metal shop or chemical plant, or it might be incidental to the occupancy and used only for cleaning and maintenance.

Careless handling of flammable liquids is perhaps the greatest single hazard in a metal-working occupancy. Oily metal parts are commonly washed in solvents that are highly volatile and flammable. Oil coolants are used for turning and milling hard metals. Hydraulic oil under extreme pressure is used to operate hydraulic presses. Finishing the product can involve spray painting. Throughout the entire fabricating process, a hazard is present not only from the existence and use of the flammable commodity but also from flammable or explosive vapors.

Plastics Manufacturing

Plastic materials consist of a combination of chemical elements that can produce a solid or liquid state and can be cast-molded, heated, or melted into a raw product that is then processed to produce a finished product. Finishing processes include the following:

- Extrusion, which consists of forcing the raw material through a die to produce a particular shape
- Injection molding, during which the plastic compound is melted and then injected through a heated nozzle into a cooled, sealed mold
- Pressing the plastic in a heated mold under pressure
- Rolling the plastic into strips

Fire and explosion are major hazards in the plastics industry. Burning plastics emit poisonous gases, generate intense heat, and produce heavy black smoke, all of which make fighting any fire extremely difficult. Most plastics present an explosion hazard when finely divided as a powder or dust.

The construction of a building in which plastics are manufactured should be noncombustible or fire-resistive and designed for that type of manufacturing. Hazardous operations should be located in a separate fire division from the nonhazardous operations. Personnel should receive comprehensive training to ensure that they not only have a thorough knowledge of their job assignments but also know how to react in emergency situations.

Chemical Hazards

Chemical hazards involve many materials, processes, and products, ranging from paint manufacture to pharmaceuticals. Inspectors must be trained to identify the chemical hazards and to determine the adequacy of storage, handling, and processing operations.

Considerations include identifying chemicals that should be stored in a building isolated from the main manufacturing plant. Proper construction of storage buildings varies, depending on the characteristics of the chemical. Some chemicals require a vented storage area because of the explosive instability of the material.

Much information on analyzing chemical hazards is available to both underwriters and engineers. NFPA publication number 49, *Hazardous Chemical Data*, lists many chemicals and their characteristics as well as appropriate precautions. If a process involves an unlisted chemical, loss control personnel need to make a thorough evaluation of the chemical and the process in which it is used.

Explosive Dusts

When mixed with air in the proper proportion, most dust particles can explode. Certain types of dust, such as grain or flour dust, are particularly volatile.

Bakeries are subject to accumulation of flour dust. Coal dust, a byproduct of mining and coal processing, is also highly explosive.

When dust is present, housekeeping is especially important. Dust accumulation on machinery bearings creates friction. The accumulation of dust on shelving and structural members can result in a flash fire.

Dust from the grinding, milling, and polishing of metal is hazardous, particularly the dust of lighter metals such as aluminum and magnesium. Wood dust or dust from large-scale wood-sanding operations can settle on structural members of the building. If this dust is jarred loose, an explosion can occur.

When operations produce a large amount of dust in the air, the dust must be removed. Suction fans, hoods, and forced ventilation should be installed to prevent a cloud of the dust from forming. Electrical motors and other electrical equipment should be dustproof and well-grounded to prevent static electricity. Electric lights should have explosion-proof fixtures. If metal grinding is involved, magnets can be used to keep the particles from escaping into the air.

Hazards of Representative Occupancy Classes[8]

The classes discussed in this section illustrate typical occupancy hazards frequently encountered in commercial property underwriting. Each occupancy is considered in isolation as if it were the only occupancy class found in the submission or renewal under consideration. Often, however, submissions include a building that has either multiple occupancies or a single occupancy including several distinct types of operations. A high-rise office building, for example, might include a restaurant on its top floor. In this case, the basic hazards of a restaurant are present, even though the risk is primarily an office occupancy. Cafeterias in other types of occupancies also introduce hazards typical of a restaurant occupancy.

Restaurants

Restaurants are a frequently encountered class of business. Underwriters will get applications for restaurants either as an insured occupancy or as a tenant in buildings they are asked to insure. Most restaurants specialize in a particular type of cuisine, and each type of cuisine presents somewhat different hazards. This situation makes it difficult to say more about restaurants as a class than that they prepare and serve food and beverages to the public. The wide variety of cooking methods and their effect on the exposure to loss make restaurants a challenging occupancy.

Restaurants vary both in their design and in the services they provide. Fast-food and take-out-only establishments cater to a clientele that places a high value on fast service, often at the expense of the quality of the food. At the opposite end of the spectrum, a few fine restaurants feature dining rooms with a small seating capacity. They rely on ambience, high-quality service, and fine food to attract patrons. Other restaurants operate banquet facilities that cater to large groups and rely on volume for their success. Restaurants such as dinner theaters or cabarets may also provide entertainment.

Ignition Sources

Fires in restaurant occupancies originate most often in cooking equipment. The type of cooking the restaurant features determines how serious this exposure is. Cooking surfaces bring together combustibles, principally in the form of food, and an intense heat source. Deep frying presents the most serious exposure because it uses a combustible cooking medium at high temperatures. Hot fat may overflow from the fryers and ignite nearby combustibles, or the fat itself may ignite. In that case, fire will spread rapidly.

The Occupancy Rating

The basic charge for restaurants is 100 percent of the basic building grade. The furniture, fixtures, and contents of restaurants are rated C-3, combustible, and S-4, susceptible to heavy damage.

Hazard Analysis

Grease is inevitable in any restaurant. It is a special problem for certain types of restaurants, especially those that rely heavily on deep frying and grills. This is especially true of fast-food restaurants, in which the bulk of the menu consists of fried foods.

All cooking equipment in any restaurant should be equipped with hoods and ducts to transfer the heat that cooking apparatus generates to the outside atmosphere. Grease from cooking tends to accumulate in the hoods and ducts, and this provides the most common source of fuel for restaurant fires. The most effective protection against fires on and near cooking surfaces is a combination of hood and duct fire suppression systems and systematic cleaning of the hoods, ducts, and filters.

Hood and duct fire suppression systems, sometimes called "Ansul systems," consist of tanks of class B extinguishing agents connected by piping to nozzles over the cooking surfaces and in the hoods and ducts. In the event of a fire, the system automatically discharges. A well-designed system will also incorporate emergency release handles located convenient to personnel who operate the cooking equipment. This setup permits manual operation of the system if the automatic discharge mechanism fails. The widespread use of hood and duct protection systems has converted restaurants from a specialty class frequently underwritten in the nonadmitted market to a mainstream class of business that many insurers now accept.

The cleaning of hoods, ducts, and filters is another important part of any restaurant loss control program. Because of its specialized nature, this task is best left to professionals. Restaurant employees can clean or replace filters, but the demands of removing grease accumulation from hoods and ducts go beyond their capabilities. It is not uncommon for underwriting guidelines to require that eligible restaurants have a contract for regular cleaning of the hoods and ducts by a professional contractor. Quarterly is the most commonly accepted interval for this process, but some underwriters will accept semiannual cleaning. Others will insist that it be done more often. Health codes in some communities also require regular cleaning by a professional.

Other considerations in restaurants include that they are frequently located in old or remodeled buildings. Remodeling often entails covering old wall surfaces with a new facade. This could result in the presence of concealed spaces. Inadequate ventilation or exhaust systems present another hazard. The building service systems, such as the heating and air conditioning systems, could be a cause of loss. Another hazard is the presence of overloaded electrical circuits and the use of extension cords. Careless disposal of cigarettes and trash is particularly hazardous. Fires often occur because an ashtray is emptied into a container with waste paper.

The extent of combustible or susceptible property in a restaurant varies depending on the type of decor. Common to all restaurant operations is the inventory of food, tables and chairs, linens, and utensils. Decor ranges from the spartan formica of fast-food operations to dinner houses with expensive draperies, wall coverings, carpeting, and upholstered furniture, all of which are subject to severe loss. The S-4 susceptibility rating also reflects the fact that in any restaurant, food commodities are subject to destruction by law in the event of even a small fire, should there be any possibility of contamination.

Since incendiary fires are a major cause of loss in this category, underwriting the restaurant's management is important. The financial condition of the owner(s) is a major consideration. Owners of restaurants might especially experience deteriorating finances if their establishments are located in a changing neighborhood in which a former business district is becoming residential or in which a new highway has changed traffic patterns.

Bowling Centers

Bowling centers provide recreational activity to their customers. Most cater to leagues, which bowl regularly at times convenient to their members. Bowling centers also offer other types of recreation. Most offer their customers video and pinball games. Some include billiard tables. A small restaurant or snack bar is a virtual certainty in a bowling center, many of which also include a bar that serves alcoholic beverages. These facilities may be operated by outside concessionaires.

At one time, bowling was the most popular participation sport in the United States. Bowling centers multiplied and became common. A decline in their popularity, however, has placed financial strain on the industry. This makes the financial condition of the applicant all the more important.

The Occupancy Rating

The basic occupancy charge for bowling centers is 125 percent of the basic building grade. The furniture, fixtures, and contents of this class are rated C-3, combustible, and S-3, susceptible to moderate damage.

Hazard Analysis

Defective wiring constitutes the most common ignition source for bowling centers. The demand for electricity is high, and bowling centers often have dedicated transformers that may be located in underground vaults on the premises. Automatic pinsetters can malfunction and overheat, creating an ignition source in close proximity to flammable pins and alleys. Adequate maintenance of electrical equipment, including refrigerators and air-conditioning, is critical.

The large open spaces that bowling centers require create a single draft area of considerable size. Concealed spaces above ceilings and behind pinsetters are common. This makes the prospect of total or nearly total loss very real. Many underwriters consider automatic fire sprinklers with a high sprinkler grading essential protection for this class.

Bowling pins and alleys require regular refinishing. At one time it was common practice for bowling centers to refinish pins on the premises. Today, off-premises refinishing of pins is the rule. Alleys, on the other hand, cannot be removed to renew their finish. The process entails sanding the hardwood surface and applying a high-gloss finish. Although urethane finishes have replaced highly flammable lacquer ones, the refinishing process continues to present a serious hazard of loss by fire. The safest method of accomplishing this necessary task involves closing the bowling center entirely during refinishing, but this is not always feasible. As an alternative to temporarily closing entirely, the bowling center might temporarily close off a section and erect a dust barrier while refinishing work is being done.

Commercial Printing

Commercial printing encompasses the production of printed material from one-page brochures to books. Printers may handle the full range of services, including distribution and mailing, or they may specialize in a particular aspect of the process. Accounts in this class might also have a design staff to assist customers in preparing the material they need to have printed. Printing often includes typesetting, although newer technology has largely displaced the more hazardous hot-lead type. If a printing operation includes bookbinding or mailing services, the underwriter should treat those operations as separate occupancies.

The Occupancy Rating

The basic occupancy charge of this class is 100 percent of the basic building grade. The furniture, fixtures, and contents of this class are rated C-3, combustible, and S-3, susceptible to moderate damage. Although the basic occupancy charge is the same as that of a restaurant and the combustibility and susceptibility ratings are the same as those of a bowling alley, this class contains different hazards from either of the others. Although the operation, materials, and hazards of this class differ markedly from those of the others, the net effect regarding the peril of fire is the same.

Hazard Analysis

Commercial printing plants contain a great deal of electrical equipment. Hot dryers with temperatures ranging up to 2,500 degrees Fahrenheit are common. Additional hazards include the presence of open gas flames and the storage and use of chemicals. Some of those chemicals are used in combination with solvents.

Printers use a variety of flammable chemicals, especially solvents for cleaning their equipment. Many inks are also flammable. Vapors from solvents and inks are heavier than air, so they tend to collect along the floor. Static electricity is a significant ignition source. Flammable liquids should be stored in accordance with NFPA standards. Employees should remove only enough for a single shift and should dispense flammable liquids from self-closing metal containers. Smoking materials also provide a source of ignition for fires. It is good practice to prohibit smoking entirely on the premises or to limit it to designated areas, preferably outdoors or in a separate fire division.

The large quantity of paper that the printing business requires contributes to the heavy fuel load. In addition to its contribution to the fuel load, paper is highly susceptible to damage by fire and water. Ideally, printers should store stocks of paper in a separate fire division from printing operations. Storage on shelves or pallets will reduce the potential for damage by water. The supply of paper in the production area should be limited to the amount required for immediate use. This is the only effective means to limit the amount of combustible material in close proximity to sources of ignition.

Grain Elevators

Grain elevators are used to store grain pending its sale or use. Farmers use grain elevators to hold grain until it can be used or sold. Grain from local grain elevators can be shipped to a larger grain terminal or grain exporter. The size of a mutually owned and operated grain elevator usually reflects the needs of the farmers in a community. Grain elevators used by grain brokers at grain terminals can be extremely large.

The Occupancy Rating

The basic occupancy charge for this classification depends on the size of the grain elevator. The charge ranges from 150 percent of the basic building grade for grain elevators with capacities of less than 250,000 bushels to 210 percent of the basic building grade for grain elevators with capacities of more than 1 million bushels. The combustibility charge for this category, which is based almost entirely on the contents, is C-2, limited combustibility. This class also has a rating of S-2, susceptible to slight damage.

Hazard Analysis

Grain dust is a major hazard in this classification, and the control of grain dust is essential. Any evidence of poor housekeeping or accumulation of dust is cause for concern. Grain elevators are subject to fires caused by spontaneous combustion and are also subject to grain dust explosions. An ignition source is static electricity caused by moving machinery. Other ignition sources are improperly grounded machinery, open motors sparking in dusty areas, sparking of waste metal not removed from grain that comes in contact with moving machinery, bare light bulbs, and lightning.

Other hazardous conditions include gasoline or LP gas that is spilled or improperly stored and flammable chemicals used in fumigation. Some of the support structures surrounding grain elevators contain potbelly stoves and portable heaters (salamanders). Malfunctioning or improperly maintained machinery or equipment can also cause losses. When requested coverage includes collapse losses, the underwriter should be aware that the location of dryers outside of buildings can expose them to heavy winds or the possibility of collapse caused by the weight of snow. Smoking is extremely hazardous in grain elevators and should be carefully controlled by management.

Summary

ISO evaluates commercial occupancies with regard to the following four factors:

- Basic occupancy charge
- Combustibility of contents, furniture, and fixtures
- Susceptibility
- Additional occupancy hazards

Contents are classified by their combustibility. The five-step scale ranges from noncombustible to rapid (or flash) burning. Contents are also evaluated based on how easily they are affected by fire, smoke, and water. The five-step susceptibility scale ranges from minimal damage to extreme loss.

Hazards fall into three categories: common hazards, which are found in virtually all occupancies; special hazards of the class, which are expected in a class but are of significant concern; and special hazards of the risk, which are not typical in the occupancy. Common hazards are housekeeping, heating and air-conditioning equipment, common electrical equipment, and lighting and smoking materials.

Ignition sources that have been responsible for losses in the past in a particular occupancy category provide insight into hazards that must be considered. In addition to the principal operation of a particular occupancy, ancillary operations such as an employee cafeteria or packing and shipping departments pose additional hazards. The analysis of occupancy hazards requires analysis of all factors, together with a determination of the manner in which the occupancy hazards are either reduced or amplified by the structure in which the occupancy is housed.

Underwriters should analyze the following five occupancy factors:

- Ignition sources
- Fuel load
- Combustibility and susceptibility of contents, furniture, and fixtures
- Interior finish of structure
- Efficiency of management, encompassing the following areas:
    - Housekeeping
    - Employee training and skills
    - Loss control programs

Chapter Notes

1. Insurance Services Office, *Specific Commercial Property Evaluation Schedule* (New York, NY: Insurance Services Office, 1995), pp. 5-9 and 6-45.
2. *Specific Commercial Property Evaluation Schedule*, p. 4-4.
3. Descriptions were obtained from *Specific Commercial Property Evaluation Schedule*, 1990, p. 4-4.
4. *Fire Protection Handbook*, 17th edition, eds. Arthur E. Cote and Jim L. Linville (Quincy, MA: National Fire Protection Association, 1991), p. 8-87.
5. *Fire Protection Handbook*, p. 8-147.
6. *Fire Protection Handbook*, p. 1-14.
7. *Fire Protection Handbook*, p. 1-52.
8. Underwriters are rarely knowledgeable about all of the hazards present in occupancies. *Best's Underwriting Guide for Commercial Lines* (BUG) (Oldwick, NJ: A.M. Best Company, continuously updated) is a comprehensive reference, and this section relies heavily on that work.

Chapter 3

Protection and External Exposure

Protection consists of those measures taken to prevent or reduce the damage done by fire. Analyzing the effectiveness of these efforts usually centers on public and private protection. Local governments, including cities, towns, counties, villages, and fire districts, provide **public fire protection** to all properties within their jurisdiction. Public fire services employ paid or volunteer firefighters, and in some cases both.

Some property owners also take steps to protect their assets from loss by fire by providing **private fire protection**. That protection can be as simple as a single fire extinguisher or a water barrel or as sophisticated as automatic fire sprinkler systems monitored from a central station, a fire brigade, or a fire company.

An **external exposure** refers to causes of loss that originate *outside* the property. For example, a normally low-hazard occupancy such as a real estate office is not low-hazard if it is located next door to a fireworks factory. Underwriters have little control over outside exposures, but they should know about the exposures and encourage implementation of measures to reduce the risk of loss that external exposures create.

Elements of Fire Protection

The goal of both public and private fire protection is to protect lives and property. **Fire protection** consists of the following three elements:

- Prevention
- Detection
- Suppression

Fire Prevention

Fire prevention includes all measures taken to reduce the likelihood of fire. Public agencies often conduct fire prevention efforts. Those agencies include the local fire service, the fire marshal, and municipal organizations with responsibility for passing and enforcing fire and building codes. These public agencies conduct inspections and update ordinances dealing with hazardous substances and conditions that could increase the incidence and spread of fire. Fire services and public agencies charged with enforcing fire and building codes also encourage businesses to implement private fire protection measures. In that way, they contribute to private fire prevention. Measures that can reduce fire losses include the following:

- Improving housekeeping
- Enforcing rules for handling hazardous substances
- Controlling ignition sources
- Conducting frequent inspections

Fire Detection

Fire detection activities include all measures and equipment used to detect fire and alert the fire service when a fire breaks out. Public sector efforts to further these goals consist mainly of communications systems used by the local fire service to transmit fire alarms. Communication equipment consists primarily of telephone, radio, and fire call-box systems. In many communities, members of the public can dial 911 to reach a single emergency response center that dispatches fire, police, and ambulance services. Private detection systems include automatic fire-sensing devices and guard services. Virtually all fires that are not caused by explosion or arson start small but grow at an exponential rate. Because the resources needed to fight a fire increase in direct proportion to its size, early detection is a vital measure to reduce the severity of fire losses.

Fire Suppression

Fire suppression includes all measures and equipment used to contain and extinguish a fire. The firefighters at the fire scene provide public fire suppression. Private fire suppression includes automatic sprinkler systems, fire extinguishers, and fire brigades. Efficient fire suppression greatly reduces loss severity, making a relatively minor inconvenience of what might have been a severe loss. Inept or ineffective suppression efforts can result in heavy or even total losses from water damage, which can be more severe than the loss from the fire itself.

Public Fire Protection Systems

Public fire protection systems consist primarily of the fire department serving the community. The quality of protection varies. Because fire department quality is such a critical factor in insurance, public protection is a crucial underwriting and pricing consideration.

Public Protection Classifications

Insurance Services Office (ISO) and its predecessor organizations have used fire defense characteristics of a community to quantify the fire protection services of towns and cities. Over the years ISO has devised a public protection classification system for rating the quality of fire protection that a community provides. The **public protection classification (PPC)** runs from class 1 to class 10, with class 1 having the highest protection and class 10 having no protection. The most recent scoring system used to evaluate public fire protection is called the **Fire Suppression Rating Schedule (FSRS)**.

The FSRS contains two major sections. In the first section, **Public Fire Suppression**, ISO develops the town class rating. This classification applies to all class-rated properties and to schedule (or specifically) rated properties that require a water flow of 3,500 gallons per minute (gpm) or less for fire suppression purposes. The second section, **Individual Property Fire Suppression**, develops a public protection classification for individual properties at which suppression requires a water flow of more than 3,500 gpm. A property might require more than 3,500 gpm because of construction, occupancy, external exposures, or unprotected wall openings. These factors might increase the amount of water needed to suppress a fire alone or in combination with the other factors.

Exhibit 3-1 shows the factors used to calculate the public protection classification and the weight that FSRS gives each. To qualify for a public protection classification of 1 through 9, a municipality must have either of the following:

- A piece of firefighting equipment that has a water pump with a rated capacity of at least 250 gpm at a pressure of 150 pounds per square inch (psi) and a water system capable of delivering 250 gpm at a fire site for two hours during the period of highest consumption
- At least one piece of firefighting equipment that has a pump capacity of 50 gpm and at least a 300-gallon water tank

Exhibit 3-1
Fire Suppression Rating Schedule

Factors Considered in the Calculation of Public Protection Classification

Factor	Percentage Weight
Water Supply	40%
Fire Department	50
Fire Alarm	10

Used with permission from Insurance Services Offices, 1980 Fire Suppression Rating Schedule (New York, NY: ISO, 1980).

A municipality that does not have either of these pieces of equipment receives a public protection classification of 10 and is considered unprotected.

A municipality that has either of the above will receive a public protection classification between 1 and 9, depending on the characteristics of its fire service rating, water supply system, and fire alarm system.

Factors considered in evaluating the **fire service rating** include the following:

- Number of engine companies
- Equipment of the engine companies
- Number of ladder companies
- Equipment of the ladder companies
- Geographic distribution of engine and ladder companies relative to the built-up areas of the municipality
- Personnel training

Factors that contribute to the **water supply rating** include the following:

- Part of the city protected by fire hydrants
- Maximum daily water consumption
- Fire flow and duration
- Ability of the water system to deliver the needed fire flow at representative locations in the city
- Condition of fire hydrants

The **fire alarm rating** depends on the following factors:

- The adequacy of the telephone system
- Devices used to record calls that report fires
- The number of operators on duty to handle fire calls
- Fire radio communication facilities
- Emergency power equipment

The rating of each municipality begins at 100 points. Credits reduce the point total for each area in which the municipality's fire suppression facilities exceed the minimum required by the schedule.

The public protection classification declines from class 10 for a city with minimal fire-suppression facilities to class 1 for a city with excellent fire-suppression facilities. Credits for fire service, water supply, and fire alarm systems do not receive the same weights in the formula. Because of the formula's operation, assigning a specific number of credits to each factor that determines the public protection classification is not possible. The number of credits needed to achieve any specified classification varies with the resources devoted to the water system, fire service, and fire alarms.

The public protection classification for individual properties, computed in Section II of the Fire Suppression Rating Schedule, depends on the firefighting facilities and water supply available to the individual property. The public protection classification for an individual property cannot be better than that of the municipality in which the property is located. It can be inferior, but not worse than class 9 if the municipality has a PPC of class 9 or better.

Effect on Individual Policy Premiums

Both public and private protection systems have an effect on the physical hazards of the risk and the fire rate for that property. A private protection system has a significant effect on the fire rate. Determining that the system is properly maintained and supervised is necessary for justifying a lower rate.

Effect on a Book of Business

Differences in protection class will affect the overall book of fire business. Underwriters must consider those differences when evaluating a risk. The differences in fire rates should account for the differences in risk between class 2 and class 10 when the book of business is large enough to be statistically credible. Since fire losses, particularly large losses, have a relatively low frequency, a very large book of fire business is required for full credibility.

Because underwriters evaluate sprinklered as well as unsprinklered risks and risks with class 1 municipal protection as well as those in protection class 10, identifying the detection and suppression elements of fire protection that are deficient or lacking is particularly important. Those elements especially affect fire severity, or the size of loss. Therefore, a book of business made up primarily of unsprinklered risks in classes 8, 9, and 10 would be likely to have more variability in loss results and therefore more "risk" in the statistical sense than a book of business of the same premium volume made up of risks with better fire protection.

For that reason, a book of fire business is usually balanced regarding protection, with the proportion of unprotected and poorly protected business kept within limits set by top underwriting management. Because of the potentially greater severity of losses, a book of fire business that is heavy in unprotected properties will usually incur higher reinsurance costs than a book of business consisting of property in low protection classes.

Other Public Protection Services

Some fire services also provide other important public protection services, including the following:

- Pre-fire planning surveys
- Salvage teams
- Arson squads

Pre-Fire Planning Surveys

Pre-fire planning surveys are important to the fire prevention efforts of commercial property accounts. These surveys include training runs by the fire service to the premises and walk-through inspections of the premises by the fire service. Surveys help the fire service personnel to become familiar with the location of major buildings and their equipment, fire hydrants, standpipes, and sprinkler system siamese connections. The **siamese connection,** sometimes called the "fire department connection," allows the fire department access to dry standpipes that supply water to hose stations and sprinkler systems. The connection is made through two pipes that extend from the building. Fire department pumper trucks draw water from hydrants and pressurize internal systems.

As the size of the industrial plant or complex increases, pre-fire planning surveys become even more important. They allow the fire service to save crucial minutes after a fire breaks out. Firefighters become familiar enough with the premises to go to the affected building and hook up their pumpers and hoses immediately. Inspections should also determine whether the pipe threads on the siamese connections are compatible with the various fire department equipment connections. Since fire services use connectors with a standard thread, a nonstandard connection would be useless during a fire.

If a business uses or appears to use hazardous materials, the local fire service should be involved in pre-fire planning. Water used to suppress a fire runs off from the fire scene and eventually drains into the ground in the surrounding area or into local waterways through storm drains. If the fire involves hazardous materials, it can pollute groundwater or local waterways and may contaminate the local drinking water supply. In several instances, that concern has prompted fire services to let a fire burn itself out rather than to risk pollution of the water supply. The fire service will work to prevent the spread of fire to adjacent properties but will not direct its hose streams onto the property involved in the fire. When this happens, a total loss becomes certain.

Design features are available to contain the spread of hazardous materials, whether it is from leakage or runoff of water used to suppress fire. They include retaining ponds and dikes around structures and areas that contain hazardous materials. Many businesses have already taken measures to contain accidental spills and leaks. If the fire services know in advance that water supplies are protected, they will be more willing to attack a fire aggressively.

Determining whether the insured and the fire service conduct pre-fire planning surveys at the property under consideration is particularly important with large commercial risks. The frequency of those surveys and their adequacy are also important. Pre-fire planning can serve as a starting point for the commercial organization's own private loss control plan.

Salvage Teams

The initial task of the fire service is to suppress the fire, but water damage can cause heavy property loss. Some fire services have specially trained **salvage teams** that use tarpaulins, drains, lifts, and similar equipment to minimize property damage caused by the water used to suppress a fire. When the contents are particularly susceptible to water damage, salvage teams might be able to reduce the severity of that damage.

Arson Squads

In recent years, the incidence of arson has increased sharply. It has become the leading cause of all fires. Arson for profit is particularly troublesome in commercial lines. This aspect of moral hazard, however, can be controlled. In communities in which vigorous investigation and prosecution efforts have been instituted, arson incidence has declined. For example, insurance company members of the Connecticut FAIR Plan have purchased specially equipped vans that state police can use to help identify a fire's point of origin. This equipment has enabled Connecticut state police to significantly increase the number of arson arrests it makes. For the arson detection efforts of the municipality to deter arson for profit, the work of the **arson squad** must be coordinated with that of the police department and the district attorney or other prosecuting agency. Only through coordinated efforts will convictions for arson be obtained. Task forces have helped focus the attention of law enforcement officials on what many considered a "victimless" crime or one of low priority.

Arson hot lines, which offer rewards for information leading to the arrest and conviction of arsonists, are used in many areas. Both urban and suburban communities have found that acts of arson cause declining areas to deteriorate even further. Small municipalities usually do not have the resources needed to form special arson squads. However, the need for arson control in small communities is often as great as that of larger communities, because arson can have a significant economic effect on municipalities of all sizes.

Private Fire Prevention Systems

Small commercial risks tend to rely heavily on public protection. Large commercial risks often provide private protection to supplement the public facilities. Fire prevention systems focus on keeping fires from occurring.

Major Elements of Private Fire Prevention

The primary goal of private fire prevention efforts is to reduce loss frequency. Following are three major elements of private fire prevention:

- Control of housekeeping
- Adherence to building codes and standards
- Fire protection planning

Control of Housekeeping

Housekeeping activities are primarily aimed at reducing fire frequency, although good housekeeping can also affect severity. Good housekeeping requires that the management of the firm be given the responsibility to establish and supervise appropriate housekeeping procedures. In large organizations, this responsibility might be delegated to lower management levels, but controls should be established to ensure that the activities are properly carried out.

Following are the eight categories of housekeeping hazards, but not all of them are present in every commercial property risk:[1]

- Smoking
- Waste cans
- Ash cans and refuse receptacles
- Packing materials and sawdust
- Old furniture and paper
- Floor oils, polishes, and cleaners
- Outdoor housekeeping
- Dumps

The National Fire Protection Association (NFPA) *Inspection Manual* recommends procedures for effectively managing each of these hazards.[2] Frequent inspections of the premises can help to ensure that the insured maintains good housekeeping standards. Proper housekeeping standards, rigidly enforced, are the foundation of a private fire prevention program. Neither public fire service inspections nor insurance company inspections are done frequently enough to fulfill this role.

Adherence to Building Codes and Standards

A private fire prevention program should consider whether building codes and NFPA standards have been met. Municipal building inspections can be perfunctory and infrequent. In addition, the municipal codes might not be as stringent as the standards set by NFPA.

Private fire prevention programs should ensure that all new construction, newly purchased existing buildings, and newly installed equipment adhere to all codes and standards that apply. The initial stages of any physical plant expansion plans should consider NFPA standards. This consideration makes adherence to the standards much more likely. The acquisition of an older building that does not comply with NFPA standards can present unique problems. For example, the cost of bringing buildings up to the current code could be prohibitive. Sometimes the fire prevention program can only note the deficiency and seek other means to reduce or control the fire hazard.

NFPA standards establish the conditions that manufacturing and industrial processes should meet. These conditions include procedures to properly store raw materials or inventory.

Fire Protection Planning

A complete private fire prevention program should include the same type of pre-fire planning that the municipal fire service provides. In large industrial complexes, pre-fire planning is often a part of an overall disaster control plan. A suggested fire control plan has the following five steps:[3]

1. Obtaining a plan of the grounds and buildings that make up the installation.
2. Plainly marking the location of all main control valves (process equipment, water supply, fuel supply, and so on); checking valves, pumps, hose houses, standpipes, and hydrants; and making sure they are easily accessible and identified on the plan.
3. Preparing a water supply plan that indicates all available water supply sources, both public and private, with their estimated capacities and available pressure. (Those sources include ponds, lakes, rivers, water mains, storage tanks, and any associated pumps.)
4. Locating on the plan all portable fire extinguishers. Equipment should be appropriate for the area in which it is located, adequate in size and number, and easily accessible.
5. Obtaining information on detection and suppression systems, even if they have not been installed. The protective and economic advantages of such equipment should make its installation feasible. All operating features of existing systems should be noted on the plan.

Fire control plans vary in length from a single page for small commercial risks to book-length for large manufacturing plants. The plan provides a starting point for training the organization's personnel in fire response. The appropriate response can greatly reduce the severity of any fire that does occur.

If the organization is large enough to have a fire brigade, all of its members should know the location of fire-suppression equipment and control valves. Employees should know not to turn off an automatic sprinkler system until they have been instructed to do so by fire service personnel. Out of ignorance, an employee could shut off the sprinkler system to prevent further water damage, only to have the fire flare up and cause a total loss.

The organization's private pre-fire planning should include regular inspection of all fire protection equipment. The automatic sprinkler and fire detection systems, standpipes, and siamese connections for automatic sprinkler systems should all be inspected.

Commercial Fire Loss Control Programs

Companies have commercial fire loss control programs to codify procedures for controlling hazards that are typical of the operation. In many instances, a company's risk manager is the catalyst for the program. In the vast majority of companies, insurer loss control personnel encourage establishment of those programs. The success of such programs varies with the zeal with which they are pursued. Management attitude is an essential ingredient in the success of the services included in those programs.

Management Attitude

A successful program for controlling fire losses will have the active support of management at all levels. A commitment to the program by senior management is the only way to ensure the active involvement of management at all levels, including the first-line supervisors. Fire loss control requires almost daily monitoring of housekeeping, faithful adherence to relevant codes and standards, effective pre-fire planning, and training. This monitoring involves so many of the company's personnel at so many levels that management commitment is vital. If senior management does not cooperate with and coordinate the program, it will fail.

Management attitude is not easy to evaluate from outside the firm. Most companies at least feign interest in fire loss control while the insurance company inspector is visiting. The state of the company's housekeeping, however, often indicates the true degree of management's commitment. An organization might have an excellent fire loss control plan on paper but not in practice. A walk through the plant might disclose cigarette butts on the floor of the woodworking shop and oily rags stored in cardboard boxes in the machine shop. Such conditions call into question the extent of management's commitment to a loss control program.

Measuring Effectiveness

Cost/benefit analysis can measure the effectiveness of a loss control program. This analysis relates the quantified benefits of any program or project to the costs incurred in that program. When the costs or benefits accrue over more than one year, future benefits and costs are discounted to their present value. This discounting procedure uses an interest rate that reflects the opportunity cost of the funds invested in the project to obtain the present value of the cost and benefit cash flows.

A project can be economically feasible only if the benefits exceed the costs. Some of the costs and benefits of loss control programs are easy to quantify, but others are more difficult. Many insureds believe that loss control programs benefit only the insurer. Showing the economic value of a loss control program to the insured can make the insured's cooperation easier to obtain.

The costs and benefits of basic loss control efforts such as housekeeping and fire protection planning are not easy to measure. The costs are usually part of other operating or capital costs, and the fire rate rarely reflects the benefits directly. However, pointing out a number of indirect costs attached to even minor fires, such as disruption of production and added cleanup and maintenance expense, can help convince the insured that loss control is beneficial.

When the loss control program includes the installation of automatic sprinklers and other fire detection and suppression systems that are reflected in the fire rates, a cost/benefit analysis can be more straightforward. The costs of a sprinkler system can be easily identified. The benefit of the reduction in the fire rate can be easily determined. Then a value can be assigned to the other less tangible benefits of a sprinkler system. Those other benefits include the following:[4]

- Prevention of costly down time and production interruptions
- Protection of workers' jobs, particularly when ordinary payroll is excluded from business income coverage
- Greater design freedom and building flexibility
- Water conservation
- Reduced frequency of workers compensation claims

Most of the costs and benefits used in the cost/benefit analysis will be estimates. At best, cost/benefit analysis is an educated guide to decision making. The safety manager who is performing this analysis will base many of the estimates on assumptions based on personal judgments. For example, one assumption might involve the loyalty of the insured's clients, should a loss to the firm occur. Regardless of the inherent uncertainty of this process, the best guess determined from it should be used to evaluate the decision to install a sprinkler system.

When evaluating the savings in the fire rate on building construction, the insured must consider that sprinklers will reduce the contents fire rate as well. A study undertaken for the federal government indicated that sprinkler system costs for government warehouses were approximately 4.64 percent of the total building cost. When the value of the contents was included, the sprinkler system costs amounted to less than 1 percent of the total value.

Available Services

Several outside resources can be used in a commercial property loss control program. An insurance company inspection service can provide important information on how improvements can be made in the risk. The insurance company can provide helpful expertise in loss control measures and can also indicate the effect that proposed changes or system installations will have on fire rates. Consultants can analyze new construction at the blueprint stage and suggest changes that would lower fire insurance rates. Brokers and fire protection consultants can also provide valuable advice.

Sprinkler system manufacturers are another source of information for analyzing the effect of sprinkler and other suppression and detection systems on fire rates. The local municipal fire service often provides inspection service and pre-fire planning information, which is of assistance to those developing and implementing the program.

Control of Loss Severity

Except for arson and explosions, most fires are small when they start. Fire suppression efforts that start early can often confine the fire to a small area and minimize the severity of a loss. The pattern of heat release in a typical fire emphasizes this point. Heat is directly responsible for much of the damage that fire causes. As fire grows, the rate at which it releases heat increases exponentially over time. With prompt discovery and an immediate alarm, the fire service can abate the fire's growth. If a fire goes unnoticed for even a short period of time, the fire service must fight a fire producing rapidly advancing heat levels. A high level of heat places firefighters at a serious disadvantage and dramatically increases the amount of water they need to suppress the blaze.

Early suppression is essential for reducing losses once a fire starts. The two primary methods of achieving early suppression are private detection systems and private suppression equipment. Early detection means prompt notice to the fire service to reduce the time that elapses before the service's initial attack. Using private suppression equipment is the most effective way to keep small problems small. It permits starting the attack between the time the alarm sounds and the time the fire service can deploy personnel and apparatus, and it can reduce the amount of water needed for suppression.

Private Fire Detection Systems

Many fires occur at night, on weekends, or during other times when commercial establishments are closed for business. Often, the first reports of fires come from passersby. For a fire to reach sufficient size to be noticed from outside the premises, it must reach a considerable size. Even immediate response on the part of the public fire service will not prevent extensive property damage. A private detection system can greatly speed the response of both private and public suppression efforts and can reduce the severity of a fire. The principal types of private fire detection systems are watch services, automatic fire detection devices, and closed-circuit television.

Watch Service Systems

A **watch service system** uses people to patrol the premises when a business is closed. The effectiveness of the watch service system depends on the quality of the personnel employed. The job of touring empty offices and plants is neither interesting nor challenging, and watch service personnel might not be conscientious in completing their rounds. The problems associated with unsupervised watch services have led to the development of systems in which watch service personnel and their activities are monitored.

The following are common types of watch service systems:

- Clock and tape systems
- Central station systems
- Tour systems
- Merchant police
- Unsupervised watch services

Clock and Tape Systems

Basic **clock and tape systems** require the watch service to make regular rounds of the premises. Clock and tape systems derive their name from the mechanical clocks originally used by watchmen making "clock rounds," and many businesses still use these systems today. The guard carries a portable clock with a keyhole in the top. Keys are mounted on the wall at various points along the guard's appointed rounds. The guard inserts each key into the keyhole on the clock and turns it to record the time that a particular station is visited. Each key has a raised number that leaves an impression on the tape or disk inside the clock. In modern systems, the traditional clock and key have been replaced with electronic stations and magnetic key cards. The guard swipes a card through a reader on the wall to record the time of the visit to each station. The record can be checked later to determine whether the guard followed the proper route.

The clock and tape system is superior to systems that provide no supervision, because the guard's performance can be monitored. The disadvantage of this type of system is that it does not provide information until after the guard's shift ends. If the guard is attacked by burglars, falls and is injured, suffers a heart attack, or for some other reason does not complete the rounds, this fact will not be known until the business reopens. The premises will be unprotected in the meantime.

When a clock and tape system is installed, the guard's tour should be designed so that the guard will visit every area of the premises at regular intervals. In a large industrial plant with several buildings, a single guard might be able to visit each station only once or twice during the night. In that situation, a fire could burn for some time without being detected. The watch service should be diligent in checking the records after each tour. The system is essentially unsupervised if the records are checked infrequently or not at all. Insurance company engineers and fire inspectors often review clock records during loss prevention surveys.

Central Station Systems

A major defect of the clock and tape system is the delay in noticing that the guard's rounds have been interrupted. A central station system remedies this defect. **Central station systems** use stations and keys similar to those of the clock and tape system. The recorded information is then sent electronically to a central station. At the central station, personnel monitor the systems at a number of properties. If a guard does not signal in at the appointed time, the central station can either telephone the guard or dispatch someone to the premises. The time that the property is unguarded by a detection system is determined by how much time the guard has before clocking in and the length of time necessary to reach the property from the central station. This response time could be lengthy for commercial properties located some distance from the central station.

A major disadvantage of the central station system is the increased cost relative to the older, portable clock and tape system. Increased cost becomes a minor consideration when a central station system is used for other purposes, such as monitoring process temperatures, waterflow alarms, and burglary alarms. When all of these monitoring services are considered together, central station monitoring of watchperson tours becomes cost-effective.

Tour Systems

The **tour system** is a compromise between the inherent time lags of a clock and tape system and the high costs of a full central station system. A tour system wires only certain stations to the central monitoring station, such as every tenth station or stations in critical locations. Selective monitoring provides an opportunity for relatively rapid response to the interruption of the guard's rounds with some reduction in cost.

With both full central station and tour systems, the stations connected to the central monitor board can send a fire alarm directly to the fire service. This feature can reduce the response time for the municipal fire service and adds a backup communication system if the local telephone system fails during the fire.

Merchant Police Systems

The systems described so far use guards employed by the protected organization. If the organization, for reasons of size, cost, or other considerations, does not use one of these systems, a merchant police guard service can be an alternative. The usual **merchant police system** uses guards who patrol a route covering a number of properties. The primary concern of merchant police is control of losses from burglary and robbery, but they also can help detect fires. Guards make regular rounds, usually after normal business hours, and often visit the interior of businesses that stay open late. After closing hours, guards drive or walk to the exterior of the property and check that all exterior doors are secure and that no other problems are visible. The merchant police approach has the following three major disadvantages:

1. The guards usually check only the exterior when the premises are closed.
2. Considerable time can elapse between visits because the guards are responsible for several properties.
3. The merchant police company employs and supervises the guards, so the insured does not have direct control of how well the property is monitored.

All types of watch service systems can deter and detect burglary in addition to fire. Because the merchant police system tends to focus on checking doors and windows after regular business hours, the system is good for catching intruders. A fire, on the other hand, could occur and spread throughout the building before the merchant police guard could detect it from outside the building. Many commercial properties are in isolated areas such as industrial and office parks where few, if any, people pass by at night and on weekends. The merchant police system can ensure only a minimal level of fire and burglary surveillance for large commercial properties if access to the interiors of these structures is restricted.

Unsupervised Watch Services

An **unsupervised watch service** consists of one or more guards who are on the premises when the business is closed. The guards often lack basic firefighting training, such as how to use portable fire extinguishers effectively. They are, however, usually reliable for calling the appropriate fire brigade or fire service as soon as they discover a fire. For small premises, fire detection will be delayed if the guard is asleep, ill, injured, or rendered helpless by intruders. Even without the occurrence of fire, the guard's illness or injury might not be discovered until the premises are reopened.

The primary disadvantage of the unsupervised watch service system is that performance cannot be monitored. The guard might have instructions to make regular rounds of the entire premises and check the floors of all buildings to minimize the time between the outbreak of fire and the first alarm. Because an unsupervised watch service might not be reliable, an unsupervised guard might be little better than no detection system at all.

Automatic Fire Detection Systems

Automatic fire detection systems consist of mechanical or electronic detectors that sense the presence of smoke or fire and sound an alarm. The major types of automatic fire detection systems are local alarm systems and remote and central station systems.

Local Alarm Systems

In a **local alarm fire detection system**, the detector is wired to an alarm bell on the exterior of the premises. The system is designed to notify employees of the fire, permitting them to take appropriate action. During the weekends or at night, the local alarm will only be successful if a passerby hears the alarm and contacts the police or fire service. Such an approach relies on unreasonable assumptions, such as that someone will hear the alarm, decide to get involved, and call the appropriate service to respond to a ringing bell or a buzzer. Though effective during working hours, the local alarm is least effective when it is needed most.

Remote and Central Station Systems

Remote and central station fire detection systems employ mechanical and electronic detection devices similar to those found in local alarm systems. Instead of sounding a local alarm bell, however, those systems transmit the alarm to a remote or central station. A **remote system** connects the devices on the premises to the local police or fire station, which monitors systems continuously.

A central station system uses detectors wired to a central station that is a private business providing this service. Some central station systems notify the municipal fire service by radio, and others use the telephone. Usually, the central station company will also dispatch a vehicle to respond to the alarm.

Types of Detectors

A variety of detectors can be wired to local alarm, remote, or central station systems. The best type of system for a particular risk depends on the size of the property and its occupancy. Detectors include the following:

- Heat detectors
- Smoke detectors
- Flame detectors
- Intrusion detectors
- Closed-circuit television monitors

Heat Detectors

Heat detectors sound alarms under abnormal heat conditions. The two major types are fixed-temperature heat detectors and rate-of-rise heat detectors.

Fixed-temperature heat detectors, also called thermostats, sound an alarm when the temperature at which they have been set is exceeded. These devices use a fusible link, a bulb, or another device that reacts to the temperature. These devices are also known as spot-type detectors.

Rate-of-rise detectors respond to sudden increases in temperature. These detectors use a thermostatic cable or pneumatic tube to detect the rapid increase in temperature.

Smoke Detectors

Smoke detectors sense the presence of visible or invisible products of combustion. For this type of detector to work properly, the smoke must be in the vicinity of the detector. The two main types of smoke detectors are ionization smoke detectors and photoelectric cells.

Ionization smoke detectors are activated by smoke particles in the air and work by ionizing air in a chamber within the detector. If smoke or pre-smoke products of combustion enter the chamber, the conduction of the air is decreased, and the alarm is triggered.

Photoelectric cell smoke detectors respond to the presence of smoke particles in the air and come in two common types. The light-scattering type sounds an alarm when smoke in the air scatters light onto a light-sensitive element. The light-interruption type projects a beam of light across the space to a receiver. When smoke interrupts the beam, the alarm is triggered.

Flame Detectors

Flame detectors sound an alarm in the presence of radiant energy. Radiant energy can be either visible or invisible to the human eye.

Intrusion Detectors

The basic purpose of an **intrusion detector** is to register the presence of burglars or other trespassers on property after the business closes. Since burglars might set fires to destroy evidence of their crimes, these detectors indirectly provide protection from fire. The three major categories of intrusion detectors are electric tapes, photoelectric cells, and passive infrared systems. Chapter 7 will discuss intrusion detectors in detail.

Closed-Circuit Television Monitors

Closed-circuit television systems that transmit pictures from cameras located throughout the premises can protect some properties. A local station on industrial premises usually monitors these systems. The closed-circuit system can detect intruders, visible smoke, and visible flame. The system can also provide additional information when other detectors transmit alarms.

Private Suppression Systems

Private fire suppression systems consist of equipment and personnel that the insured uses to suppress a fire before the municipal fire service arrives. For isolated commercial properties, a private suppression system could be the only fire service available.

These systems fall into the following four major categories:

- Portable fire extinguishers
- Standpipe and hose systems
- Automatic sprinkler systems
- Fire brigades

Portable Fire Extinguishers

Portable fire extinguishers permit employees to control the fire while waiting for the fire service to arrive. Employees may even be able to extinguish small fires. The type of extinguisher to be used depends on the type of fire.

NFPA has developed four categories of fires:[5]

1. *Class* A includes fires involving ordinary combustible materials such as wood, cloth, paper, rubber, and many plastics. The suppression of class A fires relies mainly on the quenching and cooling effects of water or solutions that contain a high water content.
2. *Class B* fires involve flammable liquids, gases, and greases. Suppression of class B fires requires a blanketing or smothering effect. Fires involving some materials that react with water but that can be smothered are in this class.
3. *Class* C fires involve energized electrical wiring or equipment. Class C fires need a suppression agent that will not conduct electricity. Using a conductive agent presents a serious life safety threat.
4. *Class D* fires occur in combustible metals, such as magnesium, titanium, zirconium, sodium, and potassium. Many of those metals react violently with water, and burning magnesium will draw oxygen from water. Extinguishing agents suitable for suppressing other types of fire are not effective on Class D fires.

Fire extinguishers should be the right type, size, and number for the type of materials and degree of hazard. They should have appropriate certification and be inspected and tested at least annually. They require maintenance, including hydrostatic testing, on a regular basis. Each fire extinguisher should carry a tag on which service technicians record the dates of maintenance. The insured should keep complete maintenance records and distribute extinguishers properly about the protected area. The appropriate types of extinguishers should be close to operations that present special hazards. A class B extinguisher, for example, should be near a workstation where flammable liquids are used. Finally, the extinguishers should be readily accessible. An extinguisher is useless unless it is within easy reach.

Standpipe and Hose Systems

Standpipe and hose systems consist of water mains with fire department hose connections inside a building. They facilitate the application of water to structure fires because firefighters can use those built-in hoses and do not need to drag hoses filled with water up many flights of stairs or over long distances. A standpipe system might have its own water supply, but many systems must rely on an external water supply. Regardless of whether the standpipe system has its own water supply, the system has a fire department connection that allows the fire service to connect a fire department pumper truck. Buildings with large floor areas, such as manufacturing buildings, shopping malls, and warehouses, can have horizontal standpipe systems. Vertical standpipes are found in most buildings over four stories.

Standpipe and hose systems can be designed for operation by the occupants of the building, by the municipal fire service, by a trained fire brigade, or by all three. If untrained personnel are to operate the hoses, the hose diameter is usually limited to one-and-one-half inches.

Types of Standpipe Systems

NFPA defines four types of standpipe systems:[6]

- Wet standpipe systems that keep the supply valve open and maintain water pressure at all times
- Standpipe systems that admit water to the system automatically by opening a hose valve
- Standpipe systems that admit water to the system by remote operation from approved control devices located at each hose station
- Dry standpipes that have no permanent water supply

NFPA has issued standards for standpipe and hose systems. Systems designed for use by trained personnel only are designated Class I systems, and those designed for untrained personnel receive a Class II designation. Class III is a third class for systems that are dual-purpose. The classes differ, in addition to their intended use, by the size of the hose, size of the pipe, and size of the water supply.

Inspection of Standpipe Systems

Underwriters should not assume that the presence of a standpipe and hose system in a structure means that the system is functional. Inspection and testing on a periodic basis, not less than once a year, are required to determine that all of the components of the system are in proper operating condition. The siamese connections should be checked regularly. These connections could have improper threads or could be clogged with refuse, rendering them useless.

A survey of 125 buildings in Los Angeles produced the following results:[7]

- Twenty-five percent could not receive water into the dry standpipes.
- Forty-five percent failed to pass the test requirements.
- Seventy percent had nonstandard threads.
- Fourteen percent had faulty standpipes.
- Twelve percent had valves that leaked excessively.
- Eight percent of the standpipes were never completely connected.

Automatic Sprinkler Systems

Automatic fire sprinkler systems are the most important part of private suppression efforts. These systems have proven their ability to outperform all other forms of public and private fire protection combined. Since the sprinkler heads respond automatically to fire, they can often control or extinguish a blaze unaided. Fire department connections also enable the fire service to hook up to the sprinkler system. The fire department's pumper trucks can greatly increase the pressure and water flow through the sprinkler heads. These systems also produce other benefits for the insured. For example, a lighter weight, less costly construction type could be adequate for an occupancy that is properly sprinklered.

According to the National Fire Sprinkler Association (NFSA), a trade group of fire sprinkler manufacturers and contractors, almost all fire sprinklers control a fire by containing the blaze at a manageable level until the fire service can arrive and extinguish it. Early suppression fast response (ESFR) sprinklers, a relatively new innovation, have proven to be particularly effective in suppressing fires. However, experience shows that automatic sprinkler systems often extinguish a blaze before the fire service arrives. The NFSA and NFPA have discontinued publishing studies that compare the experience of sprinklered and unsprinklered properties, because the frequency of small fires in sprinklered risks that are never reported distorts the results. Sprinklers sometimes act so fast that no one bothers to report an alarm. In other cases, even though a hostile fire triggered the alarm, the fire service arrives to find no fire, and the incident is considered a false alarm.

The Value of Automatic Sprinklers: Two Case Studies

The 1992 Los Angeles Riots

The performance of automatic fire sprinklers during the April 1992 civil disturbance in Los Angeles reveals their potential for controlling fires.[8] The riots claimed 58 lives and caused 2,383 injuries. Fire services responded to more than 2,000 vehicle and trash fires and 5,273 structure fires. Between 600 and 700 buildings were destroyed, and another 759 sustained serious damage. More than 1,000 businesses suffered serious damage to their premises or lost them entirely. Although the Fire Sprinkler Advisory Board of Southern California identified at least 111 incendiary fires that struck 65 sprinkler-protected properties, 63 of those properties survived with no more than minor damage. The value of property that was not destroyed totaled more than $187,500,000. Of the two sprinkler-protected properties that became total losses, one had a partial sprinkler system that protected only the basement. Fire on the unprotected first floor overwhelmed the sprinkler system from above. The other total loss was a supermarket whose manager worried too much about water damage. He turned the sprinkler system off after it had extinguished one fire. A second round of arson destroyed the building the next morning.

The owner of a variety store took another approach. After the first fire, he let the sprinklers run until the sprinkler service contractor arrived to service the system. He persuaded the technician to leave spare heads on site so that he could restore the system himself. Arsonists struck three more times, and the owner reset the system on each occasion. When order returned to South Central Los Angeles, the store remained standing with minor damage, and the owner still had sprinkler heads to spare.

In a department store, arsonists started nine fires simultaneously. Twenty-two sprinkler heads responded and made fire service intervention unnecessary. In fact, fire services responded to only two fires in sprinklered properties, and they attacked only one of the fires with hose streams. Firefighters at the other location found a wastebasket fire under a desk, shielded from sprinkler heads. The fire was extinguished when firefighters overturned the desk, enabling water from the sprinklers to reach the fire.

Automatic sprinkler systems fail in about one-third of the serious fires that strike sprinkler-protected properties. Poor maintenance is almost always the cause, and more often than not the water supply has been turned off. What makes California, and especially Los Angeles, different is Subchapter 5, Title 19 of the California Code, which requires periodic inspection and maintenance of sprinkler systems by a qualified contractor. To comply with the code, the property owner must also select primary and secondary service contractors for the system. An owner who fails to comply faces a choice of removing the sprinkler system or losing his or her certificate of occupancy. A Los Angeles ordinance known as Regulation 4 contains substantially the same provisions.

The 1991 One Meridian Plaza Fire

The One Meridian Plaza fire occurred in February 1991 in Philadelphia, when fire struck a thirty-nine-story office building and raged out of control for nineteen hours. The blaze started on a Saturday night while the building was unoccupied. Oily rags had ignited by spontaneous combustion. A passerby turned in an alarm, but by the time the fire service arrived, the fire had become an inferno. To compound the problem, the building's water system was inadequate, and a design defect rendered the standpipe system useless above about the eighth floor. Trapped on a floor above the fire with no water, three firefighters called for help, but it arrived too late. Faced with a fire he could not control, the chief on the scene made the difficult decision to recover the remains of the fallen firefighters and evacuate the building.

Officials in the Philadelphia Fire Department then consulted the contractor who had installed a sprinkler system for the thirtieth-floor tenant. The contractor and fire department devised a strategy of using fire service pumpers to draw water from a neighboring building and boost pressure at the sprinkler heads to seventy-five psi. The fire consumed nine floors of a fully fire-resistive building. In addition to the three firefighters who died from smoke inhalation, twelve other firefighters were injured. Yet when the fire reached the sprinkler-protected thirtieth floor, it was extinguished by the water discharge from only *three* heads.

Every expert who has studied the One Meridian Plaza fire agrees that an automatic sprinkler system would have confined the blaze to the floor of origin. The Philadelphia building code has required sprinklers in all high-rise structures since 1986, but it exempted existing buildings. Many building codes require state-of-the-art protection for new structures but contain a grandfather clause that exempts older buildings.

At one time, sprinkler systems could be categorized as either "wet" or "dry," which described the content of the system's distribution pipes. Now, in addition to those two approaches, there are a variety of approaches to delivering fire extinguishment materials through sprinkler systems.

Wet Pipe Systems

A **wet pipe system** is a network of water-filled pipes with various sprinkler heads installed at intervals along the pipes. The sprinkler heads are distributed across the area to be protected, usually in a grid pattern. The type of head used depends on the occupancy's requirements and the location of the head in the system.

To be classified as wet pipe, a sprinkler system must have a dedicated water supply that is not used for any purpose other than suppressing fires. The water supply for the system can be supplemented by the fire department connection, thereby increasing water availability and pressure. The system is activated when the fire heats the fusible link or other device on the sprinkler head. Since water is in the pipe, water flow is instantaneous. The system might also include supervisory alarm devices to monitor the condition of valves as well as water supply components and to sound an alarm when one or more sprinkler heads open. Exhibit 3-2 shows the design of a typical wet pipe system.

The piping is filled with water under pressure that is immediately discharged when a sprinkler operates. The water continues to flow, controlling or extinguishing a fire, until it is shut off.

Dry Pipe Systems

Because wet pipe systems have water in the pipes, they are subject to damage under freezing conditions. In many warehouses and other occupancies, heat is not maintained during the winter. The **dry pipe system** can be used in these buildings since it does not contain water in any of the pipes above the dry pipe control valve. The **risers** (the vertical piping connecting the water supply and the horizontal feed mains), mains, and branch lines in this system are filled with pressurized air or nitrogen. The air pressure forces the water to remain at the level of the control valve. When a sprinkler head opens, the air pressure is released, permitting water to enter the piping system. The water will flow only out of those heads that have been actuated by the fire.

The dry pipe system includes an unavoidable lag factor. When a sprinkler head is opened in the dry pipe system, air or nitrogen is immediately released. The water must flow from the dry pipe control valve to the head, giving the fire time to grow or spread. With dry pipe systems, more sprinkler heads are usually required to control a fire.

Deluge Systems

A **deluge system** uses sprinkler heads that are always open. A separate detection system is connected to a deluge valve. When the deluge valve opens, water is discharged from every head in the system connected to that valve, creating a "deluge" of water. This system is employed in occupancies with severe fuel hazards that could result in a quickly spreading fire. Such occupancies include premises where flammable liquids are stored or used, as well as cooling towers, explosives, or ordnance plants, and aircraft hangars. Since deluge systems discharge large quantities of water, the water supply capacity must be sufficient.

Deluge systems require time for the water to flow from the deluge valve to the open heads. The delay produced is the same as found in dry pipe systems. The **preprimed deluge system** has been devised to eliminate this lag and improve the system's performance. This system has water in the risers and horizontal pipes, right up to the sprinkler heads, with the head openings plugged with rubber stoppers. When the deluge valve opens, the water pressure pushes out the stoppers.

Exhibit 3-2
Sprinkler System Installation

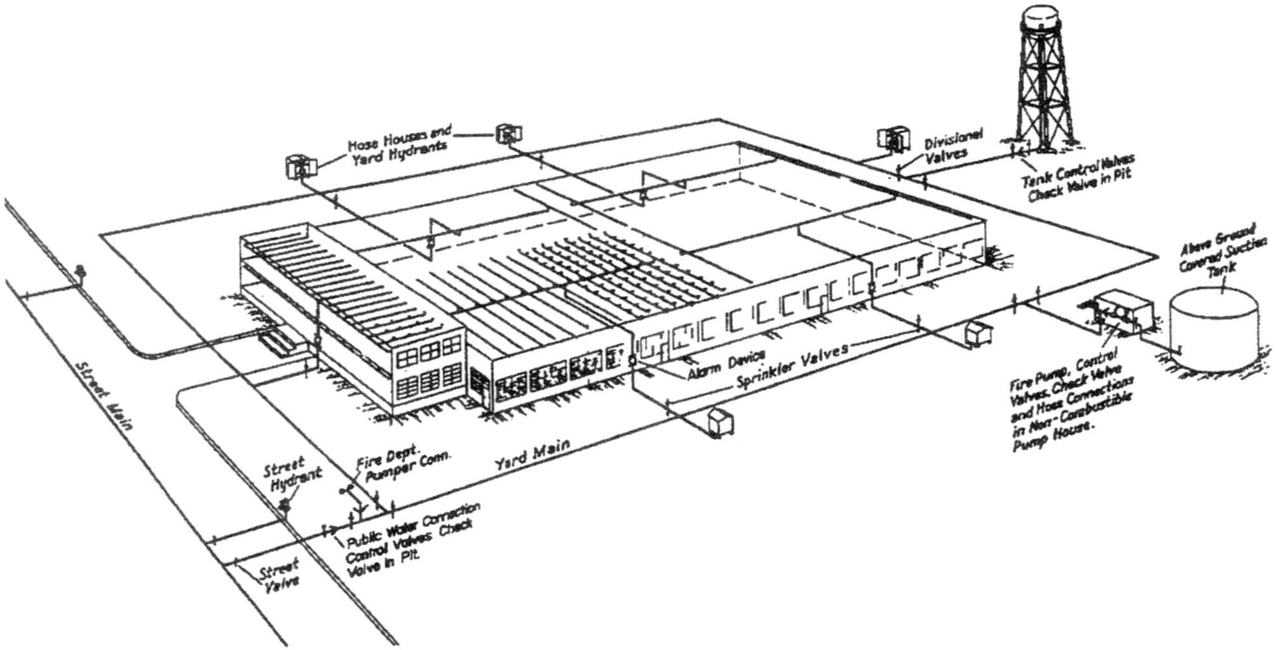

A typical sprinkler installation showing all common water supplies, outdoor hydrants, and underground piping.

Reprinted with permission from *Loss Prevention Data*, Book 2, Norwood, MA: Factory Mutual Engineering Corp., 1997, 2-8N, p. 3.

Preaction Systems

The **preaction system** is used in occupancies in which accidental discharge caused by damage to sprinkler heads or piping could cause heavy damage to the contents. The system combines some of the elements of both the wet and dry pipe systems. The sprinkler heads have fusible links, and the pipes are filled with air or nitrogen under pressure. The water is held back by a preaction valve triggered by a separate fire detection system rather than by a standard dry pipe control valve. If a sprinkler head is damaged, the release of the air or nitrogen pressure causes an alarm to sound. The separate fire detection system prevents water from entering the system unless it detects a fire. The preaction system is often used in occupancies such as computer centers, where water damage is a severe hazard.

The preaction system can also provide time for the occupants to fight the fire with portable fire extinguishers. If the fire gets out of control, the preaction valve opens and sends water to all sprinkler heads that have opened.

Water Supply

The most reliable water source results from connecting the sprinkler system directly to a public or private water main. The reliability of the water supply then depends only on the underlying water system. If it is public water, the FSRS rating for that municipality includes an analysis of the water supply. Any private water supply system can be evaluated using a similar technique. If the reliability of the main water supply is questionable, then a secondary water source should be considered.

Fire pumps can be hooked up to suction tanks to provide a water source for the system. A hydropneumatic tank that forces water into the system under air pressure is another possible water source. A third source is a gravity tank located on the roof of the structure or on a separate tower. The height of the gravity tank provides an acceptable head pressure for the water. These systems require periodic maintenance, and in some climates, the water in the tank and standpipe must be kept from freezing.

Other Types of Automatic Sprinkler Systems

Depending on the occupancy, specialized sprinkler systems using extinguishing agents other than water are available. A detailed description of those systems is beyond the scope of this text, but following are brief descriptions of some of them:

- **Water spray** or **"fog" systems** discharge droplets of water with a predetermined pattern, particle size, velocity, and density. They are most commonly used to protect certain types of electrical equipment and tanks containing flammable liquid or gas.

- **Air foam systems** include a wide variety of systems using both ordinary foam and high-expansion foam. Fixed foam systems are often used to protect aircraft hangars, petrochemical storage areas, and various other hazardous occupancies.
- **Carbon dioxide systems** dilute oxygen to a point at which it will no longer support combustion. Carbon dioxide systems can be installed so that they flood an entire room or are directed to a particular area such as a dip tank, a spray booth, or a kitchen's cooking equipment.
- **In-rack sprinkler systems** are used to protect property stored in a high-rack configuration by the installation of sprinkler heads within the racks. Sprinkler lines descend from the branches above the rack, and heads are installed on those lines. The sprinkler systems are more effective because the heads are closer to the commodities they protect.

  Although they have proven to be effective, in-rack sprinklers suffer from several drawbacks. They are more expensive to install, and they limit the flexibility owners have to configure their storage racks to take advantage of business opportunities as they emerge. In-rack sprinklers are also susceptible to damage from materials-handling equipment. This increases both repair costs and the frequency of sprinkler leakage losses. In addition, in-rack sprinklers reduce but do not eliminate the need to modify the sprinkler system to meet the requirements of NFPA 13, Standard for the Installation of Sprinkler Systems, when stored commodities change. Those disadvantages have prevented in-rack sprinklers from extending sprinkler protection to a large number of warehouses.
- **Early suppression fast response (ESFR) sprinkler systems** were developed by the fire suppression industry to help solve the problem of high-challenge fires. ESFR sprinkler systems can protect high-rack storage without the need for in-rack sprinklers.

  Standard sprinkler systems are based on a concept that relies on low-density discharge over a relatively large area. Their goal is to control a fire until the fire service can arrive to suppress it. Although standard sprinklers often suppress small fires, they can only contain a larger blaze. Standard sprinklers produce small drops of water that cannot penetrate the thrust of the fire plume—the hot upward flow of gases, smoke, and flame that a fire generates. Very little water reaches the fire itself, and some severe fires produce a plume that actually drives water away from the fire.

  At 50 psi, the standard pressure for sprinkler systems, ESFR sprinklers have a discharge rate that is 150 percent higher than standard sprinklers. They also produce a mixture of large drops (2 mm in diameter) and small drops (less than 1 mm in diameter). The smaller drops dissipate heat, which is the way standard sprinkler systems operate. The larger drops can penetrate the fire plume, reach the source of the fire, and extinguish it without fire service intervention. To achieve the discharge velocity this requires, ESFR sprinklers have to protect a smaller area than standard sprinklers. They deliver a heavier flow of water to a smaller area.

Another advantage in using ESFR sprinklers is that they eliminate the need to modify the system every time the protected commodity changes. The ESFR design standard employs a worst-case scenario. Research has identified the amount of water needed to suppress a fire in high-challenge commodities—the required delivered density (RDD). Tests can calculate the RDD for any commodity. They can also determine how much water from a sprinkler system penetrates the fire plume and is available to suppress the fire—the actual delivered density (ADD). An ESFR sprinkler system meets the requirements of NFPA 13 as long as the system's ADD exceeds the RDD of the protected commodity. This means that a system designed for a high-challenge commodity also satisfies NFPA 13 for any other commodity with an equal or lower RDD.

- **Halogenated agent systems** use halocarbons to disrupt the chemical reaction of fire. Halon systems are common in computer rooms, magnetic-tape storage vaults, electronic control rooms, and storage areas on large cargo aircraft, and for specific applications systems such as printing presses, dip tanks, spray booths, and oil-filled electric transformers.

The Future of Halon Systems

When they were introduced, halon systems seemed to be the ideal fire protection. They extinguished fires quickly and at low cost. Halons are neither corrosive nor conductive, so they do not damage the property they protect. They are, however, chlorofluorocarbons (CFCs) that deplete the layer of ozone in the upper atmosphere. In 1987, all of the developed nations subscribed to the Montreal Protocols, which mandate phasing out halon production before the year 2000. American manufacturers, which accounted for more than 75 percent of halon production capacity, ceased all production by 1995. Halon fire suppression agents are still available, but new supplies are not. When the current stock is exhausted, there will be no way to replenish it.

Chemical companies are developing halon substitutes, but these substitutes are not as effective. As fire extinguishants, halons are unique. They disrupt the chemistry of fire, while all other extinguishing agents attack the physics of fire. The substitutes now coming to market work only at much higher concentrations than halons. Fire suppression systems will need more of the new agents, and conversion will be expensive. Research at the University of New Mexico Center for Global Environmental Technologies (UNMCGET) has identified a family of new agents called "geminal dibromides" that are promising. Unfortunately, their introduction is at least several years away, and they will probably not be available to recharge existing halon systems. In the meantime, halon can be purchased from halon recyclers. Until a better solution presents itself, the use of water sprinklers is the best approach for new installations.

Supervision of Automatic Sprinkler Systems

An automatic sprinkler system can be effective only if the maintenance and supervision of the system are properly performed. The probability of failure of an automatic sprinkler system has been estimated at .004 for all fires and .006 for fires large enough to actuate the system.[9]

Sprinkler system supervisory devices can alert the insured or a central station service to valves that are closed when they should be open, as well as to the actuation of sprinkler heads in response to a fire. Sprinkler supervision devices include the following:[10]

- Water flow alarms that sound when one or more sprinkler heads have opened
- Gravity tank supervision, including low- and high-water level alarms and alarms signaling the failure of water-heating systems in tanks subjected to freezing temperatures
- Devices indicating loss of pressure in pressure tank systems
- Devices indicating the loss of electric or steam power to water pumps
- Water supply valve monitors that indicate the condition of each valve in the system
- Devices registering the air or gas pressure in dry pipe sprinkler systems

A significant cause of failure in automatic sprinkler systems is human error. Human error results from either closing the sprinkler system water control valves before a fire breaks out or prematurely closing the valves before a fire is under control. Sprinkler system components can be monitored by using electrical contact switches that relay the condition of the system components to a local, remote, or central station monitor. Many insurers require sprinkler valves to be locked in an open position to prevent improperly closed valves.

Automatic sprinkler control valves should be inspected weekly or monthly if they are locked in the open position. Fire pumps should also be inspected, and preferably operated, weekly. Weekly checks should also be made of gravity tanks, including their water level. The weekly check should also include the condition of sprinkler heads. Some of the heads can become covered with paint, dust, or other substances, effectively insulating the fusible link. A head in this condition will respond late or not at all.[11]

The sprinkler leakage hazard can be handled by careful maintenance of the sprinkler system and by the assurance that sprinkler heads are of the appropriate design, located where they will not be easily damaged, and properly maintained. In areas where exposing sprinkler heads to accidental damage is unavoidable, heads can be enclosed in cages or provided with other guards to prevent damage that could cause sprinkler leakage. The preaction system discussed earlier is another method of reducing the chance of loss from this hazard.

Misperceptions Concerning Sprinkler System Use

Several misperceptions held by the general public impede a more widespread use of sprinklers. A common misperception is that sprinklers should not be used to protect certain occupancies because the potential for water damage is too great. These buildings include libraries, museums, data-processing centers, and historic structures. Such concern is unwarranted. Fire sprinklers actually reduce the amount of water needed to suppress a fire in two ways. First, sprinkler systems attack the fire in its early stages, before large quantities of water are needed to suppress the fire. Second, fire sprinklers use water more efficiently than fire service hose streams, applying it only to the immediate area of the blaze. Fire services must wet down property in the fire's path and use additional water to protect firefighters. Hoses also deliver water at a much higher rate than sprinklers. A single one-and-one-half-inch fire hose discharges substantially more water than all the sprinklers that are actuated in response to more than 75 percent of all fires. A common shower head might discharge as much water as fifty fire sprinklers.

Another misperception is that when one sprinkler operates, they all do. This is true of deluge systems, but those systems are far from typical. Four or fewer sprinkler heads respond to more than 75 percent of all fires. On average, fire in a sprinkler-protected property actuates fewer than two heads. One is often enough to suppress a fire completely.

A fourth misperception is that accidental discharge from sprinkler systems is a serious problem. Fewer than one sprinkler head in one million will ever leak because of a manufacturing defect. The most common cause of unintended sprinkler discharge is temperatures that build up and heat the head's fusible link to its rated temperature. Physical damage to the heads, commonly caused by ladders or other maintenance and repair equipment, is the second leading cause. In any event, sprinkler leakage damage is insignificant compared to loss from fire that sprinklers can and do prevent.

Fire Service Procedures

The effectiveness of an automatic sprinkler system will be greatly enhanced if the system is coordinated with the response of the municipal fire service or industrial fire brigade. The fire department connection on the sprinkler system should be checked to determine that it is operable, clean, and of the proper thread design. The connection can be checked as part of the fire service pre-fire planning survey. Fire service response will be much more efficient if such a survey has been conducted. The underwriter can determine whether a survey has been conducted, the date of the last survey, and whether any significant changes have occurred in the risk since the most recent survey. Exhibit 3-3 shows a typical pre-fire survey diagram. The diagram shows sprinklered and nonsprinklered areas, water supply points, and the location of the fire department connection. Information such as that shown on this diagram can save the municipal fire service much valuable time.

Combined Standpipe and Automatic Sprinkler Systems

In 1971, NFPA adopted provisions for the combination of standpipe and sprinkler systems. Although automatic sprinklers are highly desirable in high-rise buildings, owners often fail to install them because of the cost. Since most structures over four floors in height must have at least a dry standpipe system, the use of standpipes as risers for automatic sprinkler systems greatly reduces the cost of providing automatic sprinkler protection.

The basic requirements for a combined standpipe and automatic sprinkler system include the following:[12]

- Riser and hose valves located in fire-resistive stair enclosures
- Separate floor control valves for sprinklers located in the fire-resistive stair enclosure
- Risers at least six inches high
- Adequate water supply for both sprinklers and standpipes

Sprinkler Protection as an Underwriting Consideration

Making a well-informed risk selection decision requires evaluating the strengths and weaknesses of a sprinkler system that protects covered property.

Exhibit 3-3
A Typical Pre-Fire Survey Form

BUILDING SURVEY FORM

ADDRESS: ____________________ DATE: ____________________

BUILDING NAME: ____________________ OCCUPANCY: ____________________

EMERGENCY PHONE NO: ____________________ NAME & ADDRESS: ____________________

OWNER OR AGENT: ____________________

OCCUPANT: ____________________

SPRINKLER: (SIAMESE) ____________________

(HOSE THREAD SIZE) ____________________

GENERAL CONTENTS: ____________________

SPECIAL HAZARDS: ____________________

ENTRY HAZARDS: ____________________

MAIN ELECTRIC SWITCH: ____________________ GAS SHUTOFF: ____________________

FUEL OIL SHUTOFF: ____________________ WATER SHUTOFF: ____________________

A.C. MAIN SWITCH: ____________________

FIRE ALARM (TYPE): ____________________ AGENT: ____________________

TYPE OF SPACE HEATING: ____________________

STRUCTURAL INFORMATION OF BUILDING

HEIGHT AND NUMBER OF FLOORS: ____________________ TYPE OF EXTERIOR WALLS: ____________________

FLOOR CONSTRUCTION: ____________________

ROOF CONSTRUCTION: ____________________ INTERIOR FINISH: ____________________

TYPE OF WINDOWS: ____________________

FIRE DOORS: ____________________

NO. OF STAIRWAYS: N __________ S __________ E __________ W __________ CENTER __________

VERTICAL & HORIZONTAL OPENINGS: ____________________

____

EXPOSURES: N __________ S __________ E __________ W __________ CENTER __________

____

BEST MEANS OF ENTRY: ____________________

ADDITIONAL INFORMATION: ____________________

____

SIGNATURE OF INSPECTION OFFICER: ____________________

STATION AND BATTALION: ____________________

FSA 130

(12/89) (A diagram of the building appears on the back of the form.)

Sprinkler systems and the factors that determine their performance are highly complex. Only a skilled professional can determine how well a sprinkler system meets the requirements of NFPA 13. The presence of at least minor deficiencies in almost all sprinkler systems also creates a need for a formal system of grading. Underwriters also have to consider cost. If each insurer had to evaluate sprinkler systems on its own, the cost could easily become prohibitive. The expense of rating the quality of sprinkler protection could easily exceed the reduction in loss costs the system delivers.

ISO inspects and rates all buildings protected by sprinkler systems. If a sprinkler system earns a fire rate credit, the building must be specifically rated. This allows underwriters to identify sprinkler-protected buildings from the rating information ISO provides. In addition to the loss cost for the specific building, the rating information includes a Rating Construction Protection (RCP) code. The first digit of the RCP code is 4 for sprinklered buildings and 1 for all other buildings.

The fact that a building is not rated as sprinklered does not mean that it does not have a sprinkler system. A building with a sprinkler system may not qualify for sprinklered rates, for example, if the sprinkler system protects only a small portion of the building. A multistory office building may have sprinklers only in lobby areas or only in the grade-floor lobby. Many older retail occupancies have sprinklers only in basements or other storage areas. ISO evaluates each sprinkler system and assigns a sprinkler grading that ranges from 0 to 100. A sprinkler grading of 100 indicates that the system fully meets the requirements of NFPA 13 with no deficiencies. A sprinkler system must earn a grading of at least 10 to qualify for a rate credit. The sprinkler grading considers six factors crucial to effective performance of a sprinkler system:

1. Water supply
2. System components
3. Testing (both initial testing when the system is installed and periodic tests to ensure that it continues to function properly)
4. Nonsprinklered areas within the building
5. Occupancy-specific requirements, such as in-rack sprinklers where required
6. Structural disadvantages, such as excessive height of a single story in the building

The sprinkler grading assesses points for each observed deficiency. Underwriters can obtain the sprinkler grading from one of three services ISO provides. The *Sprinklered Property Report Service* (SPRS) analyzes the six major areas that determine the sprinkler grading, with a by-item description of points charged for deficiencies in each area. The *Automatic Sprinkler Grading Report* (ASGR) is a copy of the worksheet ISO used to calculate the sprinkler grading. It contains technical information on the sprinkler system, and it is useful when the underwriter wishes to discuss the quality of the sprinkler system, with a loss control representative. In addition to the sprinkler grading, the *Business Underwriting Report* (BUR) includes a brief description of the occupancies in the building, the total floor area of the building in square feet, the percentage of the building's area devoted to each occupancy, and a general description of the building's construction. Some underwriters elect to rely on the BUR in lieu of ordering an inspection by their own loss control staff or an outside agency.

Fire Brigades

Some large industrial establishments are located far from municipal services. Because of the time that fire service response requires, those establishments sometimes establish a fire brigade. A **fire brigade** is a fire service, and the underwriter should evaluate it that way. Since the personnel in the fire brigade often have other duties in the plant, operating the brigade is in many ways similar to the operations of a volunteer fire service. In plants in which the fire brigade members have no other duties, brigade members can be the equivalent to full-time fire service members.

The fire brigade's efficiency depends on the following:

- The training of its personnel
- The amount and type of firefighting equipment
- The size and reliability of the water supply

Fire brigades range from little more than an organized attempt to use portable fire extinguishers until the municipal fire service arrives to fully organized engine and ladder companies that are able to deal with most fires on their own and require help only for large fires.

External Exposure

External exposure is the fourth major element property underwriters must analyze. **External exposure** refers only to fires that originate outside the insured premises. This source of loss is significant, because a fire in one building often spreads to adjacent structures. NFPA regards exposure fires as a separate cause of structure fires. The building in which the fire might start is referred to as the exposing property.

From 1988 through 1992, exposure fires accounted for 6.7 percent of all structure fires and 9.4 percent of accidental structure fires in the United States.[13] They caused 4.4 percent of all fire damage and almost 7 percent of accidental fire damage during that period. Therefore, no evaluation of an individual risk is complete unless it considers the potential for fire loss that originates outside the insured premises.

External exposure is much more difficult to analyze than construction, occupancy, and protection. Lack of information is the biggest problem. Because the underwriter usually has no direct contact with the owner of the exposing property, the information needed for analysis is difficult to obtain. Underwriters obtain some of the needed information by asking the producer specific questions or by ordering a loss control report. Exhibit 3-4 shows a portion of an inspection form that develops exposure data. Assessing external exposure requires considering the construction, occupancy, and protection of the exposing building as well as of the building being insured.

Construction

To evaluate exposures properly, the underwriter must consider the construction of both buildings. Buildings that have greater resistance to fire require less distance from other structures. In some locales, building codes require as much as seventy feet between frame apartment buildings. Fire-resistive buildings, on the other hand, require no separation for fire safety. Fire rates, in fact, do not include an exposure charge for fire-resistive structures. Many underwriting guidelines also adopt that approach. Building codes and underwriting guidelines almost always require some degree of separation between other types of buildings. The required distance increases as the quality of construction decreases. Masonry buildings require more distance from exposures than do buildings constructed of noncombustible materials, and frame buildings require more distance than masonry.

Consider the example in Exhibit 3-5 of a brick real estate office. Assume that on each side of the office is an empty lot and that on the far side of each lot is an additional building, one frame and one brick. In the diagram, each of the neighboring buildings appears to be the same distance from the real estate office. Which building creates the greater external exposure to the real estate office? From a construction standpoint, the exposing frame building is more likely to burn than the brick building, so the frame building presents a greater exposure to the real estate office.

The construction of the real estate office, however, should not be disregarded. Will the brick office catch fire if the frame building is burning? The answer to this question depends on the distance between the two buildings and the

Exhibit 3-4
Loss Control Engineering—External Exposures

Attachments

Number	Type	Square Feet
____	☐ Porches	________
____	☐ Garage	________
____	☐ Fireplace	
____	☐ Balconies	
____	☐ Car Ports	________
____	☐ Out Bldgs.	________
____	☐ Other	

Neighborhood and Locale

☐ Average
☐ Below Average
☐ Improving
☐ Deteriorating
☐ Stable

☐ Mercantile
☐ Urban
☐ Congested
☐ Outside Corp. Limits
☐ Suburb
☐ Factory/Warehouse
☐ Isolated

Public Protection

____ No. Hydrants within 500 feet

____ Feet to Nearest Hydrant

____ Distance to Fire Dept. (miles)

Private Protection

☐ Sprinklers
☐ Standpipe
☐ Extinguishers
☐ Fire Alarm
☐ Detection System
☐ Watchman
☐ Other
☐ None

Air Conditioning

☐ Central ☐ Window

Exposures	**North**	**South**	**East**	**West**
Height (Stories)				
Construction	☐ Masonry ☐ Frame ☐ Other	☐ Masonry ☐ Frame ☐ Other	☐ Masonry ☐ Frame ☐ Other	☐ Masonry ☐ Frame ☐ Other
Occupancy and Name				
Distance				
Condition	☐ Avg. ☐ Below Avg.	☐ Avg. ☐ Below Avg.	☐ Avg. ☐ Below Avg.	☐ Avg. ☐ Below Avg.

Interior Stair, Aisle and Floor Condition ____________________

____

Exterior Fire and Liability Hazards, Including Windstorm: ____________________

____

____

Exhibit 3-5
Diagram for Determination of Exposure to Insured Building

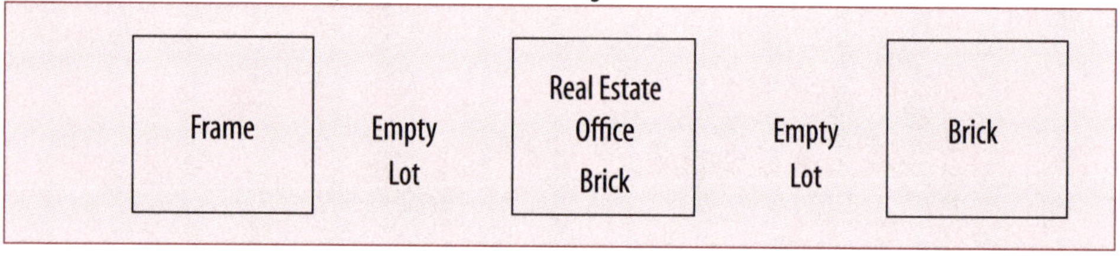

construction variations of the real estate office. The closer the burning frame building is, the more likely the brick building is to ignite. Construction variables such as windows, doors, and the type of roof on the real estate office are just as important. A window or wooden door that faces the frame building would obviously reduce the ability of the real estate office to resist an exposure fire from the frame building. A shingled roof or A-frame construction would make the real estate office more susceptible to exposure fires than if the roof were flat or constructed of fire-resistive material.

The relative heights of the exposing and exposed buildings are also important in evaluating external exposure. When the exposing building is taller than the exposed building, the chance of an exposure fire increases. Suppose the frame building were two stories high and the real estate office were only one story. A flat roof on the office building would serve as a good receptacle for flaming embers from fire in the frame building. If the frame building were several floors higher (and relatively closer to the brick building), its collapse would be an additional exposure to the real estate office.

Underwriters can develop guidelines for separation distances between buildings based on the type of construction. Construction that is more resistant to fire requires less separation from exposing structures than less fire-resistive construction does. Frame buildings, for instance, require more distance than brick. The guidelines might also require greater separation when the insured building is less able to resist fire than is the exposing building. Exhibit 3-6 presents an example of a guideline for separation from exposing structures. Based on this guide, the frame building in the previous example should be at least thirty feet from the brick real estate office. At this distance, the underwriter might feel that disregarding the frame building as an exposure is prudent. Construction features of the real estate office might, of course, alter this decision. The addition of windows, doors, or a combustible roof to the real estate office can make the exposure more serious.

The decision could be different if the underwriter is insuring the frame building against loss by fire. The exposing brick building is still only thirty feet

Exhibit 3-6
Separation Distances (Protection Classes 1-8)

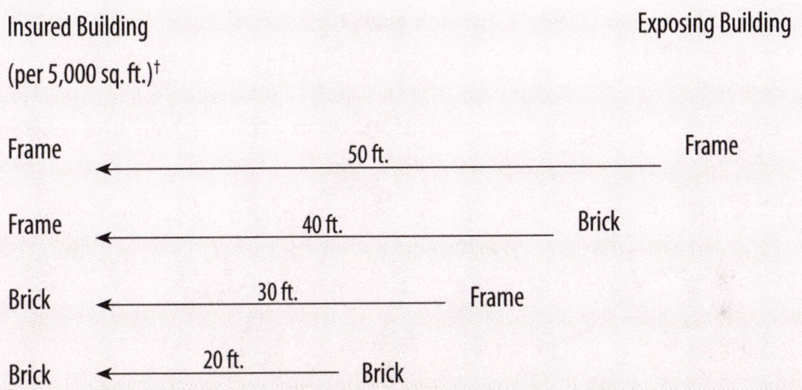

† Increase distance 10 feet for each additional 2,500 sq. ft. of floor area. For unprotected areas (Protection Classes 9-10), increase distance 50 percent.

from the exposed frame building. The guideline, however, requires forty feet because the insured building is more likely to catch fire if the exposing building burns.

The underwriter should focus on construction variables. Features that do not meet standards for the type of construction will be cited as deficiencies. Construction features are an important part of the assessment of exposures. One technique for handling deficiencies is to downgrade the construction of the insured building. The underwriter might, for instance, treat a brick building as frame if it has large windows, wooden doors, or a combustible roof. Below-standard features might make a building more susceptible to fire and, for example, can give a brick building many of the loss characteristics of frame construction. Treating it as frame then becomes a reasonable approach. The underwriter must evaluate the effect of an external exposure in relation to the insured property. This evaluation includes construction deficiencies of the insured property.

Lack of adjacent or surrounding buildings does not always mean that a risk is free of external exposures. An empty lot that is filled with overgrown, dry grass is a hazardous exposure. Combustible materials or debris close to the building would also constitute an exposure hazard.

Occupancy

Just as occupancy affects the susceptibility to a fire loss, the occupancy of an exposing building can also affect the exposed building. In the real estate office example, assume that the frame building houses a restaurant. Such a high-risk occupancy can present an exposure hazard even if the distance between the structures is greater than the guidelines require.

The underwriter must consider the combustibility of the contents and the amount of heat that the contents will release if burned. The intense heat radiating from a blaze in a nearby building can also cause an exposure fire. The nature of the contents and operations in an exposing building is an important consideration in assessing exposures.

Thus far, the analysis has concerned the exposure between separate buildings. Exposure is also a consideration within multiple-occupancy buildings. Exhibit 3-7 shows a typical one-story shopping center.

Exhibit 3-7
Diagram for Determination of Exposure to Insured Store in Shopping Center

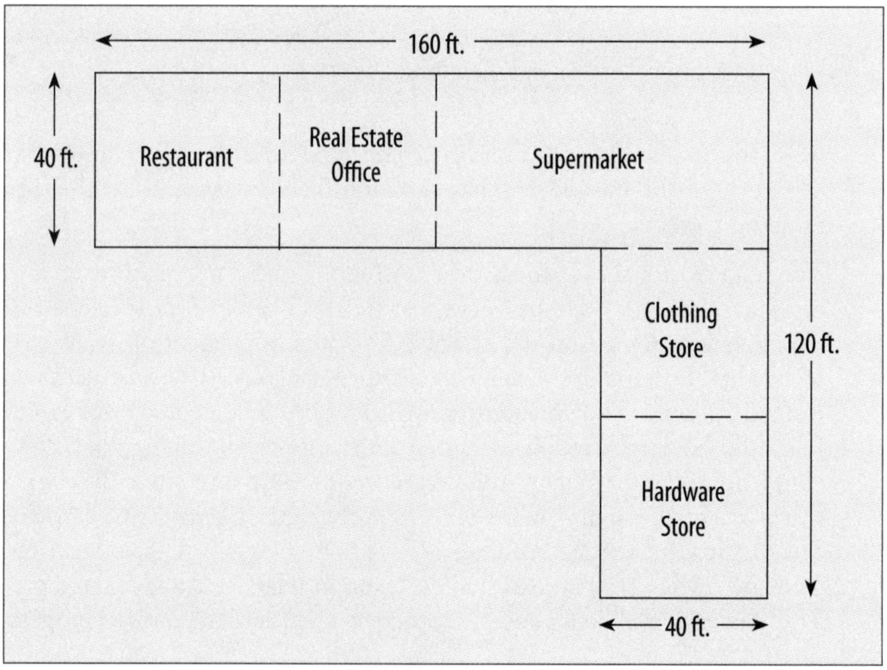

Assume that the building is owned by one person or corporation, but that each separate business is operated independently and that space is leased from the owner. If asked to insure the contents of the real estate office, the underwriter should consider the exposures from the other occupancies. In this case, the real estate office is exposed by a supermarket and a restaurant. The exposure is much more prominent than in the previous example, since the real estate office shares common walls with two other occupancies. The underwriter must consider the same factors—construction, occupancy, and protection—in evaluating the exposures in a multiple-occupancy building.

In a multiple-occupancy building, distance is not a factor, since the occupancies might be adjacent (except to the extent that one occupancy is adjacent and another is two occupancies away). Construction, however, is important. A fire-resistive building will be a less hazardous risk for fire insurance than a frame building, but this is only the first consideration. Assuming that the building in Exhibit 3-7 is of fire-resistive construction, the next factor the underwriter should consider is the nature of the walls between the real estate office and the adjacent businesses. Are the construction materials and the thickness of the walls sufficient to withstand combustion until the fire service arrives? Are the parapets high enough to keep the embers from blowing from one section of the building to another? Is the roof constructed of a material that will resist combustion?

A restaurant exposes the real estate office, and the restaurant also shares a common wall with the real estate office. The proximity of a hazardous occupancy in this example makes the adequacy of the construction even more important. The real estate office must therefore be a separate fire division from the restaurant to reduce the exposure to an acceptable level. If this cannot be accomplished, the underwriter, from a practical point of view, will be insuring a restaurant at rates developed for an office occupancy.

Besides the protective items already discussed in conjunction with construction, the underwriter must also consider the water supply, the response of the fire service, and the accessibility of the premises for the firefighters.

Underwriting Principles, the other text for this course, discusses determining the probable maximum loss (PML) on a building and its contents. Construction, occupancy, and protection can each contribute to the establishment of a PML less than 100 percent. In the example of the multiple-occupancy shopping center, the underwriter, by analyzing each of the COPE factors, can determine whether the probable maximum loss of this particular building will be less than 100 percent. If the construction of the building is fire-resistive with rated walls between each occupancy, each with two-foot parapets extending through the roof in a protected area, the underwriter can surmise that in the event of a fire the entire building probably will not burn. The question, therefore, becomes how much of the building—or better, how much of the *value* of the building—is likely to be damaged in the event of a fire. The underwriter must determine the probable maximum loss. Most insurance companies provide guidelines to their underwriters to enable them to establish uniform and fairly accurate PMLs.

Protection

Protection has an important effect on exposure. The distance guidelines shown in Exhibit 3-6 reflect the quality of the fire service and water supply as well as the construction of the buildings. The average response time of the fire service is also an important consideration. The public protection class reflects this factor. In unprotected areas (classes 9 and 10), measuring the fire service response with any certainty might not be possible. The guide in Exhibit 3-6 reflects this fact by increasing the required distance by 50 percent.

Several forms of protection can be effective in reducing the chance of exposure loss. The first and perhaps most important is clear space. **Clear space** does more than eliminate fire exposure; it also gives the fire service room in which to operate. Several factors can defeat the purpose of clear space. Dry grass, high winds, or areas cluttered with combustible materials or debris can increase rather than reduce the chance of an exposure fire.

Automatic sprinkler systems within the exposed building also protect against exposure fire. A sprinkler system within the exposing building can have the same effect if it functions properly. Underwriters cannot evaluate exposing buildings' systems directly. Published fire rates can, however, assist the assessment of sprinkler systems in exposures.

The wall and roof construction can help to reduce exposure fires, but the effectiveness of a noncombustible wall can be reduced or eliminated by unprotected openings such as glass windows or wooden doors. To protect such openings, ordinary windows can be replaced with glass blocks or wired glass. Automatic steel shutters can be placed over plain plate windows. Wooden exterior doors can be replaced with automatic fire doors. Outside sprinklers can be placed over openings. A protective wall or fence can even be constructed between the exposing and exposed buildings.

The value of any of these methods of protection depends on an adequate response from the fire service. After thirty minutes, the exposing building could be burning out of control, so the effectiveness of any protective device on the exposed building cannot be relied on.

Factors Influencing the Severity of External Exposures

The *Fire Protection Handbook* summarizes the factors that influence the severity of an exposure fire on a building. In addition to the temperature and the duration of the exposing fire, these include the following three factors:[14]

1. Exposing building
   a. Type of construction of exterior walls and roofs.
   b. Width of exposing building.
   c. Height of exposing building.
   d. Percentage of openings in exposing wall area. Exterior walls that are combustible or that do not have sufficient resistance to contain the fire should be treated as having 100 percent openings.
   e. Ventilation characteristics of the burning roof.
   f. The fuel dispersion, or surface-to-volume ratio of the fuel.
   g. The size, geometry, and surface-to-volume ratio of the room involved.
   h. The thermal properties, conductivity, specific heat, and density of the interior finish.
2. Exposed building
   a. Type of construction of exterior walls and roofs.
   b. Orientation and surface area of exposed exterior walls.
   c. Percentage of openings in exterior wall area.
   d. Protection of openings.
   e. Exposure of interior finish and combustibles to the radiation, convection, and flying firebrands of the exposing fire.
   f. Thermal properties, conductivity, specific heat, density, and fuel dispersion of the interior finish materials and the building contents.
3. Site and protection features
   a. Separation distance between exposing and exposed building.
   b. Shielding effect of intervening noncombustible construction.
   c. Wind direction and velocity.
   d. Air temperature and humidity.
   e. Accessibility for fire-fighting operation.
   f. Extent and character of fire service operations.

Control of External Exposures

Existing exposures can be controlled by good construction with modifications such as fire walls, fire doors, special barriers, and parapets. Good water supply, quick response from the fire service, and internal and external automatic sprinkler systems are additional methods of controlling exposure.

Although several protective devices are available, underwriters have relatively little control over external exposures. A good water supply and a quick response from the fire service help, but underwriters cannot be guaranteed of either. Underwriters cannot realistically ask the owner of an exposing building to rebuild it with better construction in order to reduce the exposure of the building being considered for fire insurance. Expecting a business in a nearby building to change its operations because it presents a hazardous exposure to the building being underwritten is also unrealistic. Nor will the insured move to a more suitable location with a better water supply and a quicker response from the fire service. A building that is otherwise acceptable because of good construction, nonhazardous occupancy, and excellent protection might be unacceptable for fire insurance because of uncontrollable external exposures.

The *Fire Protection Handbook* summarizes several methods by which the external exposure hazard can be reduced, given two buildings. These include the following:[15]

- Clear space between buildings
- Total automatic sprinkler protection
- Blank walls of noncombustible materials
- Barrier walls (self-supporting) between the exposed building and the exposing building
- The extension of exterior masonry walls to form parapets or wings
- Automatic outside water curtains for combustible walls
- The elimination of openings by filling them with equivalent construction or glass block panels
- Wired glass in steel sash (fixed or automatic closing) in openings
- Automatic or deluge sprinklers outside over openings
- Automatic (rolling steel) fire shutters on openings
- Automatic fire doors on door openings
- Automatic fire dampers on wall openings

Summary

The two types of fire protection are public and private. Municipalities provide public fire protection to all properties within their jurisdiction. Property owners provide private fire protection. Both public and private fire protection involve prevention, detection, and suppression.

Fire prevention activities include all measures designed to reduce fire frequency or severity before the outbreak of fire. Fire-detection activities include all measures and equipment designed to notify firefighting personnel of the fire. Fire suppression activities include all measures used to contain and extinguish a fire.

Municipal fire services are evaluated according to the ISO Fire Suppression Rating Schedule. This schedule evaluates three major aspects of the fire service: water supply, fire service personnel and equipment, and fire alarms.

Private fire prevention efforts can be categorized as control of housekeeping, adherence to building codes and standards, and fire protection planning.

Private detection systems are designed to reduce loss severity by speeding the response of firefighting personnel and equipment. These systems can be either manual or automatic. Manual systems include guards, hired either by the property owner or by a merchant police system. These guards can be supervised either by a central station system or by a clock and tape. Automatic detectors can be connected either to a local alarm or to a central or remote station. Private suppression systems include portable fire extinguishers, standpipe and hose systems, automatic sprinkler systems, and fire brigades.

Protection is a variable in underwriting decisions. Both private protection and public protection affect rates. Since unprotected risks are likely to have greater variability in loss results than protected risks are, protection is a consideration in the composition of a book of business.

External exposures are difficult to underwrite because information about them is not readily available, and the owner of the exposing property has no incentive to correct identified deficiencies. Despite those obstacles, underwriters should learn as much as possible about these exposures and evaluate the account's desirability in light of them. Measures can, in many instances, be taken to control external exposures through safeguards taken on the insured's premises.

Chapter Notes

1. *NFPA Inspection Manual*, 4th ed. (Boston, MA: National Fire Prevention Association, 1976), pp. 33-38.
2. *NFPA Inspection Manual*, pp. 33-38.
3. J. V. Grimaldi and R. H. Simonds, *Safety Management*, 3d ed. (Homewood, IL: Richard D. Irwin, 1975), p. 549.
4. Raymond J. Casey, "Convincing Consumers to Install Automatic Sprinklers," *Fire Journal*, March 1971, pp. 35-36, 41.
5. *NFPA Inspection Manual*, pp. 277-278.
6. *Standard for the Installation of Standpipe and Hose Systems* (Boston, MA: National Fire Protection Association, 1974), p. 4.
7. Paul R. Lyons, "Dry Standpipe Survey in Los Angeles," *Fire Journal*, May 1969, pp. 65-66.

8. The Fire Sprinkler Advisory Board of Southern California, August 1992.
9. Bert M. Cohn, "The Validity of Trade-offs for Automatic Sprinkler Protection," *Fire Protection News*, August 1974, pp. 1-4.
10. John L. Bryan, *Automatic Sprinkler and Standpipe Systems* (Boston, MA: National Fire Protection Association, 1976), pp. 362-370.
11. Bryan, pp. 76-78, 205-207.
12. James M. Hammack, "Combined Sprinkler System and Standpipes (Some Random Thoughts)," *Fire Journal*, September 1971, p. 68.
13. National Fire Protection Association, Quincy, MA, 1994.
14. *Fire Protection Handbook*, 15th ed. (Quincy, MA: National Fire Protection Association, 1981), pp. 5-18, 5-19.
15. *Fire Protection Handbook, p. 5-20.*

Chapter 4

Underwriting Direct Exposures: Introduction and Fire

To analyze a property's exposure to direct loss, an underwriter must evaluate the property's construction, occupancy, protection, and external exposures (the four COPE factors). Once the COPE factors have been analyzed, the underwriter can assess the coverages and causes of loss.

Several factors influence the size of the loss an insurer can expect to sustain from any covered cause of loss. The provisions of the policy that insures the property define the insurer's obligations. Commercial property forms limit the amount the insurer must pay to the extent of the insured's insurable interest. In many cases that amount is less than the full value of the covered property. When several persons have different insurable interests in the same property, on the other hand, the sum of those interests may be greater than the value of the property itself. Other policy provisions govern the methods used to determine the value of insured property. The most common valuation provisions are replacement cost and actual cash value, but other valuation clauses may be appropriate for some accounts and used in some insurance contracts. The underwriter must understand how the policy provisions for placing a value on insured property affect the amount the insurer will have to pay in the event of loss.

Underwriters use the value of the covered property to determine whether the insured carries an adequate amount of insurance and to measure the largest loss they can expect to sustain. Adequate insurance to value is a key factor underwriters use to obtain a premium commensurate with the risk of loss assumed. The traditional tool insurers have used to obtain the desired relationship between the value of insured property and the amount of insurance has been the coinsurance clause. Today, however, many insurers have made insurance to value an integral part of the risk selection process. Underwriters use the policy limit, the amount subject, and the probable maximum loss to measure the most severe loss they are likely to sustain on an account. Management attitude toward controlling losses and the financial condition of the business are also important factors to consider in property insurance.

Underwriters have to understand what fire is and how it causes damage to property. Fire is a complex chain of chemical reactions that requires heat, fuel, and oxygen to sustain itself. It spreads mainly by radiated heat and causes damage to property by the heat, smoke, and gases it produces, which are often corrosive, toxic, or abrasive. Efforts to suppress fire, particularly the use of water to do so, also contribute significantly to the extent of fire losses.

Policy Provisions Affecting the Amount of Loss

To evaluate the exposure to direct property damage, underwriters must determine how much the policy will obligate the insurer to pay if a loss occurs. The insurable interest of all entities who might be insured, the relationship of the amount of insurance the policy provides to that value, and the largest loss anticipated help the underwriter determine the maximum exposure to loss and the acceptability of the submission.

Insurable Interest

Subject to the limits of coverage, coinsurance provisions, and the deductible, standard commercial property forms limit recovery to the amount of the insured's insurable interest at the time of loss. Underwriters must consider how various types of joint ownership will affect how much of a loss a policy must pay. The least complex form of ownership is a **fee simple estate**, in which a single person has outright ownership of property. There are several ways in which more than one person may own the same property. In a **joint tenancy**, two or more persons own property. The owners are called joint tenants. A **tenancy by the entireties** is a special type of joint tenancy available only to a husband and wife. A joint tenancy is similar to a fee simple estate, except that there is more than one owner. The terms of the joint tenancy determine the insurable interest of each joint tenant, but this form of joint ownership does not present any special problems for underwriters. A person who owns property in fee simple estate or as a joint tenant has the right to use the property during his or her lifetime. That right passes to the owner's estate when the owner dies.

A **life estate** gives a person the right to use the property during his or her lifetime. Such a person becomes known as a life tenant. This form of ownership, however, terminates on the death of the life tenant and cannot be passed to his or her estate. Every life estate also creates a **remainder estate**, which is held by a **remainderman**. On the death of the life tenant, the remainderman usually acquires a fee simple estate in the property. When the person who grants a life estate to another is also the remainderman, the estate is called a **reversionary estate**, and the person who holds it a **reversioner**. A life estate may be sold, but ownership of the property passes to the remainderman on the death of the original life tenant. The principal problem in insuring a life estate is the existence of two independent insurable interests. Courts have valued both a life tenancy and a remainder estate in the same property at the full value of the property. This creates a situation in which the sum of the insurable interests is equal to twice the value of the insured property. When each party insures the property separately, courts have ruled that each is entitled to recover its full value for a total loss. Insurers have an obligation to compensate both the life tenant and the remainderman as though no other insurance covered the loss. This remains true even when a single insurer covers both interests.

In life tenancy situations, insurers might be compelled to pay some multiple of the property's full value for a single loss. Judges believe this requirement does not violate the principle of indemnity, even though the sum of the insurable interests exceeds the value of the property. The insurer has also collected multiple premiums for a single exposure. Some courts have extended this rationale to disputes involving policies that separately cover individuals holding an undivided joint interest in the same property and to a leasehold interest. The reasonable expectations of policyholders have played a major role in these court decisions. Paying premiums, even duplicate ones, entitles parties holding distinct interests in the same property to recover the total amount. Some underwriters believe that recovery for a loss should be limited to the respective interests of all parties combined and that multiple recoveries permitted by the courts do not contradict the spirit of the principle of indemnity.

The solution to having insured recoveries exceed the value of the property is to cover all parties holding an insurable interest under a single policy with the same insurer. The exceptions are leasehold interest coverage and errors and omissions insurance for secured creditors. Destruction of the subject of a life estate, for example, subjects the life tenant to a loss equivalent to its full value but also eliminates the rights that the remainderman holds in the same property. Underwriters should recognize the validity of two separate losses for the same amount in this situation and the possibility of combined losses in excess of the property's total value. In circumstances such as these, separate policies are effective in providing adequate coverage for both insureds, but this also creates the possibility of duplicate recovery for partial losses.

Secured creditors also have an insurable interest in property that secures a debt. A mortgagee provides the most familiar example. When property is pledged as security for a loan, the lender stands to suffer a loss from damage to or destruction of the property. A secured loan gives the lender the right to take the property pledged to secure the loan if the borrower defaults. In many cases, the lender will not lend money without security. The most common method of covering the interest of a secured creditor is by adding that creditor to the borrower's property insurance as a mortgagee or an additional named insured. Standard property forms give secured creditors greater rights than the insured to recover for a loss, which is rarely a genuine concern to the underwriter. Secured creditors also place coverage in their own right. The most common is contingent coverage that applies only if the borrower's insurance is not in force on the date of loss.

Policy Provisions for Valuing Losses

The method prescribed by the policy provisions for placing a value on covered property is important for determining the acceptability of a new submission or a renewal and for properly underwriting property coverage. Property insurance underwriters have traditionally relied on actual cash value (ACV) as the most accurate measure of loss. As insurance has evolved, however, new concepts for measuring the value of covered property have emerged. Other measures used in valuing insured property are stated amount, replacement cost, functional replacement cost, and market value. When the insured and the insurer cannot agree on an approach to determine the value should a total loss to the property occur, they might agree to insure it for a specific sum. This technique is applied in two slightly different ways. With **stated amount**, a coverage limit is selected as the maximum coverage limit that is subject to valuation on an actual cash value at the time of a loss. With a **valued policy**, the underwriter and the insured agree before a loss occurs what the value of the property will be at the time of loss, provided the loss is total.

Most underwriters today regard **replacement cost**, the cost of replacing damaged property with new property, as the valuation most appropriate to property insurance in general and to commercial property coverage in particular. When replacement cost coverage first appeared, it raised concerns about violating the principle of indemnity and creating a moral hazard. The principle of indemnity demands that insurance restore the insured as nearly as possible to the position he or she would have enjoyed had no loss occurred. Using actual cash value as a measure of insurable interest in property insurance presumes that new property is more valuable than old and that replacing old property with new is a betterment, which violates the principle of indemnity. Insuring property to its actual cash value eliminates this perceived inequity by reducing reimbursement for any loss by the amount of the property's depreciation. Age, use, deterioration, and obsolescence cause property to depreciate. The definition of actual cash value as replacement cost less depreciation is almost universal. In practice, however, attempts to measure actual cash value do not produce consistent results. In most cases, it is easy to measure the replacement cost of property. The amount of depreciation, on the other hand, is open to debate.

The replacement cost option in commercial property forms fully reimburses the insured for any losses sustained, eliminates uncertainty in loss adjustment, and creates a contract that fulfills the customer's reasonable expectations. Actual cash value applies legal concepts to measure value; replacement cost relies on economic concepts. New property is no more useful or productive than similar old property. A business rarely earns higher profits, for instance, by using new machines than it could earn with older equipment that is in good condition. From this perspective, replacement cost is a better measure of indemnity than is actual cash value. It comes closer to restoring the insured to the condition that would have prevailed had the loss not occurred. Actual cash value coverage requires insureds to make an additional investment to achieve the same level of earnings they would have attained had there been no loss. Insuring to replacement cost provides a business with the resources needed to restore its earning power without the need to invest additional funds.

Occasionally, the replacement cost option fails to meet the insured's requirements or the underwriter's goals. Replacing damaged or destroyed property with like kind and quality might be either impossible or unacceptable to the policyholder. The cost of repairing or finding a new replacement capable of performing the same function might be substantially greater or less than the cost of replacing the property with like kind and quality. For example, a business might rely on obsolete but well-maintained and perfectly functional machinery. The only replacement available might be modern with technological improvements and considerably more expensive. On the other hand, the owner of an office building might be content to replace plaster on wire lath walls with drywall, which provides the same utility as plaster but at a substantially lower cost.

Replacement cost coverage might fail to provide an adequate amount of insurance or impose an unnecessary expense. **Functional replacement cost** measures the amount of loss by the cost of similar property that performs the same function. Insurance based on functional replacement cost provides an amount of insurance adequate to preserve the economic utility of the insured enterprise without increasing the amount of insurance solely to satisfy the coinsurance provision. Property valuation under the functional replacement cost approach can be more or less than replacement cost. The underwriter evaluating either replacement cost or functional replacement cost coverage for obsolete equipment should be certain that maintenance is satisfactory and should monitor the account closely.

Sometimes a business uses property that it would not replace should it suffer a serious loss. Shifting demographics sometimes leave an existing location poorly suited to the insured's operations. However, loyalty to customers may prompt the business to remain. Sometimes a business can earn an adequate return because it has amortized the property fully and does not incur any capital costs. Sales potential, on the other hand, might not justify any new investment. In the event of a serious loss, sometimes the best option open to the insured is to abandon the operation. When the insured can relocate to another site, replacement cost coverage is often the best approach. Policy forms no longer require the insured to rebuild on the same site to recover the full replacement cost. Although there is no coverage for any additional expense caused by rebuilding on a different site, the insured may do so and still recover the full value of the loss at replacement cost. The recovery, however, will be limited to the cost of rebuilding on the insured site.

In some instances, a firm will make a business decision to close down at a particular location after a serious loss. These businesses need adequate coverage for partial losses and are still entitled to recover for a total loss. Because of the coinsurance clause, insuring to replacement cost requires a higher limit than the insured really needs. Despite the insured's purchase of a replacement cost coverage form, recovery is limited to ACV when the insured does not actually replace the property. This results in a higher premium that places an unnecessary burden on the insured. In this case, the underwriter and the insured should consider using a market value endorsement or actual cash value. Although standard forms filed by ISO do not include a market value endorsement for buildings, functional valuation forms serve the same purpose.

The insured can recover functional replacement cost for any property that is repaired or replaced after a loss. If the insured chooses not to repair or replace the damaged property, these forms pay the cost of market value, or actual cash value, or what it would have cost to restore the property. Many insurers have developed proprietary forms that modify this approach in order to better meet the needs of the market niches they serve.

Underwriting property that is not adequately maintained poses a special problem. Valuation at less than replacement cost affords the underwriter a valuable tool for encouraging loss control on this type of property. Because maintenance deficiencies indicate that management's commitment to preventing and controlling losses is not adequate, these deficiencies signify a substandard risk. The underwriter might feel compelled either to decline the account or to create an additional incentive to prevent or control losses. Providing coverage that reimburses losses at less than their full value achieves the desired result in the same manner as would applying a higher deductible. Market value is sometimes an appropriate tool for encouraging loss prevention and control. However, standard ISO forms include market value only as an option on the functional valuation forms, which could defeat the underwriter's purpose by agreeing to pay the functional replacement cost of repaired or replaced property.

Insurance to Value

Establishing property values allows the underwriter to determine whether the amount of insurance requested is adequate. The insurance industry recognizes that profitable underwriting requires a relatively high ratio of policy amount to the actual property value. The ratio is traditionally 80 to 90 percent. The coinsurance clause has been the principal means that insurers have used to achieve this ratio between the amount of insurance and the value of the covered property. The insured agrees to insure the property for a specified percentage of its value. If the amount of insurance when a loss occurs is less than the product of the coinsurance percentage and the value of the property, the insured cannot recover the full amount of the loss. Insureds who fail to satisfy the insurance-to-value requirement suffer a coinsurance penalty when a loss occurs. Many insurers now recognize the benefits of establishing adequate insurance to value as a basic underwriting criterion. In an effort to pay lower premiums, many small businesses purchase insurance in amounts that expose them to coinsurance penalties if a loss occurs. Coinsurance penalties persist because insureds do not understand the insurance requirements and consequently do not increase the policy face amount as values increase in response to inflation.

ISO's businessowners policy, as well as independent forms aimed at the same market, does not include a coinsurance provision. Small businessowners are often less sophisticated about their insurance needs and found the coinsurance clause confusing. The 1997 version of the ISO businessowners coverage form includes an insurance-to-value provision, but it is not coinsurance.

Businesses often either insure property at more than one location or insure more than one type of property at a single location. A retailer may, for example, operate several stores at different locations. A business that owns its building often insures both the building and its contents under the same policy. In this case underwriters refer to the building as one item of insurance and the personal property as another. The insured in these cases may choose to apply a separate amount of insurance to each covered item. This type of coverage is called **specific insurance**. A single amount of insurance applies to one item of property at one location. **Blanket insurance** provides a single amount of insurance to cover a class of property at more than one location, more than one item or class of property at a single location, or both. A single limit may apply, for instance, to both building and contents at one location or to buildings at more than one location. A blanket limit becomes more appropriate as the number of locations increases and the proportion of the total value each location represents declines. It allows the insured who has more than one location to carry a limit that is high enough to cover a total loss at any one location but is still less than the full value of the covered property. Blanket insurance requires a minimum of 90 percent coinsurance and is written at the 80 percent coinsurance rate (which is higher than the 90 percent coinsurance rate).

Requirements for insurance to value and coinsurance penalties have not encouraged all insureds to purchase adequate amounts of insurance. As a result, they have not eliminated the additional expense of adjusting losses when a coinsurance penalty applies. When the amount of insurance is less than adequate, adjusters have to devote more time and effort to negotiating a settlement, and claims result in disputes that are more likely to end up in court. This damages the insurer's relationships with its customers, agents, and brokers. It also creates a need to charge higher premiums to the majority of policyholders who do not suffer a loss.

Unless insurers aggressively enforce insurance to value as a fundamental underwriting requirement, the premium for a book of business can become inadequate. Experience has shown that efforts to persuade insureds to purchase adequate insurance to value can be successful if the idea is properly presented. The most productive programs rely on policyholder education, the comprehensive review and upgrading of all renewal business, and a requirement of full insurance to value for new submissions. Offering guaranteed replacement cost coverage has proven effective in improving customer satisfaction and underwriting results in personal lines. This innovative coverage has just begun to appear in a few narrowly defined commercial lines markets. It is too early to determine how effective it will be. To establish adequate insurance to value, underwriters must accurately estimate the total value of all insured property. This process can be considerably easier and less expensive than many insurance professionals assume.

Determining at policy inception whether the policy provides adequate insurance does not completely resolve the insurance-to-value problem. The underwriter must also consider the effects of inflation. When adequate insurance to value is an underwriting requirement, each renewal demands a new appraisal of the values exposed to loss and a determination of the amount of coverage required. Vendors offer building and contents valuation services that make this job easier for insureds, agents, and underwriters.

The inflation guard option of the building and personal property coverage form provides another means of addressing insurance to value by proportionally increasing the amount of insurance throughout the policy period. Increment options are 2, 4, and 6 percent. The present rate of inflation and the rate anticipated during the policy period must be considered. The underwriter should remember that increases in the cost of repairing or replacing buildings and business personal property usually outpace the Consumer Price Index, the most frequently cited measure of inflation. Also, though helpful in adjusting values during the policy period, the inflation guard option will not remedy inaccurate initial values.

Measures of Potential Loss Severity

Another important consideration in evaluating property loss exposures is determining the largest loss that the insured might incur as the result of a single event. Underwriters usually use three measures to make this determination:

1. Policy amount
2. Amount subject
3. Probable maximum loss (PML)

Each measure is the sum of separate values for every coverage the policy provides. Both amount subject and PML provide more accurate measures of the true exposure to a single loss than does the policy amount. Because the calculations of amount subject and PML include subjective elements, however, general agreement on precisely what each means does not exist. Different underwriters arrive at different estimates of amount subject and PML for the same or similar risks. Estimates by any two underwriters with a common employer, however, should be consistent if not identical because insurance companies ordinarily establish rules for determining both values.

Policy Amount

The amount of insurance the policy provides (or its limit of liability) is the easiest to calculate and the only one on which underwriters tend to agree. However, the amount of insurance is also the least useful figure for determining potential loss severity. Blanket insurance can complicate the calculation by providing a single amount of insurance for multiple properties at one or more locations.

Amount Subject

Amount subject measures the exposure to a single loss and varies by cause of loss. Because their perspectives differ, the insurer and the insured might have differing opinions about the amount subject. For fire insurance, the amount subject is almost always the value of all insured property exposed within a single fire division. This could be part of a building, an entire building, or several buildings. Underwriters often use the expression "within four walls" to explain the concept of amount subject. This description is generally accurate, but it implies that the calculation is more precise than it actually is. It requires subjective judgment to measure the boundaries of a fire division. Where there are no fire walls, adjacent buildings of frame, masonry, or noncombustible construction might constitute a single fire division. Not all underwriters agree about what constitutes an acceptable fire wall. Not all insurers apply the same rules concerning how much distance between buildings is considered enough to create separate fire divisions.

To create separate fire divisions between buildings that abut each other, some underwriters insist on fire walls with parapets that extend at least four feet above the roof. Others accept fire walls that extend only to the underside of a noncombustible roof. An insurer may or may not accept a lower parapet height when there is clear space between exposing buildings. The amount of clear space needed between buildings also varies from one insurer to another. At one extreme, an insurer might insist that any building close enough to generate an exposure charge in the rate schedule constitutes part of the same fire division. Others may divide two buildings into separate fire divisions with much less clear space between them. The insurer's underwriting policy reflects the values individual insurers apply to make these judgments. Two insurers looking at the same account may arrive at very different estimates of the amount subject.

Internal fire walls can also divide a single building into several separate fire divisions. Underwriters typically apply the same standards to fire walls within a building as they do to fire walls between structures that adjoin one another and that have no intervening space. Fire walls within fire-resistive structures need not extend through the roof, which acts as a full fire stop. Effectively partitioning a modified fire-resistive building into multiple fire divisions might require parapets, but the parapets generally need not be as high as those for noncombustible, masonry, or frame structures.

Underwriters must also consider how ventilating systems and electrical conduits affect the ability of a fire to spread from one part of a building to another. Heat and products of combustion can spread very quickly through the ducts of ventilating systems. Ventilation ducts that pass through fire walls should be equipped with automatic dampers. Conduits for electrical wires and telephone lines pose a similar threat, although their smaller size makes them less able to transmit heat. The primary concern when conduits pierce fire walls is having firestopping to prevent heat from penetrating the fire wall.

When determining the amount subject, the underwriter must consider all insurance that the insurer writes within a single fire division. The insurance company might insure the owner of a building and its tenant separately or separately insure several tenants in a multiple-occupancy structure. The insurer might have to pay the face amount of all policies that insure property within a single fire division.

Probable Maximum Loss

Probable maximum loss (PML) is the underwriter's estimate of the largest loss likely to occur. This concept is more controversial and subjective than amount subject. To many underwriters, PML is meaningful only for fire-resistive buildings and their contents. For other types of construction, such as frame, underwriters consider PML equal to the amount subject and make only one calculation. Some underwriters assign a PML equal to the maximum value exposed in any two adjacent fire divisions that are separated by fire walls breached by protected openings. Other underwriters might calculate a PML at less than the full value exposed within a single fire division. Amount subject considers the benefit of horizontal fire divisions, but PML includes the effects of building features that impede the vertical spread of fire from one floor to the next. Underwriters disagree on the best method for determining PML and on whether to modify the PML calculation to reflect differences in the quality of various types of fire-resistive construction.

Underwriters often calculate PML based on the assumption that anything that *can* go wrong *will* go wrong. For example, an underwriter might assume that the automatic fire sprinklers will not be maintained and fully functional to actuate when a fire occurs and that firefighters will not respond to the alarm in a timely manner. Underwriters often refer to the protection available to a property as "lines of defense." Insurer underwriting guidelines might specify that PML be calculated presuming that the first two lines of defenses have failed (the sprinkler system and the fire service, in the example above). Insurance company underwriting guidelines vary considerably on this issue, and many insurers ask their underwriters to consider worst-case scenarios but permit their underwriters considerable flexibility in determining what those are.

For fire-resistive construction, insurer underwriting guidelines might establish PML as the value of a certain number of floors, expressed as maximum and minimum values. One insurer, for example, established a PML that ranged from three to five floors for full (not modified) fire-resistive construction in which all walls, floors, and roofs have at least a two-hour fire-resistive rating. The insurer reserved the lower end of the fire-resistive rating scale for less hazardous occupancies or properties protected by a sprinkler system with a higher grading. The insurer also regarded two or more floors connected by unprotected openings as a single floor for PML calculations but accepted automatic fire sprinklers installed only at the vertical openings as adequate protection. For modified fire-resistive construction (one-hour fire-resistive rating), the PML ranged from five to eight floors. In divided masonry and noncombustible construction, the insurer established a basic PML at two fire divisions, assuming that at least one fire door would fail. While these underwriting guidelines are specific, underwriters at this insurer were granted some flexibility in calculating PML, based on individual risk conditions.

To establish an accurate PML for a fire-resistive building, the underwriter must also consider how a fire can spread vertically from floor to floor, and how fire can damage property on the floors that the fire never reaches. It is sometimes helpful to think of fire-resistive floors as horizontal fire walls that inhibit the vertical spread of fire, similar to the way in which fire walls contain the horizontal spread of fire. Vertical conduits and ducts for ventilating systems can spread fire from floor to floor in a high-rise building in the same way in which they can allow fire to travel horizontally from one fire division to another. Fire can also travel up the outside of a fire-resistive building, moving from floor to floor by radiating heat through the windows to floors above the fire. This is a significant cause of damage in most severe high-rise fires.

The fact that a fire is contained within one or two floors of a fire-resistive building does not limit damage to property on those floors. When a bomb struck New York's World Trade Center on February 26, 1993, the resulting smoke circulated throughout six buildings. Smoke from a fire can produce the same result. Water used to suppress a fire will flow to floors below the fire floor by gravity, carrying soot and debris with it. All of the ensuing damage from smoke and water is part of the fire loss. In setting the PML, the underwriter must allow for smoke and water damage on floors the fire never reaches.

Accurately calculating the amount subject and PML is also important for complying with state insurance codes and for satisfying reinsurance arrangements. Statutes generally prohibit an insurance company from exposing more than 10 percent of its policyholders' surplus to a single loss net of authorized reinsurance. Because amount subject measures this single loss exposure for property insurance, a liberal calculation of a high-value property could endanger the insurer's financial condition. Most insurers are of sufficient financial size or have adequate reinsurance programs that writing too large an account and violating regulatory constraints are not problems. For some weakly capitalized insurers, this constraint would be a concern because insurance regulators will penalize insurers that exceed what is considered to be a prudent risk retention on any one account. Because underwriting guidelines typically adopt a conservative net line, expressed as limits of liability that fall within the underwriter's authority, a line underwriter would have to exceed his or her own authority by a considerable amount before violating the 10 percent rule.

Probable maximum loss also influences the availability of both treaty and facultative reinsurance. Reinsurers have designed many property treaties to facilitate writing large amounts of insurance on a single risk while limiting the reinsurer's exposure within the PML.

Probable maximum loss is not the only term underwriters use to describe the largest loss that can reasonably be expected. It is simply the term used most often and most widely accepted. To clarify their own statement of this concept, some underwriters will use other similar terms. Maximum possible loss and maximum probable loss, which are both abbreviated MPL, have appeared from time to time. Underwriters can also expect to encounter the term maximum foreseeable loss. Probable maximum loss is a concept that can accommodate a wide range of definitions. Faced with the same account, different underwriters will assign different values to the PML. Underwriters might legitimately often use other terms to convey the concept of a loss larger than the probable maximum loss, but the difference is often only semantic. One underwriter, for example, may assign a PML to an account and then proceed to calculate a higher maximum foreseeable loss. A more conservative colleague might ignore the concept of maximum foreseeable loss entirely but assign a PML higher than the first underwriter's PML. Thus, PML is a concept that each insurer will apply according to its own underwriting policy. By its nature, PML produces different values when applied by different underwriters. It is not at all surprising that several terms have emerged to express refinements of the concept that individual insurers consider important.

Analyzing the Management and Financial Condition of a Business

Evaluating the overall competence and attitude of a prospective insured's management toward loss control is essential in underwriting commercial lines. This evaluation helps the underwriter determine the quality of the account.

Financially healthy businesses can cope with changing economic cycles. Underwriters must know how a contraction of the economy can affect exposure to property loss. If the sales decline while production temporarily continues, inventory accumulates unexpectedly. If the collection of accounts receivable drops off, cash flow might diminish, creating pressure to contain expenses. Contraction of the economy has both a physical effect and a financial effect on property loss exposures. The sudden and unexpected accumulation of inventory alters the storage configuration of finished goods or merchandise held for sale. The probable frequency and severity of loss increase. The total value at risk also increases and becomes concentrated. The cost of any loss that does occur becomes greater, and small accidents can cause severe financial consequences. Orderly storage arrangements suddenly become cramped, and aisles narrow.

These conditions might occur during an economic expansion and be only temporary because the increasing level of sales would move inventory or provide funds to acquire additional storage facilities.

When the economy stagnates, money is tight. When cash flow declines and expenses continue, the importance assigned to loss prevention and loss control might diminish as the insured delays necessary maintenance or repairs. Putting less emphasis on loss control materially alters the quality of the account, gives rise to a moral hazard, and increases physical and morale hazards. The situation is more serious when the slowdown in turnover results from changes that make the insured's inventory less desirable to consumers. The permanent reality of technical obsolescence replaces the transient conditions of a contracting economy. Although few policyholders intentionally destroy their property to collect insurance, the possibility of this happening cannot be ignored. Underwriters need to evaluate the effects of increased concentration of values, deferred maintenance, and deterioration of the quality of storage arrangements.

Fire as a Covered Cause of Loss

Fire is a form of oxidation, which is a chemical reaction. The chemical reactions that constitute fire and the physical processes that accompany these reactions vary considerably. For example, the temperature required for combustion decreases as atmospheric pressure increases. All forms of oxidation release energy in the form of heat. The difference between fire and other forms of oxidation is in the speed at which the reaction occurs. Fire develops rapidly, progressing quickly to a stage at which it generates enough heat to produce another reaction independent of any outside source. This uninhibited chain reaction enables a fire to become self-sustaining.

Exhibit 4-1 illustrates the three components of fire: oxygen, fuel, and heat. In the exhibit, the three components of fire are presented as a triangle. Together and in the right proportions, the components of the fire create a chain reaction. Each occurrence of the chemical reaction creates all the conditions needed for another occurrence. This causes the reaction to continue until some outside force interrupts it. A self-sustaining fire will therefore continue to burn until some external force acts to suppress it or until it runs out of fuel load. Each of the three sides of a triangle touches the others; if any one side were removed, the other two would collapse. Similarly, if any of the three components of fire were not present, a fire could not burn.

Exhibit 4-1
The Fire Triangle

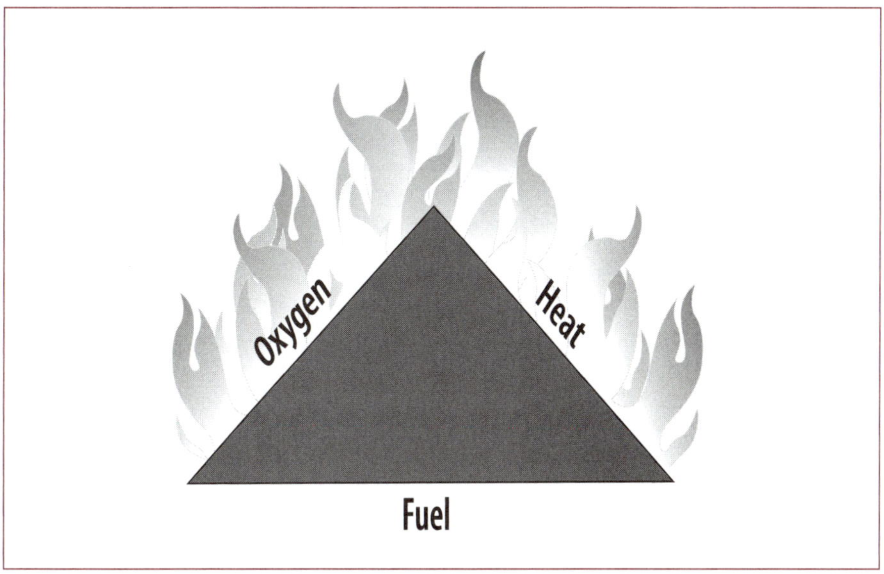

Fire and Heat

Heat plays a dual role in fires. It is needed to ignite the fire; likewise it is a product of the fire. Often, in their early stages, fires do not produce enough heat to sustain the chemical reaction, so removing the heat source is sufficient to extinguish the blaze. However, the rate of heat release grows dramatically and can quickly allow the fire to become self-sustaining. Controlling sources of heat is a key to preventing fires and limiting losses. This section discusses sources of heat for ignition and basic safety considerations associated with each.

Heating and Cooking

Heating and cooking accounted for 11.4 percent of all nonresidential fires in 1994. Exhibit 4-2 presents data from the National Fire Incident Reporting System (NFIRS) by cause of fire that will be helpful in this discussion and the discussions that follow.

Exhibit 4-2
Causes of Reported Fires, 1994

	Residential				Nonresidential			
Cause	Fires	Deaths	Injuries	$ Loss	Fires	Deaths	Injuries	$ Loss
Incendiary/ suspicious	11.8%	9.8%	10.4%	15.4%	24.2%	8.8%	15.9%	25.0%
Children playing	4.7	8.1	11.0	4.7	2.6	—	2.1	0.6
Smoking	4.7	15.7	9.7	4.5	3.5	11.4	5.0	1.9
Heating	13.5	9.6	8.1	10.5	5.2	7.3	6.3	5.4
Cooking	18.5	6.0	19.8	8.7	6.2	4.9	8.2	2.7
Electrical wiring	7.9	7.8	6.2	10.2	8.3	5.7	9.8	9.4
Appliances	6.1	2.8	4.7	4.3	4.6	—	7.8	2.1
Open flame	5.5	3.4	6.1	4.8	8.3	9.8	10.1	6.0
Other heat, spark	1.3	1.2	1.2	1.2	1.6	2.4	1.7	1.2
Other equipment	1.3	1.5	1.5	2.1	6.2	8.1	13.8	9.5
Natural causes	1.9	0.3	0.6	2.9	2.8	—	4.3	4.0
Exposure	3.7	0.3	0.6	3.2	5.5	—	0.6	2.9
Unknown	18.2	32.3	19.1	26.4	19.7	38.2	13.5	26.9

Note: Columns of figures may not add up to 100 percent because of the effects of rounding.

Sources: U.S. Fire Administration; National Fire Incident Reporting System (NFIRS).

Central heating equipment creates three sources of accidental ignition: (1) heat generated during normal operation of the unit, (2) malfunction that accidentally ignites fuel outside the unit's combustion chamber, and (3) flues that vent products of combustion. Forced-air heating units require ducts to circulate heated air throughout the premises. If they are not properly placed and insulated, these ducts can pose a threat to combustibles. Local space heaters also produce heat capable of igniting nearby combustibles. Since permanently installed equipment such as gas-fired radiators, hot blast heating units, stoves, and fireplaces have flues and ducts, that equipment presents dangers similar to central heating units.

The first step in controlling ignition from permanently installed heating equipment is ensuring that the equipment is properly installed and maintained. The equipment requires proper insulation and adequate clearance from combustible materials and surfaces, including walls, floors, and ceilings.

Allowing adequate space for air circulation around ducts and especially flues limits the potential for accidental ignition because air dissipates the waste heat escaping from the system. Qualified technicians or mechanics should perform periodic maintenance of heating equipment, at least annually. Permitting untrained or inexperienced personnel, such as the insured's own maintenance staff, to do maintenance work on heating equipment increases the likelihood of fire.

Employees and contractors, including electricians and plumbers, can also create problems in heating systems by disturbing the insulation or the ductwork that provides circulation for heating. Management must ensure that workers restore or replace all insulation disturbed after their work is done and that they install nothing in the insulating spaces provided for heating equipment. Safety for flues and chimneys, especially those for coal-burning or wood-burning heating equipment, requires periodic cleaning by qualified professionals.

Portable heaters cause many accidental fires. The portability of these heaters makes controlling this exposure inherently difficult. One common cause of fires from portable heaters is placing the heaters close to combustibles. Another cause is the inability of some heaters to shut off automatically after tipping over.

Maintaining adequate clearance for portable heaters is difficult but not impossible. The most effective protection lies in safe design. Two excellent design features are a low profile that minimizes the potential for the unit to tip over and a safety device that shuts the unit off if it leans too far from a vertical position. Because the most serious exposures arise from the use of portable heaters in spaces containing combustibles, such as office supplies and clothing, limiting use of portable heaters to unheated spaces free of combustibles is an effective control.

Electric or propane-fired equipment is the safest for indoor use. Modern kerosene heaters do not present a significant fire hazard, but ample ventilation is necessary to make them safe for heating indoor areas. Salamanders and other homemade stoves burn waste materials to provide heat. One common form of salamander consists of a fifty-five gallon drum with ventilation holes punched in its sides near the bottom. Using salamanders on construction sites is especially dangerous. The scrap wood customarily used as fuel produces sparks that can travel a considerable distance and ignite combustibles.

Cooking equipment, a leading cause of accidental fires, creates exposures similar to those created by permanently installed heaters. Grease that accumulates on cooking equipment and in flues places highly combustible material in close proximity to a source of intense heat. Although some cooking fires start in or on the cooking equipment itself, most occur in the hoods and ducts that carry grease-laden heated air and the products of combustion to the atmosphere. Like central heating plants, cooking equipment requires proper insulation and adequate clearance from combustible materials and surfaces. This equipment is typically installed in rooms with finished walls, as opposed to the unfinished areas of heating plants. Filters limit but do not eliminate grease buildup, which places flammable material close to a source of heat. Employees should regularly clean the filters, and professionals should clean hoods and ducts frequently. Many communities have revised their health and fire codes to require periodic hood and duct cleaning in restaurants.

Hood and duct fire suppression systems also offer effective protection against fire losses that originate in cooking equipment. These systems, sometimes called Ansul systems, are similar to automatic fire sprinklers. Instead of water they contain an extinguishing agent suited to class B fires, typically carbon dioxide (CO_2) or foam. A well-designed system includes extinguisher heads over all cooking surfaces, especially deep fat fryers and grills, as well as extinguisher heads in the hoods and ducts. Like water sprinklers, a hood and duct protection system responds automatically to fire. The system should also be equipped with a manual release for emergency operation. All kitchen staff should be trained to operate the emergency discharge mechanism and should know where to find it. Large kitchens may contain several separate hood and duct fire suppression systems, each protecting a separate area. A large system may also have more than one manual discharge handle. For maximum effect, the hood and duct protection system should automatically close a cutoff valve in the fuel line to the cooking equipment as soon as it discharges. This removes a source of heat that might allow a fire to flare up again after the system has suppressed it.

Smoking Materials

Smoking materials and matches are significant causes of accidental fires, but their significance is declining because health concerns and an activist attitude among nonsmokers have made tobacco use less socially acceptable. Many establishments have made their premises smoke-free. Health codes further restrict smoking in certain occupancies, including all retail occupancies in most areas. Many state and local governments now prohibit smoking in most indoor public areas. Most businesses that permit smoking restrict it to designated areas and provide ashtrays. Two types of ashtrays provide very effective protection against fires that start in smoking materials: open ashtrays or smoking stands that contain sand, and self-closing receptacles made of fire-resistant materials.

Establishments that permit smoking on-premises, especially bars and restaurants, can improve safety by emptying ashtrays separately into self-closing, fire-resistant containers and segregating those containers from linens and other refuse.

Welding, Brazing, Soldering, and Cutting

Welding, brazing, soldering, and cutting, collectively referred to as "hot work," are processes for joining or cutting metals by applying heat. In welding, the metals to be joined are heated until a small portion at the joint melts, allowing the joints to fuse as they cool. Brazing and soldering heat the materials to be joined and introduce a filler that melts and forms the joint by fusing to the pieces as they cool. Cutting is a hot process that uses welding equipment to cut metal objects by melting. All of these processes can use either an open flame (acetylene) or heat generated electrically (an arc).

The underwriter must be familiar with the processes that the insured or applicant employs, the hazards that those processes create, and the protective measures specific to each. Processes that burn gas to produce a flame are an especially dangerous form of friendly fire because of the high temperatures they require, their highly flammable gas fuels, and the frequent presence of an independent supply of oxygen. Welding, cutting, and brazing also create sparks that can travel as far as thirty feet horizontally and smolder for hours.

Analyzing and controlling hot work in production processes are easy because the work is typically confined to a fixed location. Precautions can be implemented for isolating combustibles and providing a safe place for the work to cool when completed. Safe use of portable welding, brazing, soldering, and cutting equipment, common equipment in construction and repair operations, involves several tasks. These tasks include clearing the work area as completely as possible of material that will burn; protecting remaining combustibles, including floors and walls; closing the area to all traffic until the work is finished and has had an opportunity to cool; and posting a fire watch until all heat from the operation dissipates. Spreading sand on floors and wetting or shielding surfaces with blankets of fire-resistant material provide the best protection to combustibles that must remain in the work area.

Electrical Equipment and Wiring

A NFPA study found that 11 percent of all structural fires were caused by electrical failures.[1] Most electrical fires start in the wiring that distributes the current. The amount of heat that the movement of electric current creates increases with the current's strength and decreases with the diameter of the conductor. The primary means of protecting against excessive heat in systems distributing electric current are as follows:

- Using wire of sufficient size (gauge) for the load it will carry to minimize the amount of heat released
- Using an appropriate breaker or fuse for the wire size
- Containing the heat with insulation
- Isolating distribution equipment from combustibles

NFPA Standard 70, the National Electric Code, specifies appropriate wire sizes (measured in American Wire Gauge [AWG]) and installation procedures for electrical distribution systems and equipment. AWG expresses the size of the wire as a number that represents its ability to carry current safely. The lower the AWG, the larger the wire and the more current it can carry safely. Electrical cords for small appliances and table lamps, for example, should not be less than 18 AWG. A 15-amp circuit, on the other hand, requires at least 14 AWG wire or cable.

Although many communities have adopted the National Electric Code by reference, local requirements might be less stringent. All electrical apparatus should be listed for its intended use by Underwriters Laboratories (UL) or a comparable nationally recognized testing laboratory and installed and used according to the requirements of NFPA 70. Newly installed electrical systems tend to cause few problems, because they are usually designed and installed properly. New systems typically provide adequate capacity for the load they will bear. Since the leading cause of electrical fires is worn-out equipment, maintenance and renewal are essential.

Electrical systems are often overloaded, encouraging the use of fuses and circuit breakers rated at a higher capacity than the wiring they protect. Installing approved electrical apparatus in an inappropriate area is another frequent problem. For example, fire can be caused by using ordinary electrical fixtures outdoors or in a wet environment or failing to use explosion-proof electrical devices where flammables (including dust) are present. Such practices could be an indication that management does not pay enough attention to controlling losses, and the account might not be desirable as a result.

Using electrically powered materials-handling equipment, such as forklifts, creates a special hazard because batteries require periodic, often daily, recharging. Wet-cell batteries produce flammable gases while recharging, which can ignite from the heat of a stray spark. Explosion and fire are common consequences of the failure to observe adequate safety precautions. Procedures that make this exposure reasonably safe include the following:

- Charging batteries in a remote and well-ventilated area
- Connecting a cable from the battery charger to the battery's positive terminal and then connecting the ground cable to a grounded surface away from the battery
- Supplying current to the battery charger only after all connections are complete

Charging from a fixed location is preferable to using portable equipment, because it prevents charging in a highly hazardous environment and it helps contain losses by isolating the operation from combustibles. Charging batteries in a sheltered outdoor location or in an empty loading bay provides an added measure of security.

Sources of Ignition in Industrial Commercial Processes

To evaluate an individual risk properly, an underwriter must consider the potential for a commercial process to generate and transmit the heat from friction, static electricity, hot liquids, and chemical reactions. Friction is the resistance to motion that occurs when two objects come in contact with one another. Overcoming this resistance releases heat, which can be a source of ignition. Moving machinery parts are a common source of dangerous friction, which can build up quickly, causing the equipment to overheat and ignite combustible parts such as belts or nearby flammable materials. Proper maintenance and lubrication can control this exposure.

Friction from other sources does not ordinarily produce enough heat to pose a danger to combustibles. However, some friction can generate sufficient heat to ignite flammable vapors or dust or to cause sparks that could fall on easily ignitable materials, such as loose trash or paper packaging materials. Proper use of materials-handling equipment and tools, especially in environments that contain airborne dust or flammable vapors, provides adequate protection.

The conditions that create friction also produce static electricity. The motion of one surface might create the buildup of a static charge that might discharge into another. The underwriter must consider the potential for sparking. One approach to reducing static electricity is to raise humidity levels. Not all sources of static electricity can be treated in this manner, however. In some instances, humidifying all areas would be difficult. High humidity also interferes with the materials handled. In some occupancies, high humidity can make working conditions intolerable. Where humidity or other natural channels of static discharge are not possible, grounding provides an avenue though which to dissipate a static charge.

Many industrial processes employ liquids hot enough to ignite combustibles that come in contact with them. Molten metals pose the most serious and obvious danger, but many industries routinely handle fluids at temperatures high enough to support combustion. These substances, including superheated steam and compounds with high boiling points, transfer heat efficiently, expanding the range of the heat source and the potential for igniting combustible materials. Insulation, containment, and adequate clearance between equipment containing hot fluids and combustibles control this source of ignition.

Because of the potential for chemicals to react with one another, underwriters should consult reference sources to determine the hazardous properties of substances when analyzing the chemicals used by a business. Certain chemical reactions, called exothermic reactions, release energy, usually in the form of heat. If heat produced by the exothermic reaction is not absorbed by its surroundings, the exothermic reaction can become self-sustaining and potentially uncontrollable. Using heat byproducts produced by planned reactions is an effective means of controlling ignition and explosion. Venting, insulation, and isolation from combustibles are alternative controls. Businesses using chemicals that react with one another must establish controls and systems to prevent accidental mixing or contact. Locating the reactants in different places is the most effective control, but it is not always feasible.

The presence of chemicals, flammable liquids, or flammable metals on the premises also demands special measures to control fire losses. Fires in flammable liquids are class B fires. The use of water to suppress a class B fire is often inappropriate and counterproductive. The insured should have an adequate supply of class B fire extinguishers available. Heavy concentrations of fuel for class B fires may also make water sprinklers inappropriate. Adequate protection may call for a separate system that contains a fire suppression agent suitable for class B fires. When a combustible metal burns, it creates a class D fire, which requires a suppression agent tailored to the fuel. Burning magnesium, for example, will draw oxygen for combustion from water. The insured should have an ample supply of the proper type of class D fire extinguishers on hand whenever there is an exposure to fire in combustible metals. If the insured installs an automatic fire suppression system, it must be capable of handling the specific type of class D fire that the combustible metal exposure presents.

Some chemical reactions cause a phenomenon called spontaneous combustion. This chemical reaction occurs when combustible material increases in temperature without any input of heat from an external source. The decay of organic matter produces heat, which could cause combustion. Coal and grains are especially susceptible to spontaneous combustion. The two most effective means of protecting organic materials against spontaneous combustion are storage in low piles and limiting the supply of oxygen. A low pile height allows the heat from decomposition to dissipate to the atmosphere. Limiting the supply of oxygen prevents decomposition, which is an oxidation process. This prevents the release of heat and removes the ignition source. Grain elevators, for example, limit the supply of oxygen by storing grain in tall silos and poking down the grain to eliminate pockets of air. Many oils are highly susceptible to spontaneous combustion because they are highly flammable and because they naturally give off heat as they decompose. Oily rags and paper pose a severe danger of fire. Experts on fire safety advise disposing of oily rags in self-closing fire-resistant containers because of the possibility of spontaneous combustion.

Other Sources of Ignition

A few fires originate from natural causes, including lightning, which, as shown in Exhibit 4-2, caused 2.8 percent of nonresidential fires. Properly used and well-maintained, a lightning arrester system will safely ground natural discharges of electricity. Exposing flammables in closed containers to sunlight or accidentally focusing the sun's rays on those containers can also cause ignition. Exhibit 4-2 shows that NFIRS has identified exposure fires as causing slightly more than 5.5 percent of nonresidential fires.

Fires originating externally to the structure have the most potential for creating a severe loss, because they have had an opportunity to grow and develop a high rate of heat release before involving combustibles located at the insured premises.

Exhibit 4-3
Estimates of Incendiary and Suspicious Fires in Structures, 1990–1995*

	1990	1991	1992	1993	1994	1995
Structural fires of incendiary or suspicious origin	97,000	98,000	94,000	84,500	86,000	90,500
Civilian deaths in structural fires of incendiary or suspicious origin	715	490	605	560	550	740
Dollar loss** in structural fires of incendiary or suspicious origin (in millions)	1,394	1,531	1,999	2,351	1,447	1,647

*Estimates based on data reported by fire departments responding to the annual National Fire Experience Survey.
**Includes direct property losses only; does not include indirect losses such as business interruption or temporary shelter costs.
Source: National Fire Protection Association estimates.

Reprinted with permission from *The Fact Book 1997: Property/Casualty Insurance Facts* (New York, NY: Insurance Information Institute, 1997), p. 67, and the following prior editions of *The Fact Book*: 1996, p. 67; 1995, p. 67; 1994, p. 72; 1993, p. 63; 1992, p. 64.

Annual surveys of fire departments by the NFPA indicate that fires of an incendiary or suspicious nature have declined in recent years. The insurance business has tried for years to draw attention to the arson problem. Those surveys show that although arson remains a significant problem, it appears to be on the decline nationally.[2] The estimates in Exhibit 4-3 might understate the problem because incendiary fires frequently destroy all evidence of their origins, and many fire investigations are incomplete or inconclusive. Some of these losses result from the insured's decision to destroy the property in order to collect the proceeds of insurance. Others are crimes directed against the property owner. The underwriting considerations are vastly different for these two causes. A careful analysis of financial information and business history might disclose an insured's willingness to cause a loss. The underwriter must decide whether a threat of arson can be accepted and at what price. As the experience of sprinkler-protected properties during the 1992 Los Angeles riots illustrates, automatic fire sprinklers can be effective protection against arson losses. Premises security arrangements are also effective against arson directed at the property owner.

Fuel for Fires

Almost any substance will burn if heated sufficiently to its self-ignition point, but some materials burn more readily than others. Those that burn at only extremely high temperatures are noncombustible. Noncombustible materials will burn, but only under extreme conditions. Aluminum is noncombustible because it burns only at temperatures of 2,300 degrees Kelvin (3,680 degrees Fahrenheit) or higher, a temperature that fire rarely attains. Materials that burn at typical fire-condition temperatures but that do not ignite readily are **combustible**. Materials that ignite easily or burn intensely are **flammable**.

Vaporization

Gases will burn in their natural state, but solids and liquids generally do not burn unless they are heated enough to convert part of the fuel into vapors. The vapors burn when mixed with oxygen in suitable proportions and when the vapors are heated to their self-ignition point. The heat that this process produces vaporizes more of the fuel, creating a rapid oxidation and chemical reaction (fire). A heated material will emit flammable vapors at temperatures well below its self-ignition point. The ease with which a material gives off flammable vapors when heated depends on its chemical composition, physical size, and shape. Although structural steel owes its popularity in the construction industry to its noncombustibility, the dust produced by grinding the steel ignites easily and is explosive.

Solids

Solids retain their size and shape under a wide range of conditions. They emit flammable vapors only at relatively high temperatures. The propensity of a substance to emit flammable vapors increases with the surface area of chemically identical materials of a given weight. Relatively lighter solids are more combustible than heavier materials having the same chemical composition. For example, a nylon lace veil will burn more readily than a chemically identical nylon winter jacket because the ratio of the veil's surface area to its weight is greater than that of the jacket.

Liquids

Because solids emit flammable vapors only at relatively high temperatures, their self-ignition points define their combustibility. Liquids, however, behave differently, emitting flammable vapors at much lower temperatures. The temperature at which vapor emissions from a flammable liquid mix with air in proportions that will support combustion is the vapor's **flash point**. For example, gasoline burns at a higher temperature than Number 2 fuel oil. However, gasoline is much more hazardous than Number 2 fuel oil because it has a lower flash point. Gasoline vapors are present in a flammable vapor-air mix at almost any temperature and will ignite when in contact with a hot surface, spark, or open flame. Under ordinary conditions, Number 2 fuel oil, on the other hand, does not produce a flammable vapor mixture with air. Liquids with a flash point below 100 degrees Fahrenheit are called Class I, or flammable, liquids. Class II, or combustible liquids, have higher flash points. Each class is divided into several subclassifications. There are other approaches to classifying flammable liquids, such as the one developed by Underwriters Laboratories.

The Fuel Load

The fuel readily available to a fire is called the **fuel load** or, sometimes, a fire load or fuel package. It consists of combustible portions of the structure and its contents. Frame construction has the greatest fuel load because almost the entire building is combustible. Ordinary masonry construction has the second greatest fuel load because of the large amounts of wood in joists and floors. Underwriters sometimes mistakenly disregard the contributions of noncombustible, modified, and fire-resistive buildings to the fuel load because their load-bearing members do not burn readily. Combustible interior partitions and wall and floor coverings are, however, common features in all forms of construction. Omitting them from the fuel load is a mistake.

Contents

Most of the fuel load in a structure consists of personal property contained within buildings. Assessing the fuel potential of contents requires evaluating both their combustibility and their arrangement. Because fluids (liquids and gases) rise when heated, contents arranged vertically will burn more readily than comparable combustible materials spread out horizontally. Vertical arrangement is typical of storage spaces, so warehouses are potentially exposed to more severe fire losses than are some other occupancies.

Waste and Trash

Virtually every business and institution produces large amounts of trash, which become a significant portion of its fuel load and include many materials that burn easily. Cleaning often involves the use of flammable liquids or removal of flammable oils used for lubrication. Many businesses accumulate trash haphazardly and then put it in one area, frequently a loading bay or dock. Good housekeeping is the most effective means of controlling the exposure to trash fires and should include the following:

- Adequate receptacles
- Safe storage on the premises
- Orderly procedures for collection
- Frequent removal of trash

Compactors located outside the building with access from inside are especially beneficial for retail and industrial occupancies that generate large amounts of combustible waste. These compactors afford a quick, easy means of disposal and provide a closed, fire-resistant receptacle.

Compacting trash also removes air pockets, which limits the supply of oxygen available to a fire. From a fire underwriting perspective, it is better to operate a compactor on a regular schedule than to wait until enough trash accumulates to require compacting. Loose trash lying in the compactor will burn more easily than compacted trash. Although the compactor itself is a fire-resistant container, fire can escape through the opening for inserting trash. The scale of the operation and the amount of trash it generates will dictate the schedule for operating the compactor. Daily compacting of all trash is a minimum requirement for a standard risk.

Dust and Lint

Dust consists of extremely small particles that are very light and have a relatively large surface area for their weight. This characteristic allows the particles to burn more easily than larger masses of chemically identical materials. Any significant amount of dust is extremely hazardous and potentially explosive when airborne, including dust from materials that are ordinarily difficult to burn. Metal dusts will burn readily, and airborne metal dusts present a serious explosion hazard. Many industrial and service operations produce large amounts of dust and lint, which are highly combustible when they settle on surfaces and can become explosive in the atmosphere. Mixing dust with combustible liquids, such as metal dust and lubricating oils, keeps dust out of the atmosphere but creates a combustible mixture on surfaces. The most effective technique for controlling this hazard is collecting dust as it is generated, removing the dust from the atmosphere, and preventing it from collecting on surfaces. NFPA has developed twelve separate standards for collecting and disposing of dust. Most apply to specific occupancies or operations. The most general standard is Standard No. 91, Exhaust Systems for Air Conveying of Materials. A business that complies with the appropriate NFPA standard generally represents a more acceptable account.

Cleaning and maintaining the dust collection system, as well as vacuuming to collect stray particles that evade the dust collection system, are necessary. Many businesses prefer sweeping to vacuum cleaning for dust removal because they believe sweeping is more effective. From a fire safety point of view, however, vacuum cleaning is superior. Sweeping stirs up dust, allowing a portion of the dust to become airborne. This creates the explosion hazard that cleaning seeks to eliminate. Safe removal of dust from some environments requires a high-efficiency particulate air (HEPA) vacuum cleaner. Enough dust may escape from ordinary vacuum cleaners to create an explosion hazard.

Fuels for Heat and Power

Fuels for heating and power can be significant causes of fires if human error or failure of the ignition system allows unburned fuel to accumulate in the combustion chamber of furnaces and boilers. Residual heat or subsequent operation might later cause an explosion or fire. Improved flame failure controls have largely eliminated this threat, but fuel remains a substantial component of the fuel load in many occupancies. Fire that reaches fuel storage tanks often breaches the tanks and ignites the contents.

Gases that are burned as fuel present the most serious hazard. Leaks of natural gas supplied by public utilities continue to cause explosions and fires. Because natural gas is colorless and odorless, leaks can be difficult to detect. To provide an early warning of a leak, most utilities add substances to the gas supply that give the gas a distinctive odor. Liquefied petroleum (LP) gas, propane, and butane are popular fuels because they are powerful, relatively clean, and portable. However, they are gases in their natural state and require storage under pressure to maintain a usable liquid form. Safety problems with these fuels arise most often when tanks are refilled, but leaks from connections between the tank and the equipment are also potential sources of fire. Relief valves that provide overpressure protection vent combustible gas to the atmosphere. Ordinary precautions for use of these fuels include storing and refilling tanks and cylinders outdoors, aggressively maintaining tanks and hoses, and immediately replacing those that show signs of wear. Occupancies that use large quantities of gas in their operations should have automatic gas detectors to warn of leaks.

Other common fuels are less susceptible than gases to accidental ignition and fire spread. Coal is organic material that ignites spontaneously, but fire prevention measures are well-known and widely followed. Low piles, generally containing less than fifty tons, permit the heat that stored coal generates to dissipate. Losses that do occur generally involve only the coal itself. Handling coal also produces coal dust, which requires the same precautions as other flammable dusts. Some large electrical power-generating equipment burns pulverized coal that is atomized in an airstream. Utilities that use this equipment are typically large, and their equipment is designed to contain explosions.

Oxygen for Fires

Oxygen must be available if a fire is to start and become self-sustaining. Understanding the role of oxygen in combustion enables the underwriter to gauge a normal or exceptional hazard when evaluating a particular risk.

Atmospheric Oxygen

Oxygen is the most plentiful chemical on earth, constituting about one-half of all matter. Almost all fires get their oxygen supply from the atmosphere, which is about 20 percent oxygen. For a substance to burn, the flammable vapors it emits must mix with oxygen in a proportion that will support combustion. If the concentration of vapor is too high, the mixture is rich and does not contain enough oxygen to burn. When the concentration is too low, the mixture is lean, and lack of fuel prevents combustion.

The concentration of fuel vapor and oxygen needed for efficient combustion varies with each fuel and the ambient temperature of the mix. All fuels burn only when the vapor-air mix falls within a specific range, called the "explosive" or "flammable" range. This range is expressed as the percentage of flammable vapors in the total mixture. The lowest concentration at which the vapors will burn is the lower limit of flammability; the highest concentration is the upper limit of flammability. Increasing the temperature of the mix widens the flammable range; that is, the lower limit is decreased, and the upper limit is increased. Elevated temperatures make every substance more flammable because the substance will burn at lower concentrations.

Airflow in Fires

Combustion occurs most efficiently at or near the middle of the flammable range. The fire is hotter there, and the flames are brighter. A vapor mix near the upper or lower limits of flammability slows the rate of combustion and produces a cooler fire with little or no visible flame. A lean mixture near the lower limit produces a smoldering, slow, relatively cool fire that releases heat and flammable vapors. The heat and vapor increase the temperature and enrich the vapor-air mix. The fire burns hotter, and the flame grows brighter. Inadequate airflow produces a rich mixture containing too little oxygen, eventually smothering the fire when the available air supply is exhausted.

The air directly above the fire becomes heated and rises along with the other flammable vapors present. This creates a low pressure area or a relative vacuum at the base of the fire. This area draws in fresh, cool air, makes the mixture leaner, and revives the flame. Unless outside forces intervene, fire tends to achieve a balance as heat produces more flammable vapors for combustion and creates a flow of air to renew the oxygen supply.

Solids vaporize quickly. Under extreme conditions, solids vaporize almost instantaneously. The airflow accelerates to become a powerful wind, and a firestorm develops. The best-known firestorm occurred in World War II when Allied bombers dropped incendiary bombs on Dresden, Germany, and the worst occurred a short time later during a similar raid on Tokyo. Firestorms occasionally develop during peacetime conflagrations (large destructive fires often called "group fires"), especially when wildfire sweeps through arid forest areas.

Low Oxygen Levels

When the vapor concentration is near the upper limit of flammability, the supply of oxygen is low, and combustion is imperfect. This combustion produces dense smoke, high levels of carbon monoxide, and sometimes other toxic gases. These fires smolder, releasing heat that builds up and raises the ambient temperature at the fire site. Even if the fire dies for lack of oxygen, the fuel can remain hot and extremely dangerous for a considerable length of time. If the fire obtains a new supply of oxygen, the fire will roar explosively to life. This explains how a large fire can suddenly burst out of a contained space. For example, a fire contained in a room can explode when the opening of a door enables fresh air to get to the fire. Firefighters combat the problems caused by smoke by venting the building from above. A hole in the roof allows smoke, heat, and fire gases to escape from the burning building. Venting allows trapped heat to escape and decreases atmospheric pressure in the fire's immediate vicinity. Although venting assists in reducing the intensity of the fire, it increases the possibility of introducing additional oxygen to the fire.

Oxygen-Rich Atmospheres

Oxygen-rich atmospheres are common in hospitals, especially in operating rooms, oxygen tents, and incubators. Gas welding, brazing, cutting, underwater tunneling, caisson work, and oxygen production, processing, storage, and transportation also create an oxygen-rich atmosphere. Elevated levels of atmospheric oxygen lower the self-ignition points of all substances and increase the rate of heat release in any fire. This combination allows fires to spread faster in an oxygen-rich atmosphere.

Analyzing the Air Supply

Air supply helps determine the potential severity of fire losses. Draft areas are the key to analyzing air supply. **Draft area** defines the boundaries of the space from which a fire can draw atmospheric oxygen. The underwriter must incorporate the size of the largest draft area into the evaluation. A draft area is similar to a fire division. Sealing the airflow through vertical openings, such as stairs and elevator shafts, effectively creates a separate draft area on each floor of a fire division. Fire doors or curtains provide effective barriers to divide a single floor into separate draft areas. In determining the size of a draft area, the underwriter should consider how existing airflow barriers will respond under fire conditions.

Fires Without Atmospheric Oxygen

A few fuels burn readily without atmospheric oxygen by obtaining their oxygen supply from other substances, including most common firefighting materials. Burning magnesium obtains oxygen from water and produces hydrogen, which burns in air and creates additional water as a product of combustion. Organic peroxides are self-oxidizing because they can draw on their own oxygen for combustion. Nitrates, nitrites, inorganic peroxides, chlorates, chlorites, and permanganates are among the chemicals capable of supplying themselves with oxygen. Chlorinating agents for swimming pools, common in health clubs and hotels, are also sources of oxygen. In the proper proportions, sodium hypochlorite, once a common ingredient in chlorinating tablets for home swimming pools, reacts explosively with water. Underwriters must identify all potential oxidizers in the operations that they are considering, drawing on their personal knowledge of the industry, inspection reports, and reference sources.

The Spread and Extent of Fire

Understanding the conditions that permit fire to start and grow does not provide a complete framework for analyzing fire's effects. To evaluate the likely severity of future losses, the underwriter must also understand how these factors interact under specific risk conditions.

Heat Spread

The amount of fuel that a fire can reach determines the extent of its spread and the extent of damage it can produce. Fire spreads by transferring heat from fuel already involved in the fire to nearby combustibles. The amount of fuel within reach of that heat determines the outer boundaries of a blaze. Heat spreads by conduction, convection, and radiation.

Conduction

Conduction is the transfer of heat from one mass to another by physical contact. This process causes a candle to burn down from the top even though heated fluids rise. Fire on one side of an object will transmit heat by conduction to the other side and to any object in contact with the heated material. For example, the handle of a spoon in a hot cup of coffee becomes hot by conduction. Conduction also enables fire to pass through solid objects like walls and break out suddenly on the opposite side of them. The thickness of a material and its ability to conduct heat determine how quickly fire can spread through it. Thicker walls, for example, conduct heat more slowly than thinner ones.

Some materials have greater resistance to the spread of heat than others; that is, they have superior insulating properties. A metal flue conducts heat quickly enough to pose a serious threat of fire to nearby combustibles. A masonry chimney conducts heat so slowly that the heat ordinarily dissipates as soon as it reaches the atmosphere. As a general rule, solids conduct heat more efficiently than gases, which is why insulated glass window units, consisting of multiple panes with a layer of air sealed between them, provide more effective insulation than plain plate windows. The ability of a material to conduct heat is a function of its cross-sectional area. The larger the cross-sectional area, the greater the ability of a solid to conduct heat. This is why a two-inch-diameter steel bar conducts more heat than a nail of the same material.

Convection

Convection is the mass movement of heat within a fluid (liquid or gas) caused by the expansion of heated material. The heated fluid becomes lighter and rises, displacing cooler fluid at the top. This explains why the upper reaches of a heated space tend to be warmer than the lower ones. It also explains why components of the fuel load that are above the fire ignite more easily and are more likely to burn than any other nearby property. The principle of convection explains the rapid spread of fire in high-rack storage configurations and in vertical flues like elevator shafts.

Radiation

Radiation is an electromagnetic phenomenon that transfers heat by moving particles equally in all directions from the source. The particles travel at the speed of light. Like light and other electromagnetic waves, radiated heat passes easily through air with little loss. Radiation stops only upon encountering an opaque object, which absorbs some of the radiation. The rate at which an object absorbs heat depends on the size and intensity of the original source; the size, shape, and color of the heated object; and the distance between the two. Darker materials absorb more heat than lighter ones do. The intensity of the radiation increases exponentially with the fire's temperature.

Flame Spread

Flames from fire may spread horizontally and vertically. There are two distinct types of horizontal flame spread. Flash flaming, in which fire spreads almost instantaneously, can spread fire to a larger area. Horizontal fire spread occurs when a fire develops and spreads slowly.

Flash Flaming

Flash flaming can spread fire suddenly over a large area in three ways. The sudden introduction of a fresh supply of oxygen, as discussed previously, is one way. Atmospheric combustibles and flashover are two other ways.

Atmospheric Combustibles

Atmospheric combustibles, such as flammable dust, vapors, and gases, can spread rapidly through an area and remain suspended in the atmosphere. They come from operations in progress at the site, evaporation of volatile liquids, and the accidental escape of gases that form a cloud. When any portion of this cloud contacts an ignition source, the entire mass ignites in a flash, spreading fire throughout the space and to nearby combustibles.

Flashover

Flashover is the rapid ignition of all or a substantial portion of the combustibles in a space containing a small, hostile fire. Flashover occurs when heat that is reflected from the ceiling and walls to the contents of the area raises the ambient temperature to the self-ignition point of all combustibles within reach. All combustibles in the room become involved as the fire's rate of heat release is increased. These conditions facilitate the fire's spread to adjacent spaces, allowing the fire to escape control. Flashover can occur quickly.

Flashover can occur, however, only if all of the combustibles in a room absorb heat at approximately the same rate and have approximately the same self-ignition point. Otherwise, the combustibles will not burst into flame simultaneously. The reflectivity of ceilings and walls and their distance from both the heat source and combustibles are also factors in determining a fire's ability to flash over.

Horizontal Spread

Fire will spread horizontally until it exhausts all available fuel, runs out of oxygen, or encounters a barrier capable of containing the heat it generates. Fire-resistive walls serve the last purpose while maintaining its structural integrity. The heat is conducted slowly enough that it radiates to the atmosphere and dissipates by convection or air circulation before it can ignite nearby combustibles. Fire can overcome the protection provided by fire walls in several ways. If the blaze continues beyond the wall's fire-resistance rating, the wall will lose its structural integrity and collapse. Horizontal structural members, roofs, and floors can collapse and bring the fire walls down with them. Many fire walls contain openings that are essential to the structure but that might not be adequately protected. Regardless of the quality of the fire wall, a fire wall with a fire door with a one-hour fire rating will have no more than a one-hour rating. Fire doors that fail to operate because they are defective or blocked open entirely negate the benefits of fire walls. Combustibles adjacent to fire walls or other conditions that impede airflow can also allow fire to spread through fire walls by radiation.

Interior partition walls of less than fire-resistive construction slow the spread of fire but cannot contain it. Frame construction does not conduct heat rapidly, so the frame construction itself burns. A metal wall conducts heat faster than the atmosphere on its other side can dissipate the heat, exposing any combustibles on the other side to ignition. Partition walls do, nonetheless, provide varying degrees of protection against horizontal spread of fire. Ordinary frame walls composed of three-eighths-inch drywall on two-by-fours have a fire-resistance rating of twenty-five minutes. Certain types of fire-resistant drywall increase this resistance to one hour.[3] Hollow metal walls covered by plaster or mineral board can have ratings as high as two hours, making them effective fire walls.

Windows and Doors

Several types of horizontal openings facilitate the spread of fire. Glass windows conduct heat, break, and then fall out when exposed to high temperatures. Windows in interior walls or doors allow the fire to spread readily between interior spaces. Outside windows can expose the exterior walls of another structure, especially if the other structure has facing windows and doors. As with fire walls, doors with a fire-resistance rating lower than the wall they penetrate compromise whatever protection the wall provides.

Ducts

Ductwork and conduits that penetrate walls provide another source of openings for the rapid spread of fire. Heating, ventilating, and air conditioning ducts pose a special problem because they are designed to move air and can help spread fire. Protective measures include automatic controls that in the event of fire exhaust all return air to the outside or introduce 100 percent fresh air into the ventilating system. Because fire can enter ducts and spread, adequate protection often requires automatic fire dampers to cut off the flow of air through the ducts if the air temperature rises above a critical level.

Electrical equipment and lines, especially metal conduits, can conduct heat through a wall. Overheating of electric cables by fire can also cause a short circuit, which can produce sparks in other parts of the system. Automatically shutting down the entire system and properly fusing circuits are the most effective protection against overheating and additional fire spread.

Partition Walls

Fire can also spread up and over partition walls and sometimes down and under them. Multiple units of frame construction might have common attics and, less often, common crawl spaces below the floor. Many buildings are divided into offices or sections after being built. Partitioning walls usually extend only to the original ceiling, leaving an air space above the ceiling through which fire can spread rapidly. Dropping ceilings or raising floors during renovations can have a similar effect.

Plenums

Many modern and refurbished buildings use suspended ceilings. They are attractive, are easy to repair, and provide easy access to utility lines that are often run in concealed spaces above them. They also create concealed spaces that can quickly transport the hot gases a fire produces from one part of the building to another. Heating, ventilation, and air conditioning (HVAC) systems in these buildings often make use of these concealed spaces. Modern HVAC systems recirculate the air in a building. They introduce air that has been heated or cooled into occupied spaces in the building, draw the air out of those spaces, and return it to be heated or cooled again. Using separate return ducts for this purpose is expensive. Engineers and architects reduce the cost of a building by using the concealed spaces above ceilings to bring air back to the heating or air conditioning system. This space is then called a return air **plenum**.

When a fire occurs, the use of concealed spaces as plenums facilitates the spread of heat, smoke, and hot gases through the HVAC system to the entire building. This can allow the fire to spread more quickly and hinders fire suppression efforts. The spread of heat and products of combustion through ducts can be controlled by the use of automatic fire dampers. This is not an option in plenums because they are essentially large, undivided spaces. The cost of installing fire dampers can be prohibitive.

There is no effective means of completely stopping the spread of fire, smoke, and hot gases through a return air plenum. Good design, on the other hand, can limit that spread to the immediate vicinity of the fire. Partition walls that penetrate the dropped ceiling divide the concealed spaces above them into smaller areas and limit the spread of hot gases and smoke. HVAC systems can also be designed to vent return air outside the building when sensors detect fire, smoke, or the high temperatures a fire produces. The HVAC system then introduces 100 percent fresh air into the building. While this supplies additional oxygen to the fire, it also removes through ventilation some of the heat the fire produces. At the same time, it vents smoke and often toxic gases produced by the fire. In this way it serves much the same function as venting the fire from above, a standard fire service procedure for fighting fires.

Vertical Spread

The vertical spread of fire from one floor to another can occur more readily than horizontal spread because heated gases rise. Compounding this natural phenomenon is that multistory buildings require openings between the floors for access (such as stairs, elevators, and escalators) and servicing (wiring, pipes, and ductwork). Hot vapors and air find and exploit any openings in the ceiling to floors above. Fire also spreads up the exterior walls and into upper floors through openings, especially windows.

Unplanned Openings

As heated air and unburned combustible vapors rise, they accumulate at the ceiling or roof. If these vapors cannot escape, a flammable air-vapor mixture develops as rising temperatures widen the range of flammability. Flashover is one possible result, but frequently the fire will burn through at the top and vent heat to the outside or the floor above. As the heated gases escape, fresh air rushes into the lower regions, creating a draft, a condition called the "stack effect." (Furnaces and wood- or coal-burning stoves depend on this effect to operate.) This often results in a total destruction of the floor that is the fire's point of origin.

Designed Openings

Any architectural design that allows heated air to escape upward and cooler air to replace it at the bottom creates a stack effect much like the chimney in a fireplace. A stack effect increases with the distance between levels. Designed openings include stairways, elevator shafts, chutes for movement of materials, and large open atriums that might run from the lowest floor to the roof. Some underwriters include high ceilings, characteristic of high-rise lobbies and theatrical stages, in that same class. Open shafts provide the greatest opportunity for fire spread, but any designed opening that permits hot air to escape upward promotes combustion.

Fire can also spread through windows and up the exterior walls of a building, as it did in the Las Vegas Hilton fire. Glass shatters under high temperatures, and different rates of expansion cause window frames to become loose and fall out during a fire. Heated air and gases rising along the exterior penetrate the windows of upper floors by two routes. In some instances, heat radiated through the window ignites combustibles inside, then the fire attacks the window from both sides, and the process repeats itself. Sometimes, however, the window fails from the pressure of the heat outside, shattering or falling out and admitting heat directly to the interior of the upper floor. Factory Mutual Engineering and Research has developed standards for window spacing to control this type of fire spread.

Life and property protection require that all multistory vertical openings in fire-resistive buildings be protected by self-closing fire doors. This practice is common for elevator shafts and stairwells, but most building owners prefer not to enclose escalators for aesthetic reasons. Escalators are usually protected by automatic sprinklers. In buildings of frame or masonry construction, fire spreads upward through unprotected openings more often than it burns through floors and ceilings.

Floor openings for services such as electricity, plumbing, heating, ventilating, and air conditioning need tight firestopping where they pass through floors, especially in fire-resistive construction. Inadequate, deteriorated, or removed insulation where ducts, pipes, and conduits penetrate floors is a principal cause of vertical fire spread from floor to floor of fire-resistive buildings. Heat can also bypass fire-resistive floors by moving between the edge of the floor and exterior curtain walls.

Damage From Fire

Fire damage results from four separate causes: (1) the fire itself, (2) heat, (3) products of combustion, and (4) fire suppression efforts.

Heat Damage

In addition to contributing to the spread of fire, heat causes substantial damage on its own. Burning materials release heat at different rates, measured by their calorific value (a calorie is the amount of heat required to raise the temperature of one gram of water by one degree Celsius). Materials with higher calorific values release more heat and create fires that are more difficult to extinguish. Damage by heat also varies with the exposed material. Even noncombustible materials are not immune.

Heat expands all matter at different rates and softens metals. Noncombustible structural members provide excellent examples of heat damage in a fire. Metal trusses, pillars, and walls of light fire-resistive construction expand at distinctly different rates when exposed to fire. They soften, bend out of shape, and collapse quickly. In heavier noncombustible construction, expansion of metal components can put pressure on exterior walls, pushing them outward until they collapse. Other metal objects warp or bend, glass shatters, and plastic warps, bends, or melts. Heat damage is often as severe as fire damage.

Two factors influence the amount of heat damage a building and its contents will sustain during a fire: the duration of the fire and the size and shape of the area in which the fire burns. The length of time a fire burns determines how much heat structural components and contents can withstand. The size and shape of the fire area control the supply of oxygen available to the fire and the amount of heat radiated back onto combustibles in the fire's path.

Duration

The most important consideration in estimating how much damage a fire will cause is the length of time it burns. In addition to allowing fire to reach a larger proportion of the combustibles in the fire space, longer duration allows a fire to attack firestops and involve adjacent fire divisions. Fire walls with two- and four-hour fire-resistance ratings are of little value against an eight- or twelve-hour blaze. Because fire services and private fire protection systems extinguish most fires before they burn out, most fire losses represent only a small proportion of the value of the exposed property. However, most underwriters consider the prospect of total loss in frame and masonry structures. In more fire-resistant construction, an underwriter might estimate how long a fire would need to destroy the structure. Although this determination does not necessarily define PML, the underwriter might find it a useful tool for analyzing exposure to fire losses.

Size and Shape of the Area

Another important factor in determining fire damage is the distance from the site of the fire to the ceiling or roof. Heated air and gases rise until they encounter an obstruction to their passage and then spread out along the obstruction's surface. A larger floor surface produces a thinner accumulation of hot gases in the upper reaches of the room. Lower ceilings encourage more rapid development of fire by bringing heat closer to combustibles. Larger areas and higher ceilings are not necessarily preferable, although fire develops more slowly in a large area and under higher ceilings.

Products of Combustion

Fire is a chemical reaction that converts fuel and oxygen into other substances, called products of combustion. Some of the products, like water, are harmless. Most, however, can do considerable damage. The principal products of combustion, other than heat, are smoke and gases that can be toxic, abrasive, and corrosive. Smoke is a cloud made up of suspended vapors from a fire with minute particles of solid matter suspended in it. Smoke permeates any material that lets air pass through it, leaving stains as well as a noxious odor and depositing suspended solids on surfaces in the form of soot. Exposure to abrasive gases has an effect similar to sandblasting, and exposure to corrosives is like an acid bath. In addition to damaging unburned contents and building components, fire in materials that give off dense smoke and toxic fumes hampers the efforts of firefighters. Common substances like polyvinylchloride, urethane, acrylics, ammonium nitrate, wool, animal fat, and rubber produce such smoke and fumes.

Fire Suppression Efforts

Underwriters generally consider damage caused by fire suppression as a necessary evil. Some of the most respected fire services have reputations for ripping out walls and ceilings, throwing undamaged combustibles through the windows of upper floors, and using massive quantities of water. Because they get the job done quickly, total damage is lower than it would be with less aggressive tactics. Most of the damage in fires arises not from the fire itself, but from the suppression efforts of fire service personnel and private fire protection equipment. Water poured onto a fire stirs up soot and ashes. In addition to requiring a cleanup, damage by water includes swelling and softening of many materials to the extent that they cannot be repaired. Automatic sprinklers are the most effective means of controlling damage from fire suppression because they limit the quantity of water required and the area over which it is applied.

Summary

Determining the quality of a commercial property submission begins with assessing the amount that the policy will obligate the insurer to pay in the event of loss. Confirming that the coverage requested provides the proper protection requires identifying the policyholder's insurable interest and the interests held by others. Policy provisions establishing the method for determining the value of insured property at the time of loss are both an underwriting consideration and a useful tool for designing a program to meet the underwriter's and insured's needs. Before making a commitment, the insurer must evaluate the largest amount the policy will probably pay, which is measured by the limit of liability or face amount. The amount subject and the probable maximum loss (PML) are approaches to evaluating a property's total exposure to loss and total likely loss. The underwriter needs to be aware of cyclical or structural changes in the insured's business that might affect the values exposed, the overall quality of the account, and the potential moral hazard.

Fire is a complex chemical reaction that starts and becomes self-sustaining only with the proper mix of fuel, heat, and oxygen. Fire generally spreads by radiated heat, destroying property directly and causing extensive damage through the heat and gases it produces as well as the efforts required to suppress it. For any combination of occupancy and construction, the following will determine how much opportunity fire has to start and spread:

- The nature of the furnishings
- Fixtures and contents
- The configuration of fixtures and contents
- The size and shape of the interior space

Chapter Notes

1. *Fire Protection Handbook*, 17th ed. (Quincy, MA: National Fire Protection Association, 1991), p. 2-22.
2. Federal Emergency Management Agency, *Arson in the United States* (Arlington, VA: TriData Corporation, August 1997), p. 9.
3. *Fire Protection Handbook*, p. 5-78.

Chapter 5

Underwriting Direct Exposures: Other Causes of Loss

Commercial property insurance involves more than underwriting fire. An effective underwriter looks at other causes of loss, paying particular attention to those having the greatest likelihood of loss in the policy forms being offered. This chapter discusses many of those causes of loss. Not every cause of loss carries equal weight. Some are too infrequent or slight to consider in the underwriting process. Underwriters must decide which causes of loss need investigation and then focus their limited resources on those key perils. Each cause of loss does not need to be studied in detail. Applying the lessons learned from investigating one cause of loss to several others is a simple matter.

The causes of loss discussed in this chapter are as follows:

- Lightning
- Windstorm
- Hail
- Riot and civil commotion
- Sinkhole collapse
- Volcanic action
- Weight of ice, snow, or sleet

- Flood
- Earthquake
- Explosion
- Vandalism and malicious mischief
- Sprinkler leakage
- Water damage
- Collapse

Lightning

Property insurance has historically paired lightning with fire. When lightning strikes, fire frequently results. Moreover, distinguishing between damage caused by fire and fire damage initiated by lightning is difficult, if not impossible. In the early days of property insurance, this difficulty led to confusion and disputes that often ended in court. Faced with a dilemma to which they could find no other equitable resolution, judges held that lighting was "fire from the sky." Obviously, therefore, the peril of fire also included lightning.

Insurers later amended their policy language to include lightning along with fire. Commercial property causes of loss forms list lightning independently from fire. Homeowners forms continue a tradition of covering "fire or lightning" as a single cause of loss. Nevertheless, lightning can and does cause insured damage without an ensuing fire.

Lightning is a significant source of ignition for fires. As a result, measures adopted to control loss by fire frequently include steps to mitigate lightning damage. Lightning arresters, which ground lightning strikes, provide an effective defense against damage to buildings and contents caused by direct lightning strikes. Although loss by fire might be the most significant concern that lightning causes, prudent underwriters should recognize other types of loss that lightning can cause.

When lightning strikes an electric line, it generates a power surge. This surge can enter buildings that the affected line serves and cause extensive electrical damage. These events rarely cause a fire, but damage by these surges can require replacement of the insured's electric system. Protection can be achieved by grounding electric service entrances in accordance with National Fire Protection Association (NFPA) Standard 70, the National Electric Code. An additional precaution is to install an external surge protector. For full protection of sensitive electrical devices, including data processing equipment and electric motors, adding interior surge protectors might be necessary.

Outside equipment, such as pumps and generators, is also susceptible to lightning strikes and should be properly grounded and protected.

Windstorm

Weather is a problem everywhere in the world, but especially in the United States. Atmospheric scientists have identified North America, and more specifically the United States, as the populated area of the planet subject to the most severe weather. Virtually every part of the U.S. is subject to some form of destructive wind.[1] Hurricanes batter the southeastern and Gulf Coast states, tornadoes routinely rip a path of destruction across the Plains states, northeasters pound New England and the northern Middle Atlantic states, and destructive Santa Ana winds tear through the canyons of Southern California.

The following three types of severe weather accounted for almost all wind-related catastrophes in the United States during the forty years between 1950 and 1989:[2]

- *Hurricanes*. Tropical storms are cyclones that produce strong gusty winds and can sometimes spawn tornadoes. **Hurricanes** are the most severe tropical storm, with winds of seventy-five miles per hour or more.[3]
- *Winter storms*. Extratropical cyclones affect wide areas of the United States, typically in the fall or winter months. Mountain-induced windstorms such as California's Santa Ana winds and Colorado's Boulder winds fall into this category. So do northeasters, severe winter storms that afflict the northeastern United States.
- *Severe local storms*. Thunderstorms and the related conditions they create occur throughout the country but characteristically affect only a small geographic area. Tornadoes, hail, and strong downburst winds are typical characteristics of these storms.

Wind Speed

Wind speed is important to underwriters. Gentle breezes rarely create any damage. Raging storms, on the other hand, usually cause severe damage to property and extensive loss of life. Recognizing this difference, courts have declined to interpret property insurance policies as covering all damage done by light winds. Courts require a wind of sufficient power to damage property in a reasonable state of repair. Although the courts prefer to avoid hard and fast rules, forty-five miles per hour is the velocity cited most often as the boundary between wind and windstorm.

Several factors affect wind. Velocity increases with height, so wind speeds recorded at high altitudes are always faster than wind speeds at low altitudes. Topography is another important influence on the force that wind exerts. Wind moves over open water and flat terrain at a uniform speed. Hills, valleys, trees, and structures, on the other hand, disrupt the movement of air. They tend to slow wind speed and to produce inconsistencies in its velocity. Velocity measurements taken behind an obstruction are lower because of shielding effects, and those taken near its edges are higher. Topography can dramatically increase wind speed over a small area by directing wind into a narrow channel. Wind gusts are localized but are important because of their high velocity and damaging effects. Wind is always faster at a height of sixty feet in a narrow channel between two buildings than in an unobstructed area at a height of ten feet.

To provide uniform wind-speed reports, weather services have adopted several conventions that eliminate inconsistencies. To evaluate wind hazards, some familiarity with the following three standards is needed:

- In the United States, wind speed is the average of wind speeds measured over a period of one minute. The international standard uses a ten-minute average. The measurement of severe wind is the shortest time that one mile of air requires to pass a fixed point.[4] This measurement indicates the maximum sustained wind and eliminates the effects of momentary gusts.
- Weather services measure wind at a standard height of ten meters (approximately thirty-three feet), sometimes called rooftop level.[5] This standard eliminates differences caused by altitude and provides a measurement at a level relevant to most uses of wind-speed reports.
- Anemometers, instruments that record wind speed, must be positioned on a flat area and clear of obstructions. Such placement eliminates inconsistencies caused by shielding and channeling effects.

Beaufort Scale

The internationally recognized **Beaufort scale** classifies wind according to velocity. It assigns both names and numbers to eighteen categories of wind and estimates the effect that winds will produce in each category. Effects range from smoke rising vertically to devastation. Exhibit 5-1 reproduces the Beaufort scale. It compares winds in different areas or seasons. Underwriters should use one aspect of the Beaufort scale cautiously. The level of damage it attributes to storms of various magnitudes is a function of much more than wind force and is by no means inevitable. Engineers and builders can design structures to resist wind damage. The South Florida Building Code, for example,

Exhibit 5-1
The Beaufort Scale of Wind Velocity

Beaufort number	Wind speed (miles per hour)	Wind name	Observable wind characteristics
0	< 1	Calm	Smoke rises vertically
1	1–3	Light air	Wind direction shown by smoke drift, but not by wind vanes
2	4–7	Light breeze	Wind felt on face; leaves rustle; vane moves
3	8–12	Gentle breeze	Twigs in constant motion; wind extends light flag
4	13–18	Moderate breeze	Raises dust and loose paper; moves small branches
5	19–24	Fresh breeze	Small, leafy trees sway; wavelets on inland water
6	25–31	Strong breeze	Large branches in motion; whistling in power lines
7	32–38	Near gale	Whole trees in motion; resistance felt in walking
8	39–46	Gale	Breaks twigs off trees; generally impedes progress
9	47–54	Strong gale	Slight structural damage (chimney pots, roof tiles)
10	55–63	Storm	Trees uprooted; considerable structural damage
11	64–72	Violent storm	Rarely experienced inland; widespread damage
12-17	73	Hurricane/ typhoon	Very rare occurrence except in tropics; catastrophic structural damage; heavy loss of life

requires construction capable of resisting winds up to 120 miles per hour.[6] This range includes velocities for which the Beaufort scale predicts devastation.

Saffir-Simpson Scale

The National Weather Service uses the **Saffir-Simpson scale**, reproduced in Exhibit 5-2 along with two lower storm classes, to measure hurricane-force winds. The scale is a useful tool for assessing the damage potential of a hurricane in progress. The Saffir-Simpson scale classifies hurricanes into five

Exhibit 5-2
Saffir-Simpson Hurricane Disaster-Potential Scale and Lower Storm Classes

TYPE

Tropical Depression	Winds >35 mph

An organized system of clouds and thunderstorms with a defined circulation.

Tropical Storm	Winds 39–73 mph

An organized system of strong thunderstorms with a defined circulation.

Category 1	Pressure	Damage	Winds	Storm Surge
Hurricane	Greater than 28.94*	Minimal	74–95 mph	4–5 feet

Damage primarily to shrubbery, trees, foliage, and unanchored mobile homes. No real damage to other structures. Some damage to poorly constructed signs. Low-lying coastal roads inundated, minor pier damage, some small craft in exposed anchorages torn from moorings.

Category 2	Pressure	Damage	Winds	Storm Surge
Hurricane	28.50–28.91*	Moderate	96–110 mph	6–8 feet

Considerable damage to shrubbery and tree foliage, some trees blown down. Major damage to exposed mobile homes. Extensive damage to poorly constructed signs. Some damage to roofing materials of buildings; some window and door damage. No major damage to buildings. Coastal roads and low-lying escape routes inland cut by rising water 2 to 4 hours before arrival of hurricane center. Considerable damage to piers. Marinas flooded. Small craft in unprotected anchorages torn from moorings. Evacuation of some shoreline residents and low-lying island areas required.

Category 3	Pressure	Damage	Winds	Storm Surge
Hurricane	27.91–28.47*	Extensive	111–130 mph	9–12 feet

Foliage torn from trees; large trees blown down. Practically all poorly constructed signs blown down. Some damage to roofing materials of buildings; some window or door damage. Some structural damage to small buildings. Mobile homes destroyed. Serious flooding at coast and many smaller structures near coast destroyed; larger structures near coast damaged by battering waves and floating debris. Low-lying escape routes inland cut by rising water 3 to 5 hours before hurricane center arrives. Flat terrain 5 feet or less above sea level flooded inland 8 miles or more. Evacuation of low-lying residences within several blocks of shoreline possibly required.

Category 4	Pressure	Damage	Winds	Storm Surge
Hurricane	27.17–27.88*	Extreme	131–155 mph	13–18 feet

Shrubs and trees blown down; all signs down. Extensive damage to roofing materials, windows, and doors. Complete failure of roofs on many small residences. Complete destruction of mobile homes. Flat terrain 10 feet or less above sea level flooded inland as far as 6 miles. Major damage to lower floors of structures near shore due to flooding and battering by waves and floating debris. Low-lying escape routes inland cut by rising water 3 to 5 hours before hurricane center arrives. Major erosion of beaches. Massive evacuation of all residences within 500 yards of shore possibly required, and of single-story residences on low ground within 2 miles of shore.

Category 5	Pressure	Damage	Winds	Storm Surge
Hurricane	Less than 27.17*	Catastrophic	>155 mph	18+ feet

Shrubs and trees blown down; considerable damage to roofs of buildings; all signs down. Severe and extensive damage to windows and doors. Complete fall of roofs on many residences and industrial buildings. Extensive shattering of glass in windows and doors. Some complete building failures. Small buildings overturned or blown away. Complete destruction of mobile homes. Major damage to lower floors of all structures less than 15 feet above sea level within 500 yards of shore. Low-lying escape routes inland cut by rising water 3 to 5 hours before hurricane center arrives. Massive evacuation of residential areas on low ground within 5 to 10 miles of shore possibly required.

*measured in inches of mercury

categories, numbered 1 through 5, based on maximum sustained wind speed and storm surge of tidal waters. Category 1 includes storms that generate winds between 74 and 95 miles per hour or a storm surge that produces waves of four to five feet above normal. Winds above 155 miles per hour and a storm surge with waves higher than eighteen feet define a category 5 hurricane. Most research on past storms reports severity using the Saffir-Simpson scale. Underwriters will find the scale a valuable tool for assessing hurricane damage potential.

Underwriters should read reports of a storm's destructive power carefully. Members of the media sometimes sensationalize a storm and exaggerate actual wind speeds. The National Weather Service might classify a storm as a tropical storm, but the public might perceive it as a category 5 hurricane. Wind-speed reports can be suspect for several reasons. First, anemometer locations might not reflect standard exposure conditions, ten meters high in open terrain. Scaling the readings to standard conditions is not easy and is at best an approximation. Adjusting reported wind velocity for shielding effects requires wind tunnel tests. Second, the equipment might need calibration. Third, the wind might be above the range the anemometer was designed to measure.[7]

Even wind speeds reported by the National Hurricane Center do not fully reflect the true action of wind on exposed property. Reconnaissance aircraft flying 500 feet above the ocean use barometric pressure to estimate wind velocity. As accurate as these barometer readings are, they tend to overstate conditions at the standard ten-meter height. The difference can be considerable. One expert estimates, for example, that a 160-mile-per-hour wind at the reconnaissance level translates to 120 miles per hour ten meters above open sea. The equivalent wind over flat terrain near the coast is 100 miles per hour.[8]

Engineers examine the quality of construction, the extent of damage, and the distribution of debris after a storm to provide the most accurate estimates of wind speed. Although the estimates are of little value in predicting the damage potential of an event in progress, they contribute substantially to minimizing damage in future storms.

Hurricanes

Hurricanes cause severe wind damage, and extensive research has been conducted to control the damage they cause. Conditions that give rise to the formation of hurricanes are seasonal. "Hurricane season" begins June 1 and lasts until November 30.

The Potential for Hurricane Damage

Since 1989, the number of severe hurricanes making landfall in North America has markedly increased. They affect principally the southern Atlantic and Gulf Coasts of the United States, the Gulf Coast of Mexico, and islands in the Caribbean. Exhibit 5-3 charts the hurricane experience of the East and Gulf Coasts over a period of eighty-four years. Pacific hurricanes, called typhoons in the western Pacific, also threaten Hawaii but rarely reach the continent of North America.

In 1989, Hurricane Hugo struck the Virgin Islands, then devastated Charleston, South Carolina, and surrounding areas. At the time, Hugo was the most expensive natural disaster ever to strike the United States. However, that distinction was short-lived. In August 1992, Hurricane Andrew swept across Florida just south of Miami, then gained force over the Gulf of Mexico before making landfall again near New Orleans. The insurance industry incurred more than $15 billion in insured losses. While damage assessment was still in progress, Hurricane Iniki struck Kauai in Hawaii. The combination made 1992 the worst year for natural disasters that the industry has ever experienced. The ten most costly hurricanes up to 1996 are shown in Exhibit 5-4.

The growing number of intense tropical storms that make landfall is only part of the story. The damage they produce has increased at an even more alarming rate. Four principal reasons for this phenomenon are as follows:

1. *Weather cycles*. Atmospheric scientists now attribute this development primarily to a natural cycle. The cycle extends over several decades, perhaps for as long as forty years. The Pacific Ocean's El Niño current and the

drought cycle in western Africa seem to exercise a strong influence over the formation of Atlantic hurricanes.

Exhibit 5-3

Hurricane Frequency Along the Atlantic and Gulf Coasts From 1886 to 1970

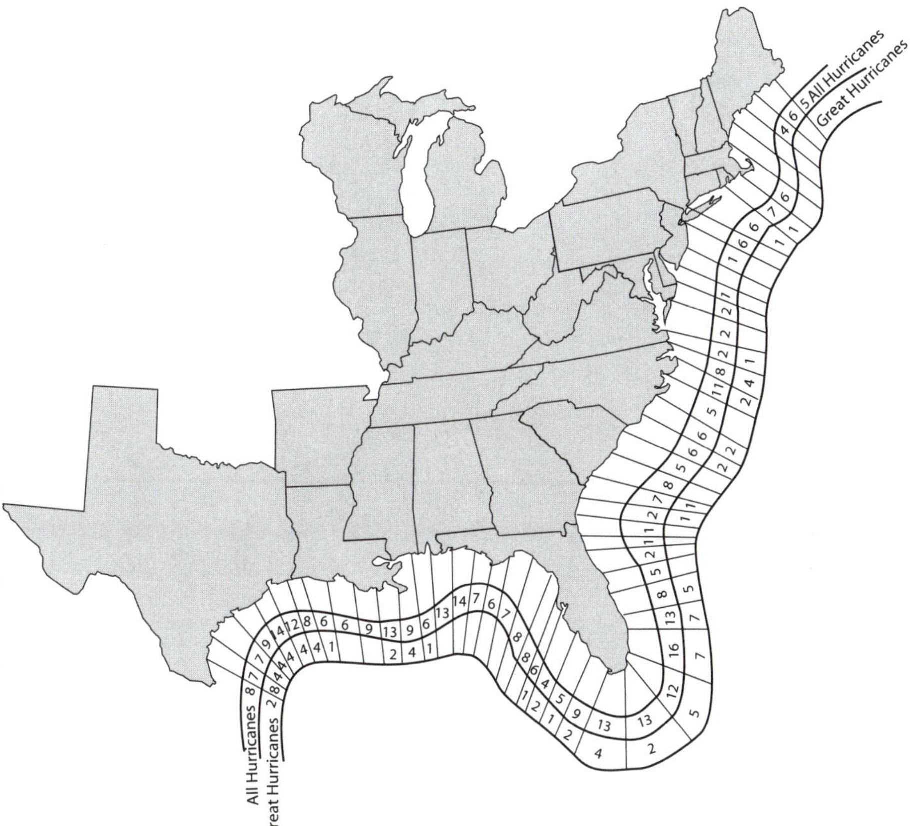

NOAA has categorized great hurricanes as having winds of 125 mph or greater.

All-Industry Research Advisory Council, *Surviving the Storm: Building Codes, Compliance and the Mitigation of Hurricane Damage*, Oakbrook, IL, 1989, p. 13.

Exhibit 5-4
The Ten Most Costly Insured Hurricanes

Hurricane	Date	Category	Place	Estimated Insured Loss (in billions)
Andrew	1992, Aug. 22-24, 25-26	4	FL, LA, MS	15.5
Hugo	1989, Sept. 17-18, 21-22	4	U.S. Virgin Islands, PR, GA, SC, NC, VA	4.2
Opal	1995, Oct. 4	3	FL, AL, GA, NC, SC, TN	2.1
Iniki	1992, Sept. 11	Unk.	Kauai and Oahu, HI	1.6
Fran	1996, Sept. 5	3	NC, SC, VA, MD, WV, PA, OH	1.6
Frederic	1979, Sept. 12-14	3	MS, AL, FL, LA, TN, KY, WV, OH, PA, NY	0.753
Alicia	1983, Aug. 17-20	3	TX	0.676
Bob	1991, Aug. 18-20	2	NC, NY, CT, RI, MA, ME	0.620
Elena	1985, Aug. 30-Sept. 3	3	FL, AL, MS, LA	0.543
Betsy	1965, Sept. 7-10	3	FL, LA, MS	0.515

Source: Insurance Information Institute, from estimates provided before 1984 by the American Insurance Association; thereafter by the Property Claim Services, division of the American Insurance Services Group, Inc.

Adapted with permission from *The Fact Book 1997: Property/Casualty Insurance Facts* (New York, NY: Insurance Information Institute, 1997), p. 79.

2. *Complacency*. The length of the natural weather cycle breeds complacency. Property owners discount weather hazards and place greater value on oceanfront property. Temperate weather conditions draw new residents and real estate developers to coastal areas. Building code enforcement officials might be less rigorous in enforcing codes, perhaps assuming that the violent storms of the past will not return. This attitude was an important factor in South Florida, which escaped major hurricanes for twenty-eight years before Hurricane Andrew. Heavy development dramatically increased the value of property exposed to a single storm.
3. *Flood insurance*. The National Flood Insurance Program has made flood insurance readily available in coastal plains, encouraging lenders to offer financing for development. These two factors have combined to spur development of coastal plains. Growth has become explosive. Exhibit 5-5

illustrates the tremendous increase in population density in hurricane-prone areas of the United States, particularly the southeast Atlantic coastal area.

4. *The greenhouse effect.* Many scientists believe that the climate is getting progressively warmer. Emissions from industrial processes, automobiles, and other fossil fuel-burning engines are raising the level of carbon dioxide in the air. Carbon dioxide reflects radiated heat back to the earth's surface, interfering with normal cooling. This process elevates temperature over a wide area. Scientists have not yet formed a consensus on the extent of the greenhouse effect. Some predict catastrophic change. Others see the greenhouse effect as moderating a new ice age that has already been in progress for thirty years. This controversy has led most atmospheric scientists to discount greenhouse gases as a significant factor in creating the more intense hurricanes of the last few years.

The higher frequency and severity of hurricanes making landfall are not new. The planet is simply returning to a period of severe weather similar to that of the 1950s and 1960s. The higher damage level results more from increased coastal development and reduced wind resistance of exposed structures than from the storms themselves. By almost every measure, Hurricane Andrew is the most destructive natural disaster ever to strike the United States. The losses it caused tripled the toll of the worst preceding disaster. It was not, however, the most powerful storm to make landfall in the United States. Hurricane Betsy (1965) and the unnamed Labor Day storm (1935), for example, were both more powerful. Had Hurricane Andrew traveled north instead of south after landfall, computer models place estimated losses in the $50 to $60 billion range. The level of damage that a hurricane produces is an equal function of the path it travels and the strength of its winds. Communities exposed to severe storms can take effective steps to mitigate damage.

The Nature of Hurricane Damage

Hurricanes cause damage in four principal ways:

1. *Wind.* Most hurricane damage results from the effect of high winds on exposed property.
2. *Wind-driven rain.* Strong winds propel rain horizontally. Wind-driven rain can penetrate structures and cause significant damage. Most of this rain enters buildings through openings that the wind creates in the roof or walls and is therefore insured as windstorm damage.
3. *Storm surge.* When a hurricane comes ashore, it drives a wall of high water before it. This is a storm surge. It threatens primarily coastal properties but

Exhibit 5-5

Growth of Population Density[1] in Hurricane-Prone Versus Other Areas of the United States: 1960-2010

Region[2]	Land Area		Population Density and Decade-to-Decade Percentage Increases						Overall Percentage Increases		
			Year								
	(Sq. Mi.)		1960	1970	1980	1990	2000	2010	1960-1990	1990-2010	1960-2010
Southeast Atlantic Coastal[3]	37,281	Pop. Density	107	141	192	245	278	301			
		% Increase	—	31.7%	36.2%	27.5%	13.5%	8.2%	128.7%	22.8%	180.9%
Other Hurricane-Prone Coastal[4]	136,914	Pop. Density	300	344	366	401	429	454			
		% Increase	—	14.6%	6.5%	9.4%	6.9%	5.9%	33.6%	13.2%	51.2%
Total Hurricane-Prone Coastal[5]	174,195	Pop. Density	259	301	329	368	396	421			
		% Increase	—	16.1%	9.5%	11.7%	7.9%	6.3%	42.0%	14.6%	62.7%
Remaining Areas of Hurricane-Prone[6] States	633,031	Pop. Density	62	73	82	91	97	102			
		% Increase	—	18.3%	12.1%	10.3%	7.0%	5.3%	46.3%	12.6%	64.8%
Total United States	3,628,066	Pop. Density	50	57	63	69	74	78			
		% Increase	—	13.3%	11.2%	9.2%	7.6%	5.6%	37.6%	13.7%	56.4%

1. Population density is the number of persons per square mile of land area.
2. Coastal means jurisdictions, mainly counties, identified by the Federal Coastal Zone Management Program or individual state coastal management programs.
3. Southeast Atlantic Coastal: NC, SC, GA, and FL (Atlantic Coast only).
4. Other hurricane-prone coastal: HI, TX, LA, MS, AL, FL (Gulf Coast only), VA, DC, MD, DE, PA, NJ, NY (Atlantic Coast only), CT, RI, MA, NH, and ME.
5. Total hurricane-prone coastal: HI, TX, LA, MS, AL, FL, GA, SC, NC, VA, DC, MD, DE, PA, NJ, NY (Atlantic Coast only), CT, RI, MA, NH, and ME.
6. Remaining areas of hurricane-prone states: Remaining areas of TX, LA, MS, AL, GA, SC, NC, VA, DC, MD, DE, PA, NJ, NY, CT, RI, MA, NH, and ME. HI and FL are considered to be entirely coastal and hurricane-prone.

Source: *The Second Report of a Coastal Trend Series—50 Years of Population Change Along the Nation's Coasts: 1960-2010*, Strategic Environmental Assessments Division, National Oceanic and Atmospheric Administration (NOAA).

can also prevent drainage and raise the levels of rivers, streams, and bays.

4. *Flooding.* The heavy rains that a hurricane produces cause flooding alone or in combination with storm surge.

Hurricane Andrew's damage was principally caused by wind. The storm produced relatively low levels of rainfall. Flooding occurred only in areas along the coast, probably influenced by proximity to canals. Since almost all the damage occurred inland and resulted from wind alone, the hurricane provided an opportunity to analyze the effects of severe winds isolated from other causes of loss.[9]

Controlling Wind Damage

Studies of hurricane damage provide valuable insight into effective means of controlling wind losses. The events of August 1992 demonstrate conclusively that the technology to limit windstorm losses is available. The location of severe winds can be predicted, and winds can be prevented from causing excessive damage.

Hurricane Andrew conclusively demonstrated the following facts:

- Commercial lines underwriters have less cause of concern about windstorm than do personal lines underwriters. One- and two-family dwellings sustained most of the damage. Commercial structures that were designed and engineered to withstand wind pressure fared very well during the storm.
- The key to a building's survival in a windstorm is maintaining the structural integrity of its "envelope," the outer walls and roof that keep weather out.
- Well-designed building codes can protect property from windstorm damage. Specifically, the South Florida Building Code, which covers the entire area affected by Hurricane Andrew, contains adequate provisions for wind-resistant construction. Structures built to code should have weathered the storm with minimal damage. The failure of too many structures to meet code requirements contributed the most to the extent of insured losses.
- Strong code enforcement is indispensable. Many of the structures in Andrew's path failed to meet wind code requirements.

The two most important factors in controlling windstorm losses are adequate building codes and their strict enforcement.

Maintaining the Envelope

Most wind damage to structures and their contents occurs when the wind load destroys the integrity of the building envelope. When wind enters a building, pressure builds up inside, causing roofs and doors to blow outward. Upward pressure lifts the roof from the structure. In extreme cases, the entire building will explode like a bursting balloon, exposing the contents to damage from two sources. Direct action of wind attacks the contents, sometimes "scouring" the interior of the building. Personal property is blown from the structure. Because heavy rains often accompany violent wind, openings created by wind action also admit water into the building. The rain often does greater damage than the direct action of the wind. The strength of the building envelope can be increased in the following ways:

- Roof anchors must be able to withstand specified wind speeds. Builders often tie the roof (rafters and ceiling joists) to the top plate of the exterior walls with nails driven through the sides of the rafters (called toe nailing). Toe nailing does not provide sufficient resistance to uplift loads. Adequate resistance requires the use of hurricane clips to secure rafters and beams to supporting columns.
- Tying the entire structure together increases the strength of the envelope and improves its wind resistance. Builders must secure roofing members not just to columns, but to the foundation as well, and builders must tie walls and columns to the foundation. Straps and J bars have proven to be effective ways of bringing about this added structural integrity.
- Windows, doors, and other planned openings need adequate protection. Strong anchors to the structure will prevent failure of the opening. Storm shutters to protect glass from airborne debris are also effective.
- Cladding, the material that makes up roofs and walls, must resist wind damage. A small failure in a building's cladding can admit wind and rain that can cause damage far in excess of the cost of wind-resistant materials.

Building Code Design

Building codes that are properly written and enforced are the most effective means of ensuring that the building envelope will endure severe wind conditions. Protecting property from windstorm damage requires well-drafted wind provisions in building codes and builders willing to follow the codes.

Three organizations provide model building codes in the United States. The Southern Building Code Congress International (SBCCI) maintains the

Standard Building Code. Communities adopting this code are located mainly in the Southeast and on the Gulf Coast. The International Congress of Building Officials (ICBO) produces the Uniform Building Code, used primarily along the Pacific Coast. The Basic Building Code, prepared by the Building Officials and Code Administrators International (BOCA), has become the standard in the Northeast and Midwest. Most communities adopt one of these codes by reference, often requiring the latest edition. A few have enacted code provisions as an ordinance.

Codes typically specify that construction must resist the force of wind at a certain velocity, called its wind design load. SBCCI, ICBO, and BOCA base their wind design loads on the most severe wind expected over a fifty-year period. An extended period of time, such as fifty years, is used to evaluate a severe but infrequent cause of loss such as windstorm. Exhibit 5-6 maps fifty years of winds for the continental United States. The South Florida Building Code, however, adopted by all communities along Hurricane Andrew's path, imposes a higher standard (120 miles per hour) than the fifty-year wind. The storm subjected property to maximum sustained winds no higher than 125 miles per hour.[10] Clearly, any structure built to code should have incurred only minimal damage. The underlying reasons for a structure's failing in a community such as this is important for underwriters to understand.

Building Code Enforcement

Reliance on performance standards is a major problem with most building codes. The standards specify wind velocity that buildings must withstand but not wind-resistive methods of construction. A few communities have adopted prescriptive codes, which, instead of specifying minimum wind design loads, provide detailed instructions for meeting code performance standards. Because the instructions often supplement the building code, prescriptive codes are also called "deemed to comply" codes. They are not actually part of the law, but interpret it to assist builders, inspectors, and plan reviewers. Builders who follow recommended practices are deemed to comply with code performance standards.

Wind code enforcement generally appears to be at a lower level than it should be. A study of Gulf Coast states disclosed that inspectors and plan reviewers are not knowledgeable about the principles of wind-resistant construction. Most builders also know little about such construction techniques.[11] Wind code enforcement improves significantly in communities that adopt prescriptive codes. Building department officials and contractors can understand them better, improving both voluntary compliance and enforcement.

Exhibit 5-6
Basic Wind Speeds for Fifty-Year Period

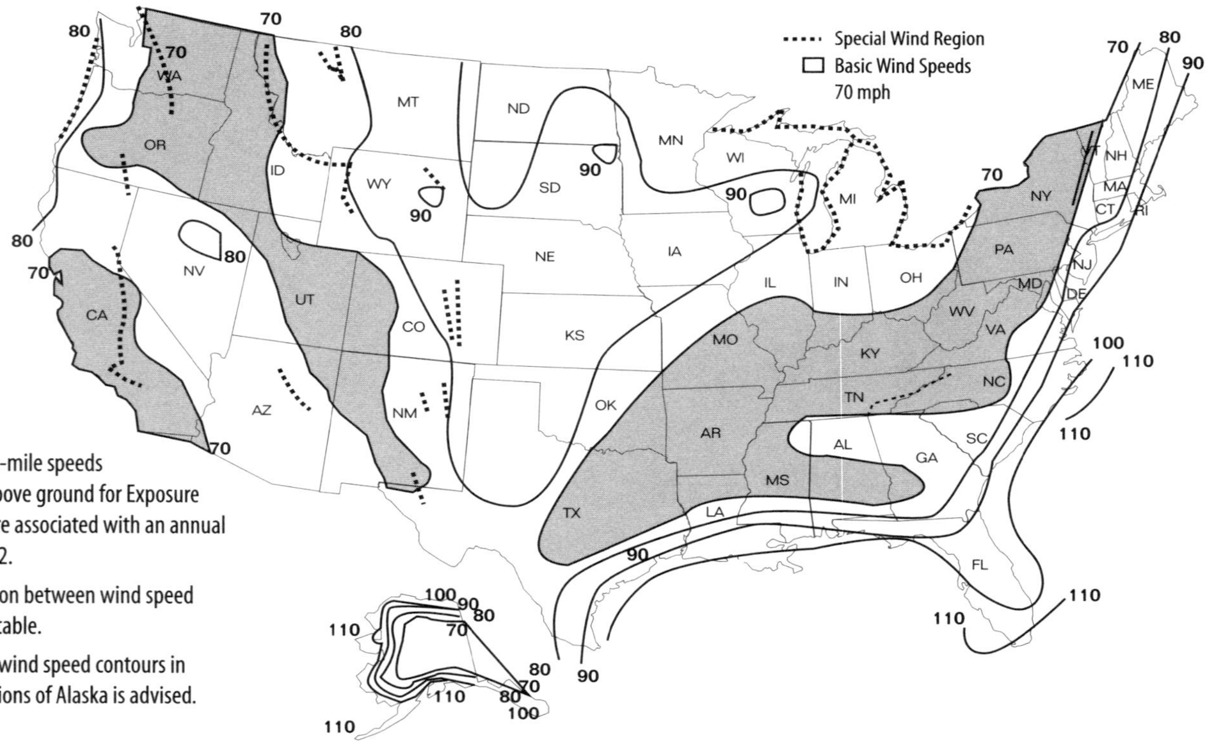

Notes:

1. Values are fastest-mile speeds at 33 ft. (10 m) above ground for Exposure Category C and are associated with an annual probability of 0.02.
2. Linear interpolation between wind speed contours is acceptable.
3. Caution in use of wind speed contours in mountainous regions of Alaska is advised.

All-Industry Research Council, *Surviving the Storm: Building Codes, Compliance and the Mitigation of Hurricane Damage,* Oak Brook, IL, December 1989, p. 28.

Case Study in Building Code Design and Enforcement

A study of two hurricanes illustrates the benefits of code design and enforcement on wind damage.[12] The two storms were nearly identical. They struck similar areas, but these two communities took different approaches to wind codes and enforcement. Consequently, the damage caused in each community was very different.

On August 18, 1983, Hurricane Alicia passed over the west end of Galveston Island, TX, producing insured losses of $1.27 billion. A little more than a year later, Hurricane Diana struck North Carolina near Kure Beach and inflicted only minor damage. The two communities were remarkably similar. Each was located on a barrier island and had about the same number of buildings. Building construction was outwardly similar. Both localities adopted the same model building code with the same provision that structures should be built to resist wind speeds up to 120 miles per hour.

The two storms were as much alike as the communities they struck. Alicia's winds ranged from 85 to 90 miles per hour and might have reached 100 miles per hour at the extreme western tip of the island. Diana produced winds in the 80-to-90-mile-per-hour range, with two weather stations reporting sustained winds in excess of 100 miles per hour. Alicia destroyed more than 1,000 of the 3,000 homes in the West Beach section of Galveston Island. Diana, on the other hand, destroyed only 10 homes. In Texas, more than 35 percent of the homes needed major structural repair because of wind damage, while only 3 percent in North Carolina needed significant repairs. Building code enforcement accounted for the differences between the effects of these storms.

Building in the West Beach area began when the area was part of an unincorporated section of the county outside the Galveston sea wall. Ironically, the National Flood Insurance Program made development of this area feasible. For several years, development proceeded without the protection of any building code, until the city of Galveston incorporated West Beach in 1975. Although the city had adopted the Standard Building Code, the code was not adequately enforced. North Carolina had also adopted the Standard Building Code. It was effectively enforced.

Underwriting Considerations for Hurricanes

Code enforcement is a key underwriting consideration for windstorm. Many commercial structures are fully engineered, meaning that engineers were involved in the design of the structure and that the structure has been designed to withstand the wind stresses that the building code specifies it should. Despite the structural strength inherent in a fully engineered structure, there are other building features an underwriter should consider. Also, many of the structures an underwriter will likely have submitted will not be engineered.

Nonengineered Structures

The design team for smaller structures often does not include engineers. Those who are part of the team might lack needed experience and training in wind loads and wind-resistant construction. A proper risk assessment requires some knowledge of the quality of local building code design and enforcement. Until recently, underwriters had to rely on the experience and expertise of colleagues in branch offices to make assessments. In 1995, Insurance Services Office (ISO), in cooperation with the Insurance Institute for Property Loss Reduction (IIPLR), began rating communities on the quality of their building codes and the level of their enforcement. The **Building Code Effectiveness Grading Schedule (BCEGS)** produces a classification, ranging from 1 to 10, that operates similarly to the community protection classifications used in rating and underwriting fire coverage. The BCEGS evaluates three major areas:

1. Administration of building codes and supporting ordinances and the qualifications of those enforcing the codes
2. Building plan review
3. Field inspection

ISO and the IIPLR expect to have all communities in the United States graded before the year 2000 but will focus first on states with a significant wind exposure.[13]

In the meantime, underwriters can use several factors to rate wind code design and compliance. A community's adoption of the latest edition of one of the three model codes is one factor. Statewide wind codes are, on the whole, superior to local codes. Prescriptive codes can also improve compliance, but they apply only to one- and two-family dwellings, which commercial lines policies rarely insure. Prescriptive codes do, however, improve code compliance for nonengineered commercial structures. Builders, inspectors, and plan reviewers have a higher level of expertise, which carries over to commercial structures.

Fully Engineered Structures

Fully engineered structures tend to comply with wind codes, but they still present a few special problems. Large expanses of glass and cantilevered walls are the most notable concerns. Underwriters should also determine whether the owner has made any material changes to the engineer's specifications.

In any severe wind, airborne debris can smash glass. Trees, shrubs, small outdoor objects like trash cans, and parts of buildings ripped off by wind all may contribute to flying debris. Large expanses of glass, common in some commercial structures, require storm shutters. In fact, code designers have begun to believe that effective protection against wind requires storm shutters over all areas exposed by glass.[14] During Hurricane Andrew, only one fully engineered structure suffered a major failure. The building featured glass walls, which shattered under the assault of flying debris. Wind entered the building and scoured its interior. Millions of dollars worth of contents simply disappeared. The original engineering specifications called for storm shutters over all exposed glass. The owners chose to eliminate them for aesthetic reasons.

Cantilevered walls are free-standing walls that have no lateral support at the top. Commercial, office, institutional, and some industrial buildings use them to conceal services like air conditioning and refuse collection. A few serve as wind breaks but are not effective against gale- or hurricane-force winds. As wind passes over and around a cantilevered wall, it creates a vacuum behind the sheltered side. The combination of direct wind action pushing the weather side and the vacuum pulling the lee side in the same direction causes the wall to fail and collapse. Cantilevered walls do not enjoy the benefit of the lateral support a roof provides to walls enclosing a structure. The absence of this support makes a cantilevered wall more susceptible to the forces of wind. Two features can improve the wind performance of cantilevered walls. First, a latticework design reduces wind force on both sides. Air passes through the wall without creating a strong vacuum on the lee side. Second, adding lateral support at the top, in the form of steel beams spanning the space the wall encloses, gives the wall added strength that can enable it to withstand the wind load.

Tornadoes

A **tornado** is a relatively small but especially violent windstorm. Tornadoes form in warm, humid, and unsettled weather. Thunderstorms and tropical storms often spawn them. They consist of winds rotating at speeds that can reach up to 300 miles per hour, creating a partial vacuum at the center of the storm, which is called its vortex. Upward velocity at the wall can exceed 200 feet per second. Condensation around the vortex produces a pale cloud that gives the tornado its characteristic funnel shape. When the tornado makes contact with the ground, it draws debris into the circulating air, and the funnel cloud darkens. An explanation of how tornadoes form is shown in Exhibit 5-7. The average tornado path is only one-quarter of a mile wide and rarely exceeds sixteen miles in length. Many are considerably shorter and narrower than average. A tornado can touch down in a backyard, pick up a lawn shed and its contents, and lift off again without damaging the fences around the yard. Yet a tornado path can be up to a mile wide and several hundred miles long. Tornadoes move forward at an average speed of forty miles per hour, but some have reached wind speeds of seventy miles per hour.

Exhibit 5-7
How Tornadoes Form

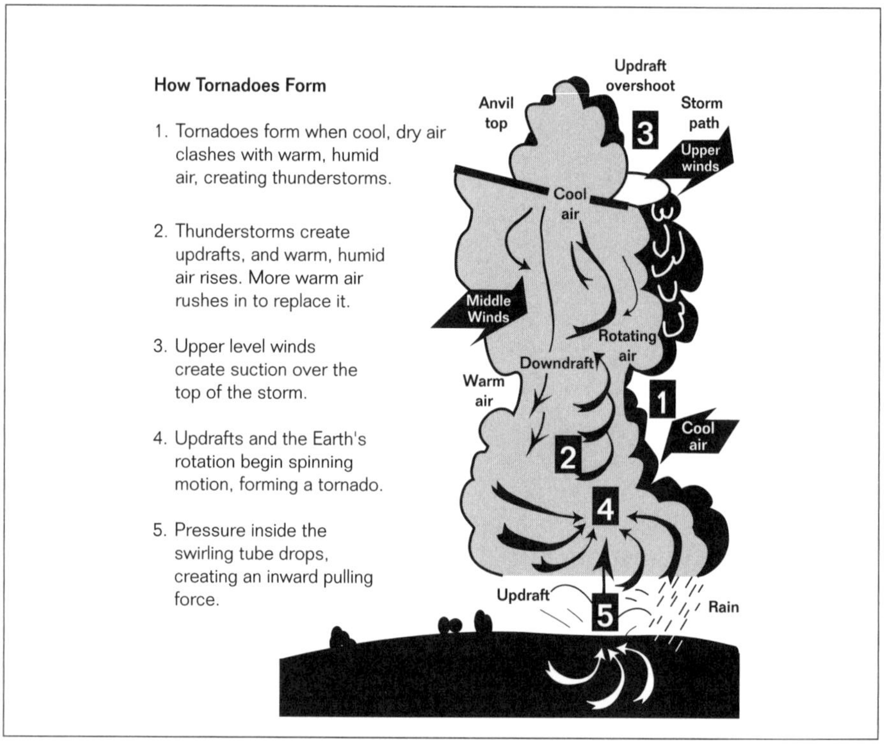

Adapted with permission from Tribune Media Services.

As with hurricanes, tornadoes can be classified based on wind speed and the destruction they cause. One classification is the **Fujita scale**. Its approach to measuring tornadoes by evaluating the damage they cause is similar in approach to the Beaufort scale. The Fujita scale is shown in Exhibit 5-8. The National Weather Service uses a similar approach that classifies tornadoes as follows:

- *Weak*. Weak tornadoes include about 69 percent of all tornadoes, cause less than 5 percent of all deaths, usually last one to ten minutes, and have winds of less than 110 mph.

Exhibit 5-8
Fujita Scale

Fujita Scale Classification of Tornadoes, Based on Damage

(F0) Light Damage 40–72 mph

This speed range corresponds to Beaufort 9 through 11. Some damage to chimneys or TV antennae; tree branches broken; shallow-rooted trees pushed over; old trees with hollow insides broken or pushed over; sign boards damaged.

(F1) Moderate Damage 73–112 mph

73 mph is the beginning of hurricane wind speed or Beaufort 12. Surfaces peeled off roofs; windows broken; trailer houses pushed or overturned; trees on soft ground uprooted; some trees snapped; moving autos pushed off the road.

(F2) Considerable Damage 113–157 mph

Roof torn off frame house leaving strong upright walls standing; weak structures or outbuildings demolished; trailer houses demolished; railroad boxcars pushed over; large trees snapped or uprooted; light-object missiles generated; cars blown off highway; block structures and walls badly damaged.

(F3) Severe Damage 158–206 mph

Roofs and some walls torn off well-constructed frame houses; some rural buildings completely demolished or flattened; trains overturned; steel framed hangar-warehouse-type structures torn; cars lifted off the ground and may roll some distance; most trees in a forest uprooted, snapped, or leveled; block structures often leveled.

(F4) Devastating Damage 207–260 mph

Well-constructed frame houses leveled, leaving piles of debris; structures with weak foundation lifted, torn, and blown off some distance; trees debarked by small flying debris; sand and soil eroded and gravel airborne in high winds; cars thrown some distances or rolled considerable distances finally to disintegrate; large missiles generated.

(F5) Incredible Damage 261–318 mph

Strong frame houses lifted clear off foundation and carried considerable distance to disintegrate; steel-reinforced concrete structures badly damaged; automobile-sized missiles carried a distance of 100 yds. or more; trees debarked completely; incredible phenomena can occur.

- *Strong.* Strong tornadoes include about 29 percent of all tornadoes, cause nearly 30 percent of all deaths, can last twenty minutes or longer, and have winds from 110 to 205 mph.
- *Violent.* Violent tornadoes include only 2 percent of all tornadoes, cause 70 percent of deaths, can last longer than an hour, and have winds faster than 205 mph.

Incidence of Tornadoes

Tornadoes occur worldwide, but most often in the United States. No part of the country is immune, but the Midwest and Southeast suffer the most tornado damage. Exhibit 5-9 illustrates the distribution of tornado activity across the United States in 1995. As shown in Exhibit 5-10, tornadoes occur year-round but exhibit a seasonal pattern with a peak in the spring. Beginning in March, the peak moves from the southern coastal states through the southern Plains states into the northern Plains states and Great Lakes area. Incidence declines from June to its lowest point in December. The appearance of tornadoes is random and completely unpredictable.

Tornado Damage

Tornadoes are destructive because of their compact size, powerful winds, and upward movement. Tornadoes produce winds that can exceed any reasonable design load. They batter a structure when wind velocity and direction change rapidly. Upward lift from these storms puts stresses on a structure that make it difficult for the structure to withstand destruction. Tornadoes commonly lift cars and heavy farm machinery from the ground and deposit the remains miles away. The most common effect of tornadoes is total destruction of any property lying directly in their path. Substantial buildings and property at the edge of a tornado's path might escape without serious structural damage. Property close to the path can sustain minor-to-severe damage. Underwriters can do little to limit the damage tornadoes inflict on individual risks.

Hail

Another product of unsettled weather is **hail**, which is small, rounded ice pellets that can often form during thunderstorms. Like tornadoes, hailstorms occur throughout the country and follow a seasonal pattern. They are also as unpredictable as tornadoes. Fortunately, damage from hail is typically much less severe than damage from tornadoes. Hail can devastate growing crops but rarely causes catastrophic damage to structures or personal property left in the

Exhibit 5-9
Total Number of Tornadoes—1995

Adapted with permission from *The Fact Book 1997: Property/Casualty Insurance Facts* (New York, NY: Insurance Information Institute, 1997), pp. 80-81.

Exhibit 5-10
Number of Tornadoes per Month, 1995

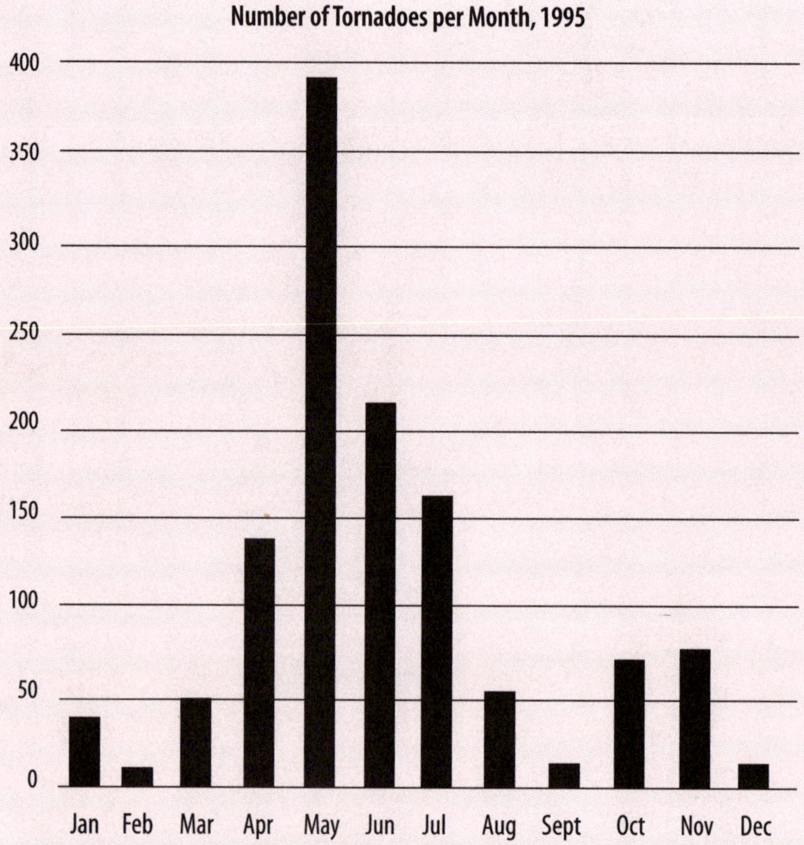

Sources: National Climatic Data Center; National Environmental Satellite, Data, and Information Service; National Oceanic and Atmospheric Administration (NOAA); and U.S. Department of Commerce.

The Fact Book 1997: Property/Casualty Insurance Facts (New York, NY: Insurance Information Institute, 1997), p. 81.

open. Roofing materials, aluminum siding, and automobiles are particularly susceptible to hail damage. Buildings with unique architectural details, such as historic buildings with copper or tin roofs and elaborate trim, can sustain severe damage. Although hailstorms are usually limited in geographic scope, some storms cause widespread damage and often account for part of the losses caused by winter storms.

Riot and Civil Commotion

Riot and civil commotion include any disruption of public order. Because riot is a crime, its definition depends on the penal code and the distinction between the two causes of loss varies by state. Property insurance covers both causes of loss. Riot losses usually result from fire and looting. Simple risk management procedures can be effective in controlling both.

The Effect of State and Federal Laws

Underwriters once used a very effective tool for limiting riot losses. They simply refused coverage in areas in which civil unrest seemed likely. This practice was termed "**redlining**" because the subject areas were outlined in red on maps. In the 1960s, riots swept major American cities, and many property owners whose property was located within the red lines had no insurance coverage. Consequently, an insurance "crisis" was declared to exist in inner-city areas. To preclude recurrence of such a situation, all states now prohibit redlining.

States define redlining as refusal to write or renew policies solely because of neighborhood, a factor called the "environmental hazard." A United States District Court in Milwaukee also held that redlining by insurers violates the Fair Housing Act.[15] The federal Department of Housing and Urban Development (HUD) is drafting regulations for providing equal access to insurance under the act's provisions. Congress has also shown an interest and in 1994 passed a law to require insurers to report their writings by ZIP Code. The law's intent is to identify areas in which redlining might be occurring.

Underwriting the Inner City

Underwriters can look for several signs that an individual risk is resistant to riot losses. The ability of automatic fire sprinkler systems to suppress fire unaided can be especially important during a civil disturbance, when fire service response might be late or absent. Premises security also plays a role in limiting losses during a riot. Given a choice, rioters choose relatively easy targets. Locks, fences, and gates can help control losses, but they lose their effectiveness as a riot becomes more severe. The more unruly the crowd, the more apt it is to tear down gates or smash through doors.

Pricing

Pricing is another tool for managing riot exposures. Inner-city accounts need not be unprofitable. Discretionary rating plans, like the individual risk premium modification (IRPM) plan, allow the premium to be adjusted for factors that the standard rate does not fully reflect. The fire station serving the insured premises might answer thirty to sixty alarms in a typical twenty-four-hour period. Standard rates assume the same public protection as another station in the same city that answers six to ten alarms within that time. Alarm frequency and the demands this frequency places on fire services is a legitimate basis for pricing the two accounts differently.

The use of discretionary rating plans requires additional attention to detail by underwriters. Those plans modify rates for essentially similar risks, a practice that might be perceived as unfair price discrimination. The application of debits and credits can keep these plans from being unfairly discriminatory. Debits or credits reflect subjective judgment, but they must be subject to objective analysis. A credit for superior housekeeping, for example, would be contradicted by an inspection that discloses large piles of uncollected trash in the loading bay. The use of discretionary rating plans also requires documentation. Information in the file must be well documented and support the underwriting decision. Through market conduct examinations, state insurance regulators investigate insurer files to ensure that all eligible accounts were included in discretionary rating plans.

Managing a Book of Business

Riot losses might be inevitable, but a catastrophic or even an unfavorable effect on underwriting results is not. Like windstorm, riot does not affect only a single account. A single occurrence almost always involves several properties separately insured by the same insurer. Such a loss situation poses a problem that goes beyond the scope of individual risk assessment. Underwriting management must monitor the book of business and hold aggregate values at risk in a single riot to an acceptable level. Management must decide exactly how large a loss it is able and willing to insure. The decision reflects management's own values.

Sinkhole Collapse

Collapse of sinkholes is a relatively new insured cause of loss. Underwriters are fortunate that sinkhole losses are infrequent. Lack of accessible information makes this coverage one of the hardest to analyze. **Sinkholes** are cavities in the ground that occur in certain parts of the country where underground rivers and streams have carved channels out of solid limestone bedrock. The walls of these caverns can become relatively weak over time. Over the centuries, they have relied on the water that fills them to distribute and support the weight of their own roofs and the earth's crust above them. They will eventually collapse from continuing erosion, but that could take millions of years.

Population growth has increased demands for water, permanently lowering the water table below the roofs of some caverns. They can collapse without warning, sometimes under no more stress than the weight of the earth's crust over them. Evaluating this exposure requires a sound knowledge of local topography and demographic trends. A local geologist might possess this specialized knowledge, but commercial underwriters are likely to be aware of sinkhole activity only after a loss has occurred or the occurrence of a sinkhole has been publicized.

Sinkholes can cause extensive and irreparable damage, as evidenced by destruction of the Corporate Plaza building in Allentown, Pennsylvania. The initial evidence that the area had a sinkhole problem arose when two city reservoirs abruptly dropped several feet and water mains broke in the vicinity of the building.[16] A sinkhole opened on February 23, 1994, under one of Allentown's newest office buildings. The twenty-foot deep and twenty-foot wide sinkhole swallowed a portion of the building and destabilized the remainder. Three-and-a-half weeks later, a demolition crew razed the seven-story, $9.5 million building by means of an implosion.

The damage caused by **mine subsidence** is similar to that caused when a sinkhole occurs. Mine subsidence occurs when tunnels of mines give way and the collapse affects the surface of the land. For years coverage has been a requirement in states that have extensive underground mining activity. Still, abandoned mine shafts and tunnels are not always easy to locate. Many of those sites were never mapped accurately. For example, a ground collapse in suburban Lyndhurst, New Jersey, within sight of lower Manhattan, threatened to swallow an entire home, after the backyard disappeared overnight.

Volcanic Action

Volcanic action had traditionally been part of the earth movement exclusion. The eruption of Mount St. Helens in 1980 made insurers reconsider that exclusion, and many insurers made ex gratia claims payments for losses stemming from the eruption.

Insurers excluded volcanic eruption because they regarded it as subject to adverse selection. That is, the eruption of a volcano is a local event, and those people who needed coverage the most would be the only ones purchasing it.

The eruption of Mount St. Helens proved how far-reaching the effects of a volcanic eruption can be. Vulcanologists were aware of the heightened volcanic activity, so the mountain was under constant watch. Nevertheless, the buildup of forces that blew off the top of the mountain was not expected. In the explosion, one cubic mile of matter was spread over 232 square miles. The eruption buried 150 miles of fishing rivers and twenty-six lakes and killed an estimated 1 million animals. Volcanic material started landslides and mudflows. A large mudflow traveled twenty-eight miles and blocked shipping channels in the Columbia River.[17]

The eruption spread volcanic ash over a wide area. Residents on the Pacific Coast and in the Northwest had to clean up the ash before it caused more damage.

State insurance regulators expected insurers to pay volcanic action losses and let the insurers as well as the public know it. Some insurance commissioners required coverage after the fact. One regulator assumed coverage under the explosion peril. Insurers took the course of least expense by paying the losses and amended their forms to include volcanic action losses.

Losses From Volcanic Action

Volcanic eruptions, which are discharges from vents in the earth's crust, cause three types of insured losses—lava flow, volcanic ash, and volcanic blast or airborne shock waves. Lava flowing from the volcano is molten rock that is hot enough to destroy anything in its path. Losses from lava occur only in the immediate vicinity of the volcano. The value of exposed property is usually low, but total losses are common. Eruptions also spread an ash cloud over a large area. Volcanic ash is highly abrasive. It can easily remove paint and other finishes from surfaces. Exposed steel, aluminum, and vinyl siding could require total replacement. Ash settles miles away from the eruption center, and its removal is expensive. Direct damage caused by volcanic blast or airborne shock waves is covered. Not covered are the indirect consequences of a volcanic eruption, specifically the cost of cleanup that is unrelated to a direct physical loss or damage to the property.

Underwriting Volcanic Action

The infrequency of loss and catastrophic nature of those losses that do occur make underwriting volcanic action difficult. In active volcanic areas, such as Hawaii, underwriters can assess loss potential. In areas in which volcanoes have long been dormant, property owners and underwriters often underestimate loss potential. Insurers writing property insurance in a state cannot refuse to insure a property because of antiredlining laws. The only practical way for insurers to avoid insuring this exposure is to refrain from writing property insurance in states with volcanoes. An insurer may also have to refrain from writing insurance in adjoining states to avoid covering the collateral damage caused by volcanic dust when eruptions do occur. Until the 1970s, volcanoes were a problem only in Alaska and Hawaii. Since then, long-dormant volcanoes like Mount St. Helens have suddenly sprung back to life and made volcanic action a current concern.

Weight of Ice, Snow, or Sleet

During the winter months, ice, snow, and sleet can accumulate on roofs. They sometimes add more weight than the structure can carry, causing partial or total collapse. Structures in areas that are regularly exposed to extremely cold winters are most susceptible. Cold snaps can also extend deep into the Sun Belt, where the design of roof structures might not provide adequate support for the snow load. Controlling losses requires proper design and good maintenance. Roofs with large, open spans are more likely to collapse under a snow load. In Connecticut, a larger, open span caused the roof of the Hartford Civic Center, a relatively new structure at the time, to collapse under a snowfall that was considered moderate for the area.

Pitched roofs help resolve the problem of ice, snow, and sleet by allowing the structure to shed some of the load. The most significant problem with these designs is the formation of ice dams. Melting snow and ice run down the roof, then freeze near the edge, especially along overhanging eaves. The formation of ice at the roof edge is called an **ice dam** and can prevent the flow of the melting snow load from being shed as intended. Water that cannot be shed can penetrate the roof, thereby damaging interior walls and ceilings.

The best way to control this type of loss is to have good insulation and adequate ventilation under the roof. Taking these precautions prevents the melting of snow and ice along the roof surface, at the bottom of the accumulation. Heat melts snow from the top, and the snow runs off without creating problems. Losses occur when heat escaping from the building melts snow from the bottom, forcing water to flow under built-up snow and ice on the roof. Having insulation above the top-floor ceiling limits the amount of heat that escapes from the interior. Ventilation disperses the heat before it can cause melting. This approach keeps the underside of the roof cold, limiting snow melt to the top of the built-up snow and ice. Additionally, there are water-resistant building materials designed to go under the lower courses of shingles near the gutters. This loss control measure can be implemented only when the roof is being built or replaced.

Flat roofs demand another approach. Insulation and ventilation can help, but water can soak through packed snow to the roof and accumulate in low areas, a condition known as ponding. Ponding concentrates weight unevenly. Uneven weight distribution can collapse one area of the roof even though the entire roof structure could bear the snow load. Flat roofs cannot shed part of the snow load, as pitched roofs can. Packed snow and ice block roof drains, keeping melted snow from running off. Repeated or heavy snowfall can make removing some of the accumulation the only way to prevent damage. Removal requires access to the roof so that the accumulation can be dealt with. Placing ladders on snowy ground is not safe, so roof access from the interior is necessary. Snow accumulation can block hatches and doors that open outward. Stairs leading to an inward-opening door provide the most effective access.

Flood

Flooding is a common event in many areas of the United States, recurring at regular intervals. Some locations flood every year, but others face no known flood hazards. Floods result from an area's receiving greater precipitation than the land can drain off, and sometimes they seem to occur unpredictably. The spring of 1997 brought flooding to Grand Forks, North Dakota, when the Red River—swollen by melting snow and a spring snowstorm—overflowed its banks. This flood caught property owners by surprise because theirs was not an area known for flooding.

Seven types of flood are common:

1. Riverine floods occur when rivers, streams, and other watercourses rise and overflow their banks. They result from either heavy rainfall or snow melt upstream in their drainage basins.
2. Tidal floods result from high tides, frequently driven by high winds offshore, and from tropical storms making landfall or passing close offshore. They affect bays and the portions of rivers along the coast.
3. Wind floods can happen whenever a strong wind holds back part of a large body of water from its normal drainage course and raises the water level. Back bays behind barrier islands are especially susceptible to wind floods. Water that cannot escape through normal channels can flow out of these bays across the barrier islands. During the winter of 1992-93, wind floods occurred repeatedly along the New Jersey shore.
4. Rising water levels downstream might prevent drainage upstream, causing a backwater flood. Backwater floods can extend for a substantial distance upstream.

5. Ice jams sometimes develop as ice thaws and begins to move downstream. They block the flow of water, causing it to back up and flood upstream areas. If the ice jam breaks suddenly, it can cause flooding downstream.
6. Accidental floods are caused by the failure of flood control systems. A dam, levee, wall, or dike might break and cause flooding downstream. Blocked floodgates and spillways cause upstream flooding.
7. Man-made topographic changes can also cause floods. For example, instead of being absorbed into the soil, rain water can accumulate on concrete and asphalt parking lots. If storm sewer drains have inadequate capacity or are blocked, water can build up and flood adjacent properties.

Measuring Flood Exposures

The U.S. Army Corps of Engineers has engaged in flood control activities for more than 125 years. Between the Mexican and Civil Wars, Col. Robert E. Lee designed and built a levee system to protect St. Louis from Mississippi River flooding. As part of the National Flood Insurance Program, the Corps has mapped areas throughout the country that are known to be subject to flooding. The National Flood Insurance Program makes the Corps's flood maps available to insurers at a reasonable price. A sample flood map appears in Exhibit 5-11. These maps divide the area into the following three zones, according to their susceptibility to flooding:

1. Zone A includes all land within the boundary of a 100-year flood, that is, areas that could possibly have a flood once every 100 years. Within Zone A, the maps mark the boundaries of the annual, five-, ten-, and fifty-year floods. In some cases, the boundaries are precise enough to identify individual properties protected by elevation.
2. Zone B falls outside the 100-year flood boundary but within the boundary of the 500-year flood.
3. Zone C designates the area exposed to minimal flood potential. The Corps sometimes refers to Zone C as an area with no known flood hazard.

Protecting Exposed Property From Flood

Not building in flood plains is the most effective way of controlling losses. Owners of property in identified flood plains can, however, take steps to protect their property. Walls and dikes can prevent floodwaters from reaching exposed property. Building strong walls and anchoring structures firmly to their foundations prevent floods from sweeping structures away. Tying down fuel tanks keeps them from floating away. Disaster planning can also be effective. During the 1992 Mississippi River floods, the owners of a carpet store

Exhibit 5-11

Flood Insurance Rate Map—Township of Willistown, Chester County, Pennsylvania

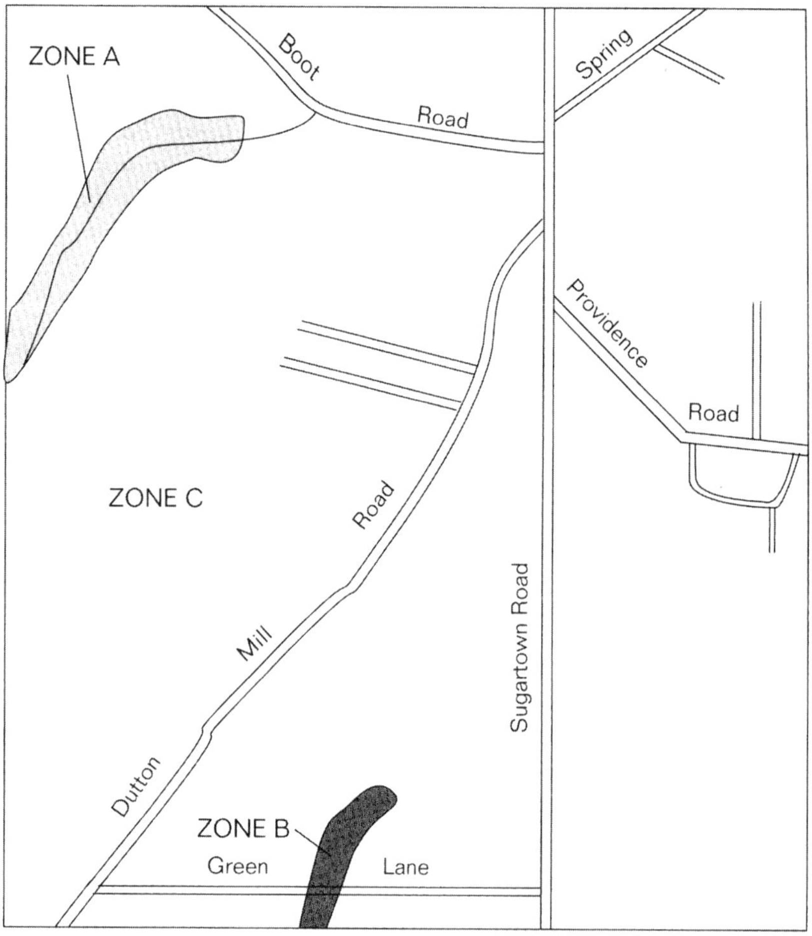

A = Areas of 100-year flood; base flood elevations and flood hazard factors not determined (light shading).

B = Areas between limits of the 100-year flood and 500-year flood; or certain areas subject to 100-year flooding with average depths less than one (1) foot or where the contributing drainage area is less than one square mile; or areas protected by levees from the base flood (medium shading).

C = Areas of minimal flooding (no shading).

Adapted from Federal Emergency Management Agency, Federal Insurance Administration.

in Des Moines, Iowa, protected their property with sandbags. When the waters receded, their stock was in great demand.

Underwriting Flood Insurance

Hazard analysis and risk selection are only part of underwriting flood insurance. Underwriters must also determine the extent of coverage they are willing to provide and the price at which they will offer it. The National Flood Insurance Program provides up to $10,000 of subsidized insurance to eligible property owners. That program offers additional insurance at actuarially determined rates. Underwriters use those rates to price flood insurance, recognizing that rates need adjustment because administrative costs might differ. Rates should allow for investment income and profit. Insurers are not required to adopt the National Flood Insurance Program's rates. They can use those published rates as a basis for their own rates and an indication of the competitive climate.

Earthquake

Although earthquakes occur throughout the United States, destructive seismic events affect only a few areas. More earthquakes strike Alaska than any other state, but the exposure is most severe in California, where exposed values are highest. The most severe earthquake recorded in the United States occurred in 1814 along the New Madrid Fault, in wilderness that became Tennessee and Kentucky. It changed the course of the Mississippi River and rang church bells as far away as Boston but caused little damage. Virtually no structures lay exposed to the earthquake at that time, but that is no longer the case. A recurrence of that event today would virtually destroy the city of Memphis. Some experts postulate that the public is totally unprepared for a devastating earthquake, which is inevitable. Exhibit 5-12 charts seismic potential for the continental United States.

Measuring Earthquakes

Seismologists measure earthquake by either magnitude or intensity. The Richter scale measures the magnitude of an earthquake by the total amount of energy it releases. It uses wave amplitude recorded on seismographs. The Richter scale measures energy release logarithmically; that is, each unit scale represents the release of ten times the energy of the next lower unit. A magnitude 6 is 10 times as powerful as a magnitude 5, 100 times as strong as a magnitude 4, and so on. There is no upper limit to the Richter scale, as shown in Exhibit 5-13. The most powerful earthquake in the United States was recorded as 9.2 on the Richter scale, as shown in Exhibit 5-14.

Exhibit 5-12
Seismic Potential for the Continental United States

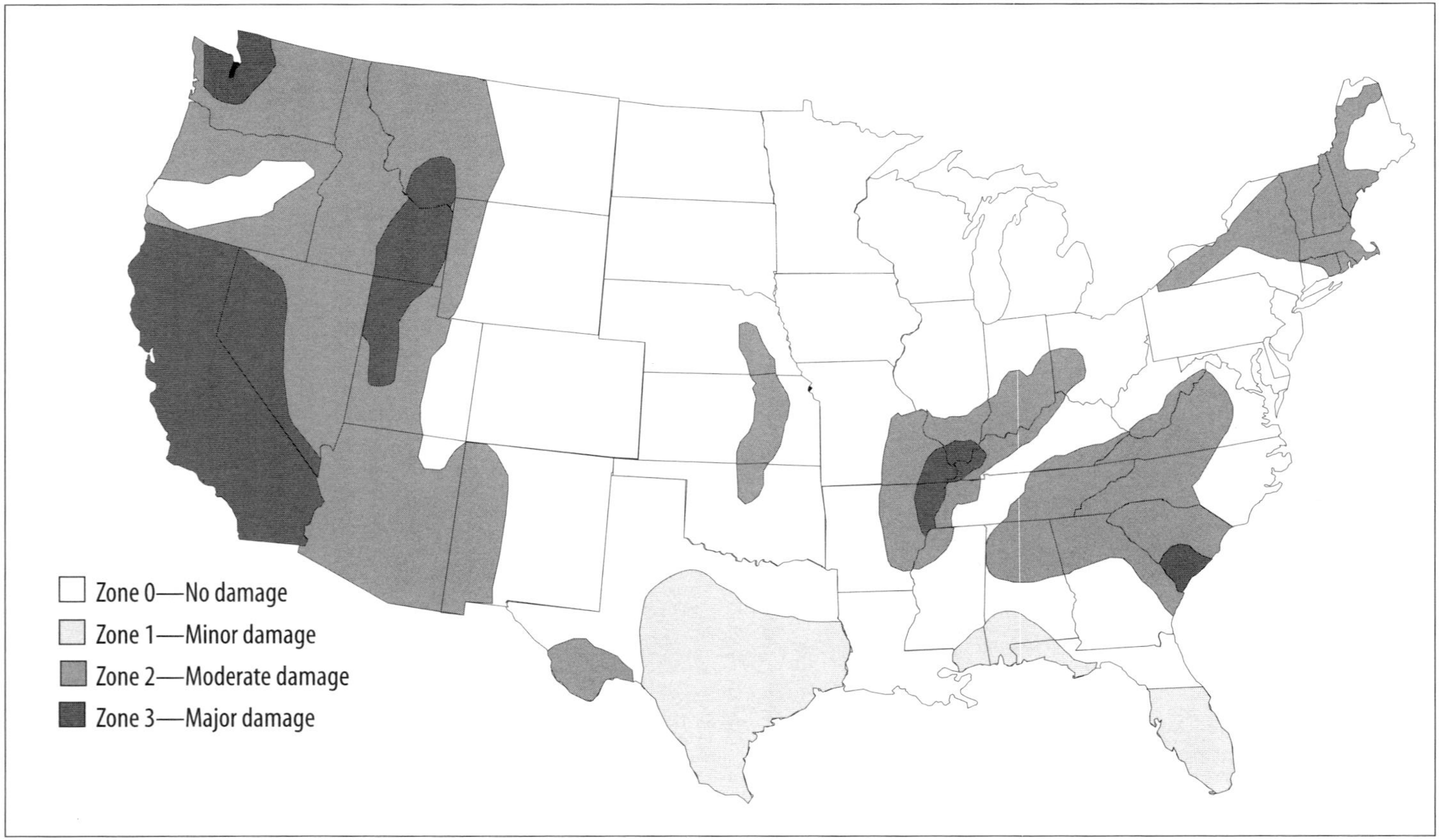

Source: John P. Drennan, *Contingencies,* January/February 1994, p. 55.

Exhibit 5-13
Earthquake Severity Measurement—Richter Scale

Richter Magnitudes	Earthquake Effects
Less than 3.5	Generally not felt, but recorded.
3.5–5.4	Often felt, but only minor damage.
5.5–6.0	Slight damage to buildings.
6.1–6.9	Can be destructive in areas where people live.
7.0–7.9	Major earthquake. Causes serious damage.
8 or greater	Great earthquake. Total destruction to nearby communities.

Source: C.W. Stover and J.L. Coffman, Seismicity of the United States, 1568-1989 (Revised), U.S. Geological Survey Prof. Paper 1527, 1993. Homepage of United States Geogogical Survey, http://wwwneic.cr.usgs.gov/neis/eqlists/bigten.html

Exhibit 5-14
Largest Earthquakes

The Ten Largest Earthquakes in the United States

	Magnitude	Date	Location
1.	9.2	March 28, 1964	Prince William Sound, Alaska
2.	8.8	March 9, 1957	Andreanof Islands, Alaska
3.	8.7	February 4, 1965	Rat Islands, Alaska
4.	8.3	November 10, 1938	East of Shumagin Islands, Alaska
	8.3	July 10, 1958	Lituya Bay, Alaska
6.	8.2	September 10, 1899	Yakutat Bay, Alaska
	8.2	September 4, 1899	near Cape Yakataga, Alaska
8.	8.0	May 7, 1986	Andreanof Islands, Alaska
9.	7.9	February 7, 1812	New Madrid, Missouri
	7.9	January 9, 1857	Fort Tejon, California
	7.9	April 3, 1868	Ka'u District, Island of Hawaii
	7.9	October 9, 1900	Kodiak Island, Alaska
	7.9	November 30, 1987	Gulf of Alaska

The Ten Largest Earthquakes in the Contiguous United States

	Magnitude	Date	Location
1.	7.9	February 7, 1812	New Madrid, Missouri
	7.9	January 9, 1857	Fort Tejon, California
3.	7.8	March 26, 1872	Owens Valley, California
	7.8	February 24, 1892	Imperial Valley, California
5.	7.7	December 16, 1811	New Madrid, Missouri
	7.7	April 18, 1906	San Francisco, California
	7.7	October 3, 1915	Pleasant Valley, Nevada
8.	7.6	January 23, 1812	New Madrid, Missouri

Continued on next page

	Magnitude	Date	Location
9.	7.5	July 21, 1952	Kern County, California
10.	7.3	November 4, 1927	west of Lompoc, California
	7.3	December 16, 1954	Dixie Valley, Nevada
	7.3	August 18, 1959	Hebgen Lake, Montana
	7.3	October 28, 1983	Borah Peak, Idaho

Note: Widely differing magnitudes have been computed for some of these earthquakes; the values differ according to the methods and data used. For example, some sources list the magnitude of the 8.7 Rat Islands earthquake as low as 7.7. On the other hand, some sources list the magnitude of the February 7, 1812, New Madrid quake as high as 8.8. Similar variations exist for most events on this list, although generally not so large as for the examples given.

In general, the magnitudes given in the list above have been determined from the seismic moment, when available. For very large earthquakes, the moment magnitude is considered to be a more accurate determination than the traditional amplitude magnitude computation procedures. Note that all of these values can be called "magnitudes on the Richter scale," regardless of the method used to compute them.

Source: C.W. Stover and J.L. Coffman, Seismicity of the United States, 1568-1989 (Revised), U.S. Geological Survey Prof. Paper 1527, 1993. Homepage of United States Geogogical Survey, http://wwwneic.cr.usgs.gov/neis/eqlists/bigten.html

The Modified Mercalli scale measures intensity, the damage that an earthquake causes to people, property, and the surface of the earth. It uses human observation, which is subjective and which could make it imprecise. Engineers, geologists, seismologists, and similar specialists now inspect all earthquake sites. They produce accurate and uniform estimates. Its accuracy and consistency make the Modified Mercalli scale a good tool for underwriters. The United States Geological Service (USGS) has used the scale since its introduction in 1931, and it is now used worldwide. Exhibit 5-15 reproduces the Modified Mercalli scale.

Damage From Earthquakes

Earthquakes occur along fault lines, where plates of the earth's surface adjoin one another. The **focus** of an earthquake is the point on the fault line at which movement of the plates begins. Its **epicenter** is the point on the surface directly above the focus. Distance from the epicenter, soil composition, and building construction all play major roles in determining the extent of damage caused by an earthquake.

Exhibit 5-15
Earthquake Severity Measurement—Modified Mercalli Intensity Scale

Modified Mercalli Intensity Scale

Intensity value	Description
I	Not felt except by a very few under especially favorable circumstances.
II	Felt only by a few persons at rest, especially on upper floors of buildings. Suspended objects may swing.
III	Felt quite noticeably indoors, especially on upper floors of buildings, but many people do not recognize it as an earthquake. Standing automobiles may rock. Vibrations like those from a passing truck.
IV	During the day felt indoors by many, outdoors by few. At night some awakened. Dishes, windows, doors rattle; wall may make creaking sound. Hanging objects swing noticeably. Sensation like heavy trucks striking building. Standing automobiles rocked noticeably.
V	Felt by nearly everyone, many awakened, a direction can be estimated. Some dishes, windows, etc., broken; cracked plaster in a few places; unstable objects overturned. Disturbances of trees, poles, and other tall objects sometimes noticed. Pendulum clocks may stop.
VI	Felt by all, many frightened and run outdoors. Persons walk unsteadily. Windows, dishes, and glassware broken; knickknacks, books, etc., off shelves; pictures knocked off walls. Church bells may ring. Some heavy furniture moved; a few instances of fallen plaster and damaged chimneys. Damage slight.
VII	Difficult to stand. Everyone runs outdoors. Hanging objects quiver. Waves on ponds, water turbid with mud. Small landslides. Damage negligible in buildings of good design and construction; slight to moderate in well-built ordinary structures; considerable in poorly built or badly designed structures; some chimneys broken at roof line. Noticed by persons driving cars.
VIII	Damage slight in specially designed structures; considerable in ordinary, substantial buildings with partial collapse; great in poorly built structures. Framed houses moved on foundations if not bolted down. Panel walls thrown out of frame structures. Fall of chimneys, factory stacks, columns, monuments, walls, towers, and elevated tanks. Heavy furniture overturned. Sand and mud ejected in small amounts. Changes in well water. Steering of cars affected.
IX	General panic. Damage is considerable in specially designed structures; well-designed frame structures thrown out of plumb; great damage in substantial buildings, with partial collapse. Buildings shifted off foundations. Ground cracked conspicuously. Underground pipes broken. Serious damage to reservoirs.
X	Some well-built wooden structures destroyed; most masonry and framed structures destroyed with foundations; ground badly cracked. Rails bent. Landslides considerable from river banks and steep slopes. Shifted sand and mud. Water splashed, slopped over bank.
XI	Few, if any, (masonry) structures remain standing. Bridges destroyed. Broad fissures in ground. Underground pipelines completely out of service. Earth slumps and land slips in soft ground. Rails bent greatly.
XII	Damage nearly total. Large rock masses displaced. Waves seen on the ground surface. Lines of sight and level distorted. Objects thrown into the air.

Distance

The force of an earthquake travels in waves emanating from the epicenter. The force of waves dissipates as the distance from the epicenter increases. The closer a building is to the epicenter of an earthquake, the more damage it will sustain, all other factors being equal. If two similar buildings stand on soil of similar composition, the one nearer the epicenter will sustain the heavier damage. Damage does not, however, always decrease as the distance from the epicenter increases. Buildings less resistant to earthquake forces might sustain more damage than stronger structures closer to the epicenter. The same is true of a comparison between similar buildings, one on loose soil and the other on firm ground but closer to the epicenter.

Soil Composition

The composition of the soil modifies the extent of earthquake damage. The force of an earthquake vibrates through the ground in the form of seismic waves. Bedrock can withstand these waves and reduces their amplitude. Loose soil magnifies wave intensity. A foundation resting on bedrock subjects a building to lower earthquake forces than a foundation on loose soil. Unconsolidated soil becomes subject to liquefaction under seismic stress; that is, the soil's consistency becomes similar to that of gelatin. Loose soil is found in landfills and where water tables are high. San Francisco's Marina District stands on landfill where the city disposed of debris from its 1906 earthquake. It was the scene of the heaviest damage sustained by the city during the Loma Prieta earthquake in October 1989. Soil liquefaction was the greatest contributor to these losses.

Construction

Most structures are designed to carry a vertical load: the weight of the structure and its contents. Earthquake subjects these structures to horizontal stress not planned for in their design. Under extreme conditions, walls and columns simply move out from under floors above them whose vertical load they should carry. On December 7, 1988, a 6.8 magnitude earthquake struck Soviet Armenia, flattening entire cities, claiming 25,000 lives, and leaving more than 500,000 homeless. Outward movement of lower-story walls from under the upper floors they supported was a major cause of damage. Soviet builders used poor construction methods to erect high- and medium-rise buildings and relied on gravity to keep the buildings upright. They made no attempt to tie floors to their vertical supports. Collapse of the Nimitz Freeway in Oakland, California, during the 1989 Loma Prieta earthquake resulted from similar construction. Different types of construction respond differently to seismic stress. Research suggests that buildings of four to six stories are at the greatest risk of damage, all else being equal, because of the seismic wave action. Also, buildings with lower levels used for parking fare even worse during earthquakes.

Frame

Properly built frame structures of up to two stories can adequately resist an earthquake. They have a strong propensity to flex and absorb shock without sustaining major damage. Builders must tie the load-bearing vertical members to the foundation. Otherwise, the entire structure will slip off the foundation during an earthquake. Wall members need firm bracing with diagonal braces or plywood sheathing. Plate glass cracks, plaster and stucco crack, and masonry veneer and chimneys might fall, but a frame building has a good chance of escaping major structural damage in an earthquake.

Masonry

Unreinforced masonry structures have little resistance to seismic force. The walls carry the vertical load without additional support. Modern mortar, made of portland cement, lime, and sand, loses its bonding ability under lateral stress. Older sand and lime mortar mixes fail even more easily. California has developed standards for effectively reinforcing ordinary masonry construction. Its statewide seismic building code incorporates these techniques.

Reinforced Concrete

Monolithic structures of reinforced poured concrete have the greatest potential for resistance to seismic stress. With proper design, they should sustain only minimal damage. However, "tilt-up" structures and structures made of precast concrete do not have the same resistance. Too often, builders do not anchor floors and tilted-up walls securely enough to poured-in-place concrete columns. Buildings in Soviet Armenia were constructed primarily of precast concrete, as was the Nimitz Freeway.

Physical Features

Underwriters must also consider the effect of the following building features on seismic resistance:

- *Shape*. Regular shape is an advantage in resisting lateral force. Square buildings fare best in an earthquake. Irregularly shaped buildings, such as those with an L or T shape, do not fare as well. Structurally separating the wings improves resistance. Long, narrow structures with rigid box-type bracing are especially susceptible to seismic force.

- *Area*. Buildings with large open areas respond poorly to the force of an earthquake. Their roof decks are frequently too flexible for their relatively rigid walls. Single-story warehouses often have large undivided areas.
- *Ornamentation*. Rigid veneers, like marble, tend to fall off flexible building walls.
- *Partition walls*. Although the trend in many office occupancies is away from individual offices, many businesses choose to divide an open area into individual offices. The greater the number of subdivisions, the greater the cost of repair if they should be damaged. In addition, the material used in partition walls varies, and some materials are more susceptible to damage than others.
- *Overhanging exposures of exposing buildings*. If adjacent buildings are taller than the insured structure, portions of the exposing building might fall during an earthquake, causing serious damage to the insured structure.
- *Pounding*. Adjacent buildings vibrate at different rates during an earthquake. They might strike each other, an event called pounding. Pounding of high-rise structures caused substantial damage during the Mexico City earthquake in September 1985.
- *Unrepaired earthquake damage*. Failure to repair damage from previous earthquakes impairs a structure's ability to withstand subsequent seismic forces. This future failure accounts for the frequency with which damaged structures collapse during a relatively minor aftershock.

High-Rise Construction

Until recently, high-rise construction over twenty-five stories was notable by its absence from areas of high seismic activity. Both steel and reinforced concrete frame structures have proved their ability to withstand earthquakes. They have adequately resisted the force of major earthquakes in California. Their ability to endure lies in special foundations that allow the building to move laterally as a unit.

Considerations for Underwriting Earthquakes

Even though seismologists cannot predict when earthquakes will occur, a great deal can be done to limit the damage they cause. California has adopted adequate seismic construction codes, but other areas of the country have not responded as well to the threat of earthquake. The Ramapo Fault is the most active fault on the East Coast. It crosses the Hudson River at Indian Point in New York State less than fifty miles north of Times Square in Manhattan. The location of the Ramapo Fault and the level of seismic activity along it have been known for generations, yet the New York Power Authority occupies Indian Point as an electric generating station with three nuclear reactors. Likewise, the V.C. Summer nuclear plant in Parr, South Carolina, was built very close to an earthquake fault. Both these instances illustrate how government and the public can disregard the potential severity of some exposures, like earthquake, when the frequency of their occurrence is extremely low.

Seismic Resistance

Earthquake underwriters should study California's seismic construction code and use it as an underwriting standard in areas prone to earthquakes. In some areas, wind codes have the same beneficial effects on frame construction. Wind and earthquake both exert lateral force on a structure. Fire-resistive structures with steel or reinforced concrete frames possess strong seismic-resistance properties.

Deductibles

A large proportion of damage in an earthquake amounts to less than 5 percent of the *value* of the insured property. This fact suggests that a relatively modest deductible can control losses paid by insurers. Standard property coverage forms express the deductible as a stated dollar amount. The causes of loss—earthquake form uses a percentage deductible that is applied to the value of the property, not to the limit of insurance. This deductible approach is designed to encourage insureds to buy a coverage amount close to the value of the property. When an earthquake occurs, underinsured policyholders are penalized by the operation of the earthquake deductible. Inadequate coverage reduces what can be recovered under the policy because of the operation of the deductible.

Explosion

Explosion is any violent expansion of gases into the atmosphere. The most common types of explosion are combustion explosions (ignition of flammable clouds) and pressure explosions (rupture of confined spaces).

Combustion Explosions

A **combustion explosion** occurs when a flammable cloud reaches an ignition source. Such clouds can consist of dust, vapor, or mist.

Combustion explosions are often classified as either deflagration or detonation, depending on the speed of the explosion. A **deflagration** is combustion that proceeds at a velocity slower than the speed of sound. Heat spreads through the material by convection, radiation, and conduction. A **detonation** is a combustion that proceeds at a rate greater than the speed of sound. The velocity of this reaction produces a shock wave similar to that of a sonic boom. This wave assists in spreading the reaction by heat compression. As the ambient pressure increases, the self-ignition point of any substance decreases.

Both types of combustion explosion are highly destructive. Detonations produce a shock wave that contributes to the overall damage, and they are much more severe than deflagrations. Clouds of gas or dust and decomposition of unstable materials (including high explosives) produce detonations. Gases, dust, mist, and low explosives (like black powder) generate deflagrations.

Dust Explosions

Dust is a common byproduct of industrial operations. Dust is any finely divided solid material. It becomes airborne easily because of its small size and the relatively light weight of its particles. Eventually, airborne dust succumbs to gravity and settles on any available surface. Almost any form of dust can become flammable.

When dust is airborne, it can achieve a combustible mixture with air that will ignite easily. The result is a deflagration occurring usually in at least two stages. The primary (or initial) explosion is typically small and causes little damage. It might only dislodge dust accumulated on surfaces, or it might breach collection systems to release additional dust, producing a larger cloud. The residual heat from the primary deflagration is often sufficient to immediately trigger a more severe secondary explosion. If ambient heat does not initiate the chain reaction, conditions that caused the primary explosion will probably prevail. Either way, the result could be catastrophic.

Grain elevators and storage facilities are good examples of risks with high potential to generate dust. The heat source can be as minimal as the friction from pulleys and belts that are used throughout the facilities.

Vapor Explosions

Vapors develop on the surface of flammable liquids. Vapors are almost always heavier than air, and they sink and travel along the floor. Over time, even a small leak can produce a sufficient concentration of combustible vapor. Furnaces, switching equipment, and other devices that can generate a spark are potential ignition sources typically found in these low areas.

Flammable gas in the atmosphere generally originates in leaks. Gas pipes and cylinders might leak because of improper installation, corrosion, or poor maintenance. Connections, joints, and valves are frequent sites of leaks. The flammable mist can eventually saturate the atmosphere and condense. When combined with air behind walls, the gas escaping from concealed lines can produce a burnable mix that might be difficult or impossible to detect. Malfunctioning equipment can vent fuel accidentally, creating another source of flammable mist.

Flammable mists occur when droplets of liquid are suspended in the air. Small leaks in pipes, fittings, and containers under pressure can produce an atomizing spray. The mist can eventually saturate the air and condense, thus forming a flammable liquid. Changes in temperature and humidity can create a flammable mist.

Storing a flammable liquid or gas under pressure creates the possibility of a boiling liquid-expanding vapor explosion (BLEVE). This type of explosion may originate as either a combustion or pressure vessel explosion, and it is frequently both. Pressure explosions commonly release a cloud of flammable gas that ignites and explodes on reaching an ignition source. This creates a fireball that is characteristic of a BLEVE.

The most common source of a BLEVE is fire that reaches a tank that stores flammable liquid or gas. Heat has two effects, both of which contribute to the initial pressure explosion. As the temperature rises, the contents of the tank expand, increasing the pressure the tank has to contain. At the same time, heat acts to soften the material the tank is made of, reducing its ability to contain pressure. When the tank fails and releases its contents, the secondary combustion explosion is nearly instantaneous. A BLEVE can also start as a combustion explosion when flammable gas or vapor escapes through a leak in the tank itself or fittings connected to the tank. The combustible cloud ignites and detonates at the first contact with a heat source. Cooling the tanks that contain flammable gas or liquid is the most effective means to protect against a BLEVE. The fire service will usually do this as soon as it arrives, but installing spray systems to cool the tanks provides a faster response and frees fire service personnel to attack the fire at its source.

Controlling Potential for Combustion Explosions

Ignition of a combustible cloud requires very little heat. Ordinary conditions suddenly become deadly sources of ignition. Friction that would be unnoticed under other circumstances can trigger a catastrophic explosion. The movement of a conveyor belt, pulley, or mechanical switch can create sufficient friction. The potential for combustion explosions can be controlled, and the damage they cause can be mitigated. Combustion explosions can occur suddenly from almost-ordinary conditions with deadly and destructive effects.

Even so, efforts to control the formation of flammable clouds and ignition sources can be effective and should be implemented.

Preventing combustible clouds from forming is the surest protection against combustion explosions. Fire can occur only when a mixture of fuel and oxygen falls within its flammable range. Two strategies to provide effective protection are as follows:

1. *Limit the supply of fuel.* A lean mixture of air and fuel contains too little fuel to burn. It falls below the lower limit of flammability and will not support combustion. Keeping flammable gas, vapor, and dust out of the atmosphere is the surest way to maintain a lean air-fuel mixture.
2. *Restrict the oxygen supply.* A rich air-fuel mixture will not burn because the concentration of fuel is too high.

Limiting the Supply of Fuel

Processes that employ flammable liquid or gas usually have a mechanism that addresses the potential for accidental discharge. Detection alarms should alert personnel to the presence of flammable gas or vapors. Proper risk management should provide written procedures that include specific instructions for evacuating personnel and shutting down operations until the danger has passed.

Collection and conveyance systems offer the most effective means of controlling dust. They remove particles at the creation point and prevent both airborne dust and hazardous surface accumulations. Although some dust will escape even the best collection systems, there should not be enough to create an airborne dust hazard. Frequent, supplemental cleaning prevents potentially hazardous surface accumulations.

Paint-spraying booths should have ventilating systems that remove flammable vapors. Newer installations integrate spraying, collection, and ventilation into a single system. Electrical equipment used in the vicinity of spray equipment and dip tanks can be a source of ignition and should meet the specifications of NFPA Standard 70 for electrical equipment.

The lack of an operational collection system demands frequent cleaning of dust-prone spaces. Vacuum cleaning is preferable, since sweeping floors and brushing other surfaces can stir up dust. The resulting cloud might constitute a serious explosion hazard.

Some highly flammable dusts are so dangerous that they require special attention. Ordinary vacuum cleaning is ineffective because it might cause an explosion within the cleaning equipment. Safe removal of these substances requires a high-efficiency particulate air (HEPA) vacuum cleaner.

Wetting dust does not effectively control the explosion potential. Although water raises the temperature required for ignition, deflagration releases so much energy that the cooling effect provides inadequate protection.

Release of flammable vapors, gases, or dust to the atmosphere is unavoidable in some processes, but a combustible cloud is not a certain result. A well-designed and carefully maintained ventilation system can reduce atmospheric flammables below combustible levels.

Ventilating systems must release flammable gases and vapors at a safe rate. The outside atmosphere must disperse them without allowing a burnable mixture to form. Venting flammable gases and vapor into the environment solves one problem but has the potential to create another one.

Federal and state environmental regulations limit emissions of many combustible fluids because they are toxic as well as flammable. Systems that remove these gases and vapors must recover them for recycling or disposal as hazardous waste.

Venting dust is never an adequate solution, because it only transfers the problem to another location. Expected frequency and severity of explosion both decrease but generally remain above acceptable levels. Environmental regulations also restrict particle emissions. Ventilating a dust-laden atmos-phere requires dust collection and disposal. NFPA Standard 91 *Exhaust Systems for Air Conveying of Materials* establishes standards for safe design and operation of atmospheric dust-collection systems.

Restricting the Oxygen Supply

Preventing combustion explosions does not end with eliminating a combustible mixture of fuel and air. A sealed inert atmosphere provides the best available protection but is not practical in most industrial operations. More realistic measures permit some dust, gas, or vapor to escape. Small pockets of burnable fuel mixed with air are inevitable, but the minor explosions that these small pockets can produce have a devastating potential. A barely noticeable primary explosion can cause a fire or a catastrophic secondary blast. Severe deflagrations typically begin this way. Eliminating this threat requires special handling of ordinary ignition sources. Electricity and friction are the most common ignition sources. They are easy to overlook and can be difficult to control.

Some processes require releasing flammable gases or vapors. They create an atmosphere that contains levels of air and fuel within the limits of combustibility. Reducing the concentration of fuel to a safe level may be neither possible nor practical. Replacing atmospheric oxygen addresses this problem effectively. The process, called inerting, substitutes an inert gas such as argon or nitrogen for oxygen, creating an asphyxiating environment. An inert atmosphere not only reduces the probability of fire to almost zero; it also requires placing both space and barriers between personnel and hazardous materials. Inerting works best in protecting highly automated processes that require little or no direct human intervention.

Controlling Sources of Ignition

Despite the insured's best efforts, a burnable mixture of combustible gas or vapors could still develop. This possibility makes measures to control sources of ignition an essential element of any program to prevent explosion losses or reduce the damage they cause. Open flames rarely pose a problem because it is so easy to recognize the hazard they create. Electricity poses the most serious threat to a potentially explosive environment. Normal operation of ordinary fixtures and equipment becomes extremely hazardous in the presence of combustible gas, vapors, or dust.

Hazardous environments require explosion-proof electrical equipment. Properly installed, that equipment will not release either sparks or excessive heat. Using any other type of electrical apparatus makes a serious loss almost inevitable.

Static electricity produces small sparks. People or property moving through the air can be an ignition source in a sensitive area. Several measures, such as the following, will minimize static electricity:

- Grounding or bonding all electrical apparatus.
- Using floor materials and coverings that do not conduct electricity.
- Installing ground wires on machinery with moving parts. Conveyors can pose a special problem.
- Requiring nonconductive clothing. The movement of shoes on carpet can create a static shock, particularly during the winter when heating systems have dried the air. Artificial fabrics can also discharge static electricity.
- Increasing humidity levels where practical.

Friction occurs when a moving object comes in contact with another surface. Friction is inherent in machinery operation. In an ordinary atmosphere, friction presents few problems because generating enough heat to initiate combustion requires enormous amounts of friction. Unwanted friction typically results from a mechanical failure. More often than not, the equipment creating the friction fails before it causes a fire.

Potentially explosive environments are different. Friction that would be unnoticed elsewhere might generate enough heat to trigger an explosion. The following protective measures reduce this threat to a manageable level:

- Keeping moving parts well oiled.
- Aligning moving parts properly for smooth movement that does not create friction. Belts, pulleys, and rollers warrant extra care.
- Enforcing a comprehensive preventive maintenance program.
- Giving unusual noises or excessive vibration immediate attention.

These measures are prudent management, and adequate attention to potential losses is necessary in any situation. They attain greater importance only because of the elevated level of hazards.

Limiting Damage Potential of Combustion Explosions

No amount of care and prevention will eliminate all combustion explosions. Businesses that face explosion potentials must recognize this and prepare for the worst. Venting, containment, and isolation provide effective damage control.

Venting

Buildings that house operations prone to explosion often incorporate pressure-relieving design features. Venting minimizes explosion damage in two ways:

1. It relieves pressure on the structure itself, thus allowing it to survive the blast.
2. It directs the force of the explosion away from other property susceptible to damage. This limits the values exposed to a potentially catastrophic loss.

Explosion vents are one common device for protecting the structure in which explosion occurs. These vents are sealed openings in the walls or roof designed to fail and blow outward under explosive pressure. Some explosion vents are panels that serve no other purpose, and others are simply doors or windows.

Some buildings incorporate roofs that act as explosion vents. A deflagration or detonation would move the roof up and out. The entire upper surface of the structure opens, directing the explosion force upward, so that the walls are left standing with minimal damage.

Venting limits the damage to buildings by relieving pressure. Escape of expanding gases drops the internal pressure to a level that the remaining structure can contain.

There are practical limits to the amount of force that explosion vents can dissipate. Although they might control a deflagration or even a minor detonation, they cannot control a severe explosion. A 1983 explosion left the Grucci fireworks factory in suburban Long Island, New York, a total loss. Sophisticated explosion vents did nothing to save any portion of the building. They also failed to protect adjacent structures.

Another reason to engineer a building to vent an explosion is to protect property outside the building. This might mean conceding total or nearly total loss of the involved structure. However, the objective is to protect other property by directing the force of the explosion toward a clear area.

Containment

Containment requires building a structure that is strong enough to contain the force of an explosion that might occur within it. This loss-reduction technique suffers from some important limitations. It is not the best choice for an occupied building because any effort to contain the force of the explosion increases the risk to anyone who is in the building at the time. By the same token, containing the force of an explosion does nothing to protect property in the same building from damage. The force an explosion can generate also limits containment. The force of the explosion might be severe and beyond the capability of the structure to contain.

Isolation

Separating operations that present an explosion hazard from other property helps minimize losses, as does isolating them from other structures on the same site. The force of an explosion dissipates rapidly with distance. Putting space between the source of an explosion and nearby property might provide effective protection. The distance required depends on the force of the anticipated explosion and the susceptibility of the property subject to damage.

Barriers can be used to direct the force of an explosion. Barriers place a substantial obstacle in the path of expanding gases and shock waves. The explosive force follows the path of least resistance, so shock waves bypass shielded property.

Pressure Explosions

Pressure explosions typically occur when pressure vessels cannot contain their internal pressure and burst. Pressure vessels that are common in most occupancies include water heaters and boilers. These devices are fired vessels, which means that they derive their pressure from heat. Some unfired vessels rely on mechanical means, such as compressors, to build and maintain internal pressure. Boiler and machinery insurance provides coverage for damage to and caused by steam boilers. Commercial property coverage forms provide coverage for explosion of other pressure vessels.

The lessons learned and experience gained by boiler and machinery underwriters can be applied to other pressure vessels as well. All pressure vessel losses are preventable through a regular program of maintenance and inspection. The leading causes of pressure vessel explosion are the failure of controls, the failure of safety devices, and failures related to the structure of the vessel.

Both primary and secondary controls govern the operation of equipment. Primary controls keep pressure within design limits. Most controls are sensitive to either temperature or pressure and shut down the equipment when tolerances are exceeded. Primary controls are designed to restart the equipment as the pressure or temperature approaches the lower boundary of its normal range.

Secondary controls shut down equipment as soon as an unsafe situation begins to develop. Good secondary controls require manual intervention to reset the equipment. This type of measure calls attention to the unsafe condition detected by the secondary control that an automatic recycling control would not.

Pressure relief devices prevent explosions by venting excessive pressure. When pressure or temperature rises above its normal operating range, relief valves open to release the pressure and then close again when pressure or temperature returns to normal. Safety valves should remain shut during normal operations. Any unplanned opening is reason to take the equipment off-line and investigate.

Some processes need high pressure and are especially susceptible to rapid increases in pressure and temperature. Since a slight variation from normal operating conditions quickly creates the possibility of an explosion, safety demands faster action than safety valves can provide. A better solution is the use of rupture discs. One end of the apparatus is designed to fail under excessive pressure. This failure immediately releases the entire contents of the pressure vessel into the atmosphere. One disadvantage of the use of rupture discs is their high cost. After they are used once, they must be repaired or replaced, which restricts their use to the most hazardous operations.

The pressure vessel structure might fail and cause an explosion for a number of reasons. Corrosion, erosion, or wear and tear can gradually thin the vessel's surface. Thermal expansion and contraction or excessive vibration might introduce cracks that weaken the vessel shell and end sheets. Whatever the cause, even a small crack, the weakened vessel can explode under even normal operating pressure. As escaping gas expands, it pushes outward at the edges of the opening and enlarges it.

Good maintenance and timely replacement of obsolete equipment offer the only protection against these types of failures. Controls designed to contain water need to have the drains used to release pressure tested and cleared regularly. Otherwise, residue or scale will build up inside and prevent proper operation. Equipment that should not contain water needs protection against condensation. Regular releases or bleeding might be enough, but some environments might require an air dryer to remove moisture from the lines. The maintenance staff should use test levers to open safety valves *under pressure* on a regular schedule. This approach does more than test for proper operation. It clears out scale and debris that can build up inside the valve and cause it to freeze shut.

If fire reaches a pressure vessel, it can cause an explosion in two ways. The vessel's contents, already under pressure, will expand as heat from the fire drives the temperature up. At the same time, heat will cause even noncombustible materials to weaken. As internal pressure increases, the vessel's ability to contain it diminishes. The problem is especially acute if the vessel's contents are combustible or flammable.

A well-designed fire safety program will address protection of pressure vessels. One measure is to place pressure vessels in a separate fire division away from combustible material and ignition sources. Processes that necessitate heating flammable or volatile fluids should use steam-jacketed vessels instead of fired vessels. The use of pressure vessels directly heated by a flame to cook flammable solvents is sometimes the most economical method to manufacture certain materials. From an underwriting standpoint, it does not afford adequate protection for life or property safety.

Vandalism and Malicious Mischief

Vandalism and malicious mischief occur randomly and unpredictably. Normally, the damage done in each act is incidental and a nuisance. Large losses can occur, however, depending on the property destroyed. For example, what started out as minor vandalism to a school led to very large losses because of the resultant removal of asbestos, replacement of damaged computer systems, and restoration of school records. Premises security measures help eliminate vandalism to the interior of buildings and their contents. Efforts to protect building exteriors from vandalism are usually not practical. Deductibles are often used to limit insured losses, which tend to have low severity and high frequency.

Sprinkler Leakage

Automatic sprinklers provide the most effective protection against loss by fire. However, they occasionally leak and cause losses. Property underwriters and the public tend to make more of sprinkler leakage damage than the exposure warrants. When sprinkler systems do leak, the damage they cause is usually limited. Domestic water lines often pose a far more serious threat but do not attract nearly as much attention as sprinkler systems do. Movies and television contribute to public misconceptions. They often depict sprinklers in comic situations. Lighting a cigar sets off every head in the building, and nothing can stem the flow of water. In truth, except for deluge systems, each sprinkler actuates individually, and only when its heat-sensing element reaches its rated temperature (ordinarily 165 degrees Fahrenheit).

Sprinkler systems leak for a variety of reasons. Freezing is the most common cause, usually as the result of heating system failure. Most sprinklers protect heated spaces. Systems designed to protect property outdoors or in unheated spaces defend against freezing by one of two means. Some systems employ a dry pipe system, in which the lines contain compressed air or an inert gas that holds back the water. When a head is actuated, the air bleeds off, allowing water to flow. Others inject an antifreeze solution into loops exposed to subfreezing temperatures. Breakdown and extended power outages are the leading causes of heat loss. Good management and prompt attention to problems that develop are enough to eliminate almost all instances of sprinkler leakage caused by freezing.

Another leading cause of sprinkler leakage is mechanical damage, usually to sprinkler heads. Lines and risers are also susceptible to damage. Any movement of material past the head can cause an accident, but forklifts and similar materials-handling equipment are the most common sources of contact damage. The movement of ladders and materials for repairs, like lumber and piping, can also damage heads in passing. Misuse of lines and risers is another source of accidental damage. No part of the sprinkler system should ever carry any load other than its own weight. For example, workers should not use parts of the system to support ladders or merchandise.

Overheating can cause heads to actuate. Some industrial equipment generates enough heat to require high-temperature heads. Their heat-sensing elements actuate at 180 degrees Fahrenheit or more. System design usually accommodates equipment that is already in place. New equipment or an occupancy change, however, might require design changes that are easy to overlook. Something as simple as a need for better illumination can cause a loss. Occasionally, installing higher wattage bulbs in fixtures near sprinkler heads has caused accidental overheating. High temperatures do not always produce immediate results; repeated exposure to high temperature for short periods can cause a head to fail. Poor installation and faulty maintenance also play a role in sprinkler leakage.

Sprinkler leakage is difficult to underwrite without a physical inspection. A significant problem in underwriting sprinkler leakage is the susceptibility of the contents to water damage. Flat steel, for instance, would fare well compared to paper goods. ISO performs physical inspections and provides sprinkler information. Underwriters should give close attention to fully sprinklered buildings that are rated by ISO as though they were nonsprinklered. Such a rating implies deficient installation or maintenance that will keep the system from performing properly.

Water Damage

Water damage occurs when water or steam accidentally escapes from pipes that are not part of a sprinkler system, or from any appliance that uses water. The principal sources of water losses are plumbing, heating and air conditioning systems, and industrial equipment that contains water. Swimming pools on the roofs or upper floors of buildings can also leak or rupture. Gravity water tanks situated on roofs pose a special concern. Water pumped into these tanks maintains pressure in water supply lines by the force of gravity. Because hydropneumatic tanks are a more modern and efficient alternative, many gravity tanks are old, and their maintenance is suspect. Some owners have abandoned gravity tanks in favor of hydropneumatic tanks but never disconnected or drained the gravity tanks.

There are several other sources of water damage losses. Pipes might burst. Tanks might leak or collapse. Apparatus using water might overflow. The site of the most serious potential loss depends on building construction and occupancy. Leaks occurring above grade level might affect a larger area of the structure. Leaks in basements may render worthless anything stored there or equipment housed there. Preventive maintenance is the key to controlling losses. Equipment that automatically fills with water warrants special attention. Failure to monitor equipment and detect a failure early can turn a small loss into a major disaster. Scuppers, built-in devices that direct water out of the upper floors of a building, can be effective but are not common in modern construction.

Collapse

Buildings collapse for several reasons other than the weight of ice, snow, or sleet. Other reasons for collapse include defective design or construction; deterioration; and weight of personnel, personal property, or water on the roof. Poor construction caused the collapse of a ceiling in the Port Authority Trans Hudson (PATH) Transportation Center at Journal Square in Jersey City, New Jersey. The plaster on a metal lath ceiling hung suspended from the reinforced concrete structure and collapsed under the weight of two PATH employees doing maintenance above it. The engineers and architects who designed this structure contemplated this load, but the contractor cut corners, omitting every fourth suspender and spreading out the rest. Vibration from passing PATH trains combined with the weight of the maintenance workers and their equipment to cause the collapse.

Any weight on a roof can cause it to collapse. Water that accumulates on flat roofs from rainfall when drains are blocked is a common cause. Regular inspection and good maintenance will prevent these losses. Many architects and engineers who design roof structures do not contemplate the load of property or people, but the users of the building do not always realize this. Some buildings have collapsed from the cumulative effect of vibration. They are usually very old structures whose builders could not anticipate modern traffic.

Collapse is also a concern during construction or renovation of an existing building. During this type of work, the building weight might be supported by only a portion of the superstructure that will ultimately support it.

Anticipating all potential causes of collapse is impossible. Underwriters might do better to concentrate on the quality of design, construction, and maintenance. Novel or unusual designs are more prone to collapse than traditional ones. The Hartford Civic Center adopted innovative designs that failed under conditions that the builder could reasonably anticipate. The ceiling of the PATH Transportation Center embodied a standard design widely used in building lobbies. Its collapse brought about numerous inspections to make sure the poor quality of workmanship did not affect similar ceilings. When a roof collapses because rain cannot run off, poor maintenance or design is the cause. Other parts of the building are likely to be affected by similar maintenance or design defects.

Summary

This chapter analyzed causes of property loss other than fire. Like fire, many of these causes of loss arise from the nature of the operations that the insured business conducts. Others arise from exposure to the forces of nature. Their evaluation depends less on the nature of the business than on the characteristics of the contents and the structure housing the contents. A few are societal factors and reflect the influence of neighbors and others on the insured's loss experience.

Lightning was once considered a type of fire. Today, commercial lines insurance treats lightning as a separate cause of loss, but homeowners forms still group it with fire. Lightning can cause damage without a fire. Protection is easily obtained if the insured adheres to the standards set by NFPA's National Electric Code.

Windstorm includes four types of severe weather: hurricanes, winter storms, tornadoes, and severe local storms. Several factors affect wind, including velocity and topography. Two scales specialize in measuring wind: the Beaufort scale classifies wind according to velocity, and the Saffir-Simpson scale measures hurricane-force winds.

Hurricanes cause the most severe wind damage. The level of damage a hurricane produces is a function of the path it follows and the strength of its winds. Hurricanes cause damage in four principal ways: wind, wind-driven rain, storm surge, and flooding. The most important factors in controlling windstorm losses are adopting adequate building codes and strictly enforcing those codes. Building envelopes are protected most effectively by incorporating properly designed and enforced building codes that require structures to hold up to aberrant wind forces. Underwriters must make certain that both nonengineered structures and fully engineered structures are properly inspected.

Tornadoes are small but violent windstorms. They are classified as weak, strong, or violent. Their appearance is random and completely unpredictable. They are destructive mainly because of their compact size, powerful winds, and upward movement.

Hail is small, rounded ice pellets that often form during thunderstorms. Like tornadoes, hailstorms are unpredictable. Roofing materials, aluminum siding, and automobiles are particularly susceptible to damage by hail.

Riot and civil commotion are actually two separate causes of loss. Insurers drew red lines on maps around areas that might experience such losses to remind underwriters not to insure property in those areas. This practice, called redlining, is now prohibited by state and federal laws. The term is still used, however, to denote any geographical underwriting discrimination. Underwriters now use pricing as a way to manage the riot exposure.

Another cause of loss is sinkhole collapse. Sinkholes occur in areas in which underground rivers and streams have carved channels out of solid limestone bedrock. This erosion causes the ground to collapse. Sinkholes cause extensive damage; evaluating this exposure requires a sound knowledge of local topography and demographic trends.

Volcanic action is another cause of loss. Until the eruption of Mount St. Helens, insurers considered volcanic action to affect only an area immediately surrounding the volcano. Insurers paid the losses resulting from the Mount St. Helens eruption, even if policies did not specify coverage for volcanic action. Insurers have since amended their forms to include volcanic action losses, such as damage caused by lava and ash. Underwriters should monitor changing geological conditions and adjust underwriting policy to changes.

The weight of ice, snow, or sleet can also cause loss. Partial or total collapse of a roof and ice dams are often the result of snow, ice, or sleet. They can be prevented with the proper roof structure design, insulation, and ventilation.

Underwriters measure flood exposures by using flood maps made available by the National Flood Insurance Program. These maps divide an area into three zones according to their susceptibility to flooding. Property can be protected from flood with walls, dikes, levees, and anchoring structures. Underwriters must determine the extent of coverage that they will provide and the price at which they will offer it.

Earthquakes can also cause much damage. Underwriters must consider the construction of buildings and the soil composition to determine the possible extent of earthquake damage.

Explosion is another cause of loss. The two most common types of explosion are combustion explosions and pressure explosions. Combustion explosions include deflagration and detonation. They can be prevented if the insured limits the amount of fuel and restricts the oxygen supply. Limiting damage potential by using techniques such as venting, containment, and isolation helps the insured reduce losses.

Pressure explosions typically occur when pressure vessels cannot contain their internal pressure and burst. Pressure vessels are common in most occupancies, and they include water heaters and boilers. The pressure vessel structure can fail for a number of reasons. A well-designed fire safety program addresses protection of pressure vessels.

Vandalism occurs randomly and unpredictably. Prevention and control of losses are often not feasible solutions. This fact suggests use of a deductible large enough to preclude coverage of most vandalism losses, which generally have low severity and high frequency.

Automatic sprinklers provide the most effective protection against loss by fire. However, they occasionally leak and cause losses. Freezing and mechanical damage are often the cause for leaks. Good sprinkler maintenance helps reduce the likelihood of leakage.

Water damage is also a cause of loss. The principal sources of loss are plumbing, heating and air conditioning systems, and industrial equipment that contains water.

Underwriters must also evaluate collapse as a cause of loss. Any weight on a roof or poor construction can cause collapse. Underwriters must concentrate on the building's design, construction, and maintenance.

Underwriters do not need to consider every cause of loss for which coverage is available. The damage resulting from some is so infrequent or so minor that adding them to the evaluation is not an efficient use of an underwriter's time. In the rare instances in which one of these causes of loss becomes a significant factor, underwriters can adapt the techniques that they apply routinely to more frequently occurring causes of loss.

Chapter Notes

1. Don G. Friedman, "Is Hugo a Forerunner of Future Great Hurricanes? (Part 1)," *Research Review*, July 1990, pp. 1-38.
2. Friedman, pp. 8-9.
3. Some scales assign a slightly higher or lower velocity to hurricane-force winds, but the differences are inconsequential.
4. Robert H. Simpson and Herbert Riehle, *The Hurricane and Its Impact* (Baton Rouge, LA: Louisiana State University Press, 1981), p. 198.
5. Simpson and Riehle, p. 204.
6. Gary G. Nichols and Sam Gerace, *A Survey of Hurricane Andrew* (Birmingham, AL: Southern Building Code Congress International, 1993), p. 2.

7. Nichols and Gerace, p. 2.
8. Dale Perry, "Deemed to Comply," panel presentation at Southern Building Code Congress International Annual Research and Education Conference, Charleston, SC, October 24, 1988.
9. Nichols and Gerace, p. 1.
10. Nichols and Gerace, p. 3.
11. Southern Building Code Congress International, *Coastal Building Department Survey* (Boston, MA: National Committee on Property Insurance, 1992), p. 2.
12. All-Industry Research Advisory Council, *Surviving the Storm: Building Codes, Compliance and the Mitigation of Hurricane Damage*, 1989, p. 3.
13. Insurance Services Office, Chief Executive Circular, "Building Code Effectiveness Grading Service To Be Introduced," Chief Executive CE-95-2, February 3, 1995, pp. 15-19.
14. See, for example, Nichols and Gerace.
15. Ziehlsdorfeder et al. v. American Family Mutual.
16. Michael E. Ruane, "For Allentown, a Blast of a Time," *The Philadelphia Inquirer*, March 20, 1994, p. A1.
17. Roger Smith, *Catastrophes and Disasters (New York, NY: Chambers, 1992), p. 211.*

Chapter 6

Indirect Loss Underwriting

Direct loss occurs when a covered cause of loss physically damages covered property. Insureds also face an exposure to the indirect consequences of a loss event. Indirect loss exposures are less obvious than direct loss exposures. Though less tangible, indirect loss exposures are just as real as direct ones and can be financially crippling. Because indirect loss exposures are more difficult to understand than direct losses, many terms have been used to describe them. These terms include time element, consequential, business interruption, business income, and extra expense. At one time, each term had a precise meaning, but general use has blurred the distinction among them, and they are sometimes used interchangeably. Underwriters should be familiar with each of these terms because they are widely used, and each has a nuance that is described later.

Fundamental to evaluating a risk for indirect loss is the acceptability of the property for direct loss coverage. An insured indirect loss cannot occur without a direct loss. Underwriters need detailed knowledge of an insured's operation to ensure that coverage amounts are adequate to enable a full recovery after a loss.

Indirect Loss Exposures

Indirect loss refers to the loss of use of property after covered property is damaged or destroyed by a covered cause of loss. **Time element loss** is another appropriate term for this type of loss because the period of time over which the loss occurs influences its severity. **Consequential loss** is any damage to property that did not result from direct action of the covered cause of loss. For example, when fire damages refrigerating equipment at a meat-packing plant, damage to the machinery is direct loss. If meat later spoils because the plant cannot use its refrigerators and cold boxes, damage to the meat would be a consequential loss. The meat spoiled as a result of a lack of refrigeration rather than from the direct action of the fire. Fire remains the proximate cause of the entire loss, but damage to the meat occurred because of damage to other property.

Business interruption is another fitting term for indirect loss exposures and was once the title of the ISO policy forms that most often provided coverage for such losses. ISO now provides coverage for indirect loss exposures through the **business income** coverage forms and the extra expense coverage forms.

For simplicity and clarity, this text uses the term "time element" to describe any exposure whose severity depends on the period of time over which loss occurs, and any loss exposures that are not time-dependent are termed "consequential."

Time Element Loss Exposures

The distinguishing characteristic of a time element exposure is that loss occurs over a relatively long period of time. The length of that period determines the severity of the loss. Although direct losses might be thought of as instantaneous, they also can occur over time. The length of that period sometimes affects loss severity. A fire that burns for three hours can be expected to cause greater damage than one that is suppressed in thirty minutes. The difference is that direct losses occur over a relatively short period of time: minutes, hours, and, in extreme cases, days. Time element losses, in contrast, usually develop much more slowly and occur over a longer period: weeks, months, or even years. The income lost from the date of loss until the business reopens and returns to the levels that would have prevailed had no loss occurred is a time element loss.

Types of Time Element Losses

Time element coverages compensate insureds for the loss of use of the property that produces income when it suffers direct loss or damage. The measure of a time element loss is the reduction of income that occurs while the insured cannot use the damaged property, *plus* the cost of substituting other property to reduce the loss. The three principal types of time element losses are business income, extra expense, and leasehold interest. Loss of a manufacturer's inventory of finished stock is so closely related to time element loss that many consider it a time element loss, but technically it is not. Because most people consider these two exposures together, loss of finished stock will be considered in this chapter.

True time element losses can be thought of as having three components:

- A length of time over which the loss occurs
- The rate at which loss occurs during that period
- The specific period of time in which the loss occurs

The Time Element

Variation occurs in the rate at which loss accrues as a function of a longer time period. Toy stores might do as much as 75 percent of their annual business within about one month. Their busy season extends from the day after Thanksgiving through Christmas Eve. To assess time element losses fully, underwriters must appreciate the effect of timing on the amount of loss. A fire that closes a toy store in January for one month might cost the business as little as 1 or 2 percent of its annual sales, but the same fire on Thanksgiving Day would have devastating effects. In the first example, fire struck during a slow period; in the second, the store had to close at the beginning of its peak season. Assessing time element losses requires evaluating two different but related time periods:

- The **period of restoration** is the length of time after a direct loss that a business needs in order to return to the condition that would have prevailed had no loss occurred. It consists of two distinct phases. The first phase is the time required to restore the property damaged or destroyed by the direct loss. To resume operations, the insured must repair, replace, or rebuild damaged property. In the second phase, the insured is ready to resume full operations but faces another problem because customers went elsewhere when the business was forced to close. To recover fully, the insured must encourage its customers to return and develop new business relationships.
- The **period of indemnity** is the length of time for which business income and extra expense forms reimburse the insured's loss. Ideally, the period of indemnity would be identical to the period of restoration, but that rarely happens. Standard business income forms limit the period of indemnity to the time required to restore the property. The true measure of the insured's loss is the time required to restore the business to its previous condition. This is usually longer than the time required to restore the property because the insured's customers have become accustomed to doing their

business elsewhere. Thus, there is often a lag between the time the property is restored following a loss and the time the insured's business income returns to the level that would have prevailed had there been no loss. In other words, the period of restoration is usually longer than the period of indemnity. An additional coverage in the ISO business income forms provides insurance for the first thirty days of this gap, but this coverage is often less than the insured needs. Coverage options that extend the period of indemnity do not fully erase this gap because they limit coverage to a fixed period of time after the end of the normal period of indemnity. If the insured cannot return its business to the level that would have prevailed had no loss occurred within that period, then part of the loss remains uninsured.

The Rate at Which Loss Occurs

The second factor that determines the severity of a time element loss is the rate at which the business sustains an insured loss. Standard business income forms express this as the **actual loss sustained**. When loss occurs, the insured must demonstrate the actual amount of loss that occurs during the period of indemnity. The actual amount of loss becomes the measure of recovery. Suppose fire strikes a toy store on Thanksgiving evening, and the business cannot reopen until December 26. The loss of sales while the store had to close minus the amount of expenses that do not have to continue equals the actual loss sustained. In this example, the actual loss sustained might equal or exceed an entire year's sales volume.

Valued forms provide an alternative approach to measuring loss of income. These forms are called "per diem" coverages because they often pay a fixed amount for each day of loss. The term "daily indemnity" is usually more understandable than "per diem." Business income forms might also pay a fixed amount for a week or a month; that is, they are weekly or monthly indemnity forms. Agents, brokers, and insureds often prefer valued forms, in which a specified dollar amount is paid, because they mistakenly believe there is never a need to prove the amount of loss under a daily, weekly, or monthly indemnity form. The insured does not have to prove the amount of business income loss if the insured is shut down completely. In this circumstance, the valued form will pay the full daily, weekly, or monthly indemnity for the period. Most losses, however, are partial losses, and partial losses will require the insured to demonstrate the amount of business income loss. Business operations continue, but at a reduced rate. Even a total shutdown usually includes some fraction of a day, week, or month. A business insured under a daily indemnity form, for example, may be shut down for thirty-seven and one-half days. The valued form will pay a proportion of the daily, weekly, or monthly indemnity that equals the reduction in the insured's business. In order to establish that proportion, the insured has to provide a reliable estimate of the amount of business that would have been conducted and a record of the actual level of business activity. While this action is often less formal and exacting than the requirements an actual loss sustained form imposes, it does create a need for the insured to prove its loss.

Extra expense insurance covers the cost of avoiding or minimizing a business income loss by paying the additional cost of continuing operations despite the direct loss. Following the bombing of the World Trade Center in February 1993, many tenants moved into temporary quarters. The added cost of doing business that way represented their extra expense loss. These losses tend to peak at two defined times: at the start and the end of the loss. The first peak occurs when the business must relocate to temporary quarters, requiring the insured to find space, move, install new telephone lines, and notify customers and suppliers of the new location. Returning to permanent quarters produces a second peak at the end of the loss.

The Period of Time in Which Loss Occurs

In a simple situation, the time element loss occurs at an even rate during the period in which the insured cannot use damaged or destroyed property. The length of that period magnifies the severity of the time element loss. This situation accurately represents some but not all time element losses that occur. Income is not usually earned at an even rate. Likewise, time element losses that result because of interruptions in income earning ability do not usually occur at an even rate.

A simple example helps to clarify the significance of this third component of time element loss. Furniture retailers usually do little business early in the week. Their sales tend to be concentrated from Thursday evening through closing on Saturday (or Sunday). A small physical loss after weekend business hours might force a furniture store to close for a few days. If the store reopens midway through normal business hours on Thursday, it would have lost half a week's business in terms of time. The effect on sales, however, would be negligible as long as weekend customers did not stay away because they assumed that the store was still closed.

Measuring Time Element Losses

Evaluating time element exposures requires a way to measure expected income and expenses that must continue during a complete or partial shutdown. Using sales as the exclusive measure of business income is tempting. The figures are almost always easy to obtain, and they have a strong intuitive appeal. However, this approach does not always produce a true measure of the loss. A retailer's business is selling. Anything that interrupts sales interrupts the business.

A manufacturer, in contrast, is in the business of converting raw stock into finished products. Because manufacturers sell mostly from inventory, sales are a poor measure of manufacturing business activity. An event might cause a serious interruption of operations but might not have an immediate effect on sales. The level of sales might not reflect the effects of the loss for several months. On the other hand, a reduction in sales does not always mean a reduction in the insured's business. A loss that is confined to a manufacturer's finished stock might reduce sales sharply but not have any effect on production. Such a loss is not treated as a time element loss because increasing the insured value of the stock to include lost profits in the direct loss is a more efficient means of insuring it. Later, this chapter discusses the appropriate methods to cover a manufacturer's loss of income from damage to or destruction of finished stock.

The most appropriate measure of business activity depends on the nature of the insured business. Following are descriptions of several types of businesses and appropriate ways to measure business activity:

- Mercantile accounts (retailers and wholesalers) depend on sales for business activity. Some service businesses are in the same position. Interruption of their sales interrupts their business. The extent to which a loss reduces sales is the best measure of their loss.
- A manufacturer's business is converting raw materials into finished goods. Manufacturers rarely sell their output as they produce it, placing it instead into inventory from which they subsequently ship orders. As a result, stopping the manufacturing process causes a loss, but sales might not reflect that loss for several months. Manufacturers shut down by a direct loss for weeks or even months might recover with no reduction in sales. The manufacturers could meet orders from inventory until repairs are complete, then replenish their stock by increasing production. The proper measure of their business activity is the net sales value of the goods they produce. **Net sales value** is the selling price of the goods the insured would have produced had no loss occurred, minus certain expenses that the insured does not incur because of the loss of production. Exhibit 6-1 presents a sample income statement that is the starting point for calculating net sales value of production in the business income report/worksheet.
- Processing is very similar to manufacturing. Processing businesses convert their input from one form to another without changing its basic character. The primary difference from manufacturers is that processing risks do not make a product from raw materials. Their output is essentially their input, but they have added value to it. They might work on finished products, raw materials, or intermediate goods. An anodizer might plate the raw stock that a customer uses to manufacture its product or plate the customer's finished stock as the last stage of production. A textile contractor

Exhibit 6-1
Income Statement—for Period 1/1 Through 12/31
Good Times Merchandise Co., Inc.

Sales			$3,000,000
Interest revenue			10,000
Total revenue			3,010,000
Cost of goods sold			1,900,000
Gross margin			1,110,000
Operating expenses			
Selling expenses			
Salaries	$200,000		
Advertising	100,000		
Sales returns and allowances	50,000	$350,000	
General and administrative expenses			
Wages	90,000		
Property taxes	40,000		
Depreciation and amortization	90,000		
Rent	85,000		
Interest on serial bonds	50,000	355,000	705,000
Income before income taxes			405,000
Income taxes			194,400
Net income			$ 210,600

might finish either the cloth its customer uses to make garments or the finished garments themselves. As with manufacturers, the proper measure of a processor's business income is the net sales value of production.

- In the real estate business, the "rental value" is the most appropriate measure of business income. Rental value includes actual rent due during the period of restoration. Business income forms also include in rental value other charges that are the landlord's obligation but that the tenant would have paid had no loss occurred. Under the terms of a lease, a tenant may agree to pay real estate taxes that the landlord would otherwise have to pay. Tenants sometimes lease entire premises under a net lease that transfers the landlord's obligations to the tenants.

  When calculating rental value, the underwriter should examine the actual rental income rather than fair market rental value. If the landlord has leased part or all of the premises at more or less than the current fair market value, the actual rent due is the measure of loss. This rule only applies, however, to the period of indemnity. If a loss permits a tenant who is paying rent above fair market value to terminate the lease, business income forms do not cover any loss that the landlord sustains after the period of indemnity expires. Coverage for this excess rental value was once available, but it seems to have disappeared from the market.

- Some service businesses are reluctant to describe their business income as sales. This is especially true for professionals such as doctors and lawyers, and other service businesses who do not like the idea of labeling their activities "sales." In this situation, the best measure of business activity is income. This measure is especially appropriate for businesses that derive their earnings from commissions such as insurance agents and brokers. As a measure of loss, income is analogous to sales.
- Schools require a special measure of business income. They derive their funds mainly from tuition and fees that students pay. They also operate some facilities, like bookstores and cafeterias, that generate income as a retail store would. Special events, like fairs, dramatic productions, and sporting events, also generate income. Insurers have traditionally lumped all income from student-related activities into a single item described as tuition. In rare instances, a school might operate an unrelated commercial venture.

Underwriters can apply these descriptions to less traditional exposures. An educational or charitable institution might, for instance, lose public funds or donations if a loss interrupts its activities. A public agency or government might fear a loss of tax revenues. Underwriters can expect to see at least one request from such an organization during their careers. They do not need to reject those requests simply because the exposure cannot be made to match the coverage provided by standard forms. The definition of covered loss under business income forms can be altered to suit the needs of public agencies and charitable institutions that derive their income from sources other than traditional business income.

Business Income Coverage

Business income forms cover the loss of the insured's net profits *plus* any expenses that must continue when a covered loss interrupts business operations. The forms also insure any added expense the insured incurs to reduce the amount of the loss that would otherwise be covered. This exposure can be divided into two distinct components. Profit reduction and the need to continue paying some expenses are losses of income. Any cost that the insured incurs to reduce the loss is a form of extra expense. Business income forms limit coverage for the extra expense exposure to the actual reduction in the loss of income. When the additional cost of maintaining normal operations is greater than the reduction in the business income loss, extra expense coverage independent of business income insurance is appropriate. The limitation in the business income (without extra expense) coverage form works to deny coverage the insured genuinely needs. The considerations for providing this coverage separately or in combination with business income coverage will be discussed later in this chapter.

The factors that underwriters must consider when evaluating a business income exposure include the following:

- Probable maximum loss
- Adequate insurance to value
- Measures available to reduce loss

Probable Maximum Loss in Business Income Coverage

The probable maximum loss (PML) for business income coverage differs from direct loss in one important respect: the value of the insured property limits a direct loss. It cannot exceed 100 percent of the value the policy places on the insured property. Assume that a policy insures a building at replacement cost for $2,500,000 and that the actual cost of replacing the structure is $2,350,729. The largest loss the underwriter can incur is the lower of the two amounts, $2,350,729. If the two figures are reversed, the answer remains the same. Insurance will not pay more than either the replacement cost of the building or the policy face amount.

In business income coverage, the policy face amount still limits the amount of loss that the insurer can incur. Replacement cost, however, has no precise equivalent. Business income coverage protects the insured against loss of net income plus expenses that must continue when a covered loss interrupts business operations. Measuring this exposure requires using accounting data that report income and expenses incurred over a comparable fixed period of time. Convention dictates that one year is used as the accounting period and that one year is used to compute business income values for coinsurance.

This practice creates a natural tendency to think of one year's full business income as a total loss, but that is not entirely true. Policy language does not limit the period of indemnity to one year. Many businesses today face a maximum period of restoration longer than one year. In extreme cases, the time required to restore the property can be several years. As a result, a business income loss can exceed total business income values for one year. The actual loss can exceed the "total loss" that serves as the basis of coinsurance.

In theory, the amount of income that the insured can lose as the result of a single covered occurrence is unlimited. The period of restoration and the level of earnings place a practical limit on the loss potential, but this limit varies from account to account. In order to form an accurate estimate of the PML for time element coverage, underwriters have to consider economic opportunities and pitfalls for the insured beyond the facts presented in the latest set of financial statements. For example, the Vista Hotel at the World Trade Center in New York City sustained severe structural damage in the terrorist bombing referred to earlier. The Vista was not able to reopen until November 1994, more than twenty months after the loss. The blast in the public parking garage under the hotel turned the first-floor lobby into a cavern and weakened columns that provided important structural support to the entire building. Repair work on the upper floors could not begin until contractors stabilized the lower levels of the structure. The nature, location, and extent of the damage caused a business income loss that continued for almost two years. A PML estimate that limited the loss potential to a single year's net income would have underestimated the loss potential.

Another area of uncertainty in computing PML for business income exposures is the rate at which the loss will occur. This uncertainty arises from two main sources. First, the calculation of business income values is based on expectations of financial performance. These estimates are less precise than the replacement values of buildings and contents. Most companies prepare full financial statements once a year. Interim statements are less precise. The period in which the loss occurs will determine the PML. Underwriters can do no more than estimate those values. Exhibit 6-2 presents examples of business income worksheets that form the basis for this estimate. (The fifth page of this form is not shown.)

The worksheets start with business income values for the twelve months preceding the policy period. This figure is an estimate because the lag in the accounting process can be as long as several months. The insured starts with the latest financial report for a full year and proceeds to project sales, production, and costs for two years on average. The true base for the estimate cannot be known until the policy year is well under way, introducing a level of uncertainty that the underwriter must consider. If sales are better or costs are lower than expected, the insured's estimate of business income values will be understated. A PML estimated from these figures will suffer from the same defect.

The extent to which the insured will continue to incur normal business expenses introduces more uncertainty into the process. The business income worksheet helps differentiate between costs that will continue and those that will not. This is not always the case. Costs deducted in computing business

Exhibit 6-2
Business Income Report/Worksheet

POLICY NUMBER:

COMMERCIAL PROPERTY
CP 15 15 06 95

BUSINESS INCOME REPORT/WORK SHEET

Your Name ______MANUFACTURER, INC.______ Date ____________

Location ____

____

This work sheet must be completed on an accrual basis.

The beginning and ending inventories in all calculations should be based on the same valuation method.

APPLICABLE WHEN THE AGREED VALUE COVERAGE OPTION APPLIES:

I certify that this is a true and correct report of values as required under this policy for the periods indicated and that the Agreed Value for the period of coverage is $ ____________ , based on a Co-insurance percentage of ____%.

Signature ______________________
Official Title ______________________

APPLICABLE WHEN THE PREMIUM ADJUSTMENT FORM APPLIES:

I certify that this is a true and correct report of values as required under this policy for the 12 months ended ________

Signature ______________________

Official Title ______________________

Agent or Broker ______________________

Mailing Address ______________________

CP 15 15 06 95 **Page 1 of 5**

Continued on next page

BUSINESS INCOME REPORT/WORK SHEET
FINANCIAL ANALYSIS
(000 omitted)

Income and Expenses	12 Month Period Ending 12/31/00 Manufacturing	Non-Manufacturing	Estimated for 12 Month Period Beginning 4/1/01 Manufacturing	Non-Manufacturing
A. Gross Sales	$ 10,050	$	$ 10,350	$
B. DEDUCT: Finished Stock Inventory (at sales value) at Beginning	- 500	XXXXXXXX	- 550	XXXXXXXX
	9,550	XXXXXXXX	9,800	XXXXXXXX
C. ADD: Finished Stock Inventory (at sales value) at End	+ 553	XXXXXXXX	+ 480	XXXXXXXX
D. Gross Sales Value of Production	$ 10,083	XXXXXXXX	$ 10,280	XXXXXXXX
E. DEDUCT:				
Prepaid Freight – Outgoing	- 0	-	- 0	-
Returns & Allowances	- 20	-	- 21	-
Discounts	- 30	-	- 32	-
Bad Debts	- 25	-	- 27	-
Collection Expenses	- 0	-	- 0	-
F. Net Sales		$		$
Net Sales Value of Production	$ 10,008		$ 10,200	
G. ADD: Other Earnings from your business operations (not investment income or rents from other properties):				
Commissions or Rents	+ 0	+	+ 0	+
Cash Discounts Received	+ 0	+	+ 0	+
Other	+ 10	+	+ 15	+
H. Total Revenues	$ 10,018	$	$ 10,215	$

	Income and Expenses	12 Month Period Ending 12/31/00 Manufacturing	Non-Manufacturing	Estimated for 12 Month Period Beginning 4/1/01 Manufacturing	Non-Manufacturing
	Total Revenues (Line **H.** from previous page)................................	$ 10,018	$	$ 10,215	$
I.	DEDUCT: Cost of goods sold (see next page for instructions)......................	- 5,725	-	- 5,900	-
	Cost of services purchased from outsiders (not your employees) to resell, that do not continue under contract.............	- 0	-	- 0	-
	Power, heat and refrigeration expenses that do not continue under contract (if **CP 15 11** is attached).......................................	- N/A	XXXXXXXX	- N/A	XXXXXXXX
	All ordinary payroll expenses or the amount of payroll expense excluded (if **CP 15 10** is attached)....................................	- N/A	-	- N/A	-
	Special deductions for mining properties (see next page for instructions)...............................	- N/A	-	- N/A	-
J.1.	Business Income exposure for 12 months......................................	$ 4,293		4,315	
J.2.	Combined (firms engaged in manufacturing & non-manufacturing operations)..............	$		$	
	The figures in **J.1.** or **J.2.** represent 100% of your actual and estimated Business Income exposure for 12 months.				
K.	Additional Expenses:				
	1. Extra Expenses – form **CP 00 30** only (expenses incurred to avoid or minimize suspension of business & to continue operations)..................			$	$
	2. Extended Business Income and Extended Period of Indemnity – form **CP 00 30 or CP 00 32** (loss of Business Income following resumption of operations, up to 30 days or the no. of days selected under Extended Period of Indemnity option)			+	+
	3. Combined (all amounts in **K.1.** and **K.2.**)..................................			$	

CP 15 15 06 95 **Page 3 of 5**

Continued on next page

"Estimated" column

L. Total of **J. and K.** .... $ ________

The figure in **L.** represents 100% of your estimated Business Income exposure for 12 months, and additional expenses. Using this figure as information, determine the approximate amount of insurance needed based on your evaluation of the number of months needed (may exceed 12 months) to replace your property, resume operations and restore the business to the condition that would have existed if no property damage had occurred.

Refer to the agent or Company for information on available Coinsurance levels and indemnity options. The Limit of Insurance you select will be shown in the Declarations of the policy.

Supplementary Information

	12 Month Period Ending 12/31/00		Estimated for 12 Month Period Beginning 4/1/01	
	Manufacturing	Non-Manufacturing	Manufacturing	Non-Manufacturing
CALCULATION OF COST OF GOODS SOLD				
Inventory at beginning of year (Including raw material and stock in process, but not finished stock, for manufacturing risks)...............	$ 1,050	$ ________	$ 1,110	$ ________
Add: The following purchase costs: Cost of raw stock (including transportation charges)..........................	+ 5,715	XXXXXXXX	+ 5,820	XXXXXXXX
Cost of factory supplies consumed...	+ 25	XXXXXXXX	+ 20	XXXXXXXX
Cost of merchandise sold including transportation charges (for manufacturing risks, means cost of merchandise sold but not manufactured by you)......................	+ 0	+ ________	+ 0	+ ________
Cost of other supplies consumed (including transportation charges)..........	+ 0	+ ________	+ 0	+ ________
Cost of goods available for sale.............	$ 6,790	$ ________	$ 6,950	$ ________
Deduct: Inventory at end of year (Including raw material and stock in process, but not finished stock, for manufacturing risks)...............	- 1,065	? ________	- 1,050	- ________
Cost of Goods Sold (Enter this figure in Item **I.** on previous page).........	$ 5,725	$ ________	$ 5,900	$ ________

income values will sometimes continue, but costs that are not deducted might not. A business income worksheet, for example, treats rent as a continuing expense and assumes that the insured will not continue to incur the cost of raw stock. The lease of the insured's premises might abate the rent after a loss, and a supply contract might obligate the insured to purchase raw stock regardless of whether the business can use it. If a loss occurs, the insured will not pay rent but will continue to buy raw stock. In this situation, expenses that the business income worksheet assumes will continue after a loss do not, and the insured continues to incur expenses that the worksheet assumes will not continue.

Calculating Probable Maximum Loss

Underwriters can estimate the PML for business income coverage in three steps:

1. Determine the most serious direct loss that is likely to occur. Chapter 4 described the process for computing PML for direct loss. When using this method for business income losses, there is no need to convert the worst foreseeable loss to a dollar value.
2. Calculate the longest period of restoration that this loss can reasonably be expected to cause.
3. Compute the largest loss of business income that the insured is likely to sustain during a period of this length. The result is the probable maximum loss that the insured might sustain.

Using Direct PML

The most important factor that determines the length of time that the insured needs to recover from a direct loss is the severity of the loss. Business income losses follow direct losses, so no indirect loss can occur without a direct loss. A small direct loss tends to have little effect on income, and a large loss tends to have serious consequences. Therefore, the direct PML is the logical starting point for estimating the business income PML. When the direct PML is used to estimate future business income losses, the dollar amount of the direct loss is not important. The extent of the damage and its location will determine how much time is necessary for repairs and how long the time element loss will continue.

The direct PML might, for example, assume total loss to a single fire division plus 25 percent of each adjoining fire division. The next-to-last step in the underwriter's calculations of the PML for direct loss identifies the fire division that produces the largest loss on this basis. The underwriter then converts the PML to a dollar amount that the underwriter can use to make a rational decision for direct loss coverage, but this step is unnecessary for determining the largest expected business income loss. Logic might suggest that another fire division affords the best basis for a sound estimate. For business income coverage, PML depends on the effect that loss of property will have on the insured's operations. The values exposed to loss do not necessarily determine this effect.

The basis of the largest expected business income loss is the worst-case loss that causes the greatest disruption to the insured's operations. The overall need for the property in the insured's business is more important than its value. The insured might be able to compensate for the loss of costly machinery, but its operations might have to be interrupted because of the loss of one inexpensive piece of machinery. Predicting which assets will have the strongest effect on the insured's earnings is often not possible. For one manufacturer, loss of production machinery will be the key. For another, it might be loss of stock in process. Elevators in a high-rise office building probably represent only a small proportion of the building's total value. Their loss, however, could cause a loss of rental income that might continue for weeks or even months. Each case requires evaluation on its own merits.

The Maximum Period of Restoration

Several factors influence the extent to which loss of a given asset will reduce the level of the insured's business activity. The extent to which the business depends on a particular piece of property varies according to the following:

- Its importance to the insured's operations
- The time required to replace it
- The availability of substitutes

Importance to Insured's Operations

Not all the property a business owns has equal importance to its operations. A manufacturer might rely heavily for its output on a single piece of equipment but might be able to continue production by using other property in a slightly different process. A larger company might have multiple production streams. Loss of any one will reduce output but will not close down the company. The insured might be able to increase the output of one line to compensate for the loss of another. On the other hand, the damaged property might be the only equipment capable of doing the job, so a shutdown caused by this and other bottlenecks would be inevitable.

Production Bottlenecks A production bottleneck exists whenever a company relies on a single piece of equipment or production line for its output. Because of a bottleneck, a small direct loss can severely interrupt the insured's business. The underwriter or loss control representative can detect the presence of a bottleneck by studying a production or process flowchart, which is simply a graph that depicts the insured's operations. Exhibit 6-3 presents a sample flowchart of a production process. This diagram depicts a production stream in which raw materials flow from storage through two separate processes. The output of Process A1 flows directly to Process AB. In the other stream, the output of Process B1 proceeds to Process B2 and then to Process AB. A bottleneck occurs because all of the output has to flow through Process AB. Any loss that interrupts Process AB will shut down the insured's entire operation.

Large businesses that have high business income values usually have production flowcharts, but flowcharts are not so common for smaller businesses. When evaluating a business income exposure, underwriters should always look for a flowchart of the production process. A flowchart provides valuable information, but one might not be available for two reasons. First, the insured might never have prepared a flowchart. Small companies whose processes are relatively simple, for example, are unlikely to have flowcharts. Lack of a flowchart is not necessarily a negative sign because the owners and managers might not need one. Because the process is familiar and not complex, a flowchart would add little to their understanding of the procedures and practices being conducted in the business. As the operation becomes more complex, the situation changes. The distinction between ownership and management becomes more pronounced. Turnover among managers and supervisors is likely to increase. Decision makers in a large, complex plant will probably not be as familiar with its processes and operations as are their counterparts at a smaller and less complex organization. Competent management in such cases demands a higher level of information, and the underwriter should not ignore the lack of an accurate flowchart.

Some businesses that have prepared flowcharts regard them as trade secrets. The insured is not willing to share the information the flowcharts contain with outsiders. Underwriters can treat such cases in different ways. One view holds that the insured's interest in protecting trade secrets is good reason to withhold information from the insurer. The underwriter should respect the insured's privacy and decide on the risk without asking for further information. Many insurers, on the other hand, regard the handling of confidential information as part of the nature of their business. Respect for the insured's privacy means holding this information in strict confidence. Underwriters should trust and respect insureds and should expect the insureds' trust and respect in return. For organizations above a certain size, underwriters decline to insure any account that fails to provide audited financial statements. Applying the same rule to flowcharts is a logical extension of this philosophy.

Exhibit 6-3
A Manufacturing Bottleneck

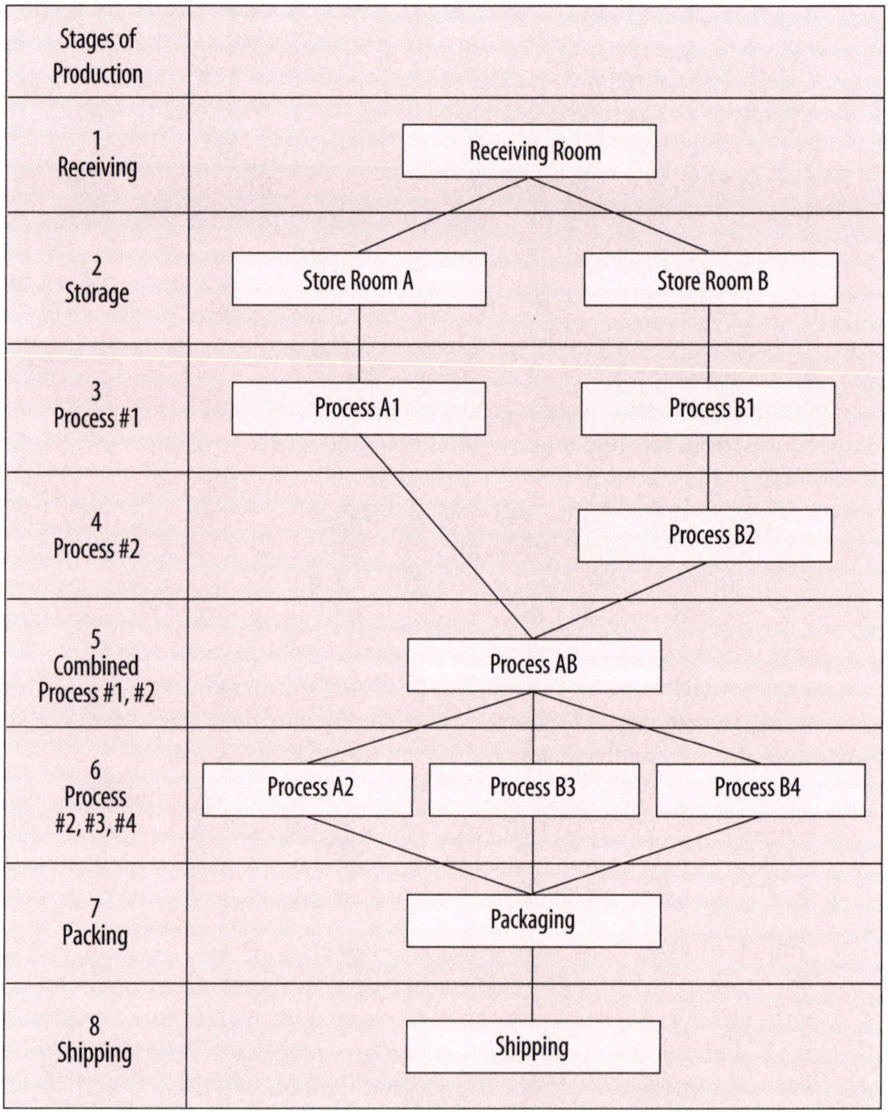

Reprinted with permission from Matthew Lenz, Jr., *Risk Management Manual* (Santa Monica, CA: The Merritt Company, 1993), p. 21.

When the insured is unwilling or unable to provide a flowchart, two options are open to the underwriter. The first alternative is to reach a decision without the information a fully informed choice requires. The other is to develop as much information as the level of the insured's cooperation will permit. In either instance, the value the insured places on privacy and proprietary information conflicts with the underwriter's need to make a well-informed decision. Insureds will often withhold information for what they perceive as very good reasons. Although the underwriter may not share the value judgments that underlie that decision, this should not be the basis for a decision to reject the account.

Most insurers adopt some combination of these two options. The principal difference lies in the point at which they insist on more complete information and cooperation from the insured. Conservative underwriters demand the trust and cooperation of the businesses they insure. They are less willing to consider an account that withholds information for reasons the underwriter does not perceive as valid. Aggressive underwriters tend to take greater risks to provide a service that is in demand. They are more willing to accept an account that provides less information, and they generally charge a higher premium to reflect the greater degree of uncertainty. The insured has the option of providing more information in return for a lower premium. Offering this type of choice increases the benefits that insurance provides for consumers.

When the insured is unwilling or unable to provide a flowchart, the underwriter may seek to develop one from other sources. This is most often accomplished by asking the loss control specialist who inspects the premises to create a flowchart. Information obtained by this method will in most situations have less value than a flowchart provided by the insured and reviewed by the loss control specialist.

Construction Bottlenecks The configuration of the insured's premises can also extend the period of indemnity. Exhibit 6-4 is the floor plan of a residential school for the blind. Section A is a residence hall that serves as a dormitory for both students and staff. When presented with this account, the underwriter estimated that the insured could rebuild any one section in six months or less. A severe fire then rendered the residence hall (Section A) a constructive total loss but caused only smoke damage to other sections of the building. Therefore, the damaged section was surrounded by portions of the building that the fire had left intact. This pattern of damage prevented the use of the heavy equipment normally used for reconstruction. Demolition of the remaining structure and removal of the debris took more than six months. The school was unable to reopen until eighteen months after the fire, a period of restoration that was three times the underwriter's estimate.

Long Production Processes The time necessary to convert raw stock into finished goods also has a strong influence on the length of the period of restoration. Raw stock moves smoothly through most production processes, with important

Exhibit 6-4
Construction Bottleneck

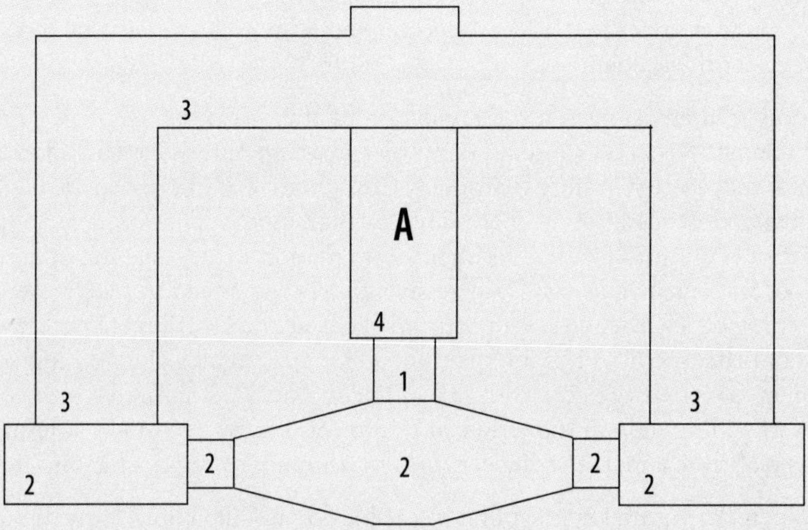

A is the building section destroyed by fire. The numbers represent the number of stories in each wing.

exceptions. The wine production process often includes aging wine in barrels for several years. Production of other alcoholic products, such as fine whiskey, can take even longer. The value of lost stock in process includes the cost of returning it to the stage of production at which the damage occurred. That is part of the direct loss. The production process is not complete, however, until the product is in the bottle. Business income coverage protects the insured against loss of net profits for that period.

Underwriters must consider the length of the production process when determining what amount of business income insurance is adequate for the values at risk. Just as most direct losses are only a small proportion of the value of the insured property, most business income losses do not stop all operations for a full accounting period. Partial losses are the rule. In the vast majority of cases, insureds will resume some operations almost immediately and full operations in less than a year. Rates reflect this fact because they are derived from past loss experience. Even when the insured can resume some operations, a long period of restoration can produce a loss larger than that assumed in the underwriter's assessment. When the insured might need more than a full year to recover from a loss, adequate insurance to value might mean a policy face amount that exceeds a full year's net income.

Incomplete Recovery A long production process could also mean that the market for the insured's product could change significantly while the insured is trying to recover. During an extended period, customer loyalty could fade, or near substitutes for the insured's product could be found. Once back in full production, the insured may find that it may never make a complete recovery because of market dynamics.

Incomplete recovery creates a problem in measuring the period of indemnity. Assuming that the insured will adjust production to the lower level of demand is reasonable. This adjustment permanently reduces the amount of stock in process. Does restoration of the property end when the insured has as much stock in process as before the loss or when the insured has enough stock in process to meet current demand? Underwriters must consider the additional cost of adjusting a loss involving incomplete recovery.

Time Required To Replace Property

Knowing how long it will take the insured to repair, replace, or rebuild damaged or destroyed property helps an underwriter determine the length of the period of restoration. In making this estimate, the underwriter must consider the possibilities of both partial losses and a total loss. As the discussion of construction bottlenecks illustrates, this process is not always simple.

Buildings Several factors, including the following, influence the time necessary to repair or replace a building:

- *Type of construction.* Frame construction requires less building time than fire-resistive construction. As a general rule, the stronger the construction, the more time it requires. Also, the same type of construction might require more time to rebuild in one geographic area than in another. The need for extraordinary wind resistance, for instance, increases construction time for some buildings in the Southeast and along the Gulf Coast.
- *Size.* Larger buildings typically require longer construction periods than smaller ones. When considering size, however, underwriters should remember that configuration can be just as important as size. Separating size into vertical and horizontal components can be useful. Consider, for example, two buildings that have the same total floor area. One is a large single-story structure, and the other has four stories. In one respect they are the same size, but the length of time needed to rebuild them will be different. Work can proceed simultaneously on all areas of the single-story building but must proceed in stages on the taller structure.
- *Quality of construction.* Not all buildings of the same type of construction are of the same quality. A simple structure with a plain exterior and

painted wallboard interior partitions needs less time to rebuild than a more elaborate building.

- *Location*. Building in a congested area requires special precautions during construction. Closing the site is generally not an option, so the builder must protect pedestrians and motorists. If the site is isolated, delivery of materials becomes a problem. One electric utility built a "mine mouth" generating station to reduce operating costs. Coal went directly from the mine into the boilers with no transportation costs. When a turbine failed, no roads were large enough to permit delivery of a replacement to the generating station. Rather than wait for several miles of new road to be constructed, the insurer opted to hire a "flying crane" to fly in the part. The added cost of expediting delivery is part of the time element loss because it reduced the down time of the generating station. By spending more money to complete repairs in less time, the insurer shortened the period of restoration and reduced the total time element loss.
- *Permits*. Rebuilding might require permits that are not easy to obtain. Rules designed to protect the environment can extend the time required to replace some buildings by months or even years. This is especially true in coastal areas, in wilderness areas, and near wetlands. The additional time required to obtain permits needed for repairs extends the period of restoration.
- *Weather*. Weather can have a strong influence on the time required to rebuild a damaged structure. It is a more important factor when construction requires several months. In areas subject to severe weather, the time of year in which a loss occurs can affect the period of restoration.

Personal Property The time required to repair or replace items of personal property can also vary considerably. The factors that exert the strongest influence over this time period include the availability of replacements and the time needed for installation.

Replacement for most personal property used in business is readily available on short notice. This might not be the case, however, when the insured uses imported or custom-made equipment. When analyzing the availability of imported machinery, underwriters should focus on how quickly the insured can obtain a replacement that will perform the same job. Imports might be readily available on short notice from domestic distributors. In that case, they are no different from domestic products. They might also require shipment from the manufacturer. Shipping will extend the time required to restore the property and the period of restoration.

Underwriters must also consider the amount of time necessary to install replacement equipment. Installation is usually not a problem, but if problems occur they are typically related to physically accessing and removing the old equipment and replacing it with new equipment. For example, a production line might be laid out in a large, horizontal arrangement. Replacing damaged equipment at or near the center can require disassembling the whole line. The process might take weeks, but the actual replacement requires only a few hours. Building configuration can also extend the time needed to replace equipment. Openings in exterior or partition walls might not allow the insured to remove damaged property and bring in a replacement. This is a common problem when heating and air conditioning systems need to be replaced. Some large production machinery might pose the same problem. The design of some modern buildings allows ready removal of portions of the building's exterior walls to expedite this type of replacement.

Availability of Substitutes

When replacing damaged or destroyed property takes a long time, the insured might not have to wait to resume full operations. In many cases, other property can be substituted. The substitute can be permanent or temporary. Four alternatives to waiting a long time for a domestic or imported replacement are as follows:

1. *Substitute equipment that is available in a shorter time.* In some cases, the insured can use similar equipment that takes less time to obtain, perhaps substituting equipment made in the United States for imports. The shortest time required to replace lost or damaged assets defines the period of indemnity. The insured does not need to replace the assets with the same brand or even with materials from the same manufacturer. This outcome, however, is not certain. The insured might assert, for example, that substituting domestic equipment for imported equipment permanently impairs the business process. If a dispute arises, it will increase the cost of adjusting losses.

2. *Maintain spares.* The insured can maintain duplicates of crucial equipment. Extra equipment that is in place and ready to use is called an installed spare. If the insured maintains duplicate equipment in storage, it is called a shelf spare. Underwriters must recognize, however, that having spares on the same premises as the equipment they are intended to replace might also increase the amount of the direct loss.

3. *Convert to a different process.* If an insured uses an obsolete process, it might have trouble replacing equipment. Manufacturers might no longer

produce the needed equipment. Used machines might not be available, or they might not restore the insured's operations. Converting to a more modern process might be the only way to expedite repairs and allow the insured to resume operations. This solution is especially practical when the loss is total or nearly total. The obsolete equipment is gone, and the insured has a chance to begin anew. If this option is realistic, the underwriter must assess its effect on moral and morale hazards. The possibility of replacing obsolete equipment with new might reduce the incentive to avoid and control losses and could increase the incentive to commit arson for profit.

4. *Use rented equipment.* The insured can sometimes reduce or eliminate a time element loss by renting replacement equipment. A portable air compressor mounted on a trailer can replace, for example, a permanently installed compressor that has been damaged or destroyed. Even replacements for components of the building, such as boilers, electrical panels, and heating and air conditioning systems, can be rented in an emergency.

Estimating the period of restoration for schools with no practical substitutes requires additional consideration. The underwriter must consider the effect of the academic calendar on the loss to a school at any level. Businesses and most institutions can resume operations as soon as they can restore the damaged property, but a school cannot. If restoration of the property extends into a new term or semester, the school will have to cancel classes during that term or semester. A school might also lose tuition income if it cannot complete repairs before the term or semester begins. The time necessary for repairs might extend the period of restoration and create a need to modify the period of indemnity.

Endorsed business income forms fill this need by extending the period of indemnity for schools to the end of the semester or term during which the insured could have restored the property. If that date is less than sixty days before the start of a new term or semester, the endorsement extends the period of indemnity until the end of the new term or semester. Underwriters must consider this additional factor when evaluating the business income exposures that schools face.

Disaster Recovery Planning and the Period of Restoration

Another factor that affects the length of the period of restoration is the extent to which the insured has prepared for a loss before it occurs. This is **disaster recovery planning**, and it is an important part of any complete risk management program. A good disaster recovery plan can dramatically reduce a time element loss.

On March 4, 1988, fire swept through the headquarters of First Interstate Bank of California in downtown Los Angeles. The blaze, one of the worst in the city's history, shut down the bank's headquarters and data center. It kept the bank in temporary quarters for four months, but branch customers hardly noticed. The timing of the loss was fortunate, but it did not determine the outcome. The loss occurred just after the close of banking hours, so First Interstate did not have to close branch office operations immediately. By the next morning, the bank's disaster control team had restored all essential functions, and the branches were able to open on time. Within three days, First Interstate was fully operational, including service at all of its automatic teller machines (ATMs).

Careful planning resulted in significant savings. In the absence of good planning, three more days would have been necessary to restore essential services and at least another week to get operations back to normal. First Interstate Bank was not the only beneficiary of careful planning. The business income and extra expense losses that its insurers incurred were also substantially lower than they might have been. Underwriters who understand the benefits of disaster planning are in the best position to assess an insured's program.

Most experts believe that the most important aspect of disaster recovery plans is simply having one. Such a plan indicates that the insured has recognized the possibility that a loss will occur and has devoted some resources to recovering from such a loss. A disaster recovery plan is part of the insured's overall risk management program. If the disaster recovery plan is to be effective, the risk management program must have clear post-loss objectives. These are goals that the insured seeks to achieve after a loss has occurred. They include survival and the maintenance of normal operations. They should be expressed as performance standards. First Interstate Bank, for instance, might have established goals of opening all branches at the start of the next business day after a loss and of having all ATMs back on line within three business days. A well-designed plan starts with establishing these goals and selects the best methods to achieve them. An effective disaster recovery plan includes three phases: pre-loss planning, emergency, and recovery.

Pre-Loss Planning Phase

The **pre-loss planning phase** includes things the insured does *before* any loss occurs. Many experts regard it as the most important phase. However, because pre-loss planning prepares for an event that might never occur, motivating management to implement this phase can be difficult. Pre-loss planning is difficult, and its need is easy for insureds to overlook. First Interstate Bank recognized the need and hired a vice president who had no responsibility other than pre-loss planning. Most insureds do not go that far. The best plans nevertheless result when one person in the organization is responsible for disaster planning. Such a decision by First Interstate Bank proved to be invaluable.

In the planning phase, the insured develops plans and makes certain that they can be implemented immediately. Plans should include arrangements for temporary quarters and backup services. Key personnel have to know their assignments. If pre-loss planning is done properly, the disaster plan is most likely to be successful. Neglect of this phase can cripple a disaster recovery plan or render it useless, which is worse.

In the planning phase, the insured should prepare a convenient off-site command room so that the disaster coordinator can start work as soon as a loss occurs. The insured should have contingency plans for temporary quarters. An account with multiple locations might be able to use other, nearby locations. In large cities, insureds can usually contract for space with companies whose only business is to provide temporary quarters. Communications are crucial in an emergency. The insured should involve the local telephone company and long-distance provider in the planning process before a loss occurs. They are important sources of information and ideas and can prepare their own plans for restoring lost service.

A business that relies on data processing should arrange for alternate facilities in its disaster recovery plan. This process includes selecting an alternate site and backing up all programs and data files off site. Many organizations protect themselves by performing this function on a regular or daily basis. Secure off-site storage and contingency computer capacity are available in most areas of the United States. Some facilities also provide emergency data processing services. Maintaining copies of all software at the backup data processing facility is often the most effective way to reduce downtime after a loss. For an additional charge, most backup data processing facilities will mount software so that it can be run immediately. Both the primary and backup computers should at least share a common operating system. Materials selected for off-site storage should include copies of the disaster recovery plan. Underwriters should assume that key personnel will lose their copies of the plan in a fire or other loss and need replacements.

Rehearsals can be an important part of an effective disaster control plan. They let everyone know what the plan demands of them. Rehearsals also provide an effective test that might be the only way to detect serious flaws in the plan before it must be implemented.

Emergency Phase

The **emergency phase** is the shortest, covering only the time at which the insured puts the disaster recovery plan into motion. Key personnel move to their assigned stations and begin carrying out their designated responsibilities. This phase can begin as soon as the right person escapes the immediate danger. First Interstate Bank had this phase well under way before the fire service had even deployed all its apparatus. Before the fire was extinguished, the bank's computer network started to come back on line. Careful planning and prompt action allowed the bank to resume all essential operations the next morning. The bank did not lose income, but this does not mean that it did not sustain a time element loss. Business income forms cover the cost of continuing operations to the extent of the reduction in the loss of income.

Recovery Phase

The **recovery phase** is the period of time during which the insured brings the business back from the emergency. Much of its success depends on the preparation that went into the planning phase. However, a business cannot simply forge ahead with a prepared disaster recovery plan when a severe loss strikes. No one can anticipate everything, and some planned actions might not achieve their goals. The insured must be ready to respond to unexpected developments. However careful and thorough the preparation, the recovery phase is not a time to regard the disaster recovery plan as inflexible or unchangeable. The insured must remain ready to react and adjust to conditions as they develop.

Planning for the recovery phase should recognize that time element losses are potentially larger than direct losses. Planning should focus on restoring normal operations as soon after a loss occurs as possible. Businesses in service industries cannot afford to let a loss interrupt their operations for a prolonged period. Rather than wait, customers will find alternate sources of services and might not return. The benefits of good disaster planning, however, do not accrue only to service businesses. Mercantile and manufacturing accounts can benefit from a well-drafted disaster recovery plan as much as and sometimes even more than service industries can.

A disaster recovery plan does not have to be elaborate to work well. A retail paint chain's disaster recovery plan consisted of simply a counter and cash register in a warehouse one block from its flagship store. When fire destroyed that store, the company was ready to conduct business at the warehouse. The morning after the loss, the company opened for business at its regular time while the fire service was still hosing down the remains of the store. It lost very little business because its customers were directed to the new location.

Maximum Loss During the Period of Restoration

One method often used to compute the PML for business income coverage is to divide the maximum period of restoration by one year and multiply the result by the coinsurance basis from the business income worksheet. Underwriters should avoid using this method, however. It is fast and easy, but the results are not reliable. It ignores the following important facts:

- The business income worksheet establishes the value for coinsurance but does not measure the exposure to loss. Certain expenses that the insured does not deduct to arrive at business income values will often cease after a loss occurs. Some expenses that the insured does deduct, on the other hand, might continue.
- Income changes from year to year, going up more often than down.
- Very few businesses earn all their income evenly over the course of a year.
- The insured is almost always in a position to take at least some steps to reduce the amount of the business income loss.
- The coinsurance basis does not include any estimate of extra expenses.

Business Income Values at Risk

In discussions of direct loss, the value at risk is reasonably clear. The physical characteristics of the property and the method for arriving at the policy values help to determine the amount exposed to a single loss. Appraisals are almost always consistent. Business income exposures do not share these characteristics. The factors that determine the value at risk and the PML are far more subjective. The underwriter must try to measure the exposure to loss of net profit *plus* expenses that must continue during the period of indemnity. As noted, the process for projecting profits and expenses is uncertain at best. Discerning which expenses will continue in the event of a loss and those that will not compounds the evaluation.

Noncontinuing Expenses

Distinguishing those expenses that will continue after a loss from those that will not is not an easy task. The extent to which expenses must continue after a loss will vary from one business to another, even within the same industry. A thorough assessment requires a level of familiarity with the insured's operations that an underwriter rarely has. Some costs normally abate after a loss, and others normally continue. For an individual risk, the underwriter can determine how far these costs depart from the norm. This determination provides a sound basis for an estimate of whether business income values will be above or below average. The coinsurance basis computed in the business income worksheet provides a useful benchmark for this process.

The cost of raw stock and other costs deducted in arriving at the basis for coinsurance in the business income worksheet do not normally continue after a loss, with some exceptions. In return for a preferred price or simply to ensure a steady supply, the insured might have agreed to purchase a certain amount of raw stock. This obligation might continue during a shutdown, regardless of whether the insured can use the materials. If this is the case, the loss does not always have to include the full cost of the raw stock that the insured would have purchased. Stopping the shipment and reimbursing the supplier for the lost sales might be possible. The insured might also be able to resell the raw materials it purchases, sometimes at a profit.

Payroll is the second major area in which the insured can reduce expenses. Most businesses reduce payroll when a loss requires a shutdown. When idled by fire or loss from another cause, most businesses lay off a large number of their employees rather than continue to pay them. The wages that this group earns are referred to as **ordinary payroll**. Ordinary payroll consists of both hourly wages and salaries paid to employees whose services are not so essential that they must continue. It does not include the earnings of any employee whose pay continues under contract or whose services the insured needs in order to resume operations.

The type of arrangement by which employers continue to pay some employees should a loss occur usually applies only to management and technical personnel. In some cases, the insured might have to extend this benefit to retain the services of skilled workers.

After a loss, the insured might need to continue paying certain employees in order to keep their services available until the business reopens. A manufacturer of high-quality shoes, for instance, must rely on skilled labor. If the insured's plant is near but not in a shoe manufacturing center, a layoff might prompt these skilled employees to relocate. They would no longer be available when the insured becomes ready to resume operations. The need to pay these employees to ensure that they will be available when operations resume makes this portion of ordinary payroll an expense that must continue following a loss.

Whether rent expense continues is a question the underwriter must answer. Commercial leases often abate rent during any time in which the insured cannot occupy the premises because of accidental loss or damage. Overhead expenses are almost always lower during recovery from a loss. These expenses include the cost of telephone service, heat, light, power, and support operations.

Insurance premiums based on sales or payroll will abate to the same extent as the rate basis. A severe loss might reduce the value at risk from direct loss and might allow the insured to purchase a lower amount of property insurance. During a long shutdown, the insured might be able to reduce costs by suspending auto insurance on a fleet that is out of service. Janitorial, delivery, and other services that the insured purchases from outsiders probably will not continue.

Underwriters must be careful not to carry these deductions too far. A serious loss might seem to reduce the insured's taxes. The property, after all, is worth less than its appraised value, and lower sales should mean lower income taxes. However, a reduction in taxes usually does not occur. Property taxes might be reduced through an appeal process, but this can be complex and is the exception more often than the rule. Income taxes will not change if the insured has an appropriate amount of business income insurance. The Internal Revenue Code defines the proceeds of property insurance as taxable income. Taxes based on payroll will be lower, but most other taxes will remain the same. Exhibit 6-5 lists expenses that might not continue after a direct loss.

Changes in the Level of Income

The basis for coinsurance in business income forms is the value for either the twelve months following the loss (under the gross earnings form) or for the policy year during which the loss occurs (under the business income form). Worksheets for estimating this value start with the one-year period preceding the current policy year. The insured has to adjust these values to reflect conditions that will prevail in the future. Because those values are estimates of future income and expenses, the values calculated on the worksheet often do not accurately measure an insured's business income exposure. The ideal selected value would consider the expected growth of the insured's business and recognize that the time element loss could occur at any time during the policy period. A loss on the last day of the policy period would require almost prophetic insight to accurately estimate values. It is this need to project values that many insureds, producers, and underwriters find frustrating about business income insurance.

Seasonal Variations in Income

Underwriters must recognize that most businesses earn more during certain parts of the year than during others. The effect of seasonal fluctuations can be highly variable. These fluctuations are more often an issue for mercantile and service accounts than for manufacturers. A manufacturer transfers its output into inventory from which it meets orders. As a result, production is much more level than sales. Businesses that buy and sell goods or provide a service

Exhibit 6-5
Possible Noncontinuing Expenses

	Actual for 19X5	Estimated Abatements	Estimated Continuing Expenses
Expenses			
Salaries	$160,000	$120,000	$ 40,000
Payroll taxes	8,000	6,000	2,000
Rent	50,000	0	50,000
Postage, etc.	1,000	0	1,000
Telephone	10,000	7,500	2,500
Depreciation on furniture and fixtures	20,000	15,000	5,000
Advertising	19,000	0	19,000
Delivery expense	6,000	6,000	0
Taxes, licenses, etc.	1,000	0	1,000
Insurance premiums	2,000	1,000	1,000
Total expenses	$277,000	$155,500	$121,500

do not have a similar experience. The proper measure of PML is a loss for the longest period of restoration that the underwriter can expect and that occurs at the start of or just before the insured's peak season.

Forming an estimate of the insured's peak season values might demand more time than the underwriter can afford. Knowing industry patterns provides a basis for a realistic estimate that does not require a great deal of research. Some insureds also experience more than one peak season in the course of a year. This type of pattern tends to mitigate the effect of seasonal fluctuations. It can produce a PML very close to the simple estimate that assumes the insured earns its income evenly throughout the year.

Reducing the Amount of Business Income Loss

When a loss occurs, the insured can probably control its size. A manufacturer with several plants might be able to increase production at an undamaged location. Directing customers to a nearby location might be a practical option for a retail chain. A small retail or service business might be able to resume operations at a new location long before repairs to its damaged premises are complete. The insured might be able to move to a new location while repairs are in progress and return when they are complete. The business might continue partial operations at the damaged premises while repairs are underway. Ideally, the underwriter should be aware of the insured's options and include them in the estimate of the business income PML. This inclusion, however, requires a degree of familiarity with local conditions that most underwriters cannot develop but that local producers can. For example, a producer might know that the local real estate market is limited and that the insured might not be able to relocate.

Insurance to Value for Business Income Coverage

Purchasing adequate insurance for the values exposed, or simply insurance to value, is an important consideration for time element coverage, but it is not as easy to measure when it relates to time element coverage as when it relates to direct loss. When this concept is extended to business income coverage, some value judgments are required. The proper way to determine how much business income coverage the insured needs is to start with the PML expressed as a dollar amount. Since this is the largest loss the insured can expect, it might appear to be the proper amount of insurance. This approach, however, fails to recognize the role of coinsurance.

To convert the PML to an amount that represents adequate insurance for the business income values exposed to loss, the underwriter should divide the PML by the coinsurance basis from the business income worksheet. For some accounts the result will exceed 100 percent because a severe loss can shut a business down for more than a year. Some businesses might also have to continue more of their expenses than the business income worksheet assumes. If the result is less than 125 percent, the number should be rounded up to the next higher coinsurance percentage for which the rules provide. The coinsurance basis should then be multiplied by the coinsurance percentage. This method produces an amount that both provides adequate insurance to exposed values and fulfills the coinsurance requirement.

A request for a higher amount of direct loss coverage than needed should cause an underwriter to seek more information. Too much insurance might indicate a moral hazard. The same is not true for time element coverages. Probable maximum loss and values at risk are both more subjective. The insured's estimate of the longest period of restoration or future business income values might be higher than the underwriter's. Extra insurance can also provide an added level of comfort that the insured considers worth the cost.

Options in Business Income Insurance

The underwriter and the insured do not have to take business income coverage as provided by the basic form. The coverage forms include options, and the underwriter can develop others.

Options for Small Businesses

Two of the options in business income coverage forms are of value mainly to small businesses. These options work well only when the longest period of restoration that the insured will face is six months or less. They have less effect on coverage than on the amount of effort the insured must expend to determine its insurance needs. They also permit the insured to obtain coverage without completing a business income worksheet. Small businesses sometimes do not want to disclose financial data in the level of detail required for completion of the worksheet. They value their privacy, and the forms allow them to protect it. These options, explained below, have the added advantage of replacing the coinsurance clause, which many insureds do not understand.

Maximum Period of Indemnity Option

Business income coverage forms offer the insured the option of limiting the period of indemnity to 120 days. When the insured selects this option, the coinsurance clause does not apply. From the underwriter's standpoint, this option limits the period of restoration for which payment will be made. In many cases, the insured will not be willing to provide the information from which the underwriter computes the PML, but this drawback is not serious. The face amount and exposed values are typically low. In most cases, the premium does not justify the time and effort needed to compute the PML.

Monthly Limit of Indemnity Option

The monthly limit of indemnity option allows the insured to limit recovery to one-sixth, one-fourth, or one-third of the face amount for each thirty consecutive days. There is a temptation to think of this option as providing coverage for a maximum loss of three, four, or six months. This is true only if the insured business earns its income evenly throughout the year. If income fluctuates, the period of indemnity varies. The coinsurance clause once again does not apply. Many underwriters refer to a business income form with this option as a valued form, but the term is not accurate. Actual loss sustained is still the measure of loss.

The monthly limit of indemnity option provides the same benefits as the maximum period of indemnity option. For a business that earns its income evenly over the course of a year, there are no significant disadvantages. Income that fluctuates from month to month, on the other hand, often makes it impossible for an insured to obtain adequate insurance for the values at risk without purchasing more insurance than needed for months when income is low. The only way to cover the month with the highest income is to purchase a total limit of three, four, or six times the highest monthly income. For a business that has a distinct peak season, this can mean purchasing more insurance than it needs for a significant portion of the year. Having coverage that is adequate for the month when income is highest means buying more coverage than needed for the other eleven months.

Limits on Coverage for Ordinary Payroll

The coverage form defines business income to include continuing normal operating expenses, *including payroll*. Many businesses know before a loss that they will not continue ordinary payroll if they shut down. By endorsement, their business income coverage can reflect this reality. This option allows the insured to delete all coverage for ordinary payroll or limit coverage to 90 or 180 days. The coinsurance basis is reduced by the amount of ordinary payroll that is no longer covered. This might have little effect on an underwriter who computes the PML for business income in detail, because the PML acknowledges that payroll will abate when a loss occurs. This option primarily affects coverage for ordinary payroll, the basis for coinsurance, and the rate. It provides a better match between exposed values and coverage for some businesses.

Valued Forms

Valued business income forms pay the insured a fixed amount for each day, week, or month that the business must close because of a covered loss. They prorate this amount for a loss that reduces the level of business activity or for a shutdown that is less than a full coverage period. These are known as daily, weekly, or monthly indemnity forms, according to the period that is the basis for recovery or payment. They also include a maximum limit for any one loss. Although they were once in general use, valued forms have become rare. In most lines of insurance, insurers must develop the valued forms themselves.

Using valued forms makes the PML easy to compute. The underwriter need only estimate the longest period of restoration, then apply the daily, weekly, or monthly value to it. However, these forms often produce an amount of insurance that is too large or too small for the exposure. Coverage is based on the assumption that the insured's income is the same for each day, week, or month, and that is rarely true. If the amount of insurance is too low, valued forms shortchange the insured when a loss occurs. When the amount of insurance is too high, the underwriter must consider the possibility of moral hazard. The underwriter cannot ignore the possibility that the insured might see the opportunity to replace falling income with an "insured" loss.

Many insureds prefer valued forms because they incorrectly believe that proving the amount of a business income loss would not be necessary. If a fire causes a business to shut down for a week, for example, the insured knows just how much the business income insurance will pay. The problem with that reasoning is that most losses are only partial. In order to recover the proper proportion of the daily, weekly, or monthly indemnity, the insured must show how much business it would have conducted and how much it actually did, so the need to prove the loss remains.

Valued forms also seem to relieve the insured of the need to complete a business income worksheet. The underwriter, however, might need the worksheet in order to evaluate the coverage properly. Completing the worksheet might be the only way to determine that insured values reflect the income the business can expect to earn in the future. With no intent to deceive the underwriter, the insured might overstate income. The owner of a small business, for instance, might equate income with receipts and overlook that expenses do not continue at the same rate when a loss shuts the business down. Underwriters must anticipate this common mistake. They can then convince insureds that worksheet completion is often necessary.

Other Time Element Coverages

Other time element coverages include the following:

- Extra expense
- Combined business income and extra expense
- Contingent business income and extra expense
- Blanket business income and extra expense
- Leasehold interest
- Manufacturer's selling price (finished stock only)

Extra Expense Coverage

Often, a business might want or need to continue to operate after a loss occurs, even when the cost of keeping the business open is more than the income it would lose by closing. Service businesses often feel that they have no choice but to continue operations. If they close, their customers will go elsewhere and might never return. The costs of continuing the business, unfortunately, often bear little or no relationship to the value of the property or the income it generates. Business income forms cover extra expense to the extent that incurring added cost reduces the loss of income. Extra expense coverage addresses the needs of insureds who must spend beyond reducing loss of income to remain viable enterprises in the short term.

The amount of extra expense insurance that an insured will need is largely a matter of speculation. In most cases, the insured will not know the cost of continuing operations until a loss actually occurs, unless the insured has done a thorough job of disaster planning. For instance, the insured can arrange for temporary quarters or to replace essential services. For a manufacturer, these arrangements might include a prior agreement to use the facilities of a competitor if a loss occurs. Exhibit 6-6 provides an example of a worksheet the

Exhibit 6-6
Extra Expense Worksheet

Expenses Necessary to Continue Business	First Month	Second Month	Third Month
Rent of temporary premises			
Cleaning temporary premises			
Labor equipping temporary premises			
Rent of temporary machinery, equipment, etc.			
Net cost of equipment, purchased			
Expense of moving equipment, etc.			
Light, power, and heat at temporary premises			
Labor at temporary premises			
Insurance expense at temporary premises			
Janitor and watchman at temporary premises			
Other expenses at or because of temporary premises (advertising, telephone, telegraph, legal, etc.)			
Total due to temporary premises			
Add payments to others for manufacturing or processing			
Add necessarily continuing expenses at original location after a loss			
Add bonuses for quick services, etc.			
Total expenses after a loss			
Deduct total of expenses which would have been incurred at the original location for the corresponding period had no loss incurred			
Extra expense insurance to be carried			

Reprinted with permission from Henry C. Klein, *Business Interruption Insurance* (Indianapolis, IN: The Rough Notes Co., 1964), p. 253.

underwriter can suggest to the insured for computing extra expense before a loss occurs.

Extra expense forms express the coverage limit in two ways. The face amount is the most that the insurer will pay for any extra expense loss. The length of the period of indemnity also limits the amount the insurer will pay. This limit is expressed as a percentage of the face amount available when the period of indemnity is a certain number of months. For example, an extra expense form might pay the following:

- 40 percent of the limit when the period of interruption is less than one month
- 80 percent of the limit when the period of interruption is more than one month but less than two months
- 100 percent of the limit when the period of interruption is more than two months

The monthly limits for extra expense are extremely flexible because there are only two rules. The increment for additional months should not be larger than the limit for the first month. Monthly limits of 20 percent, 60 percent, and 100 percent would, for example, be inappropriate in most cases. This rule reflects the fact that extra expense in the first month tends to be larger than in subsequent months. The highest monthly limit must also equal 100 percent. Otherwise, the insured would be unable to collect the full amount of insurance. With these two rules in mind, the underwriter can construct any combination of monthly limits the insured needs. For example, the full limit can be available for a one-month period of restoration.

Combined Business Income and Extra Expense Coverage

The insured can also elect to apply a single limit to both the business income and extra expense coverages. This option recognizes that the two coverages overlap to a certain extent. An insured that buys enough of each coverage often has more total coverage than it needs. When writing this coverage, underwriters should evaluate each of the components separately. The value at risk and the PML do not change simply because one form provides both coverages. The premium will be lower because the combined form eliminates duplicate coverage.

Contingent Business Income and Extra Expense Coverage

Frequently, the income of one business depends on the property of another. This is called a contingent business income or extra expense exposure. Contingent business income and extra expense coverage insures the loss that results when another business sustains a direct loss. Three situations that might create this type of exposure are as follows:

- A **leader location** is another business that attracts customers who then visit the insured's premises. Leader locations include large department stores in downtown shopping areas and malls. Smaller stores depend on these leaders to draw traffic and will suffer a loss of income if the leader location closes.
- A **contributing location** is a key supplier that provides raw materials, supplies, or services that the insured business needs. It is often a sole supplier on whom the insured depends completely. The insured might or might not have access to another source.
- A **recipient location** is one that buys all or a large part of the insured's output. The insured might or might not be able to make up lost income by sales to other customers.

Writing contingent time element coverage requires underwriting the other business just as if it were the insured. The underwriter must analyze the same physical, financial, morale, and moral hazards. This analysis presents two major problems. More often than not, the underwriter has no direct contact with the other business. Information can be difficult to obtain, and underwriters have little influence over hazards they observe. When dealing directly with its own insured, an insurer can offer suggestions to reduce the chance of loss. For contingent time element coverage, however, underwriters must often accept conditions as they discover them. Obtaining access to the information that forms the basis for the decision can also be a problem. For example, an inspection might be out of the question, or financial statements might not be available.

The underwriter must also consider the effect that shutting down the other business will have on the insured's income. Leader locations have become less important in recent years, but they can still have a major effect. A few years ago, a large discount chain failed and closed its stores. One anchored a mall with another large store and several small stores. Before the mall found another anchor tenant, almost every one of the small stores had gone out of business. Even the other anchor store, a branch of one of the country's largest chains, lost money. Although contingent business income forms do not insure losses caused by bankruptcy, the consequences of business failures illustrate the outcome that an underwriter can expect loss from a covered cause to produce. Today, large stores are becoming less significant, as consumer tastes have shifted and specialty stores and boutiques command a larger share of the market than previously was the case. This trend makes customers more likely to return to small stores near a large one that has closed. Yet in many communities, closing one large magnet store can virtually destroy a mall or downtown shopping area. The trend toward several major stores in shopping malls has also reduced the exposure leader locations create. More often than not, loss of a single magnet store has little effect on total traffic at a mall.

For contributing and recipient locations, the underwriter must consider whether the insured could find other sources of supply or other outlets for its output. These can reduce or even eliminate a loss of income. However, finding other sources or outlets is not always possible. Automobile parts manufacturers, for example, often locate their plants adjacent to the automobile assembly plants, presenting the underwriter with both a contributing and a recipient location. Any loss that interrupts one company's business will have the same effect on the other. The customer often does not have enough storage to use another source of supply, and the supplier often has no way to deliver its output to other customers. Exhibit 6-7 illustrates a flowchart an underwriter can use to analyze these effects.

As with other business interruptions, the insured might be able to make some adjustments in its products or processes to mitigate loss. Contingent business income and time element forms will pay the cost of these changes, similar to the way in which forms covering loss that occurs on the insured's premises do.

Blanket Business Income and Extra Expense Coverage

Sometimes, the same company owns both contributing and recipient locations. A company might, for example, produce parts of its product at three separate plants and assemble them at a fourth. A loss at any one plant might shut down all four. The insured might purchase separate business income coverage for one location. The policy will then respond only to income lost at the location of the direct loss. The insured will have no coverage for the loss it sustains when the other three plants must close. A retail store's sales might also depend heavily on stock stored in a separate warehouse. Business income coverage on the store will respond only for damage to stock in the store. Separate coverage on the warehouse does not make sense because the insured does not make any sales there. Although loss at the warehouse can cause a loss of income, the warehouse itself has no business value associated with it. Blanket business income and extra expense coverage solve this problem. Each covers loss of income from direct damage to any covered location. Underwriting blanket coverage is similar to underwriting specific coverage.

Leasehold Interest Coverage

A leasehold interest is created when the insured derives a financial benefit

Exhibit 6-7
External Flow

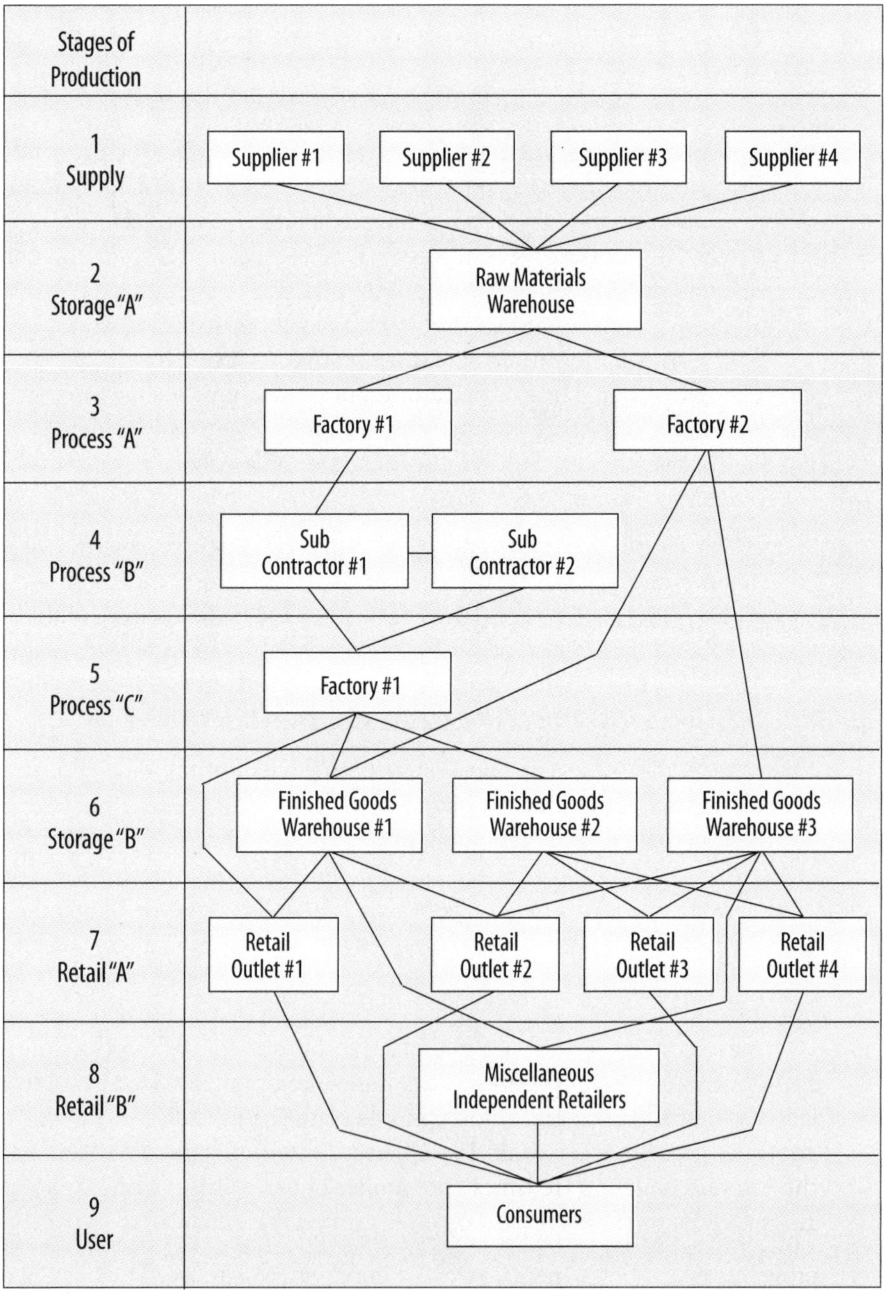

Reprinted with permission from Matthew Lenz, Jr., *Risk Management Manual* (Santa Monica, CA: The Merritt Company, 1993), p. 22.

from a lease. Many leases contain a fire clause that allows the lessor to terminate the lease when a covered cause of loss damages the premises. The leasehold interest can arise from three situations:

- The lease might charge rent that is below fair market value. If the landlord cancels the lease because of a covered loss, the insured will have to pay higher rent for the same or comparable space.
- The insured might have prepaid rent or paid a bonus to obtain the lease. At the start of the lease, the insured might have had to pay the last month's (or several months') rent in advance. Tenants sometimes pay a bonus to obtain a lease on favorable terms. These payments are not ordinarily refundable if the landlord cancels the lease because of damage to the leased premises.
- The tenant might have installed improvements and betterments. These are fixtures that become part of the real estate as soon as they are installed. They belong to the landlord (or lessor). The tenant has the exclusive right to use them during the term of the lease but may not remove them without the landlord's permission.

In the first case, the value of the leasehold interest can be computed from the difference between the rent the lease calls for and fair market rental. This difference is the monthly leasehold interest. The total value is the monthly leasehold interest times the number of months remaining in the lease, minus interest. Knowing the total value relieves the insurer of the need to make monthly payments over an extended period. It is the net present value of a series of payments equal to the monthly leasehold interest. It is the amount the insured would need to hold at interest to draw a monthly payment equal to the monthly leasehold interest for the remaining term of the lease. The calculations are complex, but underwriters need not perform them. Leasehold interest forms provide a set of tables that contain factors that allow computing the total leasehold for a given term at a specific interest rate. The rules also provide a formula that underwriters can use for other terms or interest rates.

For a bonus or prepaid rent, the payments are amortized over the life of the lease. For a five-year lease, for example, one-sixtieth of the amount of the bonus or prepaid rent would be assigned to each month. The total value of the interest is this figure times the number of months remaining in the lease.

The same approach is used to compute the value of the insured's right to use improvements and betterments, with one important difference. The original cost of the improvements and betterments is amortized from the date they were installed to the date the current lease expires. When the tenant first installs them, the value of the leasehold interest is the cost of the improvements. This value declines at an even rate over the term of the lease. If the insured renews the lease, the value of the leasehold increases, but not to the full cost of the improvements. Exhibit 6-8 illustrates the value of a leasehold interest in $30,000 of improvements installed at the start of a five-year lease that the parties renew twice. It shows the value of the leasehold interest at the start of each year of each lease. Over the term of the first lease, the value of this interest declines at the rate of $500 per month, or $6,000 per year. It declines at half that rate during the term of the second lease, and one-third that rate over the term of the third lease. On the day each lease expires, the value of the leasehold interest is reduced to zero.

Exhibit 6-8
Value of Improvements and Betterments Over Three Five-Year Leases

Year	Leasehold Interest	Year	Leasehold Interest	Year	Leasehold Interest
X1	$30,000	Y1	$15,000	Z1	$10,000
X2	$24,000	Y2	$12,000	Z2	$8,000
X3	$18,000	Y3	$9,000	Z3	$6,000
X4	$12,000	Y4	$6,000	Z4	$4,000
X5	$6,000	Y5	$3,000	Z5	$2,000

Manufacturer's Selling Price Coverage

Manufacturers convert raw materials into finished stock. Loss of finished stock does not interrupt their business, yet it presents a significant economic loss to the business. The insured might view the loss of sales that results from damage to finished stock as a loss of income, but this type of loss is not covered by business income insurance.

The proper way to insure this exposure is with the manufacturer's selling price endorsement. This endorsement sets the value of the insured's finished stock at the selling price of finished stock minus any discounts and expenses the insured did not incur. This is the same approach used in the building and personal property coverage form to establish the value of stock sold but not delivered. The difference is that the manufacturer's selling price endorsement applies this value to stock the insured has not sold.

Consequential Loss Coverages

When a loss occurs, the insured might sustain damage to property that goes beyond the direct action of the covered cause of loss. The exposures that underwriters will usually encounter arise from building codes and interruption of services provided from a site other than the insured's premises.

Building Codes

Almost every community has some form of law regulating the construction of commercial buildings. These codes change frequently, but in most cases existing structures do not have to comply with the new provisions. Exemptions for structures in place before a code change takes effect are known as grandfather clauses. Underwriters refer to exempted buildings as nonconforming occupancies. Operation of building code provisions can increase the amount of loss the owner of a nonconforming occupancy faces.

Some building codes require demolition of the undamaged portion of a structure that sustains a certain amount of damage. The codes often impose this requirement only on nonconforming occupancies. The extent of damage that triggers this type of requirement is often high, for example, 50 percent or 75 percent. It can also be low, 10 percent, for instance, if the code authorities regard the nonconforming occupancy as especially hazardous. This type of building code requirement creates two exposures for which insurance is available separately. One coverage applies to the value of the undamaged portion of the building. Its effect is to convert a partial loss to a total loss. A second coverage insures the cost of tearing down the undamaged portion of the structure when codes prohibit rebuilding. These two exposures exist only in tandem, so insuring them together makes sense.

The exemption that a grandfather clause provides might terminate when the insured improves the building. In extreme cases, the termination provision applies to any work that requires a building permit. Making any improvements to the property requires the insured to bring the entire property into full compliance with current codes. More often, damage beyond a defined extent removes the exemption. To repair the damage from a covered cause of loss, the insured might have to make substantial improvements. This is especially true in areas in which wind and seismic codes are an important issue, but the problem can arise anywhere.

To evaluate losses caused by changes in building codes, underwriters must know what local codes require and whether the insured structure meets current code standards. If the code will demand demolition of undamaged portions of the building, a total loss becomes much more likely. Damage to the extent that will require full replacement might be within the PML. In such a case, the underwriter must set the PML at 100 percent of the structure's value. Coverage for the cost of demolishing any part of the structure that remains sound after a loss does no more than increase the value at risk. In most cases, the need for this coverage implies that a total loss is within the PML, which must then include demolition cost. The underwriter must decide to provide coverage at 100 percent of the PML or decline the account.

Coverage for code improvements raises some important issues. Both the value at risk and the PML increase to reflect the higher value of the better quality structure the code requires. Once again, the underwriter must decide whether this is an acceptable exposure. In addition, the prospect of getting a better building that needs no grandfather clause might create a moral hazard.

Off-Premises Power Failure

Almost any business can incur a consequential loss, a business income loss, or an extra expense loss if services provided from outside the premises fail. Power and telephone outages are common concerns. A consequential loss occurs when lack of power, light, heat, or refrigeration damages property. A business income or extra expense loss occurs when the outage interrupts the insured's business or increases operating costs. The ISO forms portfolio includes two endorsements that address this type of loss:

- Utility Services—Direct Damage
- Utility Services—Time Element

The first endorsement, which is attached to building and personal property forms, covers damage to the insured's property as the result of interruption of service to the insured's premises; the second endorsement, which is attached to business income forms, covers the insured's business income losses. The outage must be the result of damage to utility property from a covered cause of loss. Coverage for damage to overhead utility lines is an option on both endorsements. The underwriter's prime concern is the expected frequency and severity of outages. Underwriting requests for off-premises power failure coverage requires local knowledge of the performance of utility companies providing service to the insured's premises. For the most part, utilities in urban and suburban areas have provided excellent service with few outages. Losses are infrequent, but they can be significant.

The underwriter must analyze the extent to which the insured depends on services such as power, telephone, or water. In the case of electric service, most insureds are unable to function without it. An uninterruptible power supply (UPS) or emergency generator might provide adequate protection against loss. These systems can be effective. During a 1977 power outage, both CBS and NBC were running network movies from their New York affiliates. CBS had a UPS, but NBC did not. The CBS movie flickered briefly but continued. NBC had to drive the videotape to its Philadelphia affiliate. The movie had an unscheduled break of more than an hour. Underwriters might want to consider a UPS as a basic requirement for this coverage if the exposure is especially severe. Many businesses seem to assume that the duration of outages will be short enough that they can make up any lost business when power returns.

Summary

Indirect losses occur as a consequence of direct loss. Business income coverage enables a business to meet continuing expenses and protect its net profits. Some businesses cannot afford to be out of business for any extended period of time because their customers will go elsewhere. For those businesses that rely on customer loyalty, such as dry cleaners and banks, extra expense coverage is available. Extra expense coverage pays for the additional expenses needed to continue operations during a business interruption.

Time and timing affect the severity of a business income loss. The longer it takes to restore the damaged property and get back into business, the greater the loss will be. A loss just before the business's peak season will have a greater effect than if the same loss occurred just after the business's prime season had passed.

Determining the appropriate amount of business income coverage requires more calculations than direct loss coverage. Estimates must be made on the expected period of restoration and the level of expenses that will continue. The coinsurance clause of the business income policy is designed to encourage insureds to carry adequate coverage amounts. Insureds must understand the operation of the coinsurance clause so that the best estimates of income and operating expense can be made. The coinsurance clause does not apply to extra expense coverage.

In addition to determining the amount of coverage the insured should carry, the underwriter needs to determine the probable maximum loss (PML) and the measures that are available to reduce losses. Calculating PML involves estimating the most serious loss likely to occur and estimating the longest period of restoration that can reasonably be expected. Each of these estimates raises many specific concerns. The extent to which the insured anticipates a business income loss and has made plans to diminish its effect lowers the PML.

Many insureds, particularly small businesses, find the business income worksheet confusing and simply do not want to complete one. The maximum period of indemnity option and the monthly limit of indemnity option eliminate the requirement for a worksheet and the coinsurance clause. Although simpler to purchase, the coverage provided by these options might be inadequate or excessive because the points implicit in the worksheet have not been considered. While involved, the business income worksheet forces the insured to consider factors that should provide a more accurate estimate of business income needs. Another option for business income coverage is to limit coverage for ordinary payroll, thereby reducing the coinsurance basis as well as the cost of the insurance.

Other time element coverages include extra expense, combined business income and extra expense coverage, contingent business income coverage and extra expense coverage, blanket business income and extra expense coverage, leasehold interest coverage, and manufacturer's finished stock coverage.

Consequential loss exposures include building codes and off-premises power failures. Building codes refer to governmental statutes regulating the type of construction of buildings within its authority. Existing structures tend not to be held to the standards presented in the updated building codes.

When a lack of power, light, heat, or refrigeration damages the insured's property, a consequential loss occurs. The ISO portfolio includes two endorsements that address this type of loss: Utility Services—Direct Damage and Utility Services—Time Element.

Chapter 7

Commercial Crime Insurance

Crime has a significant effect on insurers that provide crime coverage. According to the Federal Bureau of Investigation, 12.1 million property offenses were committed in 1995. This number equates to 4,593 property crimes for every 100,000 United States inhabitants. The 1995 crime rate dropped 1 percent from the 1994 rate and 11 percent from 1991 rate. The value of the property stolen in 1995 totaled $15.1 billion. Crimes against property committed in 1995 can be categorized as follows:[1]

- Larceny-theft 66 percent
- Burglary 22 percent
- Motor vehicle theft 12 percent

Employee crime is estimated to cost American businesses $40 billion annually. Surprisingly, only an estimated 20 percent of American businesses carry employee dishonesty insurance.[2]

These are the direct costs of crime. The indirect costs include the cost of police protection, private protection, and insurance premiums related to crime coverage.

Coverage for crime perils is not limited to the commercial crime insurance coverage forms offered by ISO and the Surety Association of America (SAA). Theft is a covered cause of loss in automobile insurance and homeowners insurance. Both inland marine and ocean marine insurance almost always cover theft, since mobile property is particularly susceptible—especially while it is in transit. The ISO causes of loss special form covers theft with the exceptions of dishonest acts of employees and property in the care, custody, and control of others. Crime insurance for smaller businesses is often provided in businessowners policies (BOPs). Although most BOPs are independently filed, they typically include employee dishonesty insurance and other basic crime coverages. With the exception of BOPs and other company-specific forms, the dishonest acts of employees are seldom insured other than through the employee dishonesty crime form (the traditional and often-used term for handling losses caused by employee theft is fidelity bonding). On many accounts, underwriters exclude theft coverage from the special causes of loss form to make a risk acceptable.

Despite the magnitude of crime losses, crime insurance combined ratios have been favorable. Loss experience for employee dishonesty (fidelity bonds) and burglary and theft is shown in Exhibit 7-1.

Exhibit 7-1
Loss Experience for Employee Dishonesty and Burglary and Theft

Employee Dishonesty (Fidelity Bonds) 1987-1996

Year	Premiums written ($1,000)	Annual % change	Combined ratio*
1987	1,008,608	+25.9	71.4
1988	979,544	−2.9	72.4
1989	928,081	−5.3	69.5
1990	898,828	−3.2	93.2
1991	837,184	−6.9	76.1
1992	851,493	+1.7	77.5
1993	894,471	+5.0	75.6
1994	905,947	+1.3	75.5
1995	925,104	+2.1	72.0
1996	915,405	−1.0	86.1

* Before dividends to policyholders.

Burglary and Theft 1987-1996

Year	Premiums written ($1,000)	Annual % change	Combined ratio*
1987	127,422	+5.3	64.8
1988	109,409	−14.1	63.7
1989	100,583	−8.1	66.1
1990	108,081	+7.5	66.1
1991	105,330	−2.5	67.4
1992	109,100	+3.6	64.1
1993	115,283	+5.7	67.2
1994	127,465	+10.6	59.3
1995	124,434	−2.4	58.6
1996	124,279	−0.1	63.2

* Before dividends to policyholders.

Used with permission from *Best's Aggregates & Averages,* Oldwick, NJ: A.M. Best Company, 1997 edition, p. 221.

Crime loss exposures can be handled through the use of loss control. The preventive measures that an insured has implemented are often evidence of the insured's attitude toward controlling crime, and underwriters generally recommend that insureds that have not implemented loss control measures do so.

The ISO crime program includes not only ISO crime coverage forms but also the SAA employee dishonesty forms so that specific insurance needs can be addressed with specific crime coverage forms. This modular approach to crime coverage can be further tailored through the use of a series of "plans." These plans correspond to the ISO crime forms that existed before ISO's adoption of modular coverage forms. Exhibit 7-2 lists the nineteen crime coverage forms available from ISO. Exhibit 7-3 summarizes the coverage plans, indicating how the forms can be packaged to meet the needs of specific types of business.

Crimes can be categorized as being committed by employees or by persons outside an organization. Crimes committed by employees are called "employee dishonesty." Crimes committed by others are categorized as burglary, robbery, or theft, depending on the nature of the crime.

Employee Dishonesty

Employee dishonesty insurance covers theft by employees. It is unique among crime insurance coverages because of the following factors:

- *Access to exposed property*. The nature of their jobs gives employees ready access to valuable property. They can learn the company's routines and schedules. They get to know their fellow employees and their habits. They can discover what controls management has in place and how well the controls work.
- *Losses can be hidden from discovery*. Unlike burglary and robbery, which by definition are visible crimes, employee theft is by stealth. The act of theft can be deliberately obscured or covered up for long periods of time.
- *Large losses are common*. The thief's access to property continues until the crime is discovered. The length of the time of access, in turn, contributes to the size of loss and, in some cases, to the number of employees involved.
- *Management controls are the primary protection*. Safes, vaults, alarm systems, and so on, are secondary defenses against fidelity losses. Monitoring revenue, merchandise, and raw material as they flow in and out of the company is the first line of defense.
- *Most losses are discovered by accident*. Despite the prevalence of management controls designed specifically to inhibit theft by employees, most employee dishonesty losses are discovered by chance.

Exhibit 7-2
Crime Coverage Forms

The following crime coverage forms are available from ISO. Several have restricted eligibility, but most are available for all accounts in the mercantile and governmental markets:

Coverage Form A—	Employee Dishonesty—Blanket
Coverage Form A—	Employee Dishonesty—Schedule
Coverage Form B—	Forgery or Alteration
Coverage Form C—	Theft, Disappearance, and Destruction (Money and Securities)
Coverage Form D—	Robbery and Safe Burglary—Property Other Than Money and Securities
Coverage Form E—	Premises Burglary—Property Other Than Money and Securities
Coverage Form F—	Computer Fraud (all property, including money and securities)
Coverage Form G—	Extortion (all property, including money and securities)
Coverage Form H—	Premises Theft and Robbery Outside the Premises—Property Other Than Money and Securities
Coverage Form I—	Lessees of Safe-Deposit Boxes
Coverage Form J—	Securities Deposited With Others
Coverage Form K—	Liability for Guests' Property—Safe-Deposit Box
Coverage Form L—	Liability for Guests' Property—Premises
Coverage Form M—	Safe Depository Liability
Coverage Form N—	Safe Depository Direct Loss
Coverage Form O—	Public Employee Dishonesty—Per Loss
Coverage Form P—	Public Employee Dishonesty—Per Employee
Coverage Form Q—	Robbery and Safe Burglary—Money and Securities
Coverage Form R—	Money Orders and Counterfeit Paper Currency

- *The insured might be reluctant to face the facts.* Employers are often unwilling to believe their employees might steal from them. This reluctance often leads to practices that contribute to opportunities for such thefts and greatly increases exposures to loss.
- *Management might be reluctant to prosecute employees who steal.* Many employers will not sign complaints or testify against their employees at criminal proceedings. The reasons for this include a wish to avoid bad press; a tendency to accept the culprit's "hard luck" story; and the desire to have the affair end quickly, especially when the employee promises restitution.

Exhibit 7-3
Summary of Coverage Plans

Plan #	Title	Coverage Forms Available	Class of Business Eligibility
Plan 1	Commercial Crime—Mercantile Entities	A, B, C, D, E, F, G, H, I, J, & O (all are optional, and each carries its own limit)	Any insured other than one eligible for a financial institution bond or plan if below
Plan 2	(Reserved for future use)	N/A	N/A
Plan 3	Storekeeper's Broad Form	A, B, C, D, & E (mandatory) (each carries its own limit)	Retail insured with a single location and not more than four employees
Plan 4	Storekeeper's Burglary and Robbery	D, E, & Q (mandatory)	Any retail insured
Plan 5	Office Burglary and Robbery	D, H, & Q plus CR 15 06 (mandatory)	Any office insured
Plan 6	Guests' Property—Safe Deposit Box	K (mandatory)	Insureds providing lodging facilities
Plan 7	Guests' Property—Premises	L (mandatory)	Insureds providing lodging facilities
Plan 8	Safe Depository	M and/or N (mandatory)	Private (nonbank) safe depositories
Plan 9	Excess Bank Burglary & Robbery	D plus CR 15 33 (mandatory)	Banking or trust institution
Plan 10	Bank Excess Securities	C plus CR 15 34 (mandatory)	Banking or trust institution
Plan 11	Commercial Crime—Governmental Entities	O or P (mandatory), plus B, C, D, E, F, G, H, I, J, & O (optional)	Any governmental entity (federal, state, county, city, town, or divisions thereof)

The following characteristics of employee dishonesty crimes pose additional problems for underwriters:

1. Losses might be frequent, but they are usually hidden until they become large. For example, an embezzler typically takes small sums of money over a long period of time and is caught only when the total is too large to continue to hide.
2. Employer reluctance to accept that some employees are dishonest creates a problem of adverse selection. Most financial institutions purchase fidelity

coverage, but only a small percentage of mercantile establishments do so. Employee crime losses are significant, and they are estimated to cost businesses more than any other form of crime. Nonetheless, employee dishonesty insurance is a profitable line for insurers and is available to most insureds.

Underwriting Employee Dishonesty

By tradition, insurers have written employee dishonesty insurance for an indefinite term. The use of a continuous policy for employee dishonesty was developed as a method for managing the insurer's overall exposure. Employee dishonesty forms provide a limit of liability that applies to all losses that occur during the policy period. Because most losses develop over a long period of time, renewing the policy each year would tend to expose the insurer to multiple limits of liability for a single loss. One technique for controlling this exposure is to issue a policy that remains in force until canceled. More recently, ISO and SAA have developed forms with a one-year term. These forms contain a "noncumulation of limits" clause that addresses the concern of insurers. Underwriters need to be aware of this issue with the forms they are using.

Insurers might rerate employee dishonesty policies periodically but assume that their relationship with the insured will be long term. Underwriters must be satisfied that certain conditions, such as the following, exist before issuing the policy:

1. Management of the insured organization must exhibit the highest moral character. Moral hazard, in other words, must be nonexistent for an organization to receive employee dishonesty insurance.
2. The insured should be profitable. Profits indicate a competent operation. Management planning and control systems should work well. The company should be financially able to respond to loss control recommendations. The corporate culture should reward positive performance.

   A new company might not be profitable because of heavy initial capitalization expenses and because markets are in developmental stages. At the very least, the underwriter must be assured that management has relevant experience in a related field.
3. Burglary and robbery loss control systems should be in place and maintained. Appropriate defenses against external crime also deter employee crime.
4. Amounts of insurance should fall within the limits prescribed by the underwriting guide.
5. Management controls should exist and be maintained. Management controls are evidence of management care and concern. Their absence is usually sufficient reason to decline the submission.

Controlling Employee Dishonesty Losses

Employee dishonesty loss control efforts require strict adherence to management controls. Listed below are controls, applicable to almost all organizations, that can be considered minimal standards for acceptability:

- The insured must screen new hires and check their references. Gaps in employment history might indicate that the job applicant was incarcerated. New hires with criminal records involving theft should be assigned tasks that present minimal theft exposure or not be hired at all. Extreme care must be taken, however, when interviewing applicants. A gap in employment could also mean that the applicant was handling child-care responsibilities, caring for a sick relative, or simply unemployed. An inquiry, such as this, of a job applicant might disclose an illness or disability, even though the law no longer allows an employer to ask directly for this information.

  Employee dishonesty coverage ceases immediately for any employee discovered to have committed a "dishonest act." Despite this language, an insured's "reasonable expectations" might lead a court to find coverage particularly when the form grants coverage for new hires while canceling it for others.
- Promotions of seasoned employees also require review, especially for promotion or transfer into a sensitive position. A significant change in responsibility level or position might require careful investigation. A dishonest manager might promote another employee to a higher position so that the two might collude. Underwriters should look for a logical progression of responsibilities.
- Underwriters should note the presence of a substance-abuse screening program as a positive sign. Drug abuse creates a situation in which employees might have to steal to satisfy their drug habit.
- Underwriters normally request a list of all employees, their positions, and their hire dates. The greater the rate and level of employee turnover, the more likely the exposures are to change.
- Termination procedures should be well defined. Employees who have worked in sensitive areas should have their password access to computer systems revoked, and keys or access cards should be returned.
- Management must remain sensitive to all employee behavior. Dramatic changes in lifestyle might indicate employee dishonesty.

Periodic Audits

Generally, audits test accounts receivable, cash accounts, inventories, and disbursements. Auditors sample the accounts and measure them against industry or company norms. Audits also provide early detection of loss. In addition, audits are a highly visible sign to all employees that management is monitoring performance. A good audit system can help prevent losses and reduce the size of any losses that do occur.

Audits should occur at least annually, although more frequent audits can be conducted if the management of the insured so desires. Unscheduled audits can be an effective means of deterring employee dishonesty. An auditor who appears unannounced or simply reviews the accounting records recently used is in a position to detect theft *before* the dishonest employee has a chance to cover his or her trail. Underwriters may insist on more frequent audits if the amount of insurance or the nature of the risk warrants them. Insurers often establish a limit threshold above which they will require that audits be conducted by certified public accountants (CPAs).

Financial institutions should have a complete CPA audit every year. A complete audit is one that is performed in accordance with generally accepted accounting principles (GAAP). This audit expresses an opinion as to the accuracy and completeness of the institution's financial statement. A CPA often issues a management letter, so-called because it is addressed to the board of directors, that indicates any weaknesses found in internal controls. Internal controls are operating procedures designed to safeguard against employee theft. The underwriter should review the response to any criticism in order to verify implementation of corrective action by the financial institution.

If an internal control deficiency is significant, it might be labeled a material weakness. A **material weakness** is one that could substantially affect the accuracy of the data in the financial statements. Management must thoroughly investigate any disclosed material weaknesses and take appropriate corrective action.

Small accounts might have no internal auditors, and the owners might regard outside audits as too expensive. To decide whether small accounts have satisfactory controls in place, the underwriter should consider whether the insured keeps accurate books and whether daily supervision by the owners can be a suitable substitute for an audit.

Division of Authority

Employees who regularly handle merchandise should not have responsibility for handling cash, and vice versa. Those employees responsible for managing cash accounts should not be responsible for auditing or reconciling those accounts. For small insureds, extensive division of authority may not be practical. In those businesses, the owner's physical presence can ensure that merchandise is paid for and that all sales go through a cash register.

Bank Statement Reconciliation

Bank statement reconciliation is the process by which the bank statement is compared to canceled checks and the check register to reveal outstanding checks and verify the accuracy of the records. At any given time, the insured's records are not likely to agree with the bank's. The insured will record checks when written and deposits as they are made. Bank records show not how much money the customer has sent out but the amounts that the bank has received. The insured's records and the bank's records will differ for two main reasons. First, time passes between when the insured draws a check and when the check clears the bank. Amounts spent by a business but not yet processed by its bank are referred to as the **float**, and some firms manage it with great care. Second, the insured will receive bank statements some time after the monthly closing dates. These statements will not reflect banking activity in the interim. Someone must account for these differences and verify that the bank's records agree with the insured's.

Under ideal conditions, the person who reconciles bank accounts should not make deposits or draw funds from the account. An employee who wanted to divert funds to his or her own use would then need an accomplice. The need for collusion makes losses less likely to occur. This division of duties might not be possible in a small business, and in a large company it might become a nuisance, and management might overlook this simple precaution.

Physical Inventories

Physical inventories confirm that the insured actually has the property shown on the books. Employees should not manage or account for any property on which they also take inventory. Many organizations have an office accounting staff responsible for taking inventory. These internal auditors should conduct a physical inventory at least once a year.

Spot Checks

Scheduled audits and inventories suffer one important drawback: employees expect them, and dishonest workers have a chance to conceal theft. For example, dishonest employees of one insurance company inflated premiums and assets. As part of the scheme, they listed the same securities as being stored in several banks. When an examination drew near, they moved the assets from one bank (and one state) to another. The plot was uncovered when the insurance departments of three states conducted unannounced audits at three offices simultaneously. With advance notice, the culprits could conceal their crime, but an unscheduled audit denied them that opportunity.

Annual Vacations

Some methods of embezzlement require daily adjustment of records. All employees who are not owners should take annual vacations of no fewer than five consecutive working days. Vacations permit reassignment of positions and let indiscretions surface. Most financial institutions establish a personnel policy that requires every employee to schedule a two-week leave each year.

Rotation of Duties

Rotation of duties involves changing responsibility for a sufficient period of time to increase the chance of discovering any irregularities or embezzlements. It is a good idea for employees to be cross-trained in different positions so that important tasks can be completed even if someone is absent from work.

Dual Control

Dual control means requiring two people to have responsibility for the same items or operations. Requiring two signatures on a check is a familiar example of dual control. Dual controls exist in most businesses but not to the extent that they exist in financial institutions, where each of the following should be subject to dual control:

- Vault
- Cash
- Investment securities
- Negotiable collateral
- Customers' property held for safekeeping
- Trusts and securities
- Unissued stock certificates
- Reserve supply of official checks and drafts
- Dormant accounts of depositors
- Unissued Series E bonds
- Unissued travelers' checks
- Safe-deposit spare keys and locks
- Spare keys to tellers' cash drawers
- Night depository safes

Consolidation and Merger

Banks and other financial institutions have tended to grow through acquisitions of similar businesses. The crime general provisions extend coverage to persons and property acquired through a consolidation or merger as long as the insurer receives notice of the acquisition within thirty days and additional premium is paid. A corporate change that expands the scope of the bank's operation might also significantly increase exposures to employee dishonesty.

If employee dishonesty coverage is provided on a scheduled basis, the coverage extension for new acquisitions does not apply. Providing automatic coverage in the case of a consolidation or merger is not in keeping with the intent of the insurer and is not permitted.

Discovery and Superseded Suretyship

Unlike losses caused by fire or windstorm, losses caused by employee dishonesty are difficult to detect. A significant period of time might elapse between the time at which a crime is committed and its discovery. Employee dishonesty insurance policies contain a discovery provision that permits claims to be made under the policy up to one year after the expiration of the policy. Discovery is not a problem if the insured renews coverage with the same insurer.

To enable insureds to change insurers, the **superseded suretyship** provision was created. A loss that occurred under a previous policy is covered by the current policy *if* the loss would have been covered by the previous policy had it not been replaced. Coverage does not apply if a gap in coverage occurred between the current and previous policies or if the coverage being provided under a new policy is not exactly the same as under the previous one. Because the insurer might be providing coverage for losses that actually occurred under a prior policy, the underwriter needs to know that management controls currently in effect are the same ones used in prior years.

Crimes Committed by Others

Property owners must contend with the possibility that their property might be taken by others or could be destroyed in an attempted theft. Crime insurance can cover money and securities as well as provide coverage for property other than money and securities. The perils insured against in crime coverage forms are theft, burglary, robbery, and disappearance. Specifically excluded from crime and other property policies are losses termed as "inventory shortages."

Crimes committed by others, as with employee-initiated crimes, can be reduced or eliminated through the use of loss control measures.

Commercial Crime Insurance Terminology

The definitions used in crime insurance policies are often different from those in general usage. Because the difference in terminology can be confusing and the terms have a specific meaning in crime insurance, the definitions of "theft," "burglary," "robbery," and "disappearance" are discussed in this section. The section also includes a brief discussion of inventory shortage as a cause of loss.

Theft

Theft generally means any act of stealing. It is a broad category that includes burglary, robbery, shoplifting, and other acts of stealth. Because theft encompasses so many types of crime, it is a relatively expensive cause of loss to insure. Individual losses tend to be small, and frequency is high. Businesses often opt to purchase a more limited form of crime insurance than theft coverage in order to reduce the cost of insurance and insure a crime loss that is more significant yet less frequent. Because of adverse selection, many underwriters have learned to treat requests for theft coverage with suspicion.

Burglary

Burglary is forcible entry into or exit from a premises, a building, a safe, or a vault with the intent to commit theft. The definition of "forcible entry or exit" includes thieves who hide within a fenced area or in a building during business hours in order to take property and force their way out after the business closes. Burglary is a "premises only" exposure, so insurance coverage applies solely to the described premises. This restriction helps assure underwriters that the physical protection and location are acceptable for the type of property and the amount of insurance requested.

Robbery

Robbery is the illegal taking of property by violence or the threat of violence against a person. Crime forms describe the person who has custody of the property as a custodian or messenger. This definition facilitates the distinction between coverage on and away from the insured's premises. A custodian is any person who is in possession of the insured's property on the insured's premises. A messenger is any person who is transporting the insured's property away from the insured's premises with the insured's knowledge and permission. Robbery also includes taking property from a custodian or messenger who has been kidnapped for that purpose.

Disappearance

Disappearance is the loss of property with no reasonable explanation. When disappearance is a covered cause of loss, coverage is extended to include situations in which the insured simply misplaces property. Coverage forms no longer use the term "mysterious disappearance," but the term persists in general usage. "Mysterious disappearance" implies that there was an opportunity for theft even if there is no evidence of it. Only Coverage Form C (theft, disappearance, and destruction of money and securities) insures against loss by disappearance, but underwriters might also be willing to include this coverage in manuscript policies.

Inventory Shortage

Most policies that provide "all-risks" coverage also include coverage for some theft losses. However, these policies exclude losses that the insured can prove only from inventory records. Inventory shrinkage is a normal event in any business. The exclusion prevents insureds from transferring this ordinary cost of doing business to an insurer. The inventory shortage exclusion eliminates coverage for a loss when the only evidence of either the existence or the size of the loss is found in the insured's accounting records.

Underwriting Other Crime Exposures

The process of underwriting commercial crime insurance requires considering the following six factors:

1. Property susceptibility
2. Location of the property
3. Nature of the occupancy
4. Moral and morale hazards
5. Police protection
6. Modifications of coverage and price

Property Susceptibility

Every piece of property has characteristics that make it more or less desirable to thieves. These characteristics are usually considered together, but underwriters should be able to recognize them separately. These characteristics are determined by the following three questions:

1. Is the property susceptible to crime?
2. Is the property fungible?
3. Is there a ready market for it as stolen property?

The size, weight, portability, visibility, and accessibility of the goods determine how susceptible they are to theft. The emphasis given to each of these characteristics is relative. An object's size or weight does not in itself preclude its theft. An extreme example is a forty-ton, steel truss bridge that was stolen from a West Virginia creek in the late 1950s. Despite this unusual experience, bulky items like bridges and buildings are viewed as having low susceptibility to theft. Jewelry, clothing, small electric appliances, precious metals, books, hand tools, and building materials, on the other hand, are highly susceptible. The higher the property's value is relative to its bulk and weight, the more attractive it becomes to thieves. What makes diamonds such an attractive target for theft is the extremely high ratio of their value to their size and bulk. Several million dollars' worth of diamonds will fit unobtrusively in someone's pocket.

Fungibility measures a property's value as an item of exchange. Money, securities, and other negotiable instruments are highly fungible. Bulk gas, bridges, and the like are considered essentially not fungible. That is, they might meet a rare exchange demand, but they are not regularly traded goods. A semitrailer truck loaded with brand-name golf balls has low fungibility. It is, however, susceptible to theft.

A ready market probably also exists for the load of golf balls; however, a combination of several factors determines a commodity's marketability. Goods that are in widespread use have more potential customers than goods used by a few. Goods that are difficult to trace are more marketable than those that are not. The economy often plays a key role, making a surprising variety of goods very marketable for a long period of time. Worldwide scarcity and accompanying high prices made copper a target commodity in the late 1960s. Insurers that provided "all-risks" coverage paid many losses caused by the theft of copper pipes from vacant or unoccupied buildings. Several television towers had their copper antenna wires ripped from deeply buried grounding.

In some instances, thieves might have had to turn to the original owner as their market because the owner was the only one interested in the stolen goods. In one case, several boxcars filled with automobile and truck engine blocks "disappeared." After months had passed with no trace of the boxcars, the thieves contacted the manufacturer. After price and delivery negotiations, the engines arrived at their original destination.

Finally, after satisfactorily answering the three key questions mentioned above, underwriters must sum up their answers in the larger question: How likely is the property to be stolen?

Location of the Property

Such features as topography, neighborhood, climate, and the local crime rate can tell underwriters what kind of losses to expect. Seasonal occupancy, typical of a resort, for example, makes crime losses more likely at certain times of the year than at others. Also, crime occurs more often in some areas than in others, and underwriters should use this type of information. Historically, cities have had a higher rate of crime than suburbs and rural areas. However, the gap between the two is closing in some areas of the country.

Statistics on local crime rates often reflect the experience of entire cities or counties, which is of little value to underwriters since not all sections of any given city are high-crime areas. The statistics are also incomplete because many victims do not report crimes, especially in the areas in which crimes occur most frequently. Underwriters who want accurate information in a form they can use must develop their own. The need to avoid unfair discrimination in underwriting makes reliable data especially important.

Nature of the Occupancy

Willie Sutton, a notorious bank robber of the 1940s and 1950s, is said to have made the following response to a reporter who asked why he chose to steal from banks when there were easier targets: "Because that's where the money is." Then as now, some occupancies are more attractive to criminals than others.

Some occupancies have a great deal of cash or other valuable property on hand. These occupancies include banks, savings and loan associations, credit unions, check-cashing services, grocery stores, stadiums, arenas, churches, and buildings where charity events are held.

Some businesses, such as public warehouses, are conducted in locations that are removed from the public or operate when there is little traffic that might deter criminals. Other businesses are so convenient that criminals can make a quick getaway. These include twenty-four-hour convenience stores and service stations.

Moral and Morale Hazards

Moral hazard and morale hazard can be present for any peril, but they are particularly important with regard to crime. A dishonest insured can readily dispose of inventory and arrange a fraudulent claim. Likewise, a lax attitude toward loss might mean that precautions and protective measures are not consistently adhered to, thereby creating an environment in which a loss is more likely to occur.

Assessing the moral and morale hazards of a crime risk requires subjective judgment, not hard-and-fast rules. The underwriter's assessment should focus on the following three areas:

1. *Ownership and management.* Experience, longevity, and cooperation are key factors in gauging moral or morale hazard. Responsible management cooperates to control crime losses and incurs the expense needed to improve and update barriers to crime.
2. *Financial and moral reputations.* Success provides an incentive to avoid losses. Newly formed or financially troubled firms might be undesirable crime risks. Although an underwriter might form an initial opinion from credit ratings, investigative reports usually supply in-depth information. In other words, financial ratings are an initial underwriting requirement that can be supplemented with outside inspection reports that include financial analysis. Financial success and the reputation of the business owners are the primary tools for evaluating moral hazards.
3. *Past loss experience.* The type, number, and circumstances of past losses offer valuable underwriting information about the moral or morale hazard of the risk. Any questionable losses should be carefully investigated.

Adverse selection is another problem that confronts crime underwriters. It is the tendency of those risks with the largest degree of exposure to purchase crime insurance. All forms of insurance present some degree of adverse selection, but probably not to the extent that it exists in crime insurance. In other types of insurance, such as fire or workers compensation, practically all risks are insured, but this is not true in crime insurance.

Insureds with sound management, good location, financial success, adequate protective devices, and favorable loss experience tend not to purchase crime insurance or, if they do, only in a nominal amount. Conversely, poor crime risks are likely to try to secure coverage to hedge against crime losses. Although adverse selection will never be eliminated, its effect can be minimized through good underwriting.

Police Protection

The quality of police protection varies by community. It is unlikely that an underwriter would have the knowledge needed to make a judgment on the caliber of the police protection in the area in which an insured is located. The FBI does maintain crime statistics by city, but these statistics do not address specific areas within a city. Producers or claim adjusters who live in a particular area can probably provide anecdotal information about the need for police protection in their community and the ability of the community to meet that need.

Modifications of Coverage and Price

Crime insurance underwriters have some latitude in modifying the proposal for insurance. In many instances, an applicant knows that the coverage desired is readily available and will turn to another insurer when refused by the first. In other cases, however, the applicant is eager to get coverage and accepts the first offer even if it is not for the broadest coverage at the lowest price. Because applicants for crime insurance need the coverage, they are likely to consider valid counteroffers made by the underwriter evaluating the account. The tools available to make marginal accounts more acceptable include making changes in coverage, limits, pricing, and the deductible and the use of endorsements requiring protective safeguards.

Coverage

Requests for policies providing broad coverage do not always meet underwriters' guidelines. Rather than reject the account outright, an underwriter might offer coverage that is less broad than was requested. Many requests for broad crime coverage must be negotiated. An account might be ineligible for theft coverage under a commercial property form with special causes of loss. As an alternative, the underwriter might offer to provide coverage under the causes-of-loss special form in combination with a theft exclusion endorsement and the applicable crime coverage form. This approach to controlling exposures for the entire account, however, does little to actually control crime exposures. Overall, transforming marginal accounts into acceptable accounts for crime insurance is difficult to do using coverage modification. When an applicant requests broader coverage than the underwriter can offer, the underwriter can often substitute more restrictive coverage. An application may, for example, request Theft, Disappearance and Destruction (Form C). If the account does not meet the underwriting criteria for this coverage, the underwriter can offer Robbery and Safe Burglary Coverage (Form Q) instead. By the same token, an underwriter can offer Robbery and Safe Burglary Coverage (Form D) when guidelines do not permit writing Premises Theft and Robbery Outside the Premises Coverage (Form H).

Coverage Limits

For most other types of insurance, the insured purchases an amount of insurance close to the value of the exposed property. In the case of crime insurance, most insureds assume that only small crime losses will occur. This fact and the desire to reduce premiums tend to reduce the policy limit and increase problems associated with underinsurance. In the case of crime insurance, underwriters might be satisfied with providing policy limits much lower than the values insured. Because of the moral hazard that too much insurance might create, most underwriters would not want to provide coverage to value even if the insured requests it.

Pricing

Because crime forms do not contain a coinsurance clause, the insured is not penalized for having inadequate limits. Losses will probably be partial, but they may still exceed the policy limits. Limits that are far less than the value of the covered property can lead to underpricing. Underwriters must consider both the limits and the values exposed to loss when pricing crime coverage.

Because policy limits tend to be low relative to the amount at risk, probable maximum loss usually equals the amount subject. Underwriters who provide commercial crime coverage should expect that losses will exceed the policy amount.

Deductibles

Crime insurance deductibles, as with other forms of insurance, shift responsibility for small losses back to the insured. Deductibles can encourage loss control, which might prevent future losses.

Deductibles are not used as underwriting tools in crime insurance as often as they might be. Large, sophisticated policyholders recognize the value of retaining small, frequent losses that can readily be contained through loss control techniques or financed with current cash flow.

Building and personal property coverage forms contain a standard deductible that can be increased. The deductible for crime insurance should be equal at least to the insured's business personal property deductible.

Extortion coverage (Form G) can be purchased with or without a loss participation clause (CR 00 08), under which the insured agrees to retain a portion of each loss. The retained portion is expressed as a percentage. The loss participation clause is in addition to any other applicable deductible. When the policy is written with the loss participation clause, the insurance company will pay up to the limit of insurance for losses that exceed the deductible, less the insured's participation. In the absence of a loss participation clause, the insurer pays up to the policy limit for losses that exceed the deductible.

Protective Safeguards

A protective safeguards endorsement is a statement from the insured that the measures taken to protect the property will be maintained during the term of the policy. Because the underwriter usually insists that protective safeguards be in place as a condition for issuing the policy, the protective safeguards endorsement states that coverage will be denied if a loss occurs and these safeguards are not present. Courts are often reluctant to enforce insurer warranties because they tend to be harsh and are accepted by insureds who believe they have few alternatives. In the case of crime insurance, courts are reluctant to dismiss the effect of protective safeguard warranties because they are clearly an essential consideration in the underwriting decision.

Controlling Other Crime Exposures

Crime loss exposures respond well to loss control efforts. As mentioned earlier, the loss control measures implemented and their diligent use are among the most telling characteristics of a good prospect for crime coverage.

Private protection measures to prevent or control loss include the following:

- Safes and vaults
- Cages, special rooms, and limited-access areas
- Indoor and outdoor lighting
- Fences and walls
- Protection of premises openings (gates, doors, windows, and skylights)
- Guard service
- Alarm systems
- Electronic surveillance systems
- Inventory control and other management activities

Loss control, or protection devices and systems, is generally thought to serve at least two important functions: to deter crime and to reduce crime losses.

A determined thief can break through any defense, given enough time. In other words, safes, vaults, fencing, and so on rarely preclude access when the thief is strongly motivated. However, protection devices and systems do make an invaluable contribution to deterrence. They often cause a thief to seek an easier target.

Although even the best protection systems will not eliminate loss, their value cannot be overemphasized in reducing the probability of loss. After moral hazard, private protection is the most important consideration in crime insurance underwriting.

Underwriting guidelines should indicate the acceptable level of protection that a particular class or location demands. Since private protection is known to reduce the likelihood of crime losses, the level of private protection required depends on the judgment of the staff underwriters. If line underwriters are not satisfied with the level of private protection recommended by the underwriting guide on a particular account, they might adjust the insurance proposal in other ways, such as by reducing the amount of coverage provided.

The two main categories of private protection devices are barriers to criminal access and detection devices. Barriers include devices that protect the premises and safes and vaults. Detection devices include guards, alarms, and surveillance systems.

Barriers to Access

Barriers to access are features of the premises that make entrance after hours or to restricted areas difficult.

Premises Protection

Physical protection devices for the premises reduce illegal entry and include door and window locks, bars, and screens. All premises are susceptible to illegal entry through doors, windows, and skylights (if present). Fencing and walls protect buildings and yard storage. Associated Locksmiths of America has developed a set of standards for premises security that underwriters can use as a guideline.

Since doors are the main entries to the premises, they should be adequately secured and constructed to resist illegal entry. The location of the door is an important consideration. Generally, back doors opening into alleys or yards are vulnerable because they are often shielded from public view. Door protection includes adequate locks, wire guards, angle iron cross bars, and sheet-metal linings.

Deadbolt locks provide the best protection for doors. When the door is closed, the bolt should penetrate at least one-half inch into the frame or jamb. Most jambs need a reinforced strike plate to provide adequate resistance to physical attack. Full security for doors that contain panes of glass requires double-cylinder locks necessitating a key for opening from both sides.

Doors that provide emergency exits can present a special problem. They are often placed in remote parts of the building, away from normal traffic patterns. Deadbolt locks are impractical because doors must open readily in case of emergency. Doors equipped with panic bars provide excellent resistance to opening from the outside but leave the door vulnerable from the inside. If egress by a thief is considered likely, alarms on the door can be effective.

Separate rooms and heavily screened cages are frequently built into premises to house especially vulnerable operations. For example, shop floors usually have cages for storage and distribution of valuable tools and dies.

Safes and Vaults

A **safe** is a movable device in which to store valuables; a **vault** serves the same purpose but is part of the premises. Safes can be built with inner as well as outer doors. The two basic categories of safes are **fire resistive** and **burglar resistive**. Fire-resistive safes are for record storage; they are not satisfactory barriers to criminals. There are several classes of burglar-resistive safes based on construction specifications and vulnerability to burglary.

Although a safe or vault offers crime security, the quality of this protection depends on the type and condition of the safe or vault. Many unlabeled and obsolete safes are still in use. Underwriters should obtain full information on declared safes before determining their adequacy as protection devices.

Staff underwriters often establish requirements for acceptability and limits of liability based on safe or vault protection. These guidelines normally follow the safes and vaults classification system used by ISO, which denotes the extent to which the safe will resist intrusion. Higher coverage limits are permissible for stronger safes and vaults.

Detection Systems

Detection systems are designed to alert the owners and others performing surveillance that a theft is in progress or has occurred. These systems are an effective deterrent to criminals. Detection can be accomplished through alarms, guard services, and surveillance systems.

Alarms

Intrusion detection systems consist of detection devices and alarms connected by a wiring network. These systems vary in sophistication, extent of coverage, and number of openings protected. The value of an intrusion alarm system depends on proper maintenance and periodic testing, but a system has no value unless it can be activated at all times when the premises are not open for business. Underwriters Laboratories (UL) classifies and rates alarm systems. Since many intrusion alarms have features that resist efforts to defeat them, UL includes this aspect in its rating.

Alarm systems can be divided into the following four classes:

1. Central station alarm
2. Police station connected alarm
3. Proprietary alarm system
4. Local alarm system

A **central station alarm** automatically transmits a signal to a central station that monitors the system at all times and keeps a record of all alarms. A **police**

station connected alarm signals a police station or central station. The common characteristic of alarms in these two classes is that they signal someone away from the protected premises. A **proprietary alarm system** sends an alarm to a monitoring station on the same premises, and a **local alarm** sounds a bell or siren at the premises.

A UL evaluation of a burglar alarm system is an important underwriting consideration for crime insurance and a factor in pricing. Underwriters Laboratories' burglar alarm certificate service involves the testing of burglar alarm products, their proper installation, and their maintenance. Insurance underwriters, unable to personally evaluate an applicant's burglar alarm system, rely on the UL certificate for the applicant's installed system. Because of this traditional reliance on UL certificates, insurers have come to demand UL certified alarm systems. Many non-UL certified systems provide good service but do not receive a premium discount because they are not UL-certified. The premium discount offered by insurers varies, based on the quality of the burglar alarm system installed, and ranges from 15 to 70 percent.

In 1996, UL introduced significant changes in how it evaluated commercial burglar alarm systems. Before 1996, UL used a "graded" approach under which burglar alarm systems either met the criteria for a specific grade or fell to the next lower grade. This approach to evaluating systems was well received by users of UL certificate information because they knew what criteria a system had to meet to earn each grade. For many insurers, their underwriting guides could simply specify which UL certificate grade was necessary to be considered for crime insurance and which UL certificate grades would enable the insured to qualify for a premium discount. While the old UL certificate grading system is discontinued now, many insurance applicants will have unexpired UL certificates reflecting the old evaluation approach. UL expects that it will take several years to reevaluate all of its existing burglary alarm installations.

UL refers to its new approach to evaluating commercial burglar alarm systems as being a "modular" approach. Under this approach, the elements evaluated have been unbundled from the old grades that previously applied. Individual UL certificates now describe the features of the specific burglar alarm system rather than assigning it a grade in which all the criteria are met. Rather than relying on the grades previously assigned by UL, insurance underwriters will have to review the certificate and determine whether the protection being certified by UL is adequate for the insurance applicant under consideration. While this change will require additional activity on the part of the insurance underwriter, it has advantages. Application of the graded system by insurers was often arbitrary in that many insurance applicants did not need the quality of protection demanded by the insurer's underwriting guidelines. Now insurance underwriters are more likely to accept applicants and give premium credits to applicants that are adequately protected, considering their occupancy. This change might lower both the cost of the applicant's insurance and the cost of loss control measures the insured uses. The grading approach tried to reflect the evolution of burglar alarm systems and technology within an existing framework, and as a result, over time, the terminology used to distinguish between grades became incomprehensible. The modular approach has all but eliminated the previously used alphabetic and numeric codes and provides clear statements of what alarm systems the insurance applicant has installed.

Guard Services

Guards or security personnel perform the following three major functions:

1. Protecting against robbery, shoplifting, and employee dishonesty during business hours
2. Controlling burglary losses after business hours
3. Protecting employees or messengers against robbery or violence while carrying money or merchandise away from the premises

Guard services that tour the premises after normal business hours deter criminal activity and detect fires. The use of guards has become more widespread since the mid-1980s, as people have become more crime-conscious.

Guards and guard dogs could be categorized as barriers to criminal access. However, for reasons of life safety and the potential costs of liability suits arising out of guard actions, guards are not usually expected to confront or apprehend intruders. They have a primary duty to detect crime and sound appropriate alarms.

Surveillance Cameras

Video surveillance is an effective protective device. These systems either supplement or supplant guards. Video surveillance systems range from small cameras attached to the walls in prominent locations within a convenience store to elaborate, complete-area coverage systems for a multistory office or business complex.

An insured might use video surveillance for vulnerable crime hazard areas such as entrances, exits, and aisles. Normally, surveillance cameras are visible, and they sometimes also act as a crime deterrent. The recording mechanism of the device should be at another location so that a criminal cannot destroy it or put it out of service. Although several types of equipment are available, cameras that operate continually are preferable to those that an employee must activate and are the type of systems often used in banks and retail stores.

Protection Against Robbery

A business can take several steps in response to the threat of robbery, both on and off the premises. Robbery is a special problem for businesses such as supermarkets that conduct a high volume of cash transactions or for businesses that are open twenty-four hours, such as convenience stores and filling stations.

Measures to protect against robbery on the premises include the following:

- **Premises robbery alarms** provide a means of securing rapid law enforcement response and apprehending the culprit. Police station connections are especially effective for this type of alarm. These alarms require a trigger, usually in the form of a panic button that employees push. Banks and some retail stores provide employees with special stacks of cash. Picking up the money releases a switch that activates the alarm. Unlike intrusion detection systems, robbery alarms should never sound a gong or siren on the premises because doing so would alert the robber to the presence of the alarm and place employees in danger.
- **Drop safes** are floor safes with slots where large-denomination bills can be put throughout business hours. They provide a secure place in which to keep cash that neither employees nor culprits can reach. They are most effective when only an armored carrier has the key or combination.
- Keeping valuable property, especially cash, out of easy reach helps deter robbery. If the robbery exposure is especially severe, an enclosed cage for cashiers might be the only effective protection.
- Guards and surveillance systems can deter robbery on the premises.

Employees who transport valuables away from the premises can take several precautions to mitigate the exposure to loss by robbery. Money is the most common target, so care taken when making bank deposits is crucial. Sometimes employees must carry property away from the premises. In some instances, property of the insured or customers must be taken for repair. Some property, such as tools and equipment, must be used away from the insured's premises. A common target for thieves, however, is the business's bank deposit.

Making frequent bank deposits limits the amount of cash an employee must carry on each trip to the bank. Carrying less money, in turn, makes the employee a less attractive target.

Businesses should avoid establishing a pattern for trips to the bank. Employees should try to make deposits at a different time each day. An employee who passes the bank on the way to lunch each day might be tempted to take the deposit at the same time. This pattern lets potential robbers know when they can find an easy target. The same rule holds true for routes. Whenever possible, employees carrying cash should avoid using the same route every time. If there is more than one exit from the premises, the employees should vary their route out of the building. Most banks now accept deposits at any branch. If the insured's bank has more than one office in the vicinity, making deposits at different branches avoids the creation of patterns that robbers might learn.

Businesses that take in large amounts of cash should take special precautions to secure them. Supermarkets, for instance, routinely employ armored couriers to make bank deposits. For smaller companies, many police departments offer escort service for bank deposits, especially late at night. Police in some communities offer this service at no cost as part of their crime-prevention programs. Other police departments might arrange for firms to hire off-duty officers as escorts.

Computer Crime

Businesses in the United States are rapidly expanding their dependency on computers to control information and assets. The ability of computers to perform many different functions simultaneously has created new industries and fostered growth in others. Underwriters must consider this dependency as a significant increase in hazard, especially because expensive data processing networks and their involvement in every facet of a company's operations create risk.

According to one authority, the six greatest computer loss exposures are (1) acts of God, (2) hardware or program failure, (3) human carelessness, (4) invasion of privacy, (5) malicious damage, and (6) theft.[3]

Malicious damage and theft are criminal acts against a business that can be committed by outsiders or by employees. Although a loss from either can be severe, the opportunity for committing computer crime is greater for insiders. For example, a disgruntled employee with the appropriate technical expertise can program data to self-destruct at some time in the future. Because all large computer installations have built-in clocks and calendar systems, an employee could resign and be employed in another part of the country before the "accident" actually occurs. This same employee can eliminate all traces of the program that caused the original accident.[4] Computer downtime (that is, the period during which a computer is not operational) is expensive. Financial loss increases exponentially with recovery time. Therefore, downtime lasting several days might result in revenue losses that exceed the financial capacity of a company.

Coverage for wrongful acts committed by employees can be covered by employee dishonesty insurance, Forms A, O, and P. Coverage for theft by persons outside the organization is provided under Computer Fraud (Form F).

Because of the large potential losses associated with computers, data processing managers and risk managers consider computer losses as possible disasters. Since insurance payments seldom provide full restitution for actual damage and because of extensive indirect costs and the potential loss of customers, prudent insureds must implement private protection and thorough management controls. Similarly, crime underwriters consider loss control essential for underwriting acceptance. The degree to which a company's management understands the magnitude of potential loss associated with its data processing system and the care that it takes in establishing and maintaining security cannot be overemphasized. Having established that management does indeed understand its exposure and has taken steps to secure information systems (IS) operations, underwriters need only establish the appropriate price for the coverage.

Underwriting Computer Crime[5]

Applications for computer fraud coverage usually request only necessary rating information. Therefore, most insurance companies have developed their own underwriting questionnaires. Most of the underwriting considerations for computer fraud resemble those for employee dishonesty. The insured must have proper separation of duties, coupled with physical loss prevention measures, to prevent unauthorized access to the insured's computer system. Also, underwriters usually recommend that the limit for computer fraud coverage equal the limit for employee dishonesty insurance. The following questions are typical of those on an insurer's application for computer fraud coverage:

- Is access to the data processing facility limited for both employees and nonemployees?
- Do employees and nonemployees use assigned passwords?
- Do those passwords change often and at irregular intervals?
- Does the security system log all entrances, and does it detect and report unauthorized access attempts into restricted or sensitive areas?
- Is access to the facility prohibited during nonworking hours?

- Do guards monitor the facility during nonworking hours?
- Do intrusion detection alarms protect the facility during nonworking hours?
- Are employee passwords and access codes purged immediately when employees resign or are fired?
- Are duplicate computer records maintained at a backup location away from the covered premises?
- Are duplicate backup records maintained at a separate facility?
- Is the physical security at the backup facility comparable to the physical security at the primary facility?
- Are programming personnel, both employees and nonemployees, prohibited from accessing the tape or disk library?
- Is a paper shredder used for destruction of computer printouts that are not needed the following day?
- Are printouts needed the following workday under the physical security previously described?
- Is there a full-time data security officer? (If not, a description of the experience and the duties of the person responsible for this job is in order.)
- Is the full-time data security officer a member of the corporate internal audit department? (If not, to whom does that person report?)
- Are programs subjected to a total test by people not involved in the program's design?
- Are program controls reviewed by auditors in the design stage?
- Are programs purchased from vendors? If so, does the internal audit staff test the programs fully before using them?
- Does the IS security staff fully investigate all vendors?
- If there are outside vendors, is prior written notice of the change in that vendor's staff required before allowing the new employees access to the facility?
- If there is any form of time-sharing for IS operations, is there a description of the measures in place to protect the integrity of the programs and their usage?
- Are the services of independent IS contractors used? If so, the following questions might be asked:
    1. Does the IS contractor carry employee dishonesty insurance on its employees?
    2. If so, is there evidence of that insurance?

3. If so, does such policy cover the loss of clients' property? (If endorsement [exclude loss of clients' property] CR 10 07 or [exclude loss of clients' property except while on your premises] CR 10 08 is attached to the contractor's policy, there is a restriction or exclusion for the loss of clients' property.)
4. Is the contractor's financial condition reviewed at least annually?
5. Does the IS auditor review the contractor's security and loss prevention measures?
6. If the contractor or its employees program software for the applicant's system, does the applicant prohibit the contractor or employees from running the system?

- Does the applicant or any of its employees engage in the wire transfer of funds? If so, answers to the following questions are necessary:
    1. If a telephone call can activate a transfer of the funds, does the applicant's bank call an employee other than the one who requested the transfer before acting on the transfer request?
    2. Does the receiving institution immediately verify the completion of the transfer of funds? If so, does such verification go to an employee other than the one who initiated the transfer?
- Are inventory records computerized? If so, and if access to those records is available to customers, the following questions might be asked:
    1. Are orders for merchandise accepted only for proven customers?
    2. Is a procedure in place to prevent the fulfillment of an order placed by someone not on the list of approved clients?
    3. Are all filled orders checked in the shipping department against the list of approved clients?

Coverage Form F does not cover all computer-related losses, such as the introduction of a computer virus into the system. Many insurance companies offer special inland marine coverage forms to protect insureds against those losses.

Controlling Computer Crime[6]

Just as with the other crime coverages discussed, computer crime underwriting and loss control concerns are similar because an effective loss control program can reduce insured losses as well as the consequences to the policyholder of uninsured losses. The following discussion presents general security recommendations that apply to the majority of data processing installations.

Personnel Security

Only highly competent data processing personnel who have been thoroughly investigated should be permitted to use or access the computer operations area. Access should be screened by guards or limited to those provided with keys, codes, or cards for entry. Visitors should be required to wear security pass badges and should be escorted while on the premises. The security department should be kept advised on a daily basis of personnel who are permitted access to the computer. Access during "phase-out periods" should be severely limited for employees who have been discharged or who are resigning under questionable circumstances. Finally, at least two persons should be in the room containing the computer hardware at all times.

Data Security

Passwords should be used and changed frequently to control computer access either from on-site terminals or from remote locations through modems.

A competent librarian should control computer tapes and storage disks. All tapes, files, and other sources of information should be duplicated and stored in fire- and theft-resistant storage areas, separate from the computer center.

Where confidential information is stored, electronic shielding might be required to prevent the "capture" of emissions. When a computer is in use, electronic emissions occur. These emissions can be "captured" by the use of special equipment, and unauthorized persons can "read" information going into or coming from the computer.

Information that travels between the computer and terminals in remote areas should be encrypted. Data might be transmitted by wire or satellites and intercepted by unauthorized parties. Encrypted data minimize the possibility of intercepted data being used against the owner.

When financial transactions are made, such as payroll check preparation or wire transfers of bank accounts, frequent internal and external audits should be made. Frequent and thorough audit trails should also be incorporated into computer programs. Programs dealing with money or sensitive data should have edits that require authorizations at the highest levels before changes are accepted.

Access Security

Computer centers and terminals should be designated as exclusion areas with suitable access controls in effect. Computer facilities, including power transformers, air conditioning equipment, and other important related installations, should be located away from areas accessible to the public.

The computer center and terminals should have adequate perimeter protection, augmented by intrusion alarms and by frequent security patrols. Access should be controlled physically by locks and alarms.

Site Security

The location of the computer center and its use should be made as inconspicuous as possible. During periods of social unrest, computer centers were thought to be likely targets of those people who wished to cripple an organization. As a consequence, computer centers are built to be unobtrusive. If the location is known, the data stored at the center or the work processed there is usually not publicized.

Precautions similar to those for any secured facility should be taken to prevent the computer center from being easily taken by force.

Backup facilities are important loss control techniques. A company might have written contracts with nearby data processing facilities to which it can transfer operations in an emergency. The three most common arrangements are as follows:

1. Another organization's excess capacity
2. A **cold site**, which is a commercial backup venture consisting of an available, properly wired, alarmed, empty computer room in which substitute leased hardware can quickly be installed
3. A **hot site**, where a third party keeps a compatible computer installed and running twenty-four hours a day for emergency users

Summary

Crime insurance covers losses intentionally caused by others. The major crime perils are theft, burglary, robbery, and disappearance, all of which are precisely defined for purposes of insurance coverage. Insurance against crime perils is increasingly accomplished by property policies that cover risks of direct loss with the causes of loss special form.

Assessing crime loss potential involves examining both the characteristics of the property subject to loss and the characteristics of the account itself. Underwriters must evaluate territory, police protection, private protection, moral and morale hazards, and adverse selection.

Types of private protection include premises protection, safes and vaults, and detection systems such as alarms, guards, and surveillance cameras.

Evaluating moral and morale hazards involves investigating the applicant's ownership and management, financial and moral reputation, and past loss experience. The problem of adverse selection is a serious one for crime underwriters; sales efforts and pricing are among the means available to mitigate it.

Employee dishonesty (fidelity) insurance covers theft by employees. It is unique among crime insurance coverages because the property exposed is accessible, losses can be hidden from discovery, the probability of severe loss is high, and management control systems are the primary loss control devices. In addition, management is often reluctant to accept that employee theft is a possibility and often refuses to prosecute employees when thefts are discovered.

When writing employee dishonesty insurance, underwriters must be satisfied that certain conditions exist, including adequate burglary and robbery loss control systems, sufficient management controls, and no moral hazard. Fidelity loss control factors include selection practices, periodic audits, monthly bank account reconciliation, divided responsibilities, physical inventories, and annual vacations for all nonowner employees.

The burgeoning use of computers has given rise to diverse and potentially catastrophic crime loss potential. Security considerations for computer installations include personnel requirements, data security, access security, location of the facility, and backup facilities. Security software requiring users to change their passwords frequently has proven to be an effective means for preventing unauthorized access.

Chapter Notes

1. *Uniform Crime Reports: 1995 Crime in the United States*, October 13, 1996, p. 36. Web site accessed on November 13, 1997: http://www.fbi.gov/publish.htm
2. Thomas K. Bourke, "Their Own Worst Enemies: What Companies Can Do To Guard Against Fidelity Losses," *Business Insurance*, June 1992, p. 56.
3. Frank Lamieux, quoted in *Summary Paper*, 1983, published by The Institutional Investor from a seminar: International Risk Management Seminar, "The Emerging Risk of Computer Disaster."
4. This illustration is alleged to have occurred within the IRS, from an interview with Carlton E. Wade, Senior Vice President, Frank B. Hall & Co. Inc., November 1983.
5. This section was taken from Dean P. Felton and Keith G. Sears, *Fidelity Bonds* (Malvern, PA: Insurance Institute of America, 1992), pp. 180-182.
6. This section was adapted from two position papers: "Protection of Electronic Data Processing Facilities" by Wallace Merrell, Sr., Loss Control Engineer, Frank B. Hall & Co. Inc., June 1980; and "Electronic Data Processing Exposures and Preventive Measures" by Peter Rollinger, Frank B. Hall & Co. Inc., October 1980.

Chapter 8

Other Property and Package Policies

This chapter addresses several miscellaneous property coverages that commercial underwriters are asked to provide. Most of these insurance coverages are categorized as inland marine, and they are discussed in the first section of this chapter. The chapter also includes discussions of boiler and machinery insurance and glass insurance. The chapter concludes with a discussion of package policies.

Inland Marine Insurance

Inland marine insurance can be perplexing to underwriters, agents, brokers, and policyholders. It has developed over the years into what some perceive as an enigma that defies logic. To understand fully what inland marine insurance is today and what it might become in the future, underwriters need to understand its origins.

The Development of Inland Marine Insurance

As its name suggests, inland marine insurance developed as an offshoot of the older ocean marine coverage. Insurance has existed in some form ever since communities started trading with one another. The earliest protection against loss grew out of ocean voyages, one of the first forms of commerce and a very hazardous undertaking. This early protection was actually a loan secured by a vessel or its cargo: **bottomry loans** financed a voyage for the ship owner, and **respondentia loans** financed the venture for the traders whose cargoes traveled aboard these ships. The loans were forgiven if misfortune befell the adventure and the ship did not return. The loans provided to finance these voyages commanded a higher rate of interest than loans that were not associated with a voyage. The difference between the normal interest rate and the interest rate charged for a voyage was called "the premium." The risk transfer in those loans had characteristics similar to insurance.

When commerce and industry began to move inland, the need for protection against loss followed. Ocean marine underwriters responded first by extending their policies to include transportation over land at either end of the ocean voyage. Eventually, they developed new products, inland marine insurance, to cover shipments that never traveled by sea. As demand for this type of coverage grew, inland marine insurance evolved into a separate specialty within property-liability insurance.

Even as marine underwriters began offering coverage for goods transported over land, businesses began to need insurance for property that remained at a fixed location. The Great Fire of London in 1666 promoted the development of fire insurance. Although both insure against damage to property, fire and marine insurance developed along very different lines. Insured vessels and their cargoes often disappeared without a trace. Marine underwriters rarely knew what caused the losses they paid, and their policies reflected the uncertainty associated with ocean voyages. Marine underwriters provided broad coverage, frequently insuring loss from virtually any cause. Fire underwriters, on the other hand, almost always knew what caused a loss, and their policies were very specific as to the perils insured and the ownership of the insured buildings and personal property.

Regulation also played a role in shaping inland marine insurance. Insurance regulation limited the types of insurance that an insurance company could offer. For instance, a fire insurance company could not sell life insurance. This regulation reflected the practice of early insurers that specialized because of the expertise needed to maintain solvency and grow. Although what was and was not an appropriate subject for fire insurance was obvious, other lines of insurance were more ambiguous. Casualty and marine underwriters were aggressive in offering new coverages and covering new exposures to loss. Fire underwriters, on the other hand, were reluctant to write new property coverage. Legislatures had to ensure that a market would exist for coverages that constituents needed. This need prompted them to define new types of property coverage as casualty insurance.

By this process certain coverages that protect against loss to the property of the insured have been defined by statute, as has been the case with casualty insurance. Crime insurance, for example, protects against loss to the insured's property by causes such as burglary and robbery and is similar to property insurance. Yet state statutes have categorized crime coverage as casualty insurance. This inconsistency simply reflects the evolution of insurance coverage. Several coverages were categorized as casualty lines of insurance because casualty insurers were more aggressive in developing new types of coverage.

For insureds with a variety of coverage needs, placing a complete property insurance program meant dealing with more than one insurer. This meant that insureds had to keep up with several policies. Having many insurers involved in an insured's insurance program increased the likelihood that insurers would deny a claim because it was more appropriately covered by another insurer's policy.

Insurance consumers also wanted broader coverage than fire underwriters were willing to provide. During the 1920s marine underwriters stepped in to fill the gap, offering "all-risks" floaters that relied on a liberal interpretation of due course of transit. Since these floaters insured property at fixed locations, they encroached on what fire underwriters considered their domain. Because these "all-risks" floaters did not exclude burglary and theft, they also covered causes of loss typically covered by casualty insurance. As a result, both fire and casualty underwriters lobbied regulators for restrictions on business that could be written as inland marine.

The Nationwide Marine Definition

As the 1920s drew to a close, marine insurers entered into agreements with their fire and casualty counterparts. Their intent was to end the competition, but voluntary agreements failed to do this. Fire and casualty underwriters then sought regulatory relief in ending this impasse. In June 1933, the National Association of Insurance Commissioners (NAIC) produced the **Nation-Wide Definition and Interpretation of the Insuring Powers of Marine and Transportation Underwriters** (or simply the Definition). The Definition clarified what underwriters could and could not write as marine insurance. The NAIC also created the Committee on Interpretation of the Nation-Wide Definition to rule on specific questions. Representatives of each of the sectors of the insurance industry made up the committee. The NAIC has revised the Definition several times since then, most recently in 1976. The Definition has the force of law in virtually every state. The Definition no longer defines the underwriting powers of insurers. The multiline laws of the

1950s ended this role of the Definition. Now it serves as a guide for classification purposes only.

The Definition, without distinguishing between inland and ocean marine, recognizes four broad classes of marine insurance:

1. Transportation, which consists of:
    - Imports
    - Exports
    - Domestic shipments
2. Instrumentalities of transportation and communication
3. Personal property floaters
4. Commercial property floaters

Transportation Insurance

Transportation insurance covers property in transit from one location to another. In general, imports and exports are ocean marine, and domestic shipments are inland marine. Transportation insurance can include coverage for the shipper, the carrier, and the consignee. The Definition restricts inland marine coverage, mainly to distinguish it from insurance on property that has a fixed location, in other words, fire insurance. The most important restriction bars insurers from providing coverage while the property is on the shipper's or consignee's premises. The Definition permits insuring cargo in the custody of a carrier from the time it is shipped until it arrives at its final destination. The covered time period includes stops at fixed locations that the carrier controls, such as a warehouse. This process of moving goods from one location to another with planned stops in between is called "due course of transit."

Instrumentalities of Transportation and Communication

Examples of **instrumentalities of transportation and communication** include the following:

- Bridges, tunnels, and similar property, including fixed property used with them
- Piers and wharves of all kinds
- Pipelines and all their equipment
- Transmission lines and property related to them
- Radio and television equipment
- Outdoor cranes and other equipment for loading and unloading

Personal Property Floaters

Personal property floaters include a wide range of special policies written for individuals. Because they are personal lines coverages, they are outside the scope of this text.

Commercial Property Floaters

Commercial property floaters include specific policies that the Definition treats as inland marine insurance. Most of these policies cover property that is mobile, that is, easily moved from place to place. In a few cases, the Definition recognizes a need for a policy form that has the same flexibility afforded mobile property to cover fixed property. Electronic data processing (EDP) coverage is an example of such a coverage form.

Filed and Nonfiled Classes

Freedom from state regulation of rules, forms, and rates has been one of the major attractions of inland marine insurance. For most classes, marine insurers do not need to obtain approval of state insurance departments for their forms and rates. This freedom has allowed insurers to respond quickly to demand for new products and services, but it is not absolute. Insurance advisory organizations file forms, rules, and loss costs for some inland marine classes. Insurers can become members of or subscribers to these advisory organizations and use their filed forms, rules, and loss costs. They may also file their own forms, rules, and rates. Those classes are called **filed** or **controlled classes**. Filed classes are subject to the same regulation of forms, rules, and rates as are other lines of insurance. Most state insurance laws require insurers to file forms and rates for the following commercial inland marine classes:

- Accounts receivable
- Camera and musical instrument dealers
- Film
- Floor plans
- Implement (equipment) dealers
- Jewelers block
- Mail
- Musical instruments
- Photographic equipment
- Physicians', surgeons', and dentists' equipment
- Signs
- Theatrical property
- Valuable papers and records

Other inland marine classes are generally free of this regulation and are called **nonfiled** or **uncontrolled classes**. Buyers find this flexibility in forms and rates attractive. It lets them negotiate coverage and price.

Inland Marine Perils

The freedom from regulation that inland marine insurance provides tends to produce forms that provide broad coverage. More often than not, inland marine forms provide "all-risks" coverage. They do not contain many of the exclusions that sometimes make it difficult for underwriters to tailor coverage to meet the needs of their clients.

Not all inland marine forms provide such broad coverage, however. The same flexibility that state insurance laws provide allows underwriters to tailor a coverage form to fit the customer's needs and can also be used to restrict the coverage the insurer will provide. For example, underwriters are free to draft a coverage form that excludes any cause of loss that the insurer is unwilling to provide. Sometimes this flexibility results in coverage forms that provide less coverage than filed commercial property forms would. A potentially more restrictive coverage form offers the insured an important advantage, however. Less generous terms often allow the insured to obtain some insurance coverage, albeit limited, when coverage might otherwise not be available at all.

The ability to mold the coverage form to the insured's needs does more than give inland marine underwriters a competitive edge; it also makes the covered causes of loss an integral part of the underwriting process. Faced with a marginal risk, an inland marine underwriter has one option that most other underwriters do not. Not only can the underwriter provide coverage to attract profitable accounts, but he or she can also restrict coverage to improve the marginal risk and price the account based on its exposures to loss.

Valuation in Inland Marine Forms

Freedom from regulation allows inland marine underwriters to place any reasonable value on the property they insure. For the most part, they use the same approaches to property valuation as commercial property underwriters, that is, actual cash value, replacement cost, and functional replacement cost. Inland marine underwriters also write valued forms. These should not be confused with the provisions of valued policy laws that a number of states have adopted. Valued policy statutes require an insurer to pay the policy limit for a total loss to real property, regardless of its true value. The amount of insurance in a valued form is sometimes referred to as the "agreed value." In commercial property insurance, the same term is used to describe an endorsement that, in effect, waives the coinsurance clause. Once again, the terms are the same, but their meanings are not.

An inland marine valued form states that the covered property is "insured for and valued at" a certain amount. In essence, the underwriter and the insured agree in advance that the insured property will be worth that amount at the time of loss. This technique is especially useful when determining that the value of the property after loss is either not possible or not practical. Determining the actual cash value of a painting after fire has reduced it to ashes, for example, is largely a matter of speculation. Valued forms resolve a difficult problem. They allow the underwriter and the insured to agree on the reasonable value of the property before loss occurs. Underwriters also use valued forms to insure property that cannot be replaced. Fine arts, historic manuscripts, and collections of rare coins and stamps are examples of irreplaceable items.

When writing a valued form, underwriters must be certain that the amount of insurance reflects a true measure of the property's value. Setting the value too low fails to provide adequate protection to the insured. A value that is too high creates a moral hazard by giving the insured an incentive to destroy the property in order to realize a gain from the insurance proceeds.

Underwriting Inland Marine Insurance

The process of underwriting inland marine coverage is similar to underwriting other property lines. The factors that the underwriter must evaluate, however, are sometimes very different. Commercial property forms, for instance, cover property at a fixed location, most often a building and its contents. Construction, occupancy, protection, and external exposure (the COPE factors) form the basis of hazard assessment. Inland marine forms, on the other hand, often protect property that moves. They cover mobile equipment or goods in transit. COPE loses its meaning when the location of the property ceases to be an underwriting factor. The nature of the coverage gives rise to other considerations that vary from one class of inland marine insurance to another.

Most inland marine forms protect the insured against direct loss or damage to the insured property. Coverage for loss of use is also included under many inland marine classes. Electronic data processing equipment has become essential to most businesses. A growing number of businesses cannot function for even a few minutes if their computers shut down. This has created the need for insurance to cover loss of business income and the payment of extra expenses because of loss to hardware, software, and media. Insureds whose businesses rely on their mobile equipment are concerned about effects to their earnings resulting from the loss of use of that equipment. Because of these concerns, inland marine underwriters often receive requests to provide coverage for loss of use of a wide variety of insured property. The coverage is similar to the business income coverage that commercial property forms provide. Many of the considerations for underwriting the two coverages are the same.

Transportation Coverage

Transportation insurance covers goods in due course of transit. The policy might insure the carrier who transports the goods, the cargo owner, or a third party who is at risk of loss while goods are in transit. To comprehend the exposure fully, the underwriter must know who the parties to a shipping transaction are and what roles they play.

The **shipper** is any party who hires another to transport cargo. Because goods are so often shipped as part of a contract of sale, the shipper can also be the seller. These two terms are sometimes used interchangeably in discussions of goods shipped by any mode. The **carrier** is the party who actually transports (or carries) the goods. The **consignee** is the person designated for delivery. The details of the transaction and common law determine which party bears the risk of loss in transit.

Four distinct classes of transportation insurance are used to satisfy the needs of shippers, consignees, and carriers:

1. The motor truck cargo-carriers liability form insures the carrier (the trucker) and covers liability for damage to goods of others carried on the insured's trucks.
2. The motor truck cargo-owners form protects against loss to the insured's property carried on the insured's own trucks.
3. Transit insurance covers the insured's property shipped on another party's trucks.
4. Mail insurance covers goods sent through the United States Postal Service.

The contract between the shipper and the carrier is a **bill of lading**. This is a multipurpose document that also serves as a receipt for goods accepted for shipment. In some circumstances, the bill of lading can also represent title to the goods.

Carriers Liability

A trucker that carries cargo for customers is a **public carrier**, a type of bailee. The law recognizes two distinct classes of public carriers: **contract carriers** and **common carriers**. The carriers' liability for the cargo they carry differs. A contract carrier agrees to carry goods for a select group of shippers under an agreement that covers more than one shipment. A trucker that agrees, for instance, to handle all deliveries for a manufacturer or a retail store is a contract carrier. Common carriers transport goods for *the public*. In essence, they carry cargo for anyone who can pay the freight. Common carriers might specialize in a certain type of shipment, such as bulk or liquid cargo, but they would service any shipper that needs goods moved. United Parcel Service (UPS), Federal Express, and Guaranteed Overnight Delivery are all examples of common carriers. A carrier can be a common carrier to some shippers and a contract carrier to others. This dual role can occur when a customer enters into a long-term agreement with a common carrier. A retail store might make this type of arrangement, for example, with UPS.

Liability of the Common Carrier

The courts hold a contract carrier liable as an ordinary bailee for hire. This means that the trucker has a duty to take the same care of the shipper's property as it would its own. Ordinary negligence is the basis of liability. The law regards a common carrier, on the other hand, as an insurer of the goods it carries. When a dispute over loss to goods in transit first came before the English courts, the judge read the bill of lading as a contract for *safe* delivery of the goods. This interpretation placed all risk of loss on the carrier. Over the years, courts have recognized five exceptions to the common carrier's liability:

1. *Acts of God.* An act of God is a natural event that causes damage to the cargo. The law considers lightning, windstorm, flood, and earthquake as acts of God. In many respects, this makes the "insurance" that a common carrier must provide very restrictive. It does not cover many of the causes of loss that underwriters would normally expect. This exception does not, however, excuse a common carrier for negligently exposing cargo to loss by an act of God. A carrier would be liable in negligence, for example, if cargo sustained damage from a flood that the driver could easily have foreseen and avoided.
2. *Act of a public enemy.* This is the equivalent of a war exclusion.
3. *Exercise of public authority.* If a public agency confiscates or condemns the cargo, the carrier does not incur any liability under ordinary circumstances. If, however, the common carrier has acted in some way to cause the seizure or condemnation, the courts might impose liability on negligence theories.
4. *Fault of the shipper.* Any act of the shipper that causes loss to the goods relieves the common carrier of liability. Improper packing is a good example. In addition, perishable cargo might spoil if the shipper changes delivery instructions en route. Such a change might be enough to excuse the trucker of liability, even if the bill of lading requires refrigerated trucks or trailers.
5. *Inherent vice of the cargo.* Inherent vice is the characteristic of being perishable, explosive, or subject to quick deterioration in the absence of special handling. Tomatoes will rot very quickly when exposed to bright sun or

high temperatures without refrigeration. Inherent vice does not excuse the common carrier who fails to provide special protection, such as refrigeration, that the bill of lading requires.

Bill of Lading

The bill of lading can limit the carrier's liability in two ways. First, the shipper might identify cargo as a less valuable commodity than it actually is. When this happens, the courts usually hold the common carrier liable only for the value of the declared commodity. In one case, for instance, a company shipped gold bullion but listed lead ingots on the bill of lading. The shipper's intent was to avoid losses by making the cargo appear to be something that was not worth stealing. The ruse fooled the common carrier, but not the thieves. The shipper sued to recover the value of the stolen gold bullion, but the court awarded only the value of an amount of lead ingots equal to the weight of the stolen gold.

The bill of lading can also limit the amount of any public carrier's liability for loss of the cargo. This is called a **released bill of lading**, or simply a "released bill." A contract carrier can achieve the same result in its contract with the shipper. The parties might express the value as a dollar amount for the entire cargo or a value for some unit of measure such as weight or shipping packages. The bill of lading might, for instance, place a value on the cargo of $.10 per pound or $50.00 per shipping package. In some situations, the bill of lading might place no value on the cargo. This places the risk of loss entirely on the owner of the cargo.

Since the U.S. Congress deregulated the trucking industry, released bills have become more common. Carriers shift the risk of loss to shippers as much as possible. Federal and state regulations still require truckers to offer full-value bills of lading but allow the carrier to pass insurance costs along to the shipper. In many instances, carriers charge a higher rate for a full-value bill of lading than their insurers charge for coverage. This higher rate helps the carrier defray the added cost of placing the insurance and encourages shippers to obtain their own coverage.

Inland marine underwriters at one time resisted insuring goods shipped under released bills of lading. The conventional wisdom was that it is better to hold carriers liable for the full value of goods shipped to give them an incentive to control losses. While this remains an underwriting concern, inland marine underwriters freely accept cargo shipped under a released bill of lading with the assumption that loss control concerns can be handled another way.

Underwriting Motor Truck Cargo Coverage

Beyond consideration of the bill of lading, underwriters will find little difference between the owners and carriers liability forms of motor truck cargo coverage. Past losses and safety programs are the most important factors to consider. To evaluate the exposure, the underwriter should ask several questions, some of which are discussed below:

- *What commodities does the insured transport?* This question might be especially difficult to answer for common carriers. They might simply accept any cargo from any customer who approaches them. Some, on the other hand, deal with a base of regular customers who ship commodities attractive to thieves. Contract carriers might paint their trucks and trailers to appear to belong to a customer. Some carriers paint their trucks to advertise the products they carry. If these products are ones often targeted by thieves, the identification of those goods makes them easier for thieves to steal. Although most underwriters will not decline an account for this reason alone, advertising goods carried is likely to increase losses enough to warrant a higher premium.
- *How well does the insured maintain the fleet?* A strictly enforced schedule of maintenance can help prevent accidents caused by equipment failure. The qualifications of the mechanics who work on the insured's fleet are very important. Mechanics should be fully trained and certified for the vehicles on which they work. An insured that operates a large fleet might be able to employ certified mechanics, but smaller fleets cannot afford a full staff. Contracting mechanical work out to qualified professionals is a positive sign for a fleet of any size.
- *Are trucks and trailers loaded properly?* Cargo that shifts while in transit might suffer damage, damage other goods, or cause a traffic accident. Loaders should receive proper training, and the insured should supervise all loading operations. Distributing the weight evenly and securing the load to prevent shifting on turns or during stops are important precautions. Allowing the shipper to load the vehicle is a common practice, but it impairs the insured's ability to control losses. The underwriter must evaluate the quality of the loading that the insured's customers practice. Loading by parties other than the insured's own staff might be a negative indicator of acceptability.
- *Does the insured provide driver training?* Since 1992, truck drivers have been required to have a commercial driver's license. This requirement has helped improve fleet safety in two principal ways. First, drivers can no longer maintain multiple licenses to conceal a history of violations and accidents. Second, they must pass both written and road tests that

demonstrate the knowledge and skill that safe operation of a truck or tractor-trailer requires. Maintaining a good safety record requires periodic retraining to reinforce good habits, correct bad ones, and keep drivers abreast of new developments.

- *Is a safe-driving program in place?* Traffic accidents damage cargo, and safe drivers are less likely to have accidents than are careless ones. A safe-driving program offers the potential to reduce losses in two ways. First, it might reward desirable conduct by providing incentives to drive safely. A cash bonus is one option, but anything that has value to the drivers can be effective. Even a simple safe-driving award will work if the drivers want to earn it. Recognition is important and effective. Good drivers are proud of their records.

  Second, a good safe-driving program includes penalties for bad driving. Drivers must understand that multiple accidents and violations will result in sanctions. Therefore, an effective safe-driving program must include discipline for a poor driving record. Dismissal is not unreasonable in extreme cases, even for drivers with seniority. A safe-driving program that includes random testing for substance abuse makes an account more desirable.

  Accurate recording and adequate control of the number of hours a driver logs are important features of a good safe-driving program. The insured should have systems in place to ensure that drivers maintain their logs accurately and do not drive too many hours. The United States Department of Transportation (DOT) has set legal limits on the number of hours that may be driven, but insureds might enforce tighter limits.

- *Do schedules put drivers under time pressure?* Many contract carriers operate delivery services for retail stores. They face the same time pressure that the retailer would if operating its own fleet. Pressure to meet schedules gives this class a higher accident frequency than any other.

  Several common carriers offer overnight delivery service. Most restrict this service to small parcels and letters, but a few carriers offer guaranteed overnight delivery of large items that other carriers will not accept. Drivers who rush to finish their deliveries by 10 A.M. as promised might have accidents that will damage cargo.

- *How familiar are drivers with the routes they travel?* When drivers follow unfamiliar routes, accidents and damage to cargo become more likely. Most public carriers follow regular routes when making over-the-road trips, often operating only between their own terminals. Local deliveries do not permit the same degree of familiarity with the route. Many common carriers accept only truckload lots and follow regular routes almost exclusively. Freight forwarders or consolidators, on the other hand, aggregate smaller shipments to make a truckload. LTL (less than a truckload) truckers will accept any cargo. The diverse routes and more frequent stops that these operations involve distract the driver and cause fatigue, thus making accidents more likely.

Regular routes become a disadvantage, however, when the cargo is a target for thieves. Truckers that carry cargoes vulnerable to theft should vary routes and schedules as much as possible.

- *How well does the insured protect sensitive cargo?* Some cargoes are easily susceptible to damage in transit, and some truckers specialize in these cargoes. Companies that transport fragile cargo like computers and tradeshow displays must take special care to avoid damage. They need highly qualified drivers and helpers and should be willing to pay premium wages to attract them.

  Truckers that routinely transport cargoes that thieves find attractive must take special precautions. Alarm systems are effective when used as intended. Alarms that engage passively whenever someone closes the cab or cargo compartment enhance security.

  Modern technology can also shift the emphasis from prevention to apprehension and recovery. High-tech systems allow trucking companies to track the location of their vehicles. Several fleet management systems are already on the market. Because they have been designed to report the precise location of vehicles in the fleet, these systems aid in recovery of stolen vehicles and their cargoes. In addition to protecting entire vehicles, some systems on the market are compact enough to be concealed inside a shipping package. This allows the shipper to track the location of an individual package and often to recover it after a theft. Fleet management systems are used to control costs in a competitive environment. The ability to control theft losses is an added benefit but is not a primary consideration. As a result, carriers are more likely to install fleet management hardware than to adopt other loss control measures that affect only incurred losses.

Underwriters can obtain most of the information needed to evaluate motor truck cargo coverage from the following three sources:

- A physical inspection
- The insured's loss history
- The insured's financial statements

When reading an inspection report, an underwriter should weigh systems and procedures as well as performance. Employees are more likely to follow procedures if they are in writing.

Loss history is a better indicator of quality in this line of business than in most others. Insureds accumulate a large number of shipments exposed to loss very quickly. This number makes the data more credible. If frequency is low, the insured is probably doing those things that the underwriter believes are important. If frequency is high, then the root cause of those losses needs to be identified.

Truckers must meet requirements of the DOT and state public utility commissions (PUCs), including evidence of insurance. Filings are made by insurers to the DOT and PUCs. These filings make the insurer responsible for some types of loss that are not covered by the policy and that are reimbursable by the insured. The insurer takes on a legal obligation to pay losses that are the insured's responsibility. The insured's financial stability takes added importance because the ability to reimburse losses that are not covered by the policy becomes a factor. In addition to the normal sources of financial information, underwriters can get access to the DOT and PUC filings. These filings are available as part of the public record, but collecting them directly might not be easy. The Central Analysis Bureau (CAB), a commercial service provider, collects the public filings and supplies them to underwriters with CAB's own analysis. CAB maintains records on over 50,000 motor carriers and grades the financial strength on a six-step scale ranging from satisfactory to dangerous. Many insurers rely on CAB for carriers' financial data.

Transit Coverage

Transit coverage protects the interest of the owners of cargo shipped on a public carrier's trucks. Discussions of inland marine insurance often use the terms "transit" and "transportation" interchangeably. The term "transit" is sometimes reserved for trip transit forms. Many insurers have no "transit" forms at all, labeling them "transportation" forms instead. They might number among them forms named "Motor Truck Cargo—Carrier's Liability Form," "Motor Truck Cargo—Owner's Form," and "Transportation Form." This variety in nomenclature, of course, causes some confusion.

For clarity, this text will refer to the broad class of inland marine transportation insurance as "transportation coverage." The type of transportation insurance that covers the owner of goods carried on another company's trucks will be called "transit coverage."

One of the first things that an underwriter must know in order to evaluate a transit exposure is who owns the cargo and who stands to lose if it sustains damage. Transit insurance often covers goods sold by the shipper to a customer. In this case, the contract of sale determines who owns the goods and who is at risk of loss while the goods are in transit. These contracts often employ standard terms such as F.O.B., to which the law assigns clearly defined meanings. Underwriters need to know what these terms mean and what that meaning implies for losses the insured can expect to incur. The principal terms of sale that inland marine underwriters encounter are F.O.B. point of origin and F.O.B. destination. Some familiarity with other terms of sale can also be useful.

F.O.B. is an abbreviation for "free on board" and requires something additional to indicate the point at which title passes. When a manufacturer or distributor sells goods **F.O.B. point of origin**, title passes when the goods are placed aboard the carrier's vehicle at the seller's premises. From that point forward they belong to the buyer (who might also be the consignee) and travel at the buyer's risk of loss. The seller no longer owns the cargo but might retain a security interest in it.

The applicant might seek coverage for three different insurable interests that sales F.O.B. point of origin might create. First, the customer owns the goods and is the party primarily at risk of loss. That interest presents few, if any, problems.

Second, the seller might also have a security interest in the goods. However, transit insurance might not be the best way to insure this insurable interest. If the shipment is lost and both the buyer and seller have transit coverage, the courts are likely to allow both to collect the full value of the cargo. Other details of the transaction might indicate that credit insurance or an installment sales floater might be a more appropriate way to insure the interest of a secured creditor.

Third, the seller might also agree to insure the cargo for the benefit of the buyer who owns it and is at risk of loss. This arrangement is perfectly legitimate. Most transit forms include a specific provision to accommodate this type of arrangement, sometimes called "insuring F.O.B. shipments." To prevent duplicate recovery, the seller's insurance applies only if the buyer has none. The underwriter must only evaluate the exposure to outgoing shipments, which might not be the same exposure as the incoming shipments present.

Contracts of sale sometimes use other expressions that are equivalent to F.O.B. point of origin. They include "ex [from] factory" and "ex mill."

F.O.B. destination means that the seller owns the goods until they arrive at the destination that the buyer specified. The seller is at risk of loss during transit. The buyer does not own the goods but does have an insurable interest.

For the reason mentioned above, the underwriter should be wary of using transit forms to insure the consignee's interest. If a loss occurs, some courts will permit both parties to recover the full value of the property. This is sometimes the underwriter's intent when separate commercial property forms insure different interests. That is rarely the case, however, when covering goods in transit.

In most cases, only the seller will seek to insure F.O.B. destination shipments. On rare occasions, the buyer might agree to insure the shipment. Because printed transit coverage forms rarely cover this exposure for the buyer, the request would require special attention. When offering this coverage, the underwriter should exercise care in drafting the endorsement or manuscript form. Insuring all incoming F.O.B. destination shipments is easy, even when the intent is to cover only those that the shipper has not insured. The language that most transit forms use to cover F.O.B. point of origin shipments under the shipper's policy provides a good model.

Sellers sometimes ship goods to market before selling them. This practice is especially prevalent in the sale of perishables like fresh produce. The shipper will send the cargo and work to find a buyer while the cargo is in transit. The most common terms of sale for these goods remain F.O.B. point of origin, but the term "rolling acceptance" is added to indicate that the cargo is already en route at the time of sale. Sellers often use the words "rolling acceptance final," but that phrase has little effect on how courts assign the risk of loss. More than one court has held that a rolling acceptance is always final. A rolling acceptance only changes the title and risk of loss, which pass to the buyer retroactively. The goods might have left their point of origin several hours or even days before the sale. The buyer nonetheless takes title at the time and place of shipment and is at risk of loss for the entire trip.

Transit forms also cover imports shipped to the insured from the time that ocean marine coverage expires. To help evaluate this exposure, underwriters should be familiar with the following three additional terms of sale, normally used only for ocean shipments:

- **F.A.S.** is similar to F.O.B. It is an abbreviation for "free alongside." The cargo must be alongside an overseas vessel. Inland marine underwriters should encounter this term only in the form of "F.A.S. port of entry." A shipper might, for instance, sell goods "F.A.S. Port Newark, N.J." or "F.A.S. cargo ship, Boston." Title and risk of loss pass when the goods are unloaded and placed on the pier or wharf next to the ship.
- **C.&F.**, which is a variation of F.O.B. point of origin, is an abbreviation of "cost and freight." Title and risk of loss pass to the buyer at the point of

origin, but the seller agrees to pay some of the shipping costs. The seller agrees to pay the freight charges that would ordinarily fall to the owner of the goods. Inland marine transit forms should never be used to cover C.&F. shipments. The buyer is at risk for the entire voyage and needs ocean marine coverage for adequate protection.

- **C.I.F.** is an abbreviation for "cost, insurance, and freight" and means that the shipper pays the freight charges *and* agrees to provide insurance for the entire voyage. The buyer nonetheless retains a contingent exposure. The shipper may fail to place insurance, or the shipper's insurer may be unable to pay a loss that occurs. Many importers seek to insure only this exposure. Once again, property coverage requires an ocean cargo policy. Inland marine forms should not pick up this exposure because they cannot properly meet the insured's needs.

Underwriting Transit Coverage

In many respects, transit coverage is easier to underwrite than motor truck cargo coverage. Underwriters know what commodities the insured ships and what the policy will cover. This knowledge affords an opportunity to evaluate any special treatment or handling that the cargo demands. On the other hand, the insured does not operate or control the trucks carrying the cargo. Once the truck leaves the premises, the insured has to trust control of losses to the carrier. Underwriters should consider several factors when underwriting transit coverage.

The nature of the goods is important. Perishables need refrigeration. Insureds who ship fragile cargoes that need special handling should consider using carriers with expertise in carrying such cargoes. Truckers that specialize in transporting computers or trade-show displays are less likely to damage such property. If the cargo is susceptible to theft, the shipper should find truckers that use alarms or one of the fleet management systems discussed earlier. A bill of lading that values the cargo adequately is a positive sign.

Insureds should pack the cargo properly before shipment. The type of cargo will determine what packing procedures the shipper should use. Corrugated boxes are fine for books but provide little protection for fragile items like electronic equipment. Styrofoam forms that hold the cargo immobile in the shipping package provide the best protection for many goods and are more effective than packing materials like paper, styrofoam "peanuts," and plastic bubble wrap. Employees who pack goods for shipment should receive training and know their jobs well.

Truckers often leave a trailer for the customer to load. The loading considerations discussed above in connection with motor truck cargo apply to trailers that the shipper loads.

Consignees should also inspect the cargo on delivery. For incoming shipments, the insured is often the consignee as well as the owner of the goods. The carrier might be liable for damage in transit by contract, under common law, or for negligence. If any shipping packages show signs of damage, the consignee should write "no waiver of concealed damage" on the trucker's receipt before signing it.

The carriers that the insured uses help determine what the insured's loss experience will be. Many trucking operations have come into being since the U.S. Congress eased regulation of the trucking industry. Carriers that have established a record of safely transporting cargo are less likely than others to cause losses or to charge the lowest rates. Insureds that engage in the false economy of selecting a trucker on the basis of price alone are likely to be below-average accounts.

The bill of lading can control losses in several ways. As noted above, it can impose special duties on the trucker. If the bill of lading requires refrigerated trailers, alarms, or cargo-recovery systems, truckers that fail to provide and maintain the protection will be liable for any loss.

Trip transit insurance covers a single shipment. It was once the only form of transit insurance, but annual and continuous forms have replaced it. Requests for trip transit forms are usually made to cover special situations. For example, an insured moving from one location to another may want its business personal property insured while in transit. Insureds who do very little shipping might choose a trip transit form and handle the insurance of each shipment separately. Underwriters should evaluate the single trip exposure just as they would an annual form.

Another use of the trip transit coverage form is to provide coverage for a single shipment when that shipment exceeds the limits in the annual transit or motor truck cargo owner's form. Trip transit coverage will fill the need, but the underwriter should consider an endorsement to increase the limits of the annual transit form for one trip only. These special exposures sometimes demand flexibility on the part of the underwriter.

Instrumentalities of Transportation and Communication

In most states, instrumentalities of transportation and communication are a nonfiled class for which the underwriter is free to choose the form and rate. Although many insurers maintain printed forms for accounts in this class, manuscript forms are common. Each demands attention to its own unique characteristics and needs. Coverage for instrumentalities of transportation and communication is a specialty line that most insurers have neither the interest nor the resources to write.

Bridges and Tunnels

Coverage forms that insure bridges and tunnels almost always cover risks of direct physical loss ("all-risks" coverage). The most widely available coverage forms include the following:

- Direct loss for completed bridges and tunnels
- Builders risk for those in the course of construction
- Business income for toll bridges and tunnels

Underwriting Bridges and Tunnels

The forms cover buildings used to operate bridges and tunnels, including toll plazas and administrative offices, as well as the bridge or tunnel itself. The leading causes of loss to bridges include damage from vehicles and ships, high winds, collapse, earthquake, landslide, and flood. In colder climates, ice also causes loss. Damage by fire in nearby buildings is a threat to some bridges, especially in urban areas.

Good control of traffic flow, clearly marked lanes, and careful maintenance provide effective protection against vehicle damage to bridges. Still, some losses remain unavoidable. They represent part of the ordinary cost of operating a bridge. In most cases, the bridge owner can recover from liability insurance covering the automobile that caused the damage.

Toll plazas and booths command special attention as the most likely site of collisions. The exposure to traffic damage is more severe on bridges with curves on the main span and ramps.

Passing vessels can severely damage bridges that cross navigable bodies of water. Runaway ships and barges, for example, have on several occasions knocked down parts of the Chesapeake Bay Bridge Tunnel, which runs from Norfolk, Virginia, to the southern tip of the Delmarva Peninsula. An insurer might seem to have good prospects for a subrogation recovery when a vessel strikes and damages a bridge, but this is not always the case. Over a wide range of circumstances, admiralty law limits the vessel owner's liability to the value of the vessel *after* a loss. Since collision with a bridge often renders the vessel a total loss, the owner effectively has no liability in many cases.

Good design and maintenance will prevent loss by high wind and collapse. The most spectacular bridge failure in United States history occurred in 1949 when high winds brought down the Tacoma-Narrows Bridge across Puget Sound. The span, nicknamed "Galloping Gertie" because of the way it swayed in the wind, employed an innovative design. It was designed to "give" with the wind and remain stable. Instead, it gyrated wildly whenever the wind exceeded forty miles per hour. High winds are fairly common in the narrows of Puget Sound, and the owners had to close the bridge frequently. The problem was caused by solid plates in the roadway that offered resistance to the wind. Two bridges with perforated steel roadbeds now span Puget Sound at the site of the original bridge. The wind that once proved so catastrophic now passes harmlessly through the open spaces in the roadbed.

Preventing flood losses is also a matter of good design and careful maintenance. Bridge design should allow the bridge to withstand a 100-year flood (a severe flood expected to occur only once every 100 years on average). The U.S. Army Corps of Engineers has recorded the boundaries and characteristics of 100-year floods for every area of the United States. Bridge owners and designers can use this information to improve safety.

Bridges in cold climates must be able to withstand the ravages of winter ice. Ice floating downstream can cause damage if it collides with bridge supports. Also, stationary ice can exert pressure on bridge supports. The underwriter should evaluate how often the water freezes and how the bridge defends against ice. Placing all supports on dry land offers the best protection, but that is not always feasible. Barriers in the water can deflect floating ice away from the structure and absorb enough of the pressure exerted by ice accumulations to prevent damage.

The most frequent cause of bridge failure during an earthquake is caused when lateral members become unattached from vertical supports because they were not securely anchored. During an earthquake, the structure must withstand powerful lateral stress that tends to move its vertical members away from each other. Horizontal members that are not firmly anchored to their vertical supports fall. This construction defect caused the collapse of the Nimitz Freeway in Oakland and the San Francisco-Oakland Bay Bridge during the Loma Prieta earthquake in 1989. It also accounted for the large-scale failure of freeway overpasses when an earthquake struck Northridge, near Los Angeles, in 1992.

Vehicle damage, floods, and earthquakes pose the most serious dangers to tunnels. The problems of vehicle damage are very similar to those which bridges face, and the same measures that protect bridges will protect a tunnel. Vehicle fires present a special problem for tunnels. The presence of firefighting equipment in the tunnel and trained firefighters help mitigate this exposure. Flooding in a tunnel causes damage from the force of the water and from the sand and debris that remain.

The Target Risk Exclusion

Most reinsurance treaties exclude loss or damage to any property on the target risk list. This list identifies properties with high values, typically bridges and tunnels, on which excess of loss underwriters have made heavy commitments to the facultative reinsurance market. To control the amount subject to a single loss, underwriters will exclude those properties from any treaty reinsurance. The target risk exclusion forces bridge and tunnel underwriters to retain their full limit or reinsure the bridge or tunnel in the facultative reinsurance market. To obtain the limits needed, underwriters use subscription policies for most large bridges and tunnels. A subscription policy is a single policy underwritten by several different insurers. Each takes a fixed share of premiums and pays a fixed share of losses.

Piers, Wharves, Docks, and Slips

Waterfront property includes commercial piers and wharves and marinas. They are eligible for marine insurance because they are essential to shipments by sea and along inland waterways. Insurers may choose to cover these exposures under commercial property forms, or as either inland or ocean marine forms. The underwriter's hazard analysis should emphasize the following:

- Overall condition
- Level of maintenance
- Quality of construction
- Age
- Level of public and private protection

The leading causes of loss are fire, explosion, wave action, ice, flood, windstorm, and collision with vessels. Fire is a special problem when underwriting piers, wharves, docks, and slips. Because these structures are located on the waterfront, it is easy to assume that there will be an ample supply of water available for fighting fires, which is not always the case. Water mains do not always extend to all waterfront properties, so fire hydrants may not be available. The length of some commercial piers places their far ends beyond the reach of shore-based hydrants. Placing water mains on the pier is not always practical, especially where severe winter weather would expose them to freezing. The fire services may be unable to use the water at the pier or wharf for fighting fires because necessary equipment for drawing water may not be available, or the water source may not be accessible to firefighting apparatus. Fire service equipment may be unable to pump salt water to extinguish fires located on property on or near the ocean. The fire services in large cities and busy ports have fire boats with crews trained to fight pier fires. Smaller communities and ports that attract lighter traffic may not have the same level of protection available.

Frame warehouses, grain elevators, and storage tanks for volatile liquids often expose commercial piers. Insureds often have little control over the goods stored in the exposing properties or even on the pier itself. Most marinas have refueling stations for boats. They pump both gasoline and diesel fuel, often from a wooden dock. The lay-up season can be a special problem for marina underwriters. Marinas might be unoccupied for several months of the year, and during these months, the marina keepers legal liability exposure might reach catastrophe levels because of the number of boats stored there during the off-season.

Pipelines

A network of pipelines transports natural gas and petroleum products throughout the United States. Gas pipelines are especially prone to severe property loss. Damage done by excavating is one of the most common causes. After a devastating pipeline explosion in Edison, New Jersey, on March 25, 1994, the New Jersey Board of Public Utilities disclosed that in 1993 the Board had recorded more than 2,600 pipeline accidents in the state. Almost 900 of these accidents were caused by damage done during excavation.

Within six months of the 1994 explosion, New Jersey adopted a law to establish a single-call clearance system for all underground utilities. Under such a system, contractors must call a special phone number *before* starting to dig, and utilities have to mark their lines within seventy-two hours following the call. A good clearance system is the best defense against damage to pipelines by excavation. Contractors might not know the identity of all utilities in the area or might consider obtaining their telephone numbers too much trouble. In the absence of a one-call clearance system, the pipeline operator should publish a number in the front of local telephone directories.

The universal one-call clearance system that New Jersey established was well designed and gave every appearance of working well from the outset. Early experience with the system, however, demonstrates that the best systems will never be entirely effective. An accident on January 9, 1995, closed down Newark Airport, the busiest of three serving the New York metropolitan area. A contractor was driving piles for construction of the monorail that now connects the terminals and parking lots. The local utility had marked the location of the airport's electrical service. This action by the utility did not stop the piles from penetrating the concrete conduit carrying the main electric cables to the airport. Severe damage at three separate places along the conduit deprived the busy airport of most of its electricity. Less than four months later, another contractor damaged a major natural gas pipeline while excavating. The second loss occurred at the site of the explosion that had prompted the one-call clearance system in the first place. In the wake of these accidents, no one argued either that the system was defective or that New Jersey needed a better system. These losses occurred despite the loss control measures that had been implemented.

A good clearance system does not, of course, eliminate the need for pipeline owners to place markers along buried pipeline rights of way. Markers typically identify the type of pipeline and display a telephone number to call before digging. Emergency crews responding to a ruptured water main would not call a clearance number and wait seventy-two hours. They might not even have time to call the operator before they start to dig. Markers to alert them to the presence of the pipeline might be the only effective protection against loss.

Radio and Television Communications Equipment

Radio and television communications equipment is the class of instrumentality that underwriters are most likely to encounter. This class includes antennas and their towers, mobile broadcasting equipment, transmitters, studios, and even the entire building housing the station. Underwriting studios, offices, and buildings presents no unique considerations. Coverage under commercial property forms is, in fact, an alternative to an inland marine form. The underwriting techniques discussed in Chapters 4 and 5 apply equally to radio and TV stations. The underwriter might have to consider one more cause of loss, electrical damage, but the underwriting process is the same. The discussion of commercial floaters that follows applies just as appropriately to mobile broadcast equipment. Antennas, towers, and sometimes transmitters, however, present their own unique set of exposures.

Broadcast stations generally locate their antennas on top of a building or a tower in the open. Antennas are expensive and subject to total loss. If a tower falls, it will have no value except salvage, and the salvage value might be less than the cost of removing the debris. Exposure to weather, in the form of wind throughout the country and ice and sleet in colder climates, is the leading cause of loss. Fire can also bring towers down, and aircraft might fly into them. Also, underwriters should always consider the possibility of damage by lightning. Antennas and towers need grounding to protect them from lightning. Auxiliary control equipment supporting the functioning of the antennae is included in the Definition. Stations place transmitters close to their antennas, on the upper floors of a building or in a small building at the base of the antenna tower, so there is often a concentration of values that are similarly exposed.

The major underwriting considerations are the quality of design, construction, and maintenance of the tower. Data on the recurrence of strong winds are available for all parts of the United States. Because wind velocity increases with altitude, wind speeds reported at a ten-meter height will require upward adjustment to reflect the true force against the tower. Underwriters must decide how strong a wind the tower design should anticipate. One way to gauge wind speed would be to evaluate its likelihood in a 50- or 100-year period. Model building codes often use the wind that recurs every 70 years, but local codes often adopt a higher design speed.

The tower must also be able to carry the load of snow, ice, and sleet. In addition to adding weight, accumulated ice will increase the surface area on which the wind can act. When a tower is shrouded in ice, the wind can exert a greater force on the structure. Adequate design requires an engineer who is familiar with wind-resistant construction. Good maintenance includes extra attention to the guy wires that stabilize many towers against lateral pressure such as that created by wind. Over time, these wires will stretch and become weaker. Proper maintenance and timely replacement of guy wires are essential to protecting transmission towers against damage by wind.

Many broadcast stations place towers and transmitters in remote locations in order to take the best advantage of topography and atmospheric conditions. The ideal location for the tower and transmitter is often in an undeveloped area that is subject to wildfires. The fact that the facility is usually isolated and unattended makes it attractive to vandals. Losses from fire and vandalism can be controlled by keeping the site around the base of the tower fenced and clear of brush.

In many ways, a remote antenna location helps control claims for loss of use. A single occurrence is not likely to involve both the remote and primary locations. The building housing the transmitter might also contain an auxiliary studio that will allow the station to remain on the air. In most areas, the station can also arrange for the use of an alternate transmitter and antenna when its own are out of service. Stations often have these reciprocal arrangements in place for routine maintenance shutdowns.

Commercial Property Floaters

The practice of referring to inland marine forms as "floaters" began because the forms often cover property that moves from place to place, or "floats," and needs insurance that will float with it. In actual practice, much of the property that commercial floaters insure stays primarily at one location. The practice of insuring such property under inland marine forms persists, but not principally because the property moves from place to place. The fact that the property can move or be moved qualifies if for treatment under an inland marine floater because it is not property at a fixed location, the focus of property insurance, and because it is exposed to loss when it is in transit. The term "floater" is not nearly as common as it once was. It still appears in the Definition, but it is disappearing from policy forms. Some inland marine insurers have begun to use commercial property forms. The need for more flexible forms and rates has, however, drawn builders risk business from commercial property to inland marine.

Equipment Floaters

Equipment floaters represent a major share of inland marine premiums. Since the early days of inland marine insurance, a variety of specialized forms has evolved. Each covered one type of equipment or a single type of business. The provisions of these specialized forms were, for the most part, interchangeable. The major difference lay in their varying descriptions of the property they insured. Over the years, the number of equipment floater forms has declined as underwriters have consolidated similar forms. Significant changes have also occurred to the approach underwriters take to insuring mobile equipment. One of the most important has been the shift from forms that set a specific limit for each piece of equipment to forms that cover all the insured's equipment under a single limit.

Blanket and Scheduled Equipment Floaters

When inland marine underwriters introduced forms to insure mobile equipment, they listed each covered item and insured it for a certain amount. Those forms are called "scheduled forms" because a schedule identifies each piece of insured equipment and the amount for which the policy insures it. The early scheduled floaters were often valued forms as well, and at one time the two terms were virtually synonymous. Underwriters viewed scheduled floaters as a means to control the exposure to loss they assumed. The schedule was one way to limit the amount subject to a single loss. Large schedules often required more than one insurer, so participating and subscription policies were common.

The availability of reinsurance, and especially of treaty reinsurance, made cooperative insuring of a policy among several companies unnecessary. Insurers were able to write larger lines net and treaty, so they could write entire schedules. In time, underwriters began to realize that they could eliminate the schedules in most cases and write a "blanket" floater instead. These forms provide a single amount of insurance and describe the types of equipment to which it applies.

Contractors' Equipment

The term "contractors' equipment" covers a wide variety of items ranging from power and hand tools to heavy equipment. Many businesses other than contractors need a form to cover their equipment. The form insures materials-handling equipment like the forklifts that many businesses use. It also covers bulldozers, graders, and cranes used in construction. Accounts in this class present underwriters with different exposures. The underwriter must consider the type of equipment, the insured's business, and the use of the equipment. One insured, for instance, might use bulldozers and graders to build a road across the level Kansas plains, but another could use the same equipment to cut a road through the Rocky Mountains in Colorado. Landslide, upset, and overturn are not factors when assessing the hazards that the first insured faces. They are very important factors when assessing the second.

Mobile cranes require special consideration because of their high value and the possibility of heavy damage from collapse of the boom. Using a crane to swing a wrecking ball during demolition operations makes the collapse exposure even more severe. Boom collapse occurs most often when the operator loads the crane beyond its rated capacity. Training and experience are the key factors for preventing this type of loss. Posting the boom capacity conspicuously on the crane can keep the operator aware of its load limits.

Contractors often lease the equipment they use, especially cranes. The lessee might be required to provide insurance on the equipment, and the lessor will buy coverage that only applies while the equipment is on the premises or "yard" of the lessor. Companies can lease contractors' equipment to lessees with or without operators. From an underwriter's perspective, companies that lease equipment with operators are more desirable than those that do not. The insured has greater control over the operators, their qualifications, and the way they use the equipment. A lessee might hire operators who are not well qualified and who might ignore the equipment owner's safety instructions.

Equipment in the insured's yard represents a high concentration of values exposed to a single loss. Fire, for instance, can spread from one piece of equipment to another, igniting the contents of fuel tanks as it spreads. In this case, the probable maximum loss equals the amount subject. Each piece of equipment might seem to be exposed independently to loss, but the underwriter cannot safely make this assumption. In cold climates, construction drops off during the winter months. As a result, the values at risk in the yard increase and remain at a high level for several months. The colder the climate the longer this situation persists. The underwriter must consider the value of all the contractor's equipment when setting the probable maximum loss and the amount subject.

Insurance to value is also a problem for contractors equipment coverage. Inland marine forms often do not contain a coinsurance clause. Because most losses are partial, the insured has an incentive to buy limits lower than full replacement cost or actual cash value. The underwriter should know the replacement cost or actual cash value of the covered equipment and insist on limits that reflect that value. Failure to do this will produce premiums that are not adequate for the risk of loss assumed.

Theft of equipment from contractor job sites cannot always be prevented, but it can be discouraged by contractors doing the following:

- Fence job sites to keep trespassers out
- Employ a guard service to patrol the site when no work is in progress
- Lock equipment whenever it is not in use
- Remove equipment from the site at the end of each day
- Engrave identification numbers on equipment to make recovery easier

Other factors that underwriters should include in the assessment of contractors' equipment accounts include the insured's financial position and loss history.

Mobile Equipment Floaters

This class includes almost any equipment that the insured moves from place to place, such as tools, patterns and dies, vending machines, and salespersons' samples. Insurers who write this class have developed forms to meet the needs of the markets they target. Underwriters can also use a generic form, sometimes called a Miscellaneous Property Form. The Definition does not include any vehicles designed for highway use, property held for sale or in the course of manufacture on the insured's premises, furniture, and fixtures. Any other type of property is an appropriate subject for this form as long as it includes transit coverage. Underwriters should refer to the Definition when a question arises. Some types of property might be eligible under another class. Antique and classic cars, for instance, are articles of rarity, antiquity, or artistic merit. They are usually insured under an antique and classic car floater, which is an inland marine form. Coverage qualifies as inland marine because it is a type of fine arts coverage.

Many companies own patterns and dies for machine parts that they use but do not manufacture. The insured might need patterns and dies to produce tools that it uses in its operations or as parts for its product. These include founding patterns and dies for machine tools. The foundry or other contractor will retain the pattern or die during production and often return it to the insured between production runs. Samples, patterns, and dies might be expensive because they are often unique. If only one exists, replacing it in the event of a loss would be expensive. This situation very often increases the insured's need for coverage and creates valuation issues that the underwriter has to address. Inside limits restrict the amount that the insurer will have to pay for loss to any single item of property. A pattern and die floater may, for example, limit coverage to $25,000 for any one pattern or die. Items that have exceptional value can be scheduled. The schedule can function only to limit the insurer's liability, or it can provide valued coverage for unique items that may be difficult or impossible to replace.

Accounts Receivable and Valuable Papers

Accounts receivable and valuable papers are two separate coverages that insure against loss of records. They are both filed classes. Commercial property forms insure accounts receivable and valuable papers, but only for the cost of blank material plus the expense of transcribing the information. Inland marine forms cover the cost of research needed to recover the lost information. Underwriters usually consider the same underwriting factors for both.

Secure backup is the best way to limit the loss from destruction of records. This backup includes maintaining duplicate copies in a secure off-premises site. Loss is unlikely to strike the two locations at the same time, so the insured will have to restore only the information entered since the last backup. Using a fire-resistant safe or vault further reduces the risk of loss. Many companies use secure document storage facilities to fill this need.

Fire is the most important cause of loss in these classes. Underwriters should evaluate the exposure by the same standards that apply to contents coverage. Other factors to consider are the insured's financial condition and potential moral hazard. Customer relations are also important for accounts receivable. Customers who place a high value on the insured's products and services will often pay what they owe when due, regardless of whether the insured can bill them. This attitude on the part of customers will reduce both uncollectible accounts and the interest that the insured will have to pay to borrow money to offset the loss of accounts receivable.

Dealers Policies

Some dealers forms are a filed class of inland marine insurance. The Definition specifically lists the following:

- Musical instrument dealers
- Camera dealers
- Furriers
- Mobile equipment dealers
- Stamp and coin dealers
- Jewelers
- Fine arts dealers

Dealers of other property may be covered under a dealers form if the property, when sold to the ultimate consumer, may itself be insured under an inland marine policy. So while not specified, computer dealers and bicycle dealers, for example, may be insured under a nonfiled inland marine form.

Policies covering the property of jewelers and furriers are called "block policies" from the French "*en bloc*," which means that they provide a combination of coverages. With the exception of mobile equipment dealers, each class faces similar exposures. Property is highly susceptible to theft and easily damaged by fire. Furs, musical instruments, cameras, stamps, coins, and fine arts are also subject to severe damage by water.

Bailee Policies

A **bailee** has temporary custody of the personal property of another. A company that accepts its customers' property in the usual course of business is a bailee for hire. Businesses that routinely take in customers' goods include dry cleaners, repair shops, jewelers, and furriers. **Block policies** insure bailee exposures for jewelers and furriers. The law holds the bailee responsible for ordinary care of the bailed property. The bailee must treat customers' goods as if they were the bailee's own. This exposure is often insured under a bailee liability or bailee customers' form. The most frequent causes of loss are fire and, if the bailee accepts high-valued goods, crime. The underwriting considerations for the bailment exposure are the same as underwriting the bailee's own property.

Electronic Data Processing (EDP) Policies

EDP policies provide four coverages for computers and related equipment:

- Direct loss to the hardware
- Media coverage on tapes and disks
- Extra expense
- Business income

Each of these coverages is similar to others already addressed. Direct loss coverage in the EDP form is similar to commercial property coverage, although its covered causes of loss are usually broader. Most EDP forms add mechanical breakdown and electrical injury as covered causes of loss. Even "all-risks" commercial property forms exclude coverage for electrical damage and mechanical breakdown. For most types of equipment, boiler and machinery insurance picks up this exposure. Media coverage is a type of valuable papers and records insurance. Extra expense and business income coverage are time element coverages similar to those discussed in Chapter 6.

The causes of direct loss that most affect the building and its contents are those that the underwriter must assess for EDP coverage. Data processing equipment is sensitive to damage by smoke. For this reason, the extent to which the computer room is isolated from the rest of the building is important.

Glass walls and sliding doors might provide adequate protection against smoke damage but will quickly fail when exposed to fire. At one time, computers were more sensitive to changes in temperature and humidity than they now are. For that reason, computer rooms often have a ventilating system separate from that of the rest of the building. A separate system often permits isolating mainframe computer systems from smoke when fire strikes elsewhere in the building. Smoke, even in the absence of fire or heat, can cause severe damage to the sensitive electronics of computers and peripherals. Therefore, isolation from the remainder of the premises is an effective loss control measure for data processing facilities. The underwriter should also consider the storage of combustibles and use of flammable or volatile solvents in the computer room. Large amounts of paper for use with printers might be present. The high level of housekeeping typical of data processing operations tends to keep this exposure under control.

Despite the suspension of halon production, many computer facilities are protected by halon fire suppression systems. Halon has been the extinguishment of choice by computer facilities because of the extensive use of electrical equipment and the concern that the computer equipment would be irreparably damaged by sprinklers. This concern might be misplaced because evidence indicates that computer equipment dries out well. A preaction system can effectively allay concerns over potential sprinkler leakage.

Insurance to value can be a problem for both extra expense coverage and media coverage. If the insured makes a low estimate of the cost of replacing the media, even a small loss can exceed policy limits. Disaster planning can be especially effective in limiting extra expense losses under computer coverage.

Builders Risk and Installation Floaters

The Definition includes builders risk and installation floaters as a single class of inland marine insurance. When builders risk forms insure buildings or other structures in the course of construction or reconstruction, installation floaters cover other property that the insured installs for other contractors. Coverage applies until the property that the insured has been contracted to install has been installed, tested, and accepted.

Buildings exposed to damage while under construction can be insured under a **builders risk** form. The decision to accept or reject builders risk submissions requires the same process as for a completed structure; that is, the underwriter must analyze the COPE hazards. During construction, however, different hazards are present that are either not present after structural completion or intensified by the construction itself.

Builders risk coverage can be provided in different ways. It can be an ISO builders risk form and endorsements included in a commercial property coverage part or it can be inland marine insurance. Inland marine builders risk forms range from preprinted forms and endorsements to elaborate manuscript contracts designed for large and complex projects. Since inland marine forms are nonfiled forms, underwriters have wide latitude in negotiating covered causes of loss, conditions, and price.

Insurance to value, always an important consideration in property insurance, is something of a paradox in builders risk. On the one hand, the completed value of a structure is determined by adding the cost of materials and labor. On the other hand, the structure's value at any point in the course of construction can be determined only if the contractor has precise specifications, keeps meticulous accounting records for the project, and can specify whether purchased and delivered materials have been installed or used.

Most projects are insured with the **completed value form**. That form stipulates the estimated 100 percent building cost at completion as the limit of insurance. The form also assumes a fairly steady accrual of value from start to finish of the construction project. As a consequence, the rate used for premium determination is arbitrarily set at either 50 or 55 percent of the regular rate.

When a building project is large enough and the contractor maintains accurate records, the contract can be written on a **reporting form** basis. Provisional amounts of insurance are set at the beginning of the project, and reports of added values are made during construction. Premium is charged only for the project's existing values. The reporting form approach is especially attractive to an insured whose structure will have minimal values exposed throughout a lengthy building period with a heavy accrual of values just before completion. An example is a factory with a completed superstructure. Some high-value items, such as moving assembly lines and overhead cranes, are only installed in the final stages of construction.

Perils Insured Against

The ISO builders risk form can be written with the basic, broad, or special causes of loss form. Most builders risk forms exclude collapse caused by the use of defective materials or methods in construction. Coverage for collapse can be added by using the builders risk—collapse during construction endorsement.

During construction, contractors occupy the incomplete structure. They solder, weld, cut, paint, and use various electrical and gasoline-driven machines. They can also have volatile gases on site. The nature of the work of contractors creates housekeeping problems such as congestion, poor storage, high probabilities of spontaneous combustion, waste disposal problems (including bonfires), and accumulations of dust, powders, and shavings. The major causes of loss covered by a builders risk form are discussed in the following paragraphs.

Fire

Fire can be hazardous during construction, especially if water delivery systems are incomplete. Public water systems, for example, could be under construction simultaneously with the building. In high-rise structures, standpipes must keep pace with each floor addition and be operable. (Often the water is not turned on until the building has been completed.)

Wood or other combustible materials are often used in construction. Even in fully fire-resistive structures, temporary partitions, scaffolding, braces, and concrete forms might be present. Plastic windbreaks and wood forms have resulted in large fires in slip-form poured concrete projects. Concrete forms are highly combustible because they are made of plywood and oiled to facilitate their release from newly poured concrete. Temporary heating devices such as salamanders are common hazards. Tar kettles are often hoisted to the roof when built-up roofs are being installed.

Windstorm

The damage done by windstorms can be extensive because all buildings under construction are in a weakened state. Walls might not yet be bonded to one another, and roofs are in various stages of completion or are still unanchored. Until windows and doors are installed and the entire structure is enclosed, even a light storm can create unusual stresses and pressures that, in turn, can lead to structural failures.

Riot, Vandalism, and Malicious Mischief

As an occasional consequence of confrontations between union and nonunion workers at jobsites, buildings under construction have suffered damage. While this seems unlikely today, union workers have been accused of vandalizing construction sites not employing union labor. Vandals are often attracted to construction sites because of the damage they can do to the materials and equipment left on the jobsite.

Collapse

In the course of construction, every building of every construction type is significantly weaker than when completed. Therefore, collapse can be a serious hazard when the structure is incomplete. Collapse during construction results primarily from faulty design, faulty welds in steel superstructures, and improper bracing and improper curing of poured concrete. The American Society of Civil Engineers (ASCE) has conducted and sponsored much research and has promulgated meticulous standards for design and construction supervision. Underwriters must be assured that design and construction supervision meet ASCE standards. A letter from the architect or engineering firm stipulating design qualifications lessens worry and assists subrogation procedures when warranted.

Day-to-day building supervision by the contractor should be supplemented, at the owner's expense, by a qualified **clerk of the works**. The clerk, usually a professional engineer, has sole responsibility for the daily supervision of each project component to ensure that materials, methodology, and quality of workmanship meet engineering specifications and ASCE standards. The clerk's authority includes the power to stop all work and to require that unacceptable work be redone.

Because of the nature of their respective responsibilities, the clerk of the works and the contractor might have conflicting interests. The contractor could face financial penalties if the work is delayed. The building owner could also be faced with additional costs caused by a delay in the structure's completion. Sometimes the mutual self-interest of the building owner and the contractor take precedence over proper construction techniques. An especially hazardous situation arises when the construction type is reinforced concrete poured in place. ASCE standards for forms and bracing must be maintained to ensure proper curing. Premature removal of supports can lead to collapse of a single floor and possibly the entire structure. The subsequent costs are incalculable, and loss of life is likely. An example is the 1978 collapse of the scaffolding inside a cooling tower under construction in West Virginia. Fifty-one workers were killed. The failure of the contractor to wait until the cement was properly cured was the suspected cause.

Underwriters can protect the insurance company's interest in such a project by insisting that an independent engineer oversee all form and bracing removal timetables and by having the policy warrant that form and bracing standards will be met.

Theft

Theft is often a requested coverage because losses from this peril can be significant. The underwriter should grant insurance against theft only when minimum loss control standards are met. Those standards might include twenty-four-hour guard service and fencing.

Earthquake and Flood

Earthquake and flood cause infrequent losses, but they should not be overlooked. Earthquake presents a problem because a building under construction could be susceptible to even a slight tremor. A flood could weaken the basic structural supports in the area of footings or foundations, causing structural collapse before the building is completed.

Breakage of Structural Components

Breakage of structural components is usually an inexpensive event. A reasonable deductible can usually reduce the losses an insurer will pay. However, when delicate and expensive machinery is involved, breakage can be costly. For example, installing a large turbine for electrical generation involves cranes and skilled riggers. A fall of only six inches can result in cracked casings, which would be a total loss to the turbine. Since a turbine can cost hundreds of thousands of dollars, potential loss severity is great. The exposure increases when the underwriter is also providing business income coverage during the course of construction for the same causes of loss. Replacement and delivery of a unique piece of machinery might take longer than a year.

Builders Risk and Probable Maximum Loss

Many structures, particularly those that are noncombustible and fire-resistive, are more exposed to loss during construction than at any other time.

When estimating probable maximum loss, the following are important underwriting considerations:

- Key structural components are exposed to an increase in hazard.
- Sprinkler protection cannot be completed before the building is fully enclosed.
- Fire walls will not, in all likelihood, have been fully closed off with approved fire doors; the same is true of vertical openings.
- Duct work will not have required dampers.
- Guards might not be fully trained or visiting all areas of the premises.
- Water for fighting fires might not be available or might not be available in sufficient quantity and pressure.
- Fire department personnel might not be familiar with the building or the area, delaying their initial response.
- Construction equipment and materials on the grounds might hamper effective firefighting efforts.

Those underwriting considerations and the hazards mentioned previously suggest that losses will generally be much greater during construction than when the building is complete and occupied. The probable maximum loss for any type of construction often approaches 100 percent. A major exception might be a housing development if the distance between dwellings is sufficient to prevent the spread of fire.

Builders Risk Selection Decisions

A building under construction introduces additional hazards. The underwriter, however, has selection, coverage, risk improvement, pricing, and deductible options to minimize the effects of these hazards. The use of deductibles can nullify the expected value of small losses. An inland marine form provides the requisite latitude for pricing each exposure to loss, and loss control services can minimize frequency and severity.

Underwriters can also include warranties in the policy requiring the following:

- Periodic waste and debris disposal and site cleanup
- Guard services
- Adherence to accepted standards, such as ASCE specifications for poured concrete, building codes, and so forth
- Adequate public water supply and adequate standpipes, extinguishers, and other private protection devices

In the final analysis, as in almost every insurance transaction, the builders risk underwriter must be satisfied that the people insured are qualified. The inherent exposures for a project under construction are reduced under the following conditions:

- If the contractor is experienced in the type of construction
- If the contractor has a skilled and stable work force
- If the project size is within the contractor's capability
- If the contractor has adequate financial resources and favorable prior loss experience

Difference in Conditions Policies

Difference in conditions (DIC) policies provide coverage for risks of direct loss but exclude the causes of loss normally insured by a commercial property form. DIC policies were developed as an effective means to afford "all-risks" coverage when state laws forbade fire insurers to offer such coverage. The policies have survived because they fill a need in the marketplace.

DIC forms do not include a coinsurance clause because the intent is not to insure the property to its full value. Instead, the design of this coverage contemplates allowing the insured to insure to probable maximum loss. This does not mean that the underwriter should ignore the ratio of the amount of insurance to the values exposed to loss. The insurer must earn premium sufficient to pay its expenses, pay losses incurred within the limits the insured has selected, and leave a reasonable amount for profit. The challenging task that underwriters face is pricing. Pricing correctly demands knowing the extent to which the policy insures to value.

The causes of loss that most commonly motivate an insured to purchase a DIC form are burglary, earthquake, and flood. Coverage for these causes of loss is more subject to adverse selection than almost any others. Insureds often ask for a DIC policy specifically because coverage is either unavailable or unaffordable using standard forms and standard rates. If coverage were provided under standard forms at standard rates, the account would likely produce an underwriting loss. DIC underwriters cannot earn a profit by providing broader coverage at lower rates with the same terms and conditions that apply to standard coverage. The underwriter must therefore select a deductible substantial enough to eliminate the routine losses that would make the account unprofitable. The deductible might be $25,000 or higher. Six- or eight-figure deductibles are not uncommon for large accounts. (The business can insure part of the DIC deductible for flood losses in the National Flood Insurance Program.)

Underwriters can also restrict the amount of insurance available for earthquake and flood. One technique is to provide inside limits for each cause of loss. For instance, the DIC form might provide limits of $20 million but restrict coverage for earthquake to $5 million and for flood to $10 million. A single inside limit might also apply to both causes of loss. Affording only partial coverage is another useful technique. A DIC form might provide full coverage for all losses in excess of the deductible from any cause except earthquake or flood. The underwriter might provide only partial coverage, perhaps 50 percent of the loss from these two causes. The insurer would, in this case, pay half of the amount by which the insured loss exceeds the deductible for earthquake or flood but would pay the full amount of loss above the deductible from any other cause.

Boiler and Machinery Insurance

Boiler and machinery insurance is more of a specialty than most other lines of insurance. Only a few insurers underwrite boiler and machinery coverage, and Hartford Steam Boiler Group has dominated this market since the introduction of the coverage. In 1996, Hartford Steam Boiler Group accounted for almost 30 percent of net premiums written for boiler and machinery insurance.[1] Other commercial lines underwriters were only marginally involved.

The situation began to change with the introduction of the businessowners policy. Boiler and machinery insurance was an option, and the program did not allow leeway for referral to a specialist. The underwriters of businessowners policies had no choice but to learn about boiler and machinery coverage. Commercial property underwriters in many companies now handle small or routine boiler and machinery accounts, leaving only large and complex risks to the specialists.

One reason that only a small number of insurers pursue boiler and machinery accounts is the need to provide inspection service that requires a certified boiler inspector. The laws of virtually every state require periodic inspection of boilers and sometimes fired and unfired pressure vessels as well. Only a certified boiler inspector may do the inspection and sign the certificate that the state law requires. To become certified, the inspector must pass a comprehensive examination developed by the American Society of Mechanical Engineers, meet an experience requirement, and work for an insurance company or government agency. States will accept inspections only by an insurance company that provides coverage for the boiler or pressure vessel. That is, the insurer must provide the service and cannot contract it out.

The purpose of this requirement is to give the party doing boiler inspections a vested interest in the condition of the equipment. States accept inspections by insurance companies that cover the boilers and pressure vessels because the companies stand to lose if the equipment fails. In a few instances one insurer will contract with another carrier to provide inspection services for the boilers and pressure vessels it insures. These arrangements are usually part of a reinsurance agreement. The company that inspects the boilers and pressure vessels actually bears the risk of loss. The insurer that issues the policy reinsures its book of boiler and machinery business 100 percent with the company that does the inspections.

Providing this inspection service is expensive, but most underwriters feel that doing so is worthwhile. Underwriting expenses for boiler and machinery are higher than for other lines, but combined ratios are consistently lower. This situation is not much different from crime insurance and suggests again that good underwriting improves profits. In the long run, underwriting expense ratios for boiler and machinery coverage have been declining, and combined ratios have been rising. The need for staff qualified to provide this service, however, limits the number of insurers that are willing to write boiler and machinery insurance. It might also limit an individual insurer's ability to write in a certain geographic area.

Boiler and machinery forms cover a single cause of loss: "an accident to an object," which is a sudden and accidental breakdown. The term **object** means the boilers, pressure vessels, and machines that the policy insures.

Boiler and machinery insurance began as an adjunct to the loss control service provided by inspectors, and to a certain extent it has remained that way. With proper maintenance, most boiler and machinery losses are preventable. The primary factors needed to evaluate an insured for boiler and machinery insurance can be determined during the inspection and include the following:

- *Age*. Well-maintained, older equipment may be as satisfactory as recently installed equipment. Age becomes an issue when the equipment has not been properly maintained or when it has become obsolete because replacement parts are difficult to obtain. Minor damage to an older boiler, for example, might require that the equipment be replaced.
- *Quality of preventive maintenance*. For some accounts, the equipment insured is significant enough to the insured's activities that personnel are dedicated to monitoring its safe operation. For other accounts, equipment maintenance is contracted out to others who perform regular evaluations. The quality of preventive maintenance is readily apparent to inspectors.
- *Qualification of operators*. The types of equipment that can be insured under boiler and machinery insurance varies considerably. Some equipment can be adversely affected by how it is operated. Constant operation or operation of the equipment near its capacity can cause it to fail. Equipment operators should know how to operate the equipment properly and when the equipment should be shutdown for service. An indication of operator qualification is evidence of training specific to the equipment and overall experience in operating similar equipment.
- *Account location*. The locality of the account affects the frequency with which it might be serviced by inspectors and the requirements for such inspections. Qualified inspectors must be available to visit the premises, and the frequency of such visits is likely to be less if the account is located in a remote area. Inspection requirements vary by state and some cities and counties have their own boiler codes. The satisfaction of these requirements might determine the number of inspector visits more so than other considerations.

Glass Insurance

Commercial multiple-peril premiums include almost all the glass coverage now written. What little glass is written on a monoline basis is combined with other miscellaneous lines of insurance for reporting purposes. Underwriters usually provide glass insurance as part of a package policy and will write it in many cases as an accommodation. Commercial property causes of loss forms insure glass against the most common causes of losses with some substantial coverage restrictions. The glass coverage form eliminates a $100 per-item and $500 per-occurrence limit applicable to some of the causes of loss included in the broad and special forms. The basic form limits glass breakage coverage to instances caused by a named peril. Businesses requesting glass coverage will probably have a particular need, and underwriters should be concerned with adverse selection. Underwriters must realize that glass coverage is primary to coverage provided under other commercial property forms.

The accounts that apply for glass insurance usually face some special exposure. An auto dealer, for example, might want coverage for vehicle damage to large panes of glass in or near the showroom. The basic and broad causes of loss forms do not cover damage by vehicles that the insured owns or operates. Other accounts might be especially subject to vandalism losses. Obtaining a premium high enough to pay losses and earn a profit is difficult, if not impossible. The underwriter must determine whether the risk of loss is acceptable for the entire account, not for glass coverage alone. For those accounts that do not face some special risk of loss, glass coverage is not needed.

Package Policy Underwriting

The term **package policy** applies to a single policy that contains two or more property and liability coverages. Examples of package policies abound today, but this was not always the case. Traditionally, and then by regulatory mandate, insurers were restricted from combining property and liability coverages into a single policy. States passed legislation in the 1950s that enabled the creation of multiline policies. Multiline laws permitted combinations of coverage that better meet the needs of policyholders. Package policies may provide a discount reflecting the reduced cost of issuing a single policy instead of several policies. Policyholders are also less likely to have gaps and overlaps in coverage.

Not all of a policyholder's exposures can be covered by a single policy. A more appropriate approach is to consider all of a policyholder's needs at one time and the policies that satisfy those needs as a single account. Insurance producers have encouraged insurers to take an "account" approach to offering insurance. Producers have long recognized client frustration at having to deal with several insurers. If several producers must be involved to meet a client's needs, there is a potential that another producer might be able to meet all of the client's insurance requirements.

The packaging of coverages makes a great deal of sense from an underwriting standpoint. The larger total premium generated by an account makes possible more in-depth investigative work on the character of the policyholder and the nature of the risk. Combining coverages into a single policy enhances the spread of risk, reduces adverse selection, and provides an opportunity for greater premium growth. By internally organizing to underwrite package policies, the insurer can increase its level of service to producers by creating a single source for all service needs.

The disadvantage of package underwriting is that underwriters cannot be selective in the coverage offered to the applicant. Applicants and producers want the insurance program accepted as a whole. As a result, underwriters are forced into a choice between all or nothing. Underwriters placed in this position may have to accept some marginal exposures in order to write the more profitable parts of the account.

Underwriting package policies depends to some degree on the kind of package policy. All package policies can be described as (1) simple combination or collection policies, (2) minimum requirement combination policies, (3) indivisible combination policies, or (4) nonstandard combination policies.

A **simple combination policy** includes two or more standard coverages in a more convenient format for the policyholder. There is no package discount, and the underwriting is the same as if separate coverages were requested. This approach provides maximum flexibility to the underwriter, who may choose not to issue the requested form but instead to offer a more restricted form if necessary. Each coverage is priced separately, and the package premium is simply a total of the premiums for the individual coverages.

In a **minimum requirement combination policy**, certain coverages are combined, and the insured must purchase the minimum required coverages. An example is the ISO commercial package policy (CPP), which requires a direct damage coverage form in the Commercial Property Coverage part (or the Inland Marine Physicians and Surgeons Coverage Form) *and* premises and operations liability for the same premises.[2] A combination of forms that do not meet these requirements might be referred to as a package but is not eligible for the package discount.

Adverse selection is reduced by requiring certain minimum coverages. The policy writing, accounting, and billing expenses are less with one package policy than with three or four separate single line (or monoline) policies. The benefits of reduction in expense costs and adverse selection are passed along to the insured in the form of a package discount, usually 15 to 20 percent.

Because of this package discount, most insurers try to limit eligibility to above-average risks. The underwriting guide or manual usually specifies what is above-average in terms of type of business and physical hazards. One inspection might provide sufficient information for property, liability, and crime loss exposures. Since there is a minimum requirement of property and liability coverages, inspections are coordinated, and expenses are reduced relative to having an inspection performed for each line of coverage.

Under the minimum requirement approach, the underwriter must not only analyze and evaluate each of the individual coverages but must also weigh the interrelationship of these diverse exposures. A single larger premium must reflect a combination of smaller premiums of varying levels of adequacy.

An **indivisible combination policy** provides a broad range of coverages on an all-or-nothing basis for a single indivisible premium. An example is the businessowners policy (BOP). Unlike the minimum requirement policy, the premium is shown only in total and cannot be separated by coverage. Indivisible combination policies permit little coverage selection by the policyholder, thus reducing adverse selection. However, such an arrangement permits little underwriting flexibility with regard to pricing and offering alternative coverages. The underwriter's challenge then is to evaluate the sum of the various exposures presented by a risk against the single premium to determine acceptability.

Nonstandard combination policies are usually manuscript contracts written to the policyholder's and the underwriter's specifications. Maximum flexibility is obtained by eliminating minimum coverages, and pricing tends to be on an individual-risk basis. This approach is limited to large policyholders.

Underwriting Considerations

Underwriting decision making is simple on a submission with no adverse exposures. Likewise, the decision is clear if the submission has no redeeming value. The decision becomes difficult when part of the package is acceptable but the balance is not. Perhaps the property loss exposures of a small manufacturer are minimal because of loss control devices, but the products liability exposure is severe because of the nature of the product. Alternatively, the premises and operations liability exposures of a dry cleaner might be excellent as demonstrated in its loss-free history, but the property exposure might be questionable as a result of the use of a solvent with a low flash point.

In these cases, the underwriter must weigh the strengths against the weaknesses, identify appropriate alternatives, then choose the best one. To do this, an underwriter can ask questions such as the following:

1. What are the respective limits of insurance of each of the sections of the package policy?
2. What are the respective premiums for each policy section? (This question is inappropriate if the package policy has an indivisible premium, thus complicating the underwriter's decision.)

3. What are the respective frequencies of loss for each major policy section?
4. What are the respective severities of loss for each major policy section?

Interrelating and sometimes conflicting exposures are those in which a low hazard for one line of coverage increases the hazard for another coverage. A business may, for example, have a choice of two production processes. One may be safer, the other more reliable. The safer process would reduce the chance of loss to the property but increase the possibility of turning out defective products. Using this process is likely to generate lower property and workers compensation losses. The price of this added safety in the workplace, on the other hand, is a higher risk of product liability losses. This dilemma might be compounded if an underwriter wants to offer suggestions to lower the exposure in one line of coverage. Reducing the losses from one source may increase the possibility of loss from another. In an extreme case, a consumer injured by a defective product might attribute part of the injury to the underwriter's loss control recommendations. Insurers should be able to assert that loss control surveys are conducted to evaluate the insured's underwriting desirability, not to certify the safety of the insured's products, services, or premises. Injured parties have brought suit against insurers on this basis in the past.

Additionally, the underwriter must determine whether the premium for the low-hazard exposures compensates for the inadequate premiums of the higher-hazard exposures. Most rating plans contain minimum rates and/or minimum premiums by coverage for low-hazard risks. They have been developed to cover the expenses of underwriting and issuing a policy, which might account for the majority of the cost in some instances. When several coverages are combined into a single package, the minimum rates, being primarily for expense purposes, might provide more than adequate premium when added to premiums for the higher-exposure lines of business.

In indivisible premium policies, the underwriter must identify unusual exposures for which an indivisible "class rate" does not develop sufficient premium. For example, one such package provided "all-risks" coverage on liquor stores at a premium that was less than would be charged for a store carrying general merchandise.

Package underwriting also provides the opportunity to investigate the management abilities and techniques as they relate to the overall loss control of the account. The package policy analysis, because it has more expense dollars available from the larger premium, enables the underwriter to look more closely at many aspects of management, including its ability to make a profit.

Some package policies are more than just a combination of monoline coverages. While most monoline policies and package versions of the monoline forms are the same, underwriters should be aware of any differences between them. Some package policies have altered the usual monoline policy provisions to broaden the coverage. The package credit provided under the commercial package policy program may also give too steep a discount, based on the insurer's own experience and may make packaging the coverages undesirable.

Summary

Inland marine insurance was introduced as a branch of ocean marine coverage. This extension soon evolved into a separate specialty within property-liability insurance.

The NAIC produced the Nation-Wide Definition and Interpretation of the Insuring Powers of Marine and Transportation Underwriters. The Definition helped clarify what underwriters may and may not write as marine insurance. The Definition recognizes four broad classes of marine insurance: transportation, instrumentalities of transportation and communication, personal property floaters, and commercial property floaters.

Marine insurers do not generally need approval from state insurance departments for their forms and rates. Because this freedom is not absolute, insurance advisory organizations file forms, rules, and loss costs for a few inland marine classes. Some insurers subscribe to these organizations, while others file their own. In many states, other inland marine classes are free from regulation and are called nonfiled classes.

Underwriting inland marine insurance is similar to underwriting other property lines. Unlike property lines, however, inland marine forms can cover mobile equipment or goods in transit. Because a loss of equipment or goods could affect a business's finances, inland marine underwriters must also provide coverage for loss of business income.

Instrumentalities of transportation and communication include bridges and tunnels; piers, wharves, docks, and slips; pipelines; and radio and television communications equipment. Coverage for most instrumentalities of transportation and communication is a specialty line that most insurers do not elect to write.

Although the term "floater" is slowly being phased out of policy forms, it is still used in the Definition. Some insurers have begun to use commercial property forms to cover property that floaters traditionally covered. Equipment floaters include blanket and scheduled equipment floaters, contractors' equipment floaters, and mobile equipment floaters.

Bailee policies provide coverage for businesses that routinely take in customers' goods, such as dry cleaners and repair shops. Electronic data processing (EDP) policies provide four coverages for computers and related equipment: direct loss to hardware, media coverage on tapes and disks, extra expenses, and business income.

Builders risk forms insure buildings during construction. Because they are incomplete, buildings under construction are more exposed to some causes of loss than they would be were the structures complete.

Difference in conditions (DIC) policies are used to insure the causes of loss that are not normally covered by other commercial property forms. Most businesses therefore purchase DIC policies to insure flood and earthquake losses.

Boiler and machinery insurance began as an adjunct to the loss control service provided by inspectors, and to a certain extent it has remained that way. The required inspection service provides the underwriter with extensive information about the subject of insurance. The principal facts the underwriter should consider are the condition of the equipment, its age, the quality of preventive maintenance, the qualifications of operators, and the location of the account.

Commercial property causes of loss forms insure glass against the most common causes of losses with some substantial coverage restrictions. The accounts that apply for glass insurance usually face some special exposure. Underwriters should realize that glass coverage is primary to coverage provided under other commercial property forms and subject to adverse selection.

However defined, package policies present underwriters with a number of challenges and opportunities. The challenge is to evaluate a number of diverse exposures in a single account. The underwriter must weigh the loss potential from these exposures to determine whether the account will be profitable on an overall basis. The opportunity exists to perform a thorough investigation on the entire account, which might not have been cost-justified if the account had been written on a monoline basis.

Chapter Notes

1. *Best's Aggregates and Averages* (Oldwick, NJ: A. M. Best Company, 1997), p. 276.
2. *Commercial Lines Manual*, Section Nine Multiline (New York, NY: Insurance Services Office, 1985), p. 2.

Index

A

B

C

D

E

F

G

H

I

J

L

M

N

O

P

R

S

T

U

V

W